The publisher gratefully acknowledges the generous support of the Ahmanson Foundation Humanities Endowment Fund of the University of California Press Foundation.

The publisher gratefully acknowledges the generous support of the Valerie Barth and Peter Booth Wiley Endowment Fund in History of the University of California Press Foundation.

*Edmund Burke and the Conservative
Logic of Empire*

BERKELEY SERIES IN BRITISH STUDIES

Edited by Mark Bevir and James Vernon

1. *The Peculiarities of Liberal Modernity in Imperial Britain,* edited by Simon Gunn and James Vernon
2. *Dilemmas of Decline: British Intellectuals and World Politics, 1945–1975,* by Ian Hall
3. *The Savage Visit: New World People and Popular Imperial Culture in Britain, 1710–1795,* by Kate Fullagar
4. *The Afterlife of Empire,* by Jordanna Bailkin
5. *Smyrna's Ashes: Humanitarianism, Genocide, and the Birth of the Middle East,* by Michelle Tusan
6. *Pathological Bodies: Medicine and Political Culture,* by Corinna Wagner
7. *A Problem of Great Importance: Population, Race, and Power in the British Empire, 1918–1973,* by Karl Ittmann
8. *Liberalism in Empire: An Alternative History,* by Andrew Sartori
9. *Distant Strangers: How Britain Became Modern,* by James Vernon
10. *Edmund Burke and the Conservative Logic of Empire,* by Daniel I. O'Neill

Edmund Burke and the Conservative Logic of Empire

Daniel I. O'Neill

UNIVERSITY OF CALIFORNIA PRESS

University of California Press, one of the most distinguished university presses in the United States, enriches lives around the world by advancing scholarship in the humanities, social sciences, and natural sciences. Its activities are supported by the UC Press Foundation and by philanthropic contributions from individuals and institutions. For more information, visit www.ucpress.edu.

University of California Press
Oakland, California

© 2016 by The Regents of the University of California

Library of Congress Cataloging-in-Publication Data

Names: O'Neill, Daniel I., 1967- author.
Title: Edmund Burke and the conservative logic of empire / Daniel I. O'Neill.
Other titles: Berkeley series in British studies ; 10.
Description: Oakland, California : University of California Press, [2016] | "2016 | Series: Berkeley Series in British Studies ; 10 | Includes bibliographical references and index.
Identifiers: LCCN 2015035745| ISBN 9780520287822 (cloth : alk. paper) | ISBN 0520287827 (cloth : alk. paper) | ISBN 9780520287839 (pbk. : alk. paper) | ISBN 0520287835 (pbk. : alk. paper) | ISBN 9780520962866 (e-edition) | ISBN 0520962869 (e-edition)
Subjects: LCSH: Burke, Edmund, 1729-1797—Criticism and interpretation. | Burke, Edmund, 1729-1797--Political and social views. | Imperialism--18th century. | Great Britain--Politics and government--18th century.
Classification: LCC JC176.B83 O34 2016 | DDC 325/.32—dc23
LC record available at http://lccn.loc.gov/2015035745

24 23 22 21 20 19 18 17 16 15
10 9 8 7 6 5 4 3 2 1

For Anastasia,
always

CONTENTS

Acknowledgments ix

Introduction: Edmund Burke's Conservative Logic of Empire 1

Chapter 1 · Burke and Empire in Context 19

Chapter 2 · The New World 47

Chapter 3 · India 92

Chapter 4 · Ireland 124

Conclusion: Ornamentalism, Orientalism, and the Legacy of Burke's Conservative Logic of Empire 168

Notes 179
Works Cited 229
Index 241

ACKNOWLEDGMENTS

In a scholarly climate filled with an ever-increasing number of books claiming that Edmund Burke was neither a conservative nor a defender of empire, this book argues that he was in fact both. Nietzsche, at least, believed that such "untimely meditations" had their place. We shall see. Of this I am sure: Interventions of this sort certainly incur a long list of debts. Indeed, these are perhaps deeper than usual when one's views are unfashionable.

In that spirit, I thank Mark Bevir, who told me about the Berkeley Series in British Studies at its inception and never wavered in his willingness to have the book reviewed for it, even when the writing took longer than I had hoped. I also thank both external readers of the manuscript, Don Herzog and David Cannadine, whose own work, as well as their reviews, made this a much better book than it otherwise would have been. Professor Herzog's *Poisoning the Minds of the Lower Orders* helped give me the courage of my convictions, while Professor Cannadine's notion of "Ornamentalism" was instrumental in broadening the conceptual framework that informs the finished product. I am also greatly indebted to Manu Samnotra for his meticulous reading of the entire book, his detailed written commentary on it, and the long hours we spent in discussion of its central arguments. Duncan Bell provided invaluable feedback on portions of the manuscript. Terry Ball has been a terrific mentor and offered sage professional advice throughout the writing process. Carole Pateman's deep understanding of and spirited commitment to democracy continue to guide all of my thinking.

The book has also benefited from being vetted at various conferences. In particular, I thank Dan Kapust for inviting me to present parts of the argument at the University of Georgia Ethics and Political Philosophy Workshop, and then again at the University of Wisconsin-Madison's conference "Theory's

Landscapes: Movements, Memories, and Moments." Dan's keen intellect and good humor have been equally valuable. I am also grateful to the members of Cornell University's Political Theory Workshop for allowing me to present my overarching argument there at an early stage in its development. Onur Ulas Ince, in particular, offered very helpful advice. The trip to Cornell also afforded me the opportunity to speak at length with Isaac Kramnick, who first taught me about Burke long ago, and who remains one of the very best interpreters of Burke's political thought. Les Thiele, my political theory colleague at the University of Florida, has been a great sounding board and a source of intellectual inspiration. Michael Goodhart has unfailingly listened to various iterations of my arguments over the years and has always made them better. The project was also improved by a wide range of colleagues, readers, discussants, conference participants, and students, including (but not limited to): Leslie Anderson, Mark Antaki, Badredine Arfi, Richard Avramenko, Lina Benabdallah, Michael Bernhard, Thomas Biebricher, Richard Boyd, Lorna Bracewell, Mauro Caraccioli, Ross Carroll, Alec Dinnin, Larry Dodd, Clem Fatovic, Jenn Forshee, Zephyr Frank, Dustin Fridkin, Iain Hampsher-Monk, Michael Hanchard, Ryan Patrick Hanley, Abdourahmane Idrissa, Helen Kinsella, Peggy Kohn, Antis Loizides, J. Maggio, Michael Martinez, Inder Marwah, Kirstie McClure, Bryon Moraski, Jeanne Morefield, Onur Muftigil, Conor O'Dwyer, Johnathan O'Neill, Ido Oren, Anthony Pagden, Christopher Parker, Brian Smith, Dan Smith, Seaton Tarrant, Ben J. Taylor, Megan Thomas, Brandon Turner, Koen Vermeir, James Vernon, Sean Walsh, Luise White, Stephen K. White, and of course the late and very much missed Victor Wolfenstein. I also thank the director of the University of California Press, Niels Hooper; Bonita Hurd for her copyediting expertise; and Bradley Depew.

My greatest debts, of course, are to my family. Anastasia, I could never have written this or any other book without your support. Cassidy and Jack, you continue to remind me daily of what matters most.

Portions of this argument have appeared previously. However, all of the material has been greatly reworked and expanded for the current volume. I acknowledge the following outlets for granting me the right to use my previous work:

Portions of chapter 2 originally appeared in Daniel I. O'Neill and Margaret Kohn, "A Tale of Two Indias: Burke and Mill on Empire and Slavery in the West Indies and America," *Political Theory* 34, no. 2 (2006):

192–228 (doi: 10.1177/0090591705279609), for which I wrote all of the material on Burke. I thank Sage Publications for permission.

Sections of chapter 3 and a small portion of chapter 1 originally appeared in "Rethinking Burke and India," *History of Political Thought* 30, no. 3 (2009): 492–523. I thank the editors of the journal and Imprint Academic for permission.

Small portions of the introduction and chapter 4 originally appeared as "Edmund Burke, the 'Science of Man,' and Statesmanship," in *Scientific Statesmanship, Governance and the History of Political Philosophy*, ed. Kyriakos N. Demetriou and Antis P. Loizides (New York: Routledge, 2015), pp. 174–192. I thank Taylor and Francis, LLC, for permission.

Finally, I thank the British Museum for permission to use William Dent's 1788 satirical print of the trial of Warren Hastings, "The Raree Show executed for the benefit of Mr Somebody at the expence of John Bull," for the cover art (© The Trustees of the British Museum; all rights reserved). A "raree show" was a form of entertainment, such as the type found at a carnival or a street show, often carried in a box or seen in a booth, which made it function like a peep show. The British Museum's description of the cartoon reads, in part: "The trial of Hastings in Westminster Hall is travestied as a raree show in a booth. On the ground spectators fight for access to the booth; on a gallery above their heads Burke, Sheridan, and Fox as clowns and zanies proclaim the attractions of the show; above their heads hang large pictorial placards on rollers, illustrating the shows to be seen within.... The three showmen are (left) Burke, in oriental dress but wearing a Jesuit's biretta and a clown's ruff; he blows a trumpet ... with a banner inscribed 'Sublimity'. Next is Sheridan, dressed as a clown, beating on a salt-box inscribed 'Attic'. On the right is Fox as Punch, larger than the other two; his hat is inscribed 'Wisdom', his body 'Argument', and his hump 'Knoledge'. Above their heads the three placards are [from left to right] 1.) 'The Prodigious Monster arrived from the East'; Hastings holds in his arms an Indian woman whom he is devouring. He tramples on the prostrate bodies of women and children. In the background a naked 'Black Secretary' with horns drives with a whip an ox with drums on its back. Two Indians appear to be in flight. 2.) 'The Oratorical Tragedy, or the Power of the pathetic over the beautiful' [an allusion to Burke's book].

> '"—he would drown the stage with tears
> and cleave the general ear with horrid Speech".'
> *Hamlet*

"Burke (right), standing in water produced by the tears of his audience, harangues seven ladies and a man, all with water spouting from their eyes. The man holds a smelling-bottle to the nose of a fainting lady. All are up to the neck in a sea of tears. 3.) 'Dancing on the Tight-Rope', Hastings dangles from a gibbet."

Introduction

EDMUND BURKE'S CONSERVATIVE LOGIC OF EMPIRE

THE FOLLOWING PAGES ADVANCE SIMULTANEOUSLY three increasingly heterodox scholarly propositions. The first two are that Edmund Burke (1729/1730–1797), was a consistently conservative political thinker and that he was a passionate defender of the British Empire in the eighteenth century. The third is that Burke's conservatism, in fact, provided the theoretical framework within which his defense of empire was built. More broadly, I suggest that the specific modes of reasoning that Burke employed to justify empire in his own time would long outlive him. Indeed, the cornerstones of what I am calling Burke's conservative logic of empire prefigured the two basic theoretical rationales for British imperialism throughout its heyday in the nineteenth and twentieth centuries.

ORIENTALISM, ORNAMENTALISM, AND CRITIQUES OF LIBERAL IMPERIALISM

Put provocatively, I argue that Burke's defense of empire was based on two theoretical strategies, one that Edward Said has called "Orientalism" and one that David Cannadine has dubbed "Ornamentalism."[1] Said's classic argument, which did much to establish the flourishing field of postcolonial studies,[2] is that historically Britain and other Western powers justified empire through a process of "Othering." This was a mode of representing non-Westerners as the embodiment of radical alterity and inferiority, characteristics that made them ripe for Western imperial domination and tutelage.[3] Said's view has more recently exerted a great deal of influence on the "new imperial history," a field whose practitioners have drawn particular attention to the ways in which those defending the British Empire sought to create and exploit racial and gender differences to justify their actions.[4]

Conversely, David Cannadine has emphasized that at its apogee, from 1857 to 1953, the British Empire was at least as much about class as it was about race and gender, and at least as much about what we might call "Saming," or the reproduction of affinities and similarities, as it was about Othering, or the production and reproduction of difference. On Cannadine's account the theoretical strategy deployed by British officialdom in the creation and defense of empire was one that sought out—and endeavored to reproduce abroad—the deeply stratified social hierarchies that defined Britain itself throughout this period. In this sense, for Cannadine the British Empire "was in large part about the domestication of the exotic—the comprehending and reordering of the foreign in parallel, analogous, equivalent, resemblant terms."[5]

When juxtaposed in this way, Said and Cannadine's arguments appear as rival interpretive frameworks for understanding how modern empires justified themselves. However, Burke deployed both of these strategies of imperial justification. Moreover, he was perhaps the most prominent canonical thinker to articulate both Ornamentalist and Orientalist defenses of empire simultaneously, and he did so from the standpoint of a theoretically consistent ideological commitment to conservatism. In this respect, while recent scholarship on theory and empire has been invaluable, it has also occluded as much as it has clarified.

On the one hand, recent work in this vein has shown that modern notions of freedom, despotism, and individualism were themselves developed in conjunction with and often served as justifications for European imperial and commercial expansion.[6] In fact, empires from the fifteenth to the nineteenth century raised fundamental problems for almost all of the contested concepts in what we now consider modern political thought, ranging from human nature, property, rights, sovereignty, and international justice, to the role of commerce, and the notions of "civilization" and historical progress.[7]

On the other hand, much of this work has focused almost exclusively on how liberalism, with its foundational theoretical premise of free and equal individuals, could nevertheless be used to underpin the construction of modern systems of domination that denied people both freedom and equality, often in the most brutal fashion imaginable. Here, scholars have provided us with crucial insights concerning the theoretical maneuvers that enabled imperialism to coexist in a symbiotic relationship with liberalism.[8] However, the single-minded focus on liberalism and empire has also led interpreters to misread the imperial arguments of the greatest modern conservative and, thus, to overlook the very different mode of justifying empire evident in his thought, as well as the legacy of his arguments in defense of empire and imperialism.

EDMUND BURKE: LIBERAL CRITIC OF LIBERALISM AND EMPIRE? ANTI-IMPERIAL HERO?

Edmund Burke plays a very curious role in the new narrative of canonical political thinkers' relationship to empire. These days, one finds Burke not only lauded for his criticisms of British imperial practice but also celebrated for his putative opposition to the project of empire writ large. Indeed, in the new literature on theory and empire, Burke—the thinker once conventionally regarded by scholars as the leading modern conservative—has, for many, thrown off that supposedly ill-fitting label and emerged as something of a hero across the spectrum of academic commentary.

For example, David Bromwich, an English professor who has written an intellectual biography of Burke, declares flatly that "no serious historian today would repeat the commonplace that Burke was the father of modern conservatism." Furthermore, he insists that Burke "was the first internationalist among British political writers," one whose various positions on empire and revolution demonstrate incontrovertibly that "coercion and cruelty never had a fiercer enemy than Burke."[9] Likewise, the author of an influential book on the theoretical turn to defending empire in the nineteenth century insists that "it is a mistake . . . to suggest that Burke was committed to the cause of imperialism," or that his views on empire should be understood as fundamentally conservative.[10] Another important scholar of Enlightenment and empire goes further still, referring to Burke as one among a number of "anti-imperialist political thinkers" he identifies in the late eighteenth century, and concludes that Burke's attempt to impeach the first governor general of Bengal, Warren Hastings, is "particularly suggestive of the failed political results of anti-imperialist crusades."[11]

In his influential book *Liberalism and Empire,* Uday Mehta takes a somewhat different approach by insisting that no eighteenth-century tradition of anti-imperialism existed, hence it would be anachronistic to pose the question of whether a given thinker like Burke was for or against empire tout court.[12] Nonetheless, Mehta argues at length that Burke effectively "shatters the philosophic underpinnings of the project of the empire."[13] Another commentator seems willing to grant that Burke might have been a conservative, but insists that the most famous tract of modern conservatism, *Reflections on the Revolution in France* (1790), should itself be understood as an anticolonial masterwork.[14] Still another simply crowns Burke "the most politically engaged eighteenth-century anti-imperialist thinker."[15]

Furthermore, contemporary commentators on Burke and empire often go on to portray him as one far more deeply committed to the self-professed liberal values of freedom, equality, inclusion, pluralism, and difference than the Lockes, Mills, and Tocquevilles of the world, whose views on empire systematically breached liberalism's core tenets. For example, Mehta treats Burke as a cosmopolitan liberal who expresses a "reverent humility" in the face of cultural, economic, and political difference that "create[s] a lateral plane" between different cultures. In this way, he argues, Burke "saw through the abusive distortions of civilizational hierarchies" along with the assumptions of racial superiority and cultural impoverishment by which the British justified their territorial expansionism and commercial greed.[16] Similarly, the author of a highly sympathetic book on Burke and Ireland describes that work as a complement to Mehta's argument, one that further explores Burke's critique of colonialism as applied to his Irish homeland.[17] Elsewhere, Burke's writings on Native Americans in the imperial context of the New World are described as "surprisingly favorable."[18]

Against the backdrop of a growing scholarly consensus that Burke was neither a defender of empire nor even a conservative, my fundamental claim is that Burke ardently defended empire—and at points its radical expansion—and did so precisely from the standpoint of a conservative worldview that rejected liberalism's central principles. Indeed, Burke would pioneer a nascent version of both Orientalist (Othering) and Ornamentalist (Saming) arguments from within a theoretically consistent ideological standpoint to develop a recognizably conservative, and deeply illiberal, logic of empire. In order to make this case, however, something first needs to be said about both the nature of Burke's conservatism and the importance he attributed to intellectual consistency.

BURKE'S CONSERVATISM AND CONSISTENCY

Burke as a Conservative

Elsewhere, I have argued that Burke understood European civilization as built on two cornerstones, organized religion and the landed aristocracy, institutionalized in the church and the nobility. Together, these two institutions served as the material embodiments of Burke's aesthetic principles of the "sublime" and the "beautiful," rooted in fear and love, respectively. I tried to show how Burke synthesized his early philosophical and historical work with the historiographical narrative of the Scottish Enlightenment (which imagined progress from "savagery," through "barbarism," to "civilization" across four stages of economic development) to articulate a unique understanding of the civilizing process. On Burke's view, the nobility and the church jointly inculcated what he referred to as the requisite degree of "habitual social discipline" necessary for "a people," proper, to emerge and be governed by a "natural aristocracy" sitting atop an ordered hierarchy of social ranks in which the masses appropriately subordinated themselves to the wiser, wealthier, and more cultivated. For Burke, the nobility did this by helping the masses to love their superiors, while the church led them to fear their betters. Only where such a system flourished did Burke recognize "civilization," as opposed to "savagery," or "barbarism."[19]

My contention was that, given this understanding of history, for Burke the French Revolution represented the end of Western civilization.[20] The revolutionaries systematically destroyed the church and the nobility, the two institutions he saw as chiefly responsible for driving the European civilizing process. Further, on Burke's view, the leaders of the French Revolution deliberately replaced these two pillars of civilization with mutually reinforcing egalitarian political institutions and social and cultural practices that encompassed the public and private spheres. In doing so, Burke argued, the revolutionaries intentionally obliterated the balanced alchemy of fear and love, sublimity and beauty, that had guaranteed European civilization, and unleashed in its stead a world of fearless, untamed "savagery."

In his later writings on the Revolution, Burke went on to decry as wholly unprecedented what he saw as the systematic attempt to break down natural authority relations within the family and to promote adultery and sexual promiscuity, a skyrocketing divorce rate, the legal equality of nontraditional families and their offspring, and an explosive growth in popular entertainment of all sorts, especially via the print medium. One of the definitive markers of the Revolution's unprecedented quality, Burke declared, was that the French were introducing a new system of democratic manners precisely to accommodate and support their new scheme of democratic politics. Thus the collapse of civilization was signified for Burke by a politically engaged hoi polloi ranging from tavern keepers and clerks to liberated women. In Burke's fevered imagination, the masses had torn themselves free from fealty to the natural aristocracy and lost all habitual social discipline. The result was a nightmare world of political equality echoed and reinforced by willful social, sexual, and cultural leveling in the private sphere that destroyed the natural moral sentiments. It was this entirely new phenomenon of thoroughgoing democratization that Burke depicted as synonymous with savagery and as signaling the end of Western civilization.

My portrayal of Burke thus painted him as a deeply conservative figure, one thoroughly beholden to the illiberal idea of natural inequality and hierarchy among human beings. It was for this reason that he favored a brand of aristocratic rule buttressed by the guiding force of an established church. In fact, Burke was entirely antipathetic to any notions of political equality, universal declarations of rights, or secularism and resolutely rejected all forms of democracy and democratization (understood as the right of the lower orders and women to vote, hold office, and take an active role in politics). He was also a fervent defender of the patriarchal family and women's inequality in the private sphere, and he defended a form of male power ultimately underwritten by force and the threat of violence, a point made long ago by one of Burke's fiercest critics, Mary Wollstonecraft.[21]

For Burke, the only approach to legitimate change was therefore a brand of incrementalism that fatalistically accepted the imperfectability of human beings and the existential inevitability of evil in human affairs. But on most fronts he resisted even that, arguing for example that the minimal franchise in eighteenth-century Britain's corrupt electoral system ought to be reduced still further, rather than expanded. Against this backdrop, Burke saw the French Revolution as a dangerously hubristic grand secular democratic scheme predicated on the absurd ideas of basic human equality and universal natural rights. He believed that such egalitarian schemes were not only unnatural, theoretically flawed, and morally repugnant but also likely to produce unintended, unforeseeable, and dangerous consequences, given human beings' limited capacity for rationality. Against them, Burke urged instead prejudice in favor of history's prescriptive hierarchical institutions, especially the nobility and the church, which he believed had rightly defended massive inequalities in private property as sacrosanct, thereby enabling a form of elite rule that he believed had led Europeans from savagery to civilization.

Burke deployed these fundamental beliefs in an attempt to conserve the basic political, social, and economic structure of the Old Regime in Britain and Europe, and also to conserve the British Empire in the New World, India, and Ireland. Of course, the most punctilious of historicists might object to the notion that such views make Burke a conservative, because he was by party affiliation a Whig, not a Tory. In addition, one might take issue with the nomenclature on the grounds of linguistic anachronism: the term *conservative* did not gain popular political currency until the nineteenth century, hence Burke cannot be the purveyor of an ideology for which no word existed at the time.[22] However, the former approach does not consider the substance of Burke's beliefs, while the latter also necessarily means that one cannot refer to any thinker as a liberal or as a contributor to liberalism before the nineteenth century, when those words were first used in a political sense. This is a step that few scholars are willing to take, and for good reason: it precludes—at the very least—talking about liberalism's relationship to the Enlightenment (or any Enlightenment thinker), the American Revolution and founding, and the French Revolution. Rather, liberalism—like conservatism—is treated like an ideological mushroom that is unconnected to any of these earlier intellectual currents and political events and that springs up sui generis in the nineteenth century. Surely this is problematic. However, if we understand modern conservatism as a substantive set of beliefs expressive of a particular political ideology, in addition to being a positional doctrine, then Burke's views on the French Revolution, as well as his earlier writings on aesthetics, culture, and history, represent the quintessential expression of conservatism *avant la lettre*. In this regard, I believe that twentieth-century conservatives and their critics have not all somehow been wildly mistaken in seeing Burke as the intellectual wellspring and founding father of modern conservatism.[23]

Burke as a Consistent Thinker

Hence I faced the conundrum of how to square this conservative version of Burke—largely focused on the French Revolution—with the kinder, gentler figure given to liberal pluralism, difference, and inclusion emerging as part of the new narrative on theory and empire. From a longer scholarly perspective, these recent interpretations have an ironic "back to the future" quality about them: For more than a century after his death the writings and speeches of the "early" Burke, which criticized the overreaching power of George III and the king's men, including their approach to the American colonies, were central to the Whig interpretation of history (while his views on the French Revolution were entirely ignored). Accordingly, Burke was seen as the forerunner of the British Liberal party. Similarly, in the first half of the twentieth century Burke served as a subject of intermittent fascination and sometime allegiance for numerous thinkers on the academic and political left.[24] From this longer view, it seems that contemporary scholars have now added a supposedly anti-imperial dimension to a character that has lived on and off for more than two centuries.

This latest interpretive turn adds yet one more layer to the long-standing "Burke problem," a dilemma akin to that which once plagued readers of Adam Smith.[25] In its Burkean variant, the question has been how to understand the relationship between his early and late work: How could the same thinker who became the touchstone for Victorian liberalism also have written such a vitriolic attack on the French Revolution, thereby producing a text that later became the bedrock of modern conservatism? Was Burke's work theoretically consistent and coherent, or hopelessly inconsistent and incoherent? The latest iteration of the "Burke problem" deepens this conundrum, by forcing interpreters to grapple with how Burke's interpretation of the French Revolution comports with his stance on empire.

Some commentators have argued that the issue of coherence versus incoherence itself makes no sense, because as a practicing politician Burke was interested not in theoretical questions but rather in defending a particular Whig party line regardless of how the various stances he took fit together.[26] However, the more general interpretive strategy has been to offer one of several theoretical master keys deemed necessary to unlock the fundamental consistency of Burke's work. These are in turn usually derived from some deeper intellectual taproot.[27]

The "Burke problem" inevitably takes on a methodological dimension, centered as it is on questions of theoretical consistency or coherence in the assessment of canonical figures in the history of political thought. This became particularly salient with the rise of Cambridge-school historicism, whose central figures issued a fundamental challenge to those attempting to knit the separate threads of a thinker's texts into a single consistent garment said to cover the entirety of his or her work, a task they usually regarded as a fool's errand, at best.[28]

However, the Cambridge school is open to a number of important criticisms on the specific issues of consistency and coherence.[29] In the absence of very good reasons for not doing so, we should strive to understand a given thinker's multiple utterances as comprising a coherent web of beliefs expressive of his or her particular understanding of the world.[30] Of course, while I think that the assumption that past (and present) thinkers aspire to intellectual coherence and consistency is an accurate one at a general methodological level, its applicability to particular thinkers obviously varies. If Edmund Burke were like Ralph Waldo Emerson and regarded intellectual consistency as a "hobgoblin," or portrayed willful intellectual inconsistency as a badge of mental superiority, then perhaps seeming contradictions between large portions of his work would not be nearly so troubling.

But this was clearly *not* the case. To the contrary, one of the basic reasons to ask whether (and if so, how) Burke's writings and speeches on empire are theoretically consonant with his work on the French Revolution is that *Burke himself* was steadfast and passionate in claiming that he was an internally coherent and consistent thinker. In fact, charges that he was either completely self-contradictory or deeply hypocritical (or both) were among those most fervently pressed by Burke's contemporaneous critics subsequent to the publication of the *Reflections on the Revolution in France*. Wollstonecraft, Paine, Price, and even members of his own Whig party excoriated Burke for his unwillingness to support the French Revolution when he had been so sympathetic to the American colonists before their own revolt, even acting at one point as London agent for the colony of New York. In addition, Burke ultimately paid a tremendous political price for his opposition to the French Revolution, because it precipitated a break with his closest political ally, Charles James Fox, and the rest of the "new Whig" faction that supported the Revolution, effectively sending Burke into political exile for the rest of his parliamentary career.

The obvious point is that Burke regarded intellectual consistency as a fundamental value worth paying the price of his own political career to defend, at length, in print. In 1791, in the immediate aftermath of charges of inconsistency regarding the *Reflections,* Burke wrote his famous *Appeal from the New to the Old Whigs* (its subtitle is: *In Consequence of Some Late Discussions in Parliament, Relative to the Reflections on the French Revolution*). In that pamphlet, Burke angrily declared that he could "justify to consistency everything he has said and done during the course of a political life just touching to its close."[31] Indeed, the pamphlet itself is Burke's extended attempt to demonstrate that his views on the French Revolution were of a piece with everything else he had said, written, or done throughout that career. Burke made this assertion after the majority of what he had to say about India, and even Ireland (not to mention America), had been set forth, and he continued to defend his consistency until his dying day.

THINKING EMPIRE AND REVOLUTION TOGETHER

As an interpretive matter, when an author claims to be intellectually consistent across the corpus of his or her work, writes extensively to justify that claim, and is willing to pay a very high practical price in the name of defending that belief, we ignore this evidence at our peril. Burke clearly saw his work on empire as congruent with his work on the French Revolution; therefore, we should begin by privileging that self-understanding rather than disregarding and casually cordoning off his corpus into hermetically sealed component parts. Unfortunately, however, interpreters who focus on Burke's view of empire tend to disregard his view of the French Revolution, and vice versa. Furthermore, those who concentrate on Burke's writings and speeches on empire generally tend to focus on either India (usually) *or* Ireland (sometimes), while most interpreters have given short shrift to Burke's views on the American colonies, and almost none of them contemplate his views on the Native Americans and African slaves in the New World.[32]

However, for the very reason that Burke regarded his own intellectual positions as forming a coherent whole, one cannot take such easy paths and must instead attempt to think through both dimensions of his work—on revolution and empire—simultaneously while also avoiding the reduction of his views on empire to a selective interpretation of what he had to say about one or another of its nodal points. That is what I undertake here. I do so not as a historian but rather as a political theorist interested in Burke's larger argument as expressed in discourse. My approach is that of one "who studies what people said was happening around them and how they tried to affect what was happening by what they said."[33] My focus is therefore largely on Burke's speeches and writings in defense of his positions, including both his public and private utterances, which I situate within debates over the meaning and purpose of empire in the eighteenth century.

One scholar who takes up the challenge of thinking about the entirety of Burke's work is the historian Richard Bourke, whose *Empire and Revolution: The Political Life of Edmund Burke* appeared as this book was already in production. While I cannot, therefore, do justice to Bourke's mammoth and extremely well-researched reconstruction of Burke in the context of eighteenth-century British party politics, I can nevertheless briefly outline our basic interpretive similarities and differences.[34] Unlike other recent interpreters, Bourke is far too sophisticated and sensitive a reader of Burke to describe him as an "anti-imperial" thinker in any fashion. Indeed, he notes that Burke "consistently upheld the authority of empire" and in fact "justified the authority of civilized empire at every stage of his career," whether in the New World, India, or Ireland. On this point we are in complete agreement. However, important differences emerge in our respective views when we move to the question of how to describe the principles that animated Burke's career-long defense of empire, as well as its connection to his position on revolution. Like others, Bourke does not consider Burke a conservative. Instead, he describes Burke as a thinker committed to the imperial "right of conquest," but one who also firmly rejected the "spirit of conquest" in favor of the "spirit of liberty" in the conduct of empire.[35]

Conversely, my reading of Burke stresses the conservative ideological principles at work in his defense of the act of conquest, while it simultaneously problematizes any attempt to draw a hard and fast distinction between the spirits of conquest and liberty in the implementation of empire. Instead, I argue that Burke deployed the substantive conservative principles outlined above to defend a specific type of liberty for some people in the empire while also denying liberty in important ways (or altogether) for others, based on his conception of the civilizing process and his assessment of the relative degree of "civilization" or "savagery" that obtained in a given locale. Tellingly, this also meant that at crucial points, especially with respect to Native Americans and African slaves, Burke was eager to defend a civilizing mission that manifested the "spirit of conquest" in stark fashion.

CHAPTER OUTLINE

In chapter 1, I begin by briefly sketching the etymology of the term *empire*, then discuss eighteenth-century Britain's ideology of empire. As David Armitage in particular has shown, that ideology centered on the notion that the British Empire was free, commercial, Protestant, and maritime.[36] At the same time, I alert the reader to the many ways in which this official ideology of empire was a rhetorical claim made by imperialists themselves and, as such, was a self-serving and blinkered depiction of imperial reality in the eighteenth century. Burke grappled with both the official ideology and the reality on the ground, and some understanding of both dimensions of the imperial enterprise is consequently a necessary prerequisite for comprehending Burke's position.

Following this, I directly confront and reject the idea that Burke was in any sense an anti-imperial or anticolonial thinker. Through extensive reference to his writings on America, India, and Ireland, I show that Burke in fact warmly embraced and defended the British Empire over the entire course of his long political career and across all three principal sites of the eighteenth-century empire. This included India, where Burke sang the praises and overlooked the atrocities of Robert Clive, whose violent conquest and subsequent brutal policies in Bengal established Britain's territorial control of the subcontinent. Along with those of his immediate successors (prior to Warren Hastings), Clive's policies also help create the conditions for a famine that would ultimately kill as many as 10 million people, or a third of Bengal's population. I make this case to put to rest the persistent tendency in recent scholarship to conflate Burke's criticisms of later imperial practice with a wholesale opposition to the project of empire, writ large. Burke often criticized empire, but he never rejected it, even in the face of the massive calamity in India it brought about. To the contrary, he regarded empire as a providential gift, one of God's greatest blessings to the British, and a thing to be deeply cherished.

Having debunked the idea that Burke was opposed to empire, I then map the broad outlines of Burke's own conception of it. I stress that Burke's position relied on two basic principles. The first was his belief that empire required unquestioned sovereignty and the necessary subordination of the imperial periphery to the metropolitan core, whether in the case of America, India, or Ireland. In Burke's conservative logic of empire, this theoretical principle of imperial hierarchy and subordination held a position of lexical priority; it was the necessary starting point for all imperial questions. However, the second of Burke's principles was his insistence that the degree of liberty and self-governance afforded to particular peoples in the empire necessarily varied greatly and, hence, required equally varied modes of governance.

In the three chapters that follow, I consider concretely what Burke's broad commitment to attuning imperial governance to the character of the governed actually meant, by taking up successively and in depth his views on the theory and practice of empire in the New World, India, and Ireland. By looking carefully at these cases, I argue that we can see in Burke's writings and speeches a fundamental and unwavering conservative logic of empire that ties them together and links them tightly to his work on the French Revolution, principally through his understanding of history as a civilizing process.

For Burke, the scope of legitimate British imperial action had to be attuned to the relative level of "civilization" (or "savagery") that obtained within a specific geographical locale. Because this was so, it enabled Burke to defend the addition of a vast new territory based on conquest in India, the so-called swing to the east. Empire in India was neither Protestant, commercial, maritime, nor free. As such, India pointed to the conceptual limits of the official ideology of empire that Armitage shows to have emerged during the sixteenth to the eighteenth century. However, because Burke's conservative logic of empire justified imperial expansion on a global scale through the simultaneous development of Ornamentalist as well as Orientalist arguments, it could surmount the theoretical difficulties posed by the official ideology. In itself, Burke's position thereby prefigured the two dominant approaches to British imperialism during the nineteenth and twentieth centuries and effectively served as a conceptual bridge linking what are conventionally referred to as the "first" and "second" British Empires.

In chapter 2, I turn to the New World and start by sketching the central theoretical conundrums posed for the British by the American crisis of the 1760s and 1770s. I then move on to consider Burke's approach to the colonies throughout the period that culminated in American independence. I show that Burke saw the American colonists in Ornamentalist terms as an offshoot of British civilization and, therefore, as a "people" proper, one built as all civilized peoples were, on the pillars of organized religion and a kind of landed aristocracy. However, Burke also pointed to a number of peculiar features of the colonial Americans as a people that created in them a propensity for rebellion. The most important of these were the nature of Protestantism in the northern colonies, the dangerous inclination toward democratic representation in the colonial legislatures, and the effects of the institution of slavery in the South. For these reasons, Burke argued for a policy of conciliation with the colonies built on the moral psychology of "sympathy" he endorsed. Such an approach stressed the importance of civilizational solidarity between Britain and colonial America built on their underlying similarity, and it looked to the resultant deep affective ties between these two peoples as the principal means of keeping the transatlantic empire together.

I then meditate at length on the Orientalist side of Burke's argument, by considering how Burke applied his logic of empire to the New World's Others—namely, its large numbers of Native Americans and African slaves. Here, I argue in successive sections that Burke rejected the notion that either of these groups was a "civilized" people and identified them instead as "savage" populations. Regarding the Amerindians, I demonstrate that Burke's understanding of them as hostile savages lacking in the institutional rudiments of civilization is a theme that goes back to his earliest writings and is one he developed extensively. It was for this reason that in the American crisis Burke adamantly rejected the use of these "savages" as allies against the colonists in war. Instead, he urged the British to make common cause with their colonial brethren to push westward into the American continent with the aim of imperial conquest and conversion—or in short, of "civilizing" the Native Americans while also thereby tightening the affective bonds between Britain and the American colonies.

As concerns the African slaves, Burke likewise argued against any proposals to offer them freedom if they would fight on the British side in the American conflict. Rather, he defended the institution of slavery throughout the American crisis, just as he had defended expanding the slave trade before the conflict. I then focus on the nature of Burke's intervention in the debate over slavery that took place near the end of his career, long after American independence had been won and in the face of a massive push to immediately abolish slavery and the slave trade. In this debate, Burke favored gradual abolition. However, a careful examination of his position shows that Burke's policy aims were identical to those that stretch back to his earliest writings. Burke's goal was principally to use organized religion as a means of "civilizing" the Africans before their emancipation, just as he had earlier urged it as the chief means of "civilizing" them and the Amerindians. When slaves were finally to be set free after their "improvement," Burke argued, they should be held to a strict behavioral code and made to demonstrate before the law that they had become civilized beings, failing which, he argued, they should be reenslaved.

Burke's long-submerged arguments about Native Americans and Africans demonstrate his willingness to deploy his Orientalist understanding of civilization—albeit in the West rather than the East—to create a theoretical concept of alterity, or "savagery," as a means of keeping the colonial empire in the New World together. As I make clear in the final section of chapter 2, this strategy interweaves with Burke's views on the French Revolution in a crystalline fashion in the 1790s, when he takes up the issue of the slave revolts in the Caribbean. Burke believed that such events as the Haitian Revolution, led by former slaves, were dangerous and horrifying proof that the French doctrine of the rights of man was an egalitarian disease that acted like a solvent on empire, by leading the savages to revolt against the civilized colonists in dreadful fashion.

Following this, I turn in chapter 3 to Burke's arguments relative to the British Empire in India. Traditionally, Burke's views on India have been at the heart of the mistaken "anti-imperial" interpretation of his thought. However, by the time we reach chapter 3, we know that this is an untenable reading of Burke's views regarding the subcontinent, as elsewhere. Thus the real question becomes: what was the basis for Burke's long and laborious crusade to impeach and convict Warren Hastings, the former governor general of Bengal, for his crimes while in office? Indeed, what did Burke believe Hastings's crimes truly were in the first place, and what made them sufficiently objectionable that he should be held accountable before the bar of Parliament? From the standpoint of Burke's conservative logic of empire, this question receives a striking answer that fundamentally challenges much recent scholarship: Burke's view of the East, in this case India, was in fact deeply Ornamentalist. Given Burke's understanding of civilization, he did not in fact see India as an exemplar of difference worth defending, but actually viewed it as a mirror image of western European civilization because, like Europe, it exhibited the definitional markers of all truly civilized societies.

I demonstrate that at a general level Burke stressed the institutional and functional similarity of organized religion and the landed nobility in India and Europe. On his account, these institutions worked to create a cultural, commercial, and even material world that was remarkably similar in both locales. I then go on to show that Burke lauded Hinduism and the Hindu caste system, as he understood them, as the quintessential expression of authentic Indian religion, and he stressed Hinduism's role in linking the worldly and divine to create a deeply stratified social hierarchy, even more effectively than was the case in Europe. Finally, we see Burke's remarkable narrowing of the conceptual distance between Europe and the subcontinent in his rendering of Muslim India, and specifically in his rejection of the tradition of "Oriental despotism" and his concomitant insistence on the importance of what he describes as the Mughal version of the British "ancient constitution." Taken together, these Ornamentalist modes of tightly analogizing India and Europe would prove central to Burke's strategy of affectively linking these two great civilizations. This can be seen in Burke's extended recourse to the moral psychology of "sympathy" that is central to his political theory, to his specific critique of British imperial practice in India, and to his attempt to punish Hastings. Such theoretical moves, in turn, enabled Burke to represent the British as the appropriate inheritors of the "civilized" Mughal Empire in India, together with its extraordinary extractive capacities. Because this was the case, Burke argued that the British should have preserved inviolate the hierarchical world of the Indian Old Regime with its landed aristocracy, organized religion, and caste system,

In the latter half of chapter 3, I argue that—because Burke saw Indian civilization in Ornamentalist terms as a mirror image of European civilization—his critique of empire in India closely resembled and in many ways anticipated his critique of the French Revolution. Burke's analysis of the failings of empire in India was tightly tied to his critique of revolution in France because he saw both events as assaults on the anciens régimes of two similar civilizations. This can be seen in three areas in particular, all of which were vital to Burke's prosecution of Hastings. The first area is Burke's detailed description of the attack on the Indian nobility and landed aristocracy. The second is his lengthy depictions of the downfall of aristocratic women in India, which are every bit as central to Burke's narrative of events in India as in France. The third relates to Burke's attempt directly to conjoin the animating spirit of illegitimate imperial excess and illegitimate revolutionary resistance, or "tyranny" and "rebellion," and thus to argue that "Indianism" and "Jacobinism" were essentially flip sides of the same theoretical coin.

In the fourth and final chapter, I take up Burke's views on the place of his homeland, Ireland, within the British Empire. I first situate Burke's biography, with its dual Protestant and Catholic elements, within the broader context of Ireland's ambiguous historical status both as a quasi-independent sister kingdom within the framework of "multiple monarchy" and as a colony subordinate to England. Ireland's imperial status gave rise to a series of commercial and political debates in the 1770s and 1780s with which Burke was deeply engaged. The most important of these were the question of an absentee tax on the owners of Irish land; the advisability of granting Ireland the ability to trade freely with the rest of the empire; and the fraught issue of the Protestant "patriot" party and Irish Volunteers' push for "legislative independence" from the British Parliament. On these issues, Burke's strident opposition to any form of absentee tax, his full-throated support of free trade for Ireland as a means of preventing the Irish from breaking away from Britain as the Americans had, and his long-standing dislike for the "Revolution of 1782" and Ireland's legislative "independence" strongly demonstrate Burke's willingness to prioritize the British Empire's survival above all other considerations related to his native land.

However, Burke also combined this unwavering commitment to empire with an equally passionate desire to alleviate the draconian penal laws imposed by the Protestant Ascendancy on four-fifths of Ireland's people, the Catholics, and to provide a small portion of the elite Catholic population with the ability to vote and hold some political offices. In order to understand Burke's arguments on this score, which combine in equal measure the goals of keeping Ireland as a subordinate part of the empire and alleviating the plight of Irish Catholics, one must turn to his view of Irish history within the parameters of his understanding of history as a civilizing process.

On Burke's view, I argue, the history of England's conquests and confiscations of Irish land, when combined with the systematic discrimination of the penal laws, had warped and transmogrified its "natural aristocracy" into something else entirely. The Protestant minority in Ireland constituted instead what Burke called a "plebeian oligarchy," one that was far too numerous to play its role in the civilizing process but which also locked out the Catholic nobility, whom he believed should appropriately be a part of any rightly constituted ruling elite. Because this was so, Burke argued, the penal laws had to be revoked entirely, and the Catholic aristocracy had to be allowed to vote and hold some political offices, in order to re-create something like a proper ruling class in Ireland.

In short, Burke saw Ireland in Ornamentalist terms, as a sister civilization possessing the required elements of organized religion and aristocracy, should they be properly cultivated. However, precisely because this was so, Burke looked on in horror during the 1790s at what he saw as the Protestant Ascendancy's reckless pursuit of exactly the wrong strategy: delaying the renunciation of the penal laws and resolutely resisting the enfranchisement of Catholic elites. The danger of such an approach, Burke believed, was that the Protestant Ascendancy would strengthen the hand of the United Irishmen, a group led by the Protestant republican Theobald Wolfe Tone, which sought a nonsectarian Ireland based on the democratic principles of universal manhood suffrage and Thomas Paine's *Rights of Man*.

As becomes increasingly evident in his work from the 1790s, Burke's greatest fear was that the Ascendancy was leading the Irish lower and middling orders of both Catholics and Protestant Dissenters to coalesce in support of the United Irishmen, who ultimately blamed Ireland's problems on the imperial connection with England and sought to sever that link forever in favor of an independent Ireland. Burke rejected such arguments because he claimed that after the granting of legislative "independence," in 1782, all of Ireland's problems were attributable solely to the Protestant Ascendancy—and thus to Ireland alone—and not England. Therefore, he spent his last years warning at length that the Ascendancy's policies were inevitably forging an alliance between Ireland's masses, the United Irishmen, and the French Revolution.

From Burke's perspective, given his understanding of civilization, this was disastrous. He believed that by discriminating against the Catholics and Dissenters the Ascendancy was waging war on the wrong enemy, their fellow Christians. In imaginatively failing to perceive the Ornamentalist civilizational solidarity between Catholic and Protestant aristocratic elites the Ascendancy also failed to recognize the rise of wholly new dangers posed by what Burke referred to by the single term *Jacobinism:* atheism, secularism, and a brand of egalitarianism underpinned by universal rights that threatened to swamp civilization under a wave of democratic fervor. For Burke, the Ascendancy's policies were alienating the Catholic majority, whose "habitual social discipline" and corresponding commitment to hierarchy and order would ordinarily lead them to defend a justly constituted ancien régime. At the same time, they were holding out the property of the aristocracy as one of the great spoils of rebellion.

Burke admitted that this strategy, which targeted the two essential institutions of the civilizing process simultaneously, was meeting with broad support in Ireland. The results, he feared, would be an alliance of the French revolutionaries with the United Irishmen in an endeavor to break the imperial connection with Britain, instill atheistic democracy, and ultimately end civilization in Ireland and England. This was a process that, he believed, had already been accomplished in France. For these reasons, as I maintain at the end of chapter 4, Burke would have favored the union of Great Britain and Ireland, which in fact occurred only a few short years after his death. Such a policy would have been the culmination of a consistent and coherent conservative logic of empire that animated Edmund Burke's political theory from the beginning to the end of his career.

CHAPTER I

Burke and Empire in Context

EDMUND BURKE WAS BORN INTO a world increasingly governed by empires and imperial rivalry. To understand Burke's conception of empire, we must begin with the definition of the term itself and what it had come to mean for the British in the eighteenth century. The English word *empire* is derived from the Latin *imperium,* whose literal meaning is "supreme power or command." Initially, *imperium* referred to the authority of a magistrate to act in the name of Rome and its citizens. Over time, therefore, the term became closely allied with sovereignty, originally understood as the power to apply Rome's laws. In the beginning there was a distinct division between the domestic and external realms subject to this power. However, eventually *imperium* (and hence *empire*) came to connote unlimited authority over both spheres. The "Roman Empire" thus came to be understood as a single extended territorial unit encompassing different political and cultural communities under one sovereign power, and our modern understanding of empire has inherited this broader meaning.[1]

The terms *colony* (and *colonialism,* etc.) derive from another Latin word, *colonus,* meaning "farmer." Here, the etymology appropriately reminds us that colonial practices are best understood as one subset of imperial practices, involving the large-scale transfer of settler populations from the metropole to peripheral territories, where the new arrivals "planted" themselves permanently in the soil while maintaining political allegiance to their home country.[2]

From this perspective we can see that eighteenth-century Britain was both imperial, as in the case of India (which had no large-scale British settler population), and colonial, as in the case of North America and (to a lesser extent) the West Indies. Ireland was a more difficult case to define in these terms. Unlike all of the other nodal points of the British Empire in the eighteenth century, it was technically a "kingdom by conquest," but one with a large and well-established colonial population by the eighteenth century.[3]

As it unfolded during the 1700s, the concept of empire underwent a transformation based on the practices and interests of British policy makers. The earlier notion of *imperium* as sovereignty or military rule (including rule over a large geographically contiguous area) expanded to cover a wider range of interwoven phenomena. The eighteenth-century British Empire included territories marked by conquest and overseas colonization, but also those linked by new networks of commerce, often coexisting in overlapping and complex fashion. Additionally, regardless of any discrete terminological division, the British actually engaged in acts of conquest not only in the "kingdom" of Ireland but also against the Native Americans in the "colonial" context and on the Indian subcontinent in the more old-fashioned and narrowly "imperial" one.[4] In order to understand Burke's overarching logic of empire, therefore, we must first come to grips with the multilayered, deeply entwined, and evolving meanings of the term *British Empire* in the eighteenth century, which provided the necessary context in which his particular conception of empire developed.

THE IDEOLOGY OF BRITISH EMPIRE IN THE EIGHTEENTH CENTURY

David Armitage has shown convincingly that Britain's dominant conception of its empire in the eighteenth century was defined by the terms "Protestant, commercial, maritime, and free." This regnant self-understanding was an "ideology"—or a specific, systematic, and contestable political interpretation—of a geographical entity that started to develop from the mid-sixteenth century. By the 1730s it included the kingdoms of England and Scotland along with Wales (collectively known as "Great Britain" after the 1707 Act of Union), as well as the "third kingdom" of Ireland.[5] This portion of the "Atlantic Archipelago," to use J. G. A. Pocock's term, was centered at London and situated along an "Anglo-Celtic frontier" that was increasingly dominated by English culture, political norms, institutions, and language throughout the period.[6] By the second quarter of the eighteenth century the settler colonies of North America and the islands of the Caribbean had also been firmly added to this archipelago, an entity whose inhabitants for the first time began to describe themselves as members of a unified "British Empire," understood as a Protestant, commercial, maritime, and free community.[7] Let us consider each of its four component themes briefly in turn.

We shall start with freedom, or "liberty," since it has been observed that the fundamental question for the British in the eighteenth century was how to reconcile *imperium* and *libertas*,[8] or how to create a unified empire based on liberty. But what was meant by *liberty*? Even though it was not universally applied even in the metropole, the British trumpeted the protection of a number of "negative" freedoms pertaining to the individual. These included the protection of life, freedom of personal movement, freedom from arbitrary arrest, and the protection of private property. The most important source of these liberties was the common law, but institutionally their defense also required the right to trial by jury and not to be taxed or subject to laws without "consent." By the eighteenth century there was also a well-established belief, supposedly traceable back to the quasi-mythical "ancient constitution" but really emerging in the seventeenth century, that political liberty could be preserved only through a mixed constitution of the one (king), the few (House of Lords), and the many (House of Commons). Such a constitution created both a balance and a separation of powers in the form of a representative government, the so-called king in Parliament. This arrangement, which greatly augmented parliamentary power, grew out of the Glorious Revolution of 1688 and was largely gospel in the metropole by the mid-eighteenth century.[9]

Closely allied to the principle of liberty in the British conception of empire was that of commerce.[10] The British depicted their empire as built on Enlightenment principles: it eschewed the conquest, subjugation, or destruction of indigenous peoples for the purpose of extracting their resources (much unlike their imperial competitors France and—especially—Spain). Instead, the basis of the British Empire was said to be trade, or *commercium*, in the widest sense of the term, one that encompassed the exchange of ideas as well as material goods. According to Scottish Enlightenment thinkers in particular, commerce was held to require freedom rather than force, and commercial interactions were understood by the British as having a profoundly humanizing and civilizing effect on all those who engaged in them. Commerce, it was believed, could in fact culminate in the alleviation and perhaps even the elimination of international conflict.[11] Within this framework, Britain saw its North American and West Indian colonies as built on the backs of intrepid colonial entrepreneurs enacting their liberty on unbroken ground and aiming, simultaneously, at material gain and spreading the civilizing fruits of what Montesquieu, a great lover of things British, praised as "sweet commerce."

This view of the New World points in turn to the importance of the doctrine of *res nullius* or *terra nullius* ("empty things" or "empty lands"), which formed the philosophical backbone of the British Empire across the Atlantic until the end of the eighteenth century. According to this theory, the British did not see themselves as the *conquerors* of indigenous peoples at all, unlike the French and Spanish. There were two dimensions to this claim. The first was straightforward: for a time, many of the lands in North America seemed literally empty, devoid of inhabitants and therefore available for anyone willing to exercise individual liberty to make their own private property. However, this argument could extend only so far, because the British quickly encountered Native Americans, both in small settlements and wandering nomadically through large territories that they had previously assumed were vacant.

This is where the second dimension of the *res nullius* claim proved essential. According to John Locke and others, the lands of the New World remained empty, notwithstanding the existence of large numbers of Native Americans on them, because most of their inhabitants did not to do what the colonists' very Protestant God had instructed, which was to enclose common lands, till and improve them, and plant themselves as well as their crops in residence on them. In the *Second Treatise,* the Calvinist Locke memorably insisted that while God gave the earth to men in common, he did not want it to stay that way. Rather, he gave it to the industrious and rational and commanded them to mix their labor with it, subdue it, cultivate it, enrich it, and divide it up into discrete individual tracts of private property. The Native Americans' failure to do this could only mean that they were irrational, incapable of understanding God's law, and therefore less than fully equal human beings, or, alternatively, that they were willfully disobeying God's commands. Either way, the British saw themselves as justified in settling on the land, because the indigenous peoples did not really own it anyway. In some instances, of course, the British did "freely" trade for or purchase the land from settled Native American tribes (who wondered at the strange beings who believed anyone could own the earth), thus "planting" themselves on the land without violently extirpating its previous inhabitants, at least in the short run.[12]

At the same time, earlier arguments drawn from feudal conquest and the obligation to spread Christianity and transform the "heathen" subjects newly under Britain's control also persisted as forms of justification for expanding empire in North America. These arguments went back to Sir Edward Coke's famous decision in *Calvin's Case* (1608), an argument that crystallized the views embedded in royal charters such as the one establishing the Virginia Company (1606), requiring Christian princes to convert all Amerindian heathens in a sort of religious crusade. For Coke, conversion remained the ultimate goal, one that was the logical extension of the absolute power that conquest legitimized. Failing their willing conversion, Coke argued, permanent war was justified over indigenous imperial subjects. This justification for westward expansion in America surfaced strongly in some quarters after 1763, with the vast new territorial acquisitions made during the Seven Years' War.[13]

That both *res nullius* arguments and those derived from conquest were predicated on a specific religious understanding of God's intentions points to the third pillar of the British Empire in the eighteenth century, its Protestantism. In the sixteenth and seventeenth centuries, thinkers such as the two Richard Hakluyts (elder and younger), Sir Walter Raleigh, and Samuel Purchas defended the aggressive expansion of English power, especially in the New World, as a means of spreading the true faith and fending off the imperial advances of Catholic Spain.[14] As Linda Colley has shown, Protestantism took on a still greater importance for the later expansion of the empire because it served as a bulwark against Catholic France, Great Britain's greatest enemy throughout the eighteenth century. The Protestant faith provided the necessary social glue to bind England, Scotland, and Wales together at home (if not Ireland, entirely) while also acting as a rallying point against French Catholicism and its closely associated political bane, monarchical absolutism. Protestantism was therefore key to the lengthy wars fought by the British against the French throughout the eighteenth century, wars that were about both imperial supremacy and domestic survival.[15]

For most of the eighteenth century the self-proclaimed free, commercial, and Protestant empire created by the British could not be based on armies conquering territory, for reasons both geographical and demographical as much as ideological. Ideologically, of course, this would be an explicit denial of liberty. However, it was also wildly infeasible. The scale of discoveries in the New World made it clear that dominating all of the world's peoples and territories through force alone was impossible for any would-be imperial power, let alone an island with a relatively small population. However, while control of the land might elude the architects of empire, control of the seas was possible and could also serve as the chief conduit for commerce.[16] First, however, the preexisting notion of maritime dominion, which implied *imperium* only over home waters, had to be replaced with the notion of *mare liberum,* or "free seas," a view of the oceanic waters that firmly solidified in the eighteenth century. The idea that nobody owned the seas opened the way for a "blue water" strategy guaranteed by the world's greatest naval power, which ensured that the ocean remained accessible to British interests at all times.[17]

The notion that the British Empire was Protestant, commercial, maritime, and free was thus a means whereby the British distanced themselves ideologically from other imperial powers, like France and Spain. But of course, Britain's own conception of empire in the eighteenth century not only was "invariably self-serving" but also failed to capture the wide gulf between the ideal of empire as articulated in theory and its actual practice on the ground,[18] as can be seen across all four of its definitional markers.

Even at the most basic level, assertions of Protestantism as definitional of British national and imperial identity willfully overlooked the case of Ireland, where four-fifths of the kingdom/colony were Catholic. And, of course, the "heathens" of the New World were not Protestants, which helps explain the continued appeal of feudal-conquest arguments in both locales. Similarly, the British could describe their empire as "free" in the eighteenth century even as they shipped and traded roughly half of all the slaves taken from Africa, or approximately 3.4 million people.[19] In this way, the vaunted "empire of liberty" effectively closed its eyes to the evils of slavery.[20]

Likewise, with respect to its exclusively "maritime" dimension, defenders of the "new imperial history" have noted that Native Americans were frequently at war with the British in North America during the eighteenth century and would no doubt have disputed any claim that Britain did not have a territorial empire before the 1760s, as would the millions of enslaved Africans and the Celts who had lost land, culture, and population since the 1600s through the expansion of British traders, colonists, and soldiers.[21] Similarly, the *beau idéal* of "commerce" was in fact "clearly both rose-colored and self-serving, mystifying or obscuring the brutal, exploitive and violent processes of 'trade' and colonization (including the immensely profitable trade in slaves)."[22] Finally, the fact that the British denied citizenship to indigenous peoples throughout large swaths of the New World, and even withheld "self-ownership" from the African slaves and their descendants who were brought to it, ensured that Britain's was in fact an "exclusionary empire" and had become so long before the addition of India to the imperial fold.[23]

These interventions are extremely important because they remind us that there is a world of difference between eighteenth-century Britons' ideological depiction of their empire and empirical reality on the ground. At the same time, the self-conception remains crucial for my purposes here, because the ultimate aim of this book is to explicate Burke's logic of empire. Burke's was a view that emerged at the tail end of the official ideology, but it crucially distinguishes itself from this view of the British Empire in important ways through Burke's simultaneous deployment of Orientalist and Ornamentalist strategies. These strategies in fact enabled Burke to staunchly defend empire and imperialism even as the shape and scale of the empire itself radically transformed.

Indeed, while the ideology of the British Empire as Protestant, commercial, maritime, and free took roughly two centuries to construct, it was descriptively appropriate—even if we overlook all of its self-contradictions—for only a much briefer time, roughly from the mid-1730s to the mid-1760s. Subsequently, the Atlantic portion of the British Empire began to unravel in the aftermath of the Seven Years' War and the coming of American independence, while vast new imperial vistas were simultaneously opened in Asia. The Empire's so-called swing to the East refers to this shift away from the Atlantic to Asia, a move once conventionally understood as marking a clean break between the first and second British Empires.[24]

However, recent scholarship has shown that British overseas expansion in the eighteenth century is better seen as a continuous process. Parts of the empire in the West and East were not only chronologically overlapping—as the British did everything they could after American independence to hold on to the old settler colonies in the West Indies and the newly acquired ones in Canada that resulted from the Seven Years' War with France—but also jointly illustrative of Britain's deepening commitment to global empire from the middle of the century onward. This commitment took very different forms but was driven above all by fear of France and the perceived requirements of national survival in response to that fear, including wealth creation through imperial expansion as well as aggression against French trade and colonies.[25] Britain's increasing global economic interests thus were neither a rejection of settlement colonies nor a rejection of attempts to regulate and control imperial trade.[26]

Nevertheless, British expansion into Asia after the Seven Years' War, coupled with lessons learned from the loss of the American colonies, did ultimately force a rethinking of empire. By the end of the long eighteenth century the empire in the East was very different from what it had been in the Atlantic. Instead of free settler peoples linked to Great Britain via commercial trade regulations and defended by naval power, the empire encompassed large numbers of non-British peoples incorporated through conquest. The preponderance of the empire's population was in provinces conquered by the East India Company's armies on the subcontinent. For this reason alone, the swing to the east had to dispense with the *terra nullius* argument, because the British had to contend with the fact of Mughal (and other) large-scale kingdoms in India. Empire in the east was an engagement with an altogether different political reality. Britain's rule in India was over large numbers of natives who in turn provided the labor, commercial, and technical expertise that enabled British trade and material extraction to flourish. In India the British also did not have to contend with representative political institutions like those that had developed in America. Rather, the British relied heavily on the active participation of a large corps of both Hindu and Muslim officials to administer laws and collect taxes from the indigenous population. In this environment, notions that the empire was free, commercial, Protestant, and maritime were clearly no longer adequate. Empire in Asia was largely territorial, not maritime, and was guaranteed by military rather than naval power. It was also a government over Hindus and Muslims, not settler Protestants, and over nonwhites as opposed to whites. In the East, a new ideology of how to rule had to be developed for a new kind of empire.[27]

As P. J. Marshall has argued, the eighteenth century was therefore a transitional period in which the British Empire was guided by two very different rationales in the West and East. During much of this period, the Atlantic empire was kept intact by a set of commercial regulations, of which the Navigation Acts were the most important. In this free, commercial, Protestant, and maritime portion of the empire, white settler colonists enjoyed a good deal of authority and autonomy that had devolved to the colonial legislatures in North America and the West Indies. In India, the empire was largely nonwhite and peopled by multiple religious communities, guaranteed by military rather than naval power, and administered autocratically, often with the collusion of Hindu and Muslim elites. Nevertheless, the two ideological rationales overlapped chronologically. The old Caribbean colonies remained profoundly important through the end of the century, as did the new ones in Canada, and the British also became increasingly active in Africa, even after the rise of the antislavery movement. Thus, the swing to the East in the later eighteenth century did not imply a move away from concern with the West. In this respect, the first and second British Empires overlapped and coexisted at the end of the eighteenth century, and both were clearly feats of design rather than absent-mindedness.[28]

Against this backdrop, Burke's great innovation was to develop a substantively conservative logic of empire that relied on his notion of history as a civilizing process to justify and defend the new global British Empire in both the West and East through the simultaneous development of Orientalist and Ornamentalist arguments. In doing so, Burke overcame the theoretical difficulties that the official ideology of the empire (as Protestant, commercial, maritime, and free) posed for the addition of India to the imperial fold, even though the British Empire on the subcontinent was not marked by any of these features. Moreover, Burke's arguments not only linked the first and second empires in a new global imperial vision but also prefigured the two dominant approaches to British imperialism during the nineteenth and twentieth centuries.

However, before making this case, it is necessary first to confront and address the increasingly entrenched mischaracterizations of Burke as an anti-imperialist either explicitly hostile to or intellectually disruptive of empire. Once some clarity has been gained on the depth of Burke's commitment to empire, it will be possible to better understand his specific conception of it.

BURKE'S EMBRACE OF EMPIRE

As noted in the introduction, a number of scholars have in recent years described Burke as an anti-imperialist or anticolonial thinker; however, such claims raise a number of serious difficulties that extend well beyond the possible problem of anachronism,[29] since Burke's work cannot be said to fit any definition of these terms. Indeed, one will search the vast corpus of Burke's writings and speeches in vain for a rejection of the British Empire, whether in the New World, India, or Ireland, and whether one conceives of empire in the loose sense of domination and control over a large and expanding territory by the metropole or more narrowly as the planting of colonies. In fact, the opposite is true. Edmund Burke cherished the British Empire and strongly defended its legitimacy even as he often sharply criticized its practical implementation. This is abundantly clear from a careful consideration of Burke's reflections on the legitimacy and desirability of empire, which themselves span the entire course of his political life.

America

From the beginning of his parliamentary career in 1765, through the late 1770s, questions relating to the status of the British Empire in the North American colonies played a leading role in Burke's thought. As a spokesman for the Rockingham Whigs' short-lived administration, in 1766, Burke defended perhaps the most momentous and broad-ranging enunciation of imperial power before the American Revolution, the so-called Declaratory Act for the American colonies, which made clear that British sovereignty over the colonies was absolute. The resolution declared that Parliament "had, hath, of Right ought to have full power and Authority to make Laws and Statutes of sufficient force and validity to bind the Colonies and People of America Subjects of the Crown of Great Britain in all cases whatsoever."[30] It was in fact in defense of this sweeping claim of imperial sovereignty that Burke made his first significant parliamentary speech. As to the question of Great Britain's right to tax the American colonies, Burke was adamant that this right necessarily followed from the nature of the imperial relationship itself. In his notes for the speech, Burke wrote of the American colonies: "I think we have the clearest right imaginable, not only to bind them Generally with every Law, but with every mode of Legislative Taxation, that can be thought on." For Burke, such a right was inherent in empire, could be "deduced from the unlimited Nature of the supreme Legislative authority," and was "very clear and very undeniable."[31]

Burke argued that the Declaratory Act formed the bedrock on which the imperial relationship with the American colonies rested, and that it necessarily encompassed the essential right of internal as well as external taxation. In America, as would prove the case for Burke with respect to all other imperial locales, the notion of the periphery's absolute subordination to the metropole was lexically prior to all other considerations. In the American case, in subsequently defending the Rockingham Whigs' position against attacks from George Grenville's supporters in his *Observations on a Late State of the Nation* (1769), Burke specifically defended Britain's *right* to internally tax the colonists, insisting that "if that very specific power of levying monies in the colonies were not retained as a sacred trust in the hands of Great Britain," then "the presiding authority of Great Britain, as the head, the arbiter, and the director of the whole empire, would vanish into an empty name, without operation or energy." Conversely, Burke held that "if Great Britain were stripped of this right, every principle of unity and subordination in the empire was gone forever."[32]

Later, throughout the growing American crisis, and despite his own increasing criticism of British imperial policy, Burke always insisted on the absolute sovereignty of the mother country as the overriding feature of the imperial relationship between Britain and the American colonies. In his *Speech on American Taxation* (1774), Burke described what he called the *"imperial character"* of Parliament as akin to "the throne of heaven," whose theoretical powers, like those of God, brooked no dissent: "It is necessary to coerce the negligent, to restrain the violent, and to aid the weak and deficient, by the over-ruling plenitude of her power.... But in order to enable parliament to answer all these ends of provident and beneficent superintendence, her powers must be boundless."[33]

Burke thus made it abundantly clear that even those on either side of the Atlantic who (like himself) were highly sympathetic to the Americans should nevertheless understand that empire was necessarily predicated on a proper understanding of the colonies' place within the imperial system. In a letter of the same year as his speech on taxation, written in his capacity as agent for the colony of New York, Burke informed his employers that empire began and ended with the fundamental principle of colonial subordination: "Every good Englishman, as such, must be a friend to the Colonies; and all the true friends to the Colonies, the only *true* friends they have had, or ever can have in England have laid and will lay down the proper subordination of America, as a fundamental, incontrovertible Maxim, in the Government of this Empire."[34]

Hence it is clear that in the American colonial case, Burke held that the British Empire was not only wholly legitimate but also legally possessed of absolute authority over its colonies. Thus, in his 1777 *Letter to the Sheriffs of Bristol*, written of course after the Americans had declared their independence, Burke could honestly claim to his constituents "that if ever one man lived, more zealous than another, for the supremacy of Parliament, and the rights of this imperial Crown, it was myself." His ultimate goal, as he put it to the Americans themselves in his *Address to the Colonists* of that same year, was always "the lasting concord, freedom, happiness, and glory of this Empire."[35] Such views should put to rest the long-standing historical canard that Edmund Burke favored American independence.

India

Lord Clive and the Violent Establishment of British Rule in India. The notion that Burke was somehow hostile to the very project of empire is principally (and more often, exclusively) drawn from his work on India, particularly his relentless attempt to prosecute, impeach, and convict Warren Hastings, the former governor general of Bengal, on charges of corrupt and despotic behavior while in office. It is therefore worth describing at some length Burke's overall view of the legitimacy and desirability of the British Empire in India in principle, before taking up in chapter 3 the nature of his brief against Hastings within the parameters of his conservative logic of empire. In this fashion, one avoids conflating Burke's often searing criticisms of imperial practice under Hastings with an outright rejection of empire on the subcontinent, a position he never adopted.

To fully understand Burke's standpoint, one must begin with a brief description of Britain's acquisition of a territorial stronghold in India through the process of armed conquest. The English East India Company had been operating on the subcontinent since the early seventeenth century, when it was created and granted a monopoly on trade with Asia by Elizabeth I. However, in the century and a half after 1600, the British were just one among a number of European powers competing with the Dutch and French for such renowned goods as Indian textiles, and doing so almost exclusively from enclaves scattered along the coast, principally Madras in the southeast, Bombay on the west coast, and Calcutta in the northeast. However, this was to change dramatically in the mid-eighteenth century.

In 1757, the Company dismissed an ultimatum issued by the new Muslim nawab of Bengal, Siraj-ud-Daula, who responded by taking the Company's settlement at Calcutta. A British force led by Robert Clive recaptured Calcutta, then, with the collusion of Mir Jafar, destroyed Siraj-ud-Daula's forces at the battle of Plassey. The following decade would see intermittent fighting, until the Company and their native sepoy allies defeated the combined forces of the nawab of Bengal, the nawab of Oudh (Awadh), and the Mughal emperor Shah Alam II at Buxar in 1764. The following year, Clive, at that point commander in chief of East India Company forces, received from the captive Mughal emperor the *diwani,* or grant of civil administration and land revenue and tax rights, over Bengal, Bihar, and Orissa. This effectively made a phenomenally rich region—with annual revenues estimated at over £3 million in the eighteenth century, as well as some 20 to 30 million people—a British province.[36]

Some recent historical treatments have stressed the stunning degree of wealth siphoning, corruption, and Indian oppression and misery that followed Clive's victory at Plassey, and the decade of the so-called Bengal revolution that followed it, overseen by Clive and his immediate successors, Henry

Vansittart and Harry Verelst. Clive went back and forth between India and England in this decade, leaving the country for the last time in 1767, five years before Hastings's appointment as governor of Bengal in 1772. And, immediately after Plassey and under Clive's direction, the Company systematically looted Bengal's treasury, filling over a hundred boats with gold and silver worth £2.5 million (estimated at over £232 million at current values), as well as £234,00 additionally for Clive himself (or roughly £22 million today). This, in startling fashion, inaugurated the British plundering of the East, a process that continued unabated throughout the next decade.[37]

Subsequently, in 1772–1773 a Select Committee of the House of Commons on Indian affairs led by John Burgoyne estimated that the "presents" alone—effectively, unsolicited bribes paid for preferential treatment—given to East India Company officials during this period were worth over £2 million at the time. Clive also kept the land grand given to him by Mir Jafar, nawab of Bengal, as a "gift," and negotiated with the Company the right to take £27,000 per year from the Bengal revenues for as long as he lived. Such facts have led historians of India to note that British imperial corruption was in fact at its highest point well before Hastings and peaked during Robert Clive's years of greatest influence, from the late 1750s to the early 1770s.[38] Nor should we underestimate the degree of suffering visited upon Indians during this period. For example, the Company used its monopoly power to drive down the wages of highly skilled textile workers in Bengal to such low levels that, according to a historian at that time, William Bolts, "instances have been known of their cutting off their thumbs to prevent their being forced to wind silk."[39]

In 1769–1770, however, the nature of Company rule in Bengal—as set in place by Robert Clive at the Battle of Plassey and directly overseen by him during two crucial periods in the previous decade (1757–1760, 1765–1767)—would reveal itself in truly devastating fashion. In that year, a drought in Bengal precipitated a famine that was brutally exacerbated by the inhumane practices of the Company. These included Company servants cornering the market on rice and purchasing grain (including seeds for the following year's crops), then selling those commodities at extortionate prices. Before this, the Company had already depleted the usual amount of available foodstuffs by replacing edible crops with poppies for opium production and indigo. Meanwhile, instead of reducing taxation during the period to provide relief to farmers and others in the region, the Company relentlessly collected its dues, which had increased dramatically after it obtained the *diwani*. As a result, even during a time of massive starvation the Company's tax revenues actually increased, and the flow of wealth out of India further undermined the ability of its people to purchase food. In all, it is estimated that as a direct result of these policies at least one-third of the entire region's population under Company control died during the Bengal famine, perhaps as many as 10 million people, victims of what has been rightly referred to as a preventable, human-made catastrophe.[40]

Burke's Defense of Clive and the Indian "State of Exception". Given the historical record, it seems surprising that, focused as they are on his vociferous criticism of Hastings, Burke's recent interpreters have neglected to mention his overwhelming support for the policies and practices of Robert Clive and his immediate successors. These were acts that Burke spoke at length about in Parliament at the beginning of his career and then again during Hastings's impeachment trial. Therefore, if one wishes to have a clear understanding of the depth of Burke's commitment to empire, notwithstanding his critique of the Company under Hastings's leadership, it would be far more apt to begin by recognizing his approval of the Bengal Revolution initiated by Clive, who is generally regarded by historians as both more corrupt and more despotic than Hastings, and whose final tenure in power was followed shortly afterward by a colossal human catastrophe that, in terms of scale, was far more devastating than anything overseen by his successor.[41]

Burke entered Parliament the year that Clive extracted the Bengal *diwani* from the captive Great Mughal; and like many of London's political elite, he would come to invest extensively in Company stock.[42] Burke also had occasion at that time to reflect on the momentous events of the Bengal Revolution in a parliamentary speech he gave in 1769, the very year the Bengal famine began, in a debate over renegotiating the terms of the Company's charter. At this stage of his career, Burke's position was one of adamant opposition to any increased parliamentary oversight of the East India Company, which he saw as an unwarranted extension of ministerial control and an unacceptable assault on its legitimate property claims. Burke spoke after the return of Clive (now Lord Clive of Plassey, MP), who had earlier in the debate described the extraordinary potential of Britain's new territorial empire in India. Speaking after Clive, Burke used the occasion to praise him and his actions establishing territorial empire on the subcontinent in lavish terms:

> He [Clive] has laid open such a world of commerce, he has laid open so valuable an Empire both from our present possessions and future operations, he

has laid open such additional manufactures, and revenue as I believe never was laid before any Committee in so short words.... The Noble Lord has shown a manly eloquence, he has shown the greatest abilities civil, and military.... If we make war shall we not conquer? If we conquer, shall we not keep? You are plunged into Empire in the east. You have formed a great body of power, you must abide by the consequence. Europe will envy, the East will envy: I hope we shall remain an envied People.[43]

Far from being something to retreat from, then, the expanding British Empire in India ushered in by Clive would be, if managed properly, a wondrous possession of potentially enormous commercial value. Burke thus regarded the new territorial empire in India as a source of national glory, global envy, and profit, all of which he clearly relished.

Crucially, Burke's assessment of Clive never changed substantially throughout his career. Speaking of Plassey in 1788, at the opening of Hastings's impeachment trial, Burke commended "the daring and commanding genius of a Clive."[44] Later in the same speech, he described Clive's return trip to India in 1765 as the mission of a great reformer, sent by a self-policing Company to clean up such widespread practices as the receiving of "presents," although Burke was forced to admit of Clive that "he himself had been a large receiver of them." This was, of course, the trip in which Clive won the *diwani* from Shah Alam II with the Treaty of Allahabad after the latter's military defeat by Company forces at Buxar. Burke describes this forced concession from the captive shah as "the great grand period of the constitutional entrance of the Company into the affairs of India." Burke's narrative of India thus focused almost exclusively on two points: the Battle of Plassey itself, and the extraction of the *diwani* in 1765. He paints Clive as an honest broker purifying the corrupt and despotic practices that had developed under Company rule in the period when he was out of the country, thereby setting India on a firm constitutional footing after 1765: "I do say that the plan which he [Clive] laid down, and the course which he pursued were in general great and well imagined, that he settled great foundations, if they had been adhered to."[45]

The theoretical effect of Burke's depiction of Clive is nothing short of remarkable. Burke's willful historical amnesia occludes the profoundly corrupt decade of imperial consolidation in Bengal that was inaugurated, driven, and initially overseen by Clive himself. By treating Clive as a reformer in 1765—neglecting the great irony that he was reforming himself—Burke also depicts the granting of the *diwani* not as a forced concession under duress, which it was, but rather as a happy agreement between two symmetrically situated and equally free parties. In this way, Burke's obfuscation of the terms of transfer legitimated the coerced concessions based on conquest that established Britain's territorial empire in India. And finally, by treating Clive as a reformer sent on a noble mission to rectify Company misdeeds in Bengal, Burke's calculus conveniently overlooked Clive's principal role in introducing and institutionalizing the sorts of despotic, avaricious, and corrupt practices and behaviors that would play a pivotal role in the subsequent death of millions of people during the Bengal famine.

It should be mentioned that the latter point cannot be chalked up to ignorance on Burke's part, because it was Hastings himself who estimated—as early as 1772—that 10 million Indians had died in the famine that took place before he ever became governor general, even as he attempted to absolve the Company of any fault for it. Similarly, even Hastings admitted that the reason the tax revenue had not diminished during the famine was "owing to its being violently kept up to its former standard" by Company servants.[46] Thus, by the time of Hastings's impeachment trial, Clive's despotic and corrupt practices were common knowledge, and a general understanding of the dreadful famine that followed directly after his rule in Bengal had been current in British political circles for nearly a generation. Indeed, for many, the source for this knowledge was the 1772–1773 Select Committee's own report on Company malfeasance in India.

In fact, Burke's future arch-enemy, Thomas Paine—who was in and around London in 1773 (when the report was published) before leaving for America the following year—was shocked and horrified by it. Shortly after arriving in his new home, Paine subsequently wrote a scathing indictment of the Baron of Plassey based on the Committee's findings, called *Reflections on the Life and Death of Lord Clive*, for the *Pennsylvania Magazine* in 1775. In the essay, Paine quotes the highly critical overview by Burgoyne, the Committee chair, of Company atrocities to support his own claims that Clive had overseen "murder and rapine" and produced "famine and wretchedness" on a grand scale. Paine's essay on Clive depicts him as a man so tormented by the memory of the bloodletting he had overseen in India that it eventually drove him to madness and suicide. In another essay, Paine would likewise decry the "artificial famine" that the British had unleashed in India. Stressing this evidence, J. M. Opal has recently shown convincingly that Paine viewed Britain as an "evil empire" largely owing to its actions in the East Indies. For this reason, Paine came to believe very early during the colonial crisis in the New World that the Americans should sever any connection with the British; hence, atrocities in India were a fundamental impetus for Paine's argument, in *Common Sense* (1776), on behalf of American independence.[47]

Later, in *The American Crisis*, written during the Revolutionary War, Paine insisted that clear proof of the British Empire's fundamental immorality could be found on the subcontinent, where "her late reduction of India, under Clive and his successors, was not so properly a conquest as an extermination of mankind." Consequently, Paine wished that for "the peace of the world... she had not a foot of land but what is circumscribed within her own island." Britain's "extent of dominion has been her ruin, and instead of civilizing others has brutalized herself," as well as those subject to British rule.[48]

Tellingly, Burke does not discuss the Bengal famine, or any other imperial atrocities during the years after Plassey and before Warren Hasting's ascent to power, at any length in the vast body of his work on India. He also adamantly opposed the very creation of the East India Select Committee in 1772. One of the few times he mentions the "dreadful famine" is in his famous *Speech on Fox's India Bill* (1783). He does so, however, only to note that "upon the heels" of this calamity *Hastings* had failed in "administering a remedy" to it when he took office in 1772. This is a statement that conveniently overlooks the reasons why the famine occurred in the first place, as well as the fact that Hastings could not have been responsible for overseeing the Company practices that led to it since he had not been in charge in Bengal the previous decade, whereas Clive had been for much of it.[49] All of this has been ignored by the vast majority of Burke scholars and scholars of empire.[50]

Surprising as these "inconsistencies" might seem to those sympathetic to Burke's position on empire, they were in fact deeply and consistently woven into the broader fabric of his conservative political theorizing. Burke always maintained that the passage of time was the catalyst for transforming might into right, according to his vaunted doctrine of prescription. This belief led Burke to endorse as wholly legitimate those property claims, regimes, titles, and rights established by possession and uninterrupted use. In the *Reflections on the Revolution in France,* Burke would argue that the doctrine of "prescription" had sanctified earlier uses of force in Europe and had, "through long usage, mellow[ed] into legality governments that were violent in their commencement."[51] In a subsequent letter to a British army officer in France, Burke expanded on the concept, telling him that "*prescription*... gives right and title. It is possible that many estates about you were originally obtained by arms, that is, by violence... but it is *old violence;* and that which might be wrong in the beginning, is consecrated by time, and becomes lawful."[52] In short, the violence and injustice at the foundational moments of the European political and economic order did not make that order illegitimate for Burke. To the contrary, in Europe originary injustice was transformed into legality and legitimacy with the passage of time.

The same was equally true for Burke of the violence that had established Britain's territorial empire in India. In a manuscript fragment from his opening speech at Hastings's impeachment trial, Burke claims that "conquest" or "force, convert[s] its own injustice, into a just title."[53] In the same speech, speaking specifically of Plassey and the events surrounding it, which included Clive's looting of the Bengal treasury, Burke linked this general maxim with the particular case of the founding of British India, maintaining that "there is a secret veil to be drawn over the beginnings of all governments. They had their origin, as the beginning of all such things have had, in some matters that had as good be covered by obscurity. Time in the origin of most governments has thrown this mysterious veil over them. Prudence and discretion make it necessary to throw something of that veil over a business in which otherwise the fortune, the genius, the talents and military virtue of this Nation never shone more conspicuously."[54]

Burke thus regarded all political foundings as violent, bloody affairs necessarily marked by injustice. Because this was so, it was better to throw a discreet theoretical veil over them so as to obscure the ugly, messy reality and brutality of conquest. However, speaking of India at the end of his parliamentary career, in 1794, Burke could nevertheless insist that whether Britain established its power on the subcontinent "by fraud or force or whether by a mixture of both" was irrelevant,[55] especially when compared with the blessings and good fortune of imperial glory secured by the wisdom, skill, and valor of Britons.

Hence we see well-known Burkean principles such as "prescription" and "prudence," so lovingly celebrated by an earlier generation of Burke's conservative scholarly admirers, hard at work in his interpretation of empire and imperialism in India. Further, what is truly remarkable in Burke's narrative is the rapidity with which he believed that the magical elixir of time effectively transformed the (best-hidden) ugliness of British conquest in India into a prescriptive claim to political legitimacy. The Bengal Revolution had been successful, and somewhere in the five years between Clive's final departure from India and Hastings's assumption of power in 1772, all that had been done, despite its ugliness, had been placed beyond the pale of criticism. As a result, even the famine that Clive's culture of corruption and despotism had done so much to cause was entirely occluded by Burke's well-wrought veil. For Burke, it was only with Hastings that imperial responsibility began. As Nicholas Dirks argues, for Burke "the history of violent conquest had to be veiled. Conquest was for Burke the 'state of exception,'" in which the sovereign stood outside and above the law and the ordinary rules of justice simply did not apply.[56]

Richard Bourke seems to accept this interpretation of Burke's position and helpfully unearths crucial archival evidence to support it. In the "Proceedings against Clive" of 1773, Burke argued in Clive's defense that "no nation ever formed a tribunal to sit and inquire by what Crimes it was they acquired an augmentation of their empire." As Bourke rightly notes in his gloss on this passage, and indeed regarding Burke's overall view of the early years following British conquest in India, for Burke "a veil of silence should be drawn over the original assertion of might, with each bloody manifestation of force consigned to oblivion."[57] For Burke, British actions before Hastings were ultimately the source of a glorious extension of empire, and the violence and suffering attendant on them were best carefully occluded from historical sight, if they could not be effaced altogether.

From Company Cheerleader to Company Critic. Given his support of Clive and the violent initial conquest of Bengal, Burke in fact commenced his serious engagement with Indian affairs in the 1770s as a harsh critic of *any* state regulatory interference in the affairs of the East India Company, which he considered an unwarranted extension of executive power. For example, in 1772–1773, while Burke was busy arguing against the East India Select Committee and defending and exonerating Clive, he was also opposing North's Regulating Bill, an early attempt to bring the Company to heel, by claiming that abuses in India were being exaggerated by North as a pretext for extending ministerial influence and patronage through the expansion of unnecessary legislation and oversight.[58] In fact, in an unpublished manuscript from June 10, 1773, Burke argued that if the Company were left to its own devices it would be capable of reforming every major disorder in India and developing "a system one of the most beautiful ever established in any place."[59]

It was only with his work on a much later Select Committee (1782–1783), which produced eleven lengthy reports on the state of British rule in India, that Burke transformed into a critic of the East India Company's behavior.[60] However, the criticism of the Company that emerged from those reports did not take on an anti-imperial cast but was explicitly meant to answer a question framed from the standpoint of how Parliament might reform the Company such that the empire could flourish. The specific query that the Select Committee was tasked with answering was "how the British Possessions in the East Indies may be governed with the greatest Security and Advantage to this Country, and by what Means the Happiness of the Natives may be best promoted."[61] And when Burke and the rest of the Committee considered the relations between the British and the Indian people, they found that "these Interests are, in Effect, one and the same."[62] That is to say, for Burke there was a natural harmony of interests between the imperial metropole and its subject peoples when those interests were rightly understood and the responsibilities and obligations of empire were handled appropriately.

Later, despite his growing criticisms of the East India Company, Burke did not argue that the Company ought to relinquish its dual role as mercantile monopoly and regnant political power. Burke maintained (unlike his friend Adam Smith) that while there was much to be said against extraordinary political power being held by a private business enterprise, it was nevertheless inadvisable to end the Company's monopoly, even though he believed it should be more closely supervised by Parliament. For this reason, he declared that owing to his "particular ideas and sentiments," he felt "an insuperable reluctance in giving my hand to destroy any established institution of government, upon a theory, however plausible it may be."[63] Which is to say, Burke's commitment to custom, historical tradition, and habit (or prescription and prejudice) led him to reject the notion that Britain should relinquish India as a colonial possession under the auspices of Company rule in favor of creating a simple free-trade arrangement between two independent sovereign entities, as the ultimate logic of Smith's argument suggested.[64]

This refusal to take the Smithian path was ineluctably bound up with Burke's notion of Providence, one of the crucial elements for understanding his embrace of empire. To be sure, Burke did sometimes admit that "circumstances" were not "very favorable to the idea of our attempting to govern India at all." Nevertheless, at the end of the day he stuck firmly by the notion that the British Empire manifested God's will acting in the world: "But there we are; there we are placed by the Sovereign Disposer: and we must do the best we can in our situation. The situation of man is the preceptor of his duty."[65] The latter portion of this phrase is frequently quoted by Burke interpreters in the abstract, without reference to its historical context. Placed in the appropriate context, it is part and parcel of Burke's insistence that the duties demanded of the British by God expressly forbade a diminution of their violently acquired empire in India. Indeed, Burke even went so far as to assert that such "conquest" was in fact "a more immediate designation of the hand of God."[66]

After his time on the Select Committee, however, Burke became perhaps the leading advocate, in the British Parliament, of strict parliamentary oversight and control of the Company. The locus classicus of this rationale was his *Speech on Fox's India Bill*. However, it is important to note that none of Burke's arguments on behalf of strict government control of the Company, any more than his strident critique of Hastings, expressed a merely reluctant acceptance of the British Empire as a fait accompli. As Burke maintained in the speech at the opening of Hastings's impeachment trial—reiterating his earlier and long-standing praise of Lord Clive and the Bengal Revolution—Providence had clearly smiled upon the British by granting them such an extensive empire. Nearly two decades after congratulating Clive on expropriating Indian land by force, Burke reasserted the claim that the British Empire was "an object, thank God, of envy to the rest of the world for its greatness and its power." But he also insisted that it was exactly for this reason that British actions would be, and should be, the subject of scrutiny.[67] Unfortunately, Burke argued, Britain's opportunity for national glory had been seriously threatened by Hastings's corruption and despotism. However, Burke maintained that the appropriate approach was not to retreat from that empire but rather to alter its wayward trajectory: "it is now for us to think how we are to repair it."[68]

In short, Burke embraced the British Empire as a glorious extension of God's plan, but he deplored the ways in which that providential gift had been bungled in practice. While he thus railed until the end of his life against the practical implementation of God's gift, less than a year before he died he could still speak glowingly of "the dominion of the glorious Empire given by an incomprehensible dispensation of the Divine providence into our hands."[69] The operative question for Burke was thus never about the theoretical legitimacy of empire per se, let alone the legitimacy of the British Empire in India or elsewhere, but rather about how empire should best be managed in a given locale, and on what basis it should be criticized and reformed if it were to be mismanaged. This conclusion is shared by those scholars who have done the most to enhance our understanding of Burke's views on India.[70]

Ireland

Finally, albeit more briefly, we also see Burke's warm embrace of empire at play in his thinking regarding Ireland, his own homeland and the third nodal point of the British Empire during his lifetime. Eighteenth-century Ireland was a deeply divided and complex place. Nominally a separate "kingdom," in reality it was in many ways a restive British colony, the still volatile portion of the Anglo-Celtic frontier that defined one of the borders of the empire's Atlantic Archipelago. We will turn to Burke's position on Ireland in depth in chapter 4 but here must briefly address Burke's commitment to empire in Ireland, owing to the fact that a number of interpreters have hailed Burke as something of an Irish national or even nascent nationalist hero for his defense of Catholics and his criticisms of the British Empire in his homeland.[71] Nevertheless, it would be a grave mistake to assume that Burke sought an end to the British Empire in his homeland, or anything like Irish independence. In fact, while Burke deplored what he regarded as the bungling of the British Empire in Ireland, he wholeheartedly defended it in principle and regarded the potential decoupling of Ireland from the empire with unequivocal dread throughout his long political career.

For example, in 1785 Burke insisted bluntly that "Ireland could not be separated from England; she could not exist without her; she must for ever remain under the protection of England, her guardian angel."[72] Likewise, in a private letter written in the 1790s he wrote that "the closest connection between Great Britain and Ireland, is essential.... At Bottom Ireland has no other choice, I mean no other rational choice.... By such a separation Ireland would be the most completely undone Country in the world; the most wretched, the most distracted and, in the end, the most desolate part of the habitable Globe."[73] Burke, the Irishman turned British MP, thus counseled his countrymen to embrace imperial governance by the British as an act of providential kindness, one that ought to be celebrated, akin to God's sending a guardian angel to a people without whose protection they would surely perish.

These were not sentiments to warm the hearts of the first defenders of the idea of a unified, nonsectarian, independent Ireland free of English imperial control—Theobald Wolfe Tone and the United Irishmen. These men, who emerged in the 1790s, were instead the intellectual followers of Burke's sworn enemy, Thomas Paine, and the first fierce advocates of Irish nationalism and independence. Indeed, as we shall see in chapter 4, Burke believed that the

United Irishmen were completely wrong about both the causes of Irish suffering and the remedies for it, which, if anything, he believed required a still closer imperial connection between the two islands, not Irish independence. Late in his life, it was this very belief that led Burke to inform the Irish Catholic leader John Keogh that, in his opinion, "Ireland cannot be separated one moment from England without losing every source of her present prosperity, and even every hope of her future."[74] And, in one of his last letters, in 1797, Burke told a member of the Irish Parliament that Ireland "is a part, which I cannot separate, even in thought, of this great Empire."[75] Given the strength of this evidence, and despite recent revisionism, there remains a strong scholarly consensus that Burke cannot be construed as an anti-imperial or anticolonial thinker in any sense of those terms with respect to Ireland.[76]

Unfortunately, none of the preceding evidence has prevented some otherwise excellent scholars of empire from pursuing unconvincing avenues of interpretation concerning Burke in an attempt to salvage a more sympathetic interpretation of his position as one of reticence toward, if not rejection of, empire.[77] However, in summing up his subject's lifelong commitment to empire across its various locales, Burke's biographer has aptly commented that Burke's faith in Providence explains why, despite Britain's imperial record of malfeasance and misrule in Ireland, America, and India, he refused to give up on the idea of empire.[78] Given all of the evidence, we should resist attempts to co-opt Burke into the forces of anti-imperialism, because "the search for a usable Burke should not be pursued at the expense of distorting his ideas to support such current shibboleths as anti-colonialism."[79] Unfortunately, as we have seen, such approaches now loom increasingly large in the scholarship on Burke and empire.

As will become evident in subsequent chapters, Burke was indeed often a harsh critic of the British Empire. However, we should never confuse his criticism of imperial practice with a full-throated opposition to empire as such, a position Burke never took.[80] Rather, Burke remained until his dying day a fervent defender of empire rightly understood. His conservative logic of empire would, in fact, lead him to celebrate and defend a particular theoretical notion of empire while simultaneously criticizing Britain's practical rule of its providential imperial possessions for deviating from the ideal he endorsed and defended. Having confronted and rejected the view that Burke was an anti-imperial or anticolonial thinker, we are now in a position to turn to his particular conception of the imperial ideal, rightly understood.

BURKE'S CONCEPTION OF EMPIRE

The notion of Britain as a unified empire that included all of its diverse possessions in America, Canada, the Caribbean, Ireland, and India began to emerge only after the Seven Years' War ended in 1763.[81] In the 1770s, survey books with the term *British Empire* in them became increasingly common, as did the sense that some sort of unity knit together this structurally diverse collection of overseas possessions and modes of governance.[82] Two dominant yet mutually reinforcing strands of thought about imperial governance emerged during this period. The first insisted on appropriate subordination to imperial authority by those subject to it, while the second was a belief that different peoples incorporated within the empire had different needs. Hence, the mainstream ideology of empire held that absolute sovereign authority and utility went hand in hand.[83] What this meant practically was that British imperial governance could take on different forms suited to different peoples. After 1763, this included the acceptance of representative assemblies under common law in the British settler communities in America and the West Indies; French civil law, religious toleration, and special treatment for the Catholic Church in Canada and Grenada; limited legislative independence for Ireland; and autocracy within the legal framework of Hindu and Muslim law in India. The British came to believe that by taking such steps and attuning their modes of governance to local requirements they could avoid the fate of Rome.[84] However, this approach to empire meant that large questions relating to such issues as uniformity and diversity, or equality and hierarchy, were brought into sharp relief in the late eighteenth century.[85]

Burke's political career ran from 1765 to the end of his life in 1797, a period that roughly spanned the end of the Seven Years' War and the formal annexation of India to the end of the eighteenth century, precisely the time of the momentous transitional period in the British Empire sketched in the first portion of this chapter. And, throughout his career, Burke was deeply concerned with how best to understand and conduct empire. Given this, it is remarkable how few commentators have given any sustained attention to delineating Burke's overall imperial conception. To the extent that it has been discussed, Burke's understanding of empire has largely been read from the standpoint of a particular view of "international relations" attributed to him by scholars of that academic discipline.[86] Fortunately, some few commentators have undertaken to situate Burke's conception of empire within the context of those eighteenth-century views of the phenomenon canvassed above.[87]

The first thing to stress about Burke's notion of empire is that it was truly global. Burke was one of the earliest thinkers to embrace the idea of a British Empire that encompassed not only Great Britain and Ireland but also the North American colonies, the Caribbean, and India. In this respect, the speed with which Burke incorporated India into his vision of empire was extraordinary.[88] Far sooner than most, Burke understood British possessions as a unified whole, despite the great differences between places such as the New World, India, and Ireland.[89] As early as 1774, for example, in his *Speech at the Conclusion of the Poll,* which outlined his notion of political representation to his Bristol constituents, Burke told them that MPs were "Members for that great *Nation,* which however is itself but part of a great *Empire,* extended by our Virtue and our Fortune to the farthest limits of the East and of the West."[90] While fully aware of the historical dangers of imperial overstretch and corruption that had plagued the Alexandrine, Roman, Spanish, and French Empires, Burke nevertheless embraced the possibility that a well-conducted empire might escape these perils.[91]

The other main points that need to be stressed about Burke's vision of empire relate to the centrality of a deeply entwined pair of features, "its preeminence and its heterogeneity."[92] Taken together, these principles led Burke to view the empire "as a diversified structure of subordination" under the sovereign authority of king in Parliament, which were understood as absolute, at least in principle.[93] Combining these points in 1773, Burke wrote, "If it be true, that the several bodies, which make up this complicated mass, are to be preserved as one Empire, an authority sufficient to preserve that unity ... must reside somewhere: that somewhere can only be in England." Thus, the colonies were "placed in a subordinate situation," as Burke put it, "not for oppression but for order." Inversion of this principle, he concluded, would "destroy the happy arrangement of the entire Empire."[94] Therefore, despite his sympathy for the colonists, Burke held steadfastly to the principle of imperial subordination announced in the Declaratory Act, until after the Americans had declared their independence.

However, because empire had to be exercised over such widely diverse populations, Burke also argued that the extent to which sovereign power *should* press its rightful claims to preeminence was highly dependent on the nature of the people over whom it was exercised. For this reason, it was both deeply contingent and variable. In his *Speech on Conciliation with America,* Burke set this forth in unmistakable fashion when he described what he called "my idea of an Empire, as distinguished from a single State or

Kingdom." His vision stressed that sovereign authority and local privileges, immunities, and exemptions from that authority could and should coexist in order for empire to flourish:

> My idea of it is this; that an Empire is the aggregate of many States, under one common head; whether this head be a monarch, or a presiding republic. It does, in such constitutions frequently happen ... that the subordinate parts have many local privileges and immunities. Between these privileges, and the supreme common authority, the line may be extremely nice. Of course disputes, often too, very bitter disputes, and much ill blood, will arise. But though every privilege is an exemption (in the case) from the ordinary exercise of the supreme authority, it is no denial of it. The claim of a privilege seems rather, *ex vi termini* [from the very meaning of the word], to imply a superior power.[95]

That is, according to Burke the British Empire was a unified entity composed of many deeply differentiated and subordinate components amenable to a wide range of special exemptions and privileges owing to their particular character and local circumstances. However, this fact did not attenuate the notion of imperial sovereignty but in fact presupposed it by definition. After all, what good was it to speak of special "privileges" if no superior power existed to supplicate and grant them in the first instance?

Burke's definition of empire thus drew simultaneously on the dual meanings of the term that had defined it historically—absolute sovereignty and rule over territories that were internally and externally differentiated from one another in complex ways. In the eighteenth century, these included not only the colonies of the New World and the vast new additions in India but also that "*internal* empire" accumulated by the English over the Welsh, the Scots—and in a far less settled fashion, the Irish. Even before it took on overseas colonies, Britain was thus "*aboriginally* an empire in the sense of a single domain, in which internal jurisdictions were differently related to the center."[96]

Burke argued that, given this fact, it would be impossible to conceive of empire appropriately if one clung to a rigid and unvarying method of treating the very different peoples who comprised it. Rather, the appropriate conduct of empire required its implementers to tailor their mode of governance to the particular features of those over whom they exercised authority. As he told the sheriffs of Bristol in 1777,

> In the comprehensive dominion which the divine Providence had put into our hands, instead of troubling our understandings with speculations con-

cerning the unity of empire, and the identity or distinction of legislative powers, and inflaming our passions with the heat and pride of controversy, it was our duty, in all soberness, to conform our Government to the character and circumstances of the several people who compose this mighty and strangely diversified mass. I never was wild enough to conceive, that one method would serve for the whole; I could never conceive that the natives of *Hindostan* and those of *Virginia* could be ordered in the same manner.... Our business was, to rule, not to wrangle; and it would have been a poor compensation that we had triumphed in a dispute, whilst we lost an empire.[97]

For Burke, the art of ruling an empire lay exactly in balancing the universality of parliamentary sovereignty with the particularity of local difference, or in balancing provincial liberty with metropolitan authority in order to create the sort of informal trust that formed the very sinews of empire.[98] Achieving this balance between authority and liberty was no easy task, as Burke recognized even at the outset of his parliamentary career: "Without subordination, it would not be one Empire. Without freedom, it would not be the British Empire."[99] Years later, however, at the opening of Hastings's impeachment trial, he nevertheless reiterated to the House of Lords that they had to strike this difficult balance in order to guarantee that, "Imperial justice which you owe to the people that call to you from all parts of a great disjointed empire."[100]

However, this historically contextualized understanding of Burke's embrace of a particular conception of empire ultimately still leaves us with a crucial set of unanswered questions. Specifically, how did Burke determine the appropriate boundaries of "liberty" within the different sites of the British Empire? Or, put differently, how far should liberty extend to different peoples, and why? Were all peoples of the empire (or all the ranks of any given people) equally free and, if not, why not? Alternatively, when should authority trump liberty, and why? And what, in the end, did it mean to treat the various peoples of the empire "justly"? Even those few scholars who have helped us understand Burke's overall conception of empire have elided these vital issues.[101]

In the chapters that follow, I argue that what makes Burke's conception and defense of empire intellectually coherent and consistent with his interpretation of the French Revolution is his underlying view of history as a civilizing process. That is, to understand what Burke meant by acting "prudently" with respect to imperial policy, or rendering "liberty" or "justice" to the diverse inhabitants of the empire, one must recognize that these terms derive their substantive meaning from Burke's assessment of the degree of "civilization" or "savagery" that obtained in the New World, India, and Ireland. These assessments, in turn, relied on arguments that were by turns both Orientalist and Ornamentalist in nature. In this way, Burke's conservative logic of empire not only would link with his interpretation of the French Revolution in ways that defended the new global reality of the British Empire in the eighteenth century, but it would also serve as a conceptual bridge for the most influential imperialist arguments in the nineteenth and twentieth centuries.

CHAPTER 2

The New World

WHEN BURKE ENTERED PARLIAMENT IN 1765, shortly after the extraordinary territorial expansion of the British Empire at the conclusion of the Seven Years' War, he stepped into a political world in which debates over empire were central. These debates would ultimately reach to the core questions of the meaning and desirability of empire itself. For his part, Burke would do everything he could to keep together and expand the British Empire in the New World. Moreover, to do so he would advance simultaneously arguments that were both Ornamentalist (reliant on the logic of Saming) and Orientalist (reliant on the logic of Othering). These arguments, through which Burke attempted to delineate the appropriate boundaries between liberty and subordination for the various peoples in America and the Caribbean living under imperial rule, were in turn tightly linked to Burke's understanding of history as a civilizing process, a process that he believed was playing out in dramatic fashion on the stage of the New World.

BURKE AND THE AMERICAN COLONIES: ORNAMENTALISM, CONCILIATION, AND SYMPATHY

The Debate over the American Colonies and Empire That Burke Inherited

As we saw in chapter 1, the British notion of empire was one wherein the metropole governed a single, unified "realm" over which the balanced constitution of king in Parliament exercised unquestioned sovereignty. Within the boundaries of the internal empire on the "British" isles this was theoretically unproblematic. Ireland was a "kingdom by conquest" whose parliamentary subordination to London was seemingly clear from 1541 onward, and the formal Act of Union with Scotland in 1707 had been an "incorporating" rather than a "federating" one, so that the Scots, too, were brought into a single realm under condition of subordination to England. However, by 1763 the British "empire" not only drew on the earlier definition of absolute *imperium* over a given realm but also referred to the second meaning of empire, understood as control over geographically distant territories of diverse population, in this case North America and the Caribbean. These settler colonies were not nominally the product of either conquest or formal incorporation but rather resulted from large-scale migration from the center and subsequent plantation in distant lands. This posed a basic question for the eighteenth-century architects of empire in London: were the British colonies in the Americas within the one indivisible "realm" of empire like the rest of the territories within the Atlantic Archipelago, or not? The 1765 Stamp Act, which was an unprecedented attempt by Britain to impose a form of internal taxation, rather than external taxation, on the American colonies for the purpose of raising revenue to pay for the massive expense of the Seven Years' War with France, brought this issue to a head.[1]

The Stamp Act raised the problem of defining empire in a particularly acute form. It pointed out clearly that the legal status of Britain's New World colonies had never been clearly determined, and it demonstrated concretely that there were two very different ways of imagining the appropriate distribution of power between the metropolitan core and the periphery of the empire. In the absence of a clear legal definition of what a colony in fact was, what unfolded in the debate between Britain and the American colonists over the next decade would therefore be nothing less than an ideological struggle over the meaning of empire itself.[2]

On the one hand, the English attempted to unify the two meanings of the term—internal sovereignty and external dominion—by using their control over far-flung territories to create the power necessary to guarantee the sovereignty of king in Parliament at home. This was necessary in order to prevent the recurrence of war within the British realm, whether that meant war with Scotland or Ireland or even another English civil war. Anything less than absolute sovereignty at the center raised fears of an *imperium in imperio*—an empire within an empire—a specter that threatened to tear the Atlantic Archipelago apart.[3]

On the other hand, by the mid-eighteenth century the American colonists no longer considered themselves members of chartered corporations granted by the Crown, but rather regarded themselves as self-governing societies. Underlying this belief were two assumptions. First, since the colonies were not represented in Parliament, they believed that their consent to such matters as taxation (and by implication, every other law) was owed not to that body but to their own colonial legislatures. Second, what became clear after a decade of intense debate was that the colonists held a vision of empire as a confederation of independent states bound to Britain via their colonial legislatures' agreements with the king alone, rather than the "king in Parliament." The result of these arguments was that the North American colonists turned to Lockean notions about their status as a distinct people represented by states. Subsequently, they would go on to define the empire as a confederacy of such independent states and, ultimately, to secede from that confederacy by declaring their independence from it.[4] Thus, in 1776 when the thirteen colonies rejected the idea that the British realm could be extended to include them, they managed to undo both dimensions of the British claim to empire in North America (as an extension of the internal sovereignty of the realm and as a form of external dominion) simultaneously.[5]

Burke would regard America's declaration of independence from the British Empire and the war that followed it as a great, avoidable tragedy. His overriding goal was to keep the colonies within the familial embrace of empire, and he would ultimately lament their loss deeply.

Burke on Britain and the American Colonies: Theoretical Sovereignty and Practical Leniency

On both sides of the Atlantic, Burke was considered a friend of the colonists, from the beginning to the end of the American crisis. This was due in large part to his attempts at seeking reconciliation between Britain and her colonies, but also because of his harsh criticism of metropolitan policies, especially those of Lord North, which he saw as doing much to precipitate the American Revolution.[6] However, rather than being "anti-imperial," Burke's approach to the American colonies would be an attempt to balance two theoretical principles simultaneously: absolute sovereignty and colonial subordination, with the need for differential treatments of peoples based on their perceived level of civilizational achievement.

We have seen that, in 1766, as a spokesman for the Rockingham Whigs, Burke defended the definitive articulation of British imperial power in the New World before the American Revolution, the so-called Declaratory Act, which made clear that British sovereignty over the colonies was absolute. Burke thus made plain that the smooth functioning of empire required a proper understanding of the colonies' subordinate place within the imperial system.[7] When reflecting on this period more than a decade later, in his *Letter to the Sheriffs of Bristol* (1777), Burke told his constituents, "When I first came into a public trust, I found your Parliament in possession of an unlimited legislative power over the Colonies. I could not open the Statute-Book, without seeing the actual exercise of it, more or less, in all cases whatsoever."[8]

At the same time, however, the passage of the Declaratory Act was paired by the Rockingham Whigs with the repeal of the Stamp Act. This speaks to the second aspect of Burke's approach to dealing with the American colonists. Indeed, Burke's understanding of the relationship between the Declaratory Act and the Stamp Act illustrates his overall approach to empire. In the case of the American colonies, Burke argued that circumstances augured against the heavy-handed assertion of legitimate imperial sovereignty, in favor of the acceptance of a broad range of justifiable privileges, immunities, and exemptions for the colonists, which had long been a part of Britain's relationship with them.[9] Burke argued that when it came to "the right of Great Britain to Tax the Colonies," there was no doubt that this was "very clear and very undeniable." However, he also insisted that such a "speculative Idea of a right deduced from the unlimited Nature of the supreme Legislative authority" even "when explained proved and admitted" was in fact "little to the purpose." The question of the extent to which an abstract imperial right to tax the colonies *should* be enforced was a complex matter to be determined by specific contextual circumstances, and it required sound political judgment. The goal, as Burke put it, was "applying as far as the rules of subordination will permit the principles of the British Constitution," and he believed that, at least when it came to the American colonists, the goal was the difficult one of attempting to "govern a Large Empire upon a plan of Liberty."[10]

The question of where to place the boundary between liberty and subordination was exacerbated, Burke agued, by the depth of Britain's large-scale imperial expansion into the New World. The British constitution could not provide a rote formula "for Governing a Tract of the world, that our Ancestors so far from knowing how to Govern did not know it existed in the Universe." Thus, Burke told his parliamentary auditors: "We cannot resort to the example of Roman or Greek colonies. Nor must we seek for it in the older part of our constitution about the method of governing an Empire, the existence of which they could not even conceive."[11] The entirely unprecedented circumstances of imperial governance in the New World necessitated an equally new approach to empire.

In his *Observations on a Late State of the Nation* (1769), Burke reiterated this point by directly confronting those of his political opponents who opposed the Rockingham ministry's attempt to synthesize absolute imperial sovereignty with the repeal of the Stamp Act. He insisted that such critics failed to understand the novel theory of empire required by unique historical circumstances: "Those who resort for arguments to the most respectable authorities, ancient or modern, or rest upon the clearest maxims, drawn from the experience of other states and empires, will be liable to the greatest errors imaginable. The object is wholly new in the world."[12] It is clear that Burke understood the problems facing Britain in the administration of its empire in the New World as requiring a de novo approach because the territory itself was so distant and largely unknown to predecessors.

In this imperial environment, or "new system," Burke therefore accepted a principle of "artificial commerce" anchored by the Navigation Acts, the series of external restraints and taxes levied on the Americans that restricted colonial trade. He did so even though he considered the acts "very alien from the spirit of liberty" because they required the exercise of metropolitan power to be enforced. Moreover, Burke warned his parliamentary colleagues that the people who were meant to obey these laws, and any others to come from London, were the "descendants of Englishmen," a vital point whose theoretical ramifications for understanding Burke's position on empire it is essential to grasp. While Burke held that Britain did indeed "have a great empire to rule," one whose colonies all need "to be held in subordination to this country," it was nevertheless crucial to recognize that "people must be governed in a manner agreeable to their temper and disposition" as this had developed historically.[13]

This point is fundamental to grasping Burke's conservative logic of empire, and it is one that he would reiterate in his famous speeches on conciliation with the American colonies. In those speeches, he sided wholly with those who claimed that British Parliament was "the *sovereign* of America," but declared that the enactment of sovereignty should be not uniform but carefully calibrated to suit the historically developed character of the peoples over whom it was exercised: "Sovereignty was not in its nature an idea of abstract unity; but was capable of great complexity and infinite modifications, according to the temper of those who are to be governed, and to the circumstances of things; which being infinitely diversified, government ought to be adapted to them, and to conform itself to the nature of things, and not to endeavor to force them."[14] Describing to his Irish friend Charles O'Hara the argument for conciliation, Burke pointed to his belief that, as a theoretical matter, "no bounds ever were set to the Parliamentary power over the Colonies." However, he insisted, "I never ask what Government may do in *Theory*, except *Theory* be the *Object*; When one talks of *Practice* they must act according to circumstances."[15]

The deeper question this gives rise to, of course, is: what circumstances did Burke consider central to an understanding of the "*Temper*" and disposition or the "Character of the Americans,"[16] such that the British should govern them according to those circumstances? To answer this query, we must return to Burke's particular understanding of civilization, a view that goes back to his earliest writings on English history and aesthetics, but which is encapsulated most succinctly in his later analysis of the French Revolution.[17] Subsequently, we will be in a position to see how Burke deployed his view of civilization and history as a civilizing process to argue for an imperial policy of conciliation based on mutual sympathy between the metropole and its North American colonies. Specifically, Burke would depict the colonies in largely Ornamentalist terms that stressed the colonies' civilizational similarity to Britain and, therefore, would advocate a policy of conciliation based on the cultivation of mutual empathetic fellow-feeling, or "sympathy," between England and its colonial periphery in the New World.

Burke's Understanding of (English) Civilization

Burke considered the American colonists, as English descendants living abroad, to be the offshoot of a great civilized society. For Burke, England itself was a particularly laudable instance of civilization, which required governance by a "natural aristocracy," a group drawn largely from men of landed wealth and status but open to those of extraordinary talents as well. Later, Burke would describe "a people"—properly understood—as existing only under circumstances where "the multitude" were governed by "the wiser, the more expert, and the more opulent," drawn from this elite.[18] As he memorably put it in the *Reflections,* it was this natural aristocracy's role in such a system to keep in place the intergenerational social compact, to specify the appropriate boundaries of conventional rights, and to knit together in harmony "those who are living, those who are dead, and those who are to be born."[19] However, Burke warned that "when you separate the common sort of men from their proper chieftains," then the "venerable object called the People" collapses into a "disbanded race of deserters and vagabonds."[20]

These views on the place of the natural aristocracy within English civilization help us to understand Burke's position on the role of elected representatives, as set forth in his oft-cited depiction of the tasks of the legislator in the *Speech at the Conclusion of the Poll,* given to his Bristol constituents in 1774. This speech is now regarded as a locus classicus of the "trustee" as opposed to the "delegate" model of representation; in the former, representatives are understood as a specialized group capable of making informed judgments owing to their rare abilities, rather than simply aggregating and validating the unreflective preferences of their constituents.[21] These views also help explain Burke's steadfast resistance to any attempt to expand the suffrage or even to reform Britain's notorious "rotten" electoral boroughs.[22] The ability of the "natural aristocracy" to do the thinking for the rest of the nation also undergirded Burke's commitment to "virtual" representation. On this theory, large chunks of the citizenry had no need to vote, Burke argued, because their interests were capable of being accounted for by the capacious understandings of the "natural aristocracy" to such a degree that they did not require "actual" representation.[23]

The natural aristocracy's power was also tightly connected with that of organized religion, and Burke specifically praised the role of an established church in England. In turn, organized religion relied upon Burke's aesthetic principle of the sublime. As Burke wrote in the *Reflections,* an established church "consecrated the commonwealth" by making certain that the state was "infused" with the "sublime principles" that exert a "wholesome awe upon free citizens; because, in order to secure their freedom, they must have some determinant portion of power." By learning to treat the state's representatives as if they were sanctified by God—according to Burke's aesthetics the ultimate power and therefore the supremely fearsome being—the common people would learn to willingly subordinate themselves to the natural aristocracy and gingerly "approach to the faults of the state as to the wounds of a father, with pious awe and trembling solicitude." Burke maintained that the power of an established church became more important as governments became more democratic and their representation more popular. As this occurred, the masses posed a greater threat of tyrannizing over their legitimate representatives from the natural aristocracy in the absence of an established church. Consecration of the church by the state ensured that the people, in making their nominations for political office, "will not appoint to the exercise of authority, as to a pitiful job, but as to an holy function." Conversely, he tells readers of the *Reflections,* in the absence of such an institutional arrangement "a perfect democracy" becomes "the most shameless thing in the world. As it is the most shameless, it is also the most fearless."[24]

On the other hand, the most famous passages in the *Reflections,* in which Burke rhapsodizes about the central importance of chivalry and nobility, and laments the downfall of Marie Antoinette, directly invoke his aesthetic principle of the beautiful. Burke insisted that it was chivalry that had "made power gentle, and obedience liberal" and "incorporated into politics the sentiments which beautify and soften private society." It did so by inculcating "a system of manners" in which beauty was literally "embodied" in sentient national symbols in order for people to learn to love the polity. As he put it: "To make us love our country, our country ought to be lovely."[25] Burke believed that chivalry and beautiful female nobility like Marie created love among the masses—that other dimension of fealty—thereby facilitating their voluntary submission to inequality and rule by the natural (male) aristocracy.

Together, an established church and landed nobility thus created the requisite level of what Burke called "habitual social discipline" necessary for the natural aristocracy to rule and civilization to flourish.[26] Given this particular understanding of civilization, we can now better apprehend Burke's specific criticisms of the heavy-handed implementation of metropolitan imperial sovereignty as doomed to fail when applied to the American colonies.

The American Colonies: Idiosyncratic Ornamentalism

A close reading of Burke's *Speech on Conciliation with America* (1775), given less than a month before the opening of hostilities at Lexington and Concord, suggests that his criticisms of British imperial policy were rooted in this particular theory of civilization. Furthermore, such a reading demonstrates the extraordinary extent to which Burke deployed an Ornamentalist interpretive strategy to depict the American colonies as a kind of English civilization abroad, albeit one with important differences that boded ill for the type of British imperial policy he saw being implemented.

In the speech, Burke stresses the importance of liberty for the American colonists, which of course was one element of the British self-conception of empire in the eighteenth century. Further, he tells his parliamentary audience in London: "The Colonists emigrated from you, when this part of your character was most predominant; and they took this bias and direction the moment they parted from your hands." Concretely, the colonists' notion of what constituted liberty was built on "English ideas, and on English principles" and therefore focused chiefly on issues of taxation. For this reason, the American colonists went to great lengths to establish the fundamental principle that the people must possess the power of the purse directly or through duly elected representatives, "or no shadow of liberty could subsist."[27]

While Burke regarded this as ultimately a mistaken notion of empire held by the colonists—their claims about taxation, after all, undermined the basic assertion of the Declaratory Act—it had been encouraged by Britain's lax mode of governance. "Whether through lenity or indolence, through wisdom or mistake,"[28] the belief that Britain lacked absolute sovereignty had taken root in the colonies, where it was aided by three additional important features of the colonial Americans, who were understood as a civilized "people." These were their "Form of Government; of Religion in the Northern Provinces; [and] of Manners in the Southern." Unfortunately, Burke believed, these cultural characteristics of American civilization were "unhappily meeting with an exercise of Power in England, which, however lawful, is not reconcilable to any ideas of Liberty, much less with theirs [and] has kindled this flame, that is ready to consume us."[29]

With respect to the first of these—and much unlike in England, where the "natural aristocracy" with its commitment to "trustee" and "virtual" modes of representation ruled in Parliament—England's civilizational offshoot in the New World had gone in a very different (and on Burke's view a very dangerous) direction. It was for this reason, Burke argued, that the colonial legislatures implicitly denied the Declaratory Act as it pertained to the relationship between taxation and representation—namely: "Their governments are popular in an high degree; some are merely popular; in all, the popular representative is the most weighty; and this share of the people in their ordinary government never fails to inspire them with lofty sentiments, and with a strong aversion from whatever tends to deprive them of their chief importance."[30] Here, Burke develops the idea that as the colonial legislatures became more popular or democratic, they more zealously guarded their freedom and resisted control from the metropole. It is no stretch to say that the Americans' "fierce Spirit of Liberty" and their obstinate refusal to hew to the dictates of British rule were in important part the concomitant of the fearless (and shameless) behavior that Burke would later describe in the *Reflections* as the quintessential effects of increasingly democratic institutions on a people.[31] By configuring their colonial assemblies along more democratic lines, the Americans were transforming their civilized character in an increasingly unruly and rebellious direction and, hence, were less willing to subordinate themselves to Britain.

But what, one might ask, of the sublime power of organized religion and, in particular, the ability of an established church to consecrate American politics such that this people would not be overcome by an excessive commitment to liberty and equality? For contingent historical reasons, Burke thought that this was impossible in America, where, unfortunately, religion actually aided and abetted the colonists' commitment to liberty as developed through democratic forms of self-government: "If anything were wanting to this necessary operation of government, Religion would have given it a complete effect." Burke insisted that religion, "always a principle of energy in this new people," was in their case paradoxically "one main cause of this free spirit."[32]

Burke points out that in America, this was because another linchpin of the British ideology of empire, its Protestantism, was highly important but sadly pernicious. Colonial Protestantism was "of that kind, which is the most adverse to all implicit submission of mind and opinion." This was especially true in the northern colonies. These churches were of course founded in the main by Dissenters from the Church of England; they therefore "sprung up in direct opposition to all the ordinary powers of the world; and could justify that opposition only on a strong claim to natural liberty. Their very existence depended on the powerful and unremitted assertion of that claim." In describing the spirit of New England, Burke remarked that while all Protestantism is by definition a form of dissent, the type practiced in "our Northern colonies is a refinement on the principle of resistance; it is the dissidence of dissent; and the protestantism of the protestant religion." Thus, while the Catholic Church and the Church of England have "generally gone hand in hand" with governments where they predominate, in the northern colonies in particular this was not the case, because there "the Church of England, notwithstanding its legal rights, is in reality no more than a sort of private sect, not composing most probably the tenth of the people." Therefore, in New England the sublime power of organized religion and an established church, which would ordinarily have helped create the kind of habitual discipline and social order antithetical to rebellion, was not simply lacking: such religion as there was actually worked in the opposite direction, and served as a chief cause of the "disobedient spirit in the Colonies." The North was, in fact, defined by a "republican Religion."[33]

In his speech, Burke recognized that there were those in his parliamentary audience who objected to such a broad description of the deleterious effect of religion practiced in the colonies, by reference to the American South, where "the Church of England forms a large body, and has a regular establishment." Burke admitted this but went on to argue that, notwithstanding this fact, "these people of the Southern Colonies are much more strongly, and with an higher and more stubborn spirit, attached to liberty than those to the Northward." The reason for this had everything to do with the nature of the southern landed aristocracy—usually that second great stabilizing force within the civilizing process—which was defined by the institution of slavery. Burke argues that while there was not in the American colonies a titled nobility, there was nevertheless a "high aristocratic spirit" among the landed elites in Virginia and the Carolinas that was directly attributable to the fact that "they have a vast multitude of slaves." For Burke, the deeply psychological reasons for this spirit were woven into the unalterable "nature of man." He contended that, going back to ancient times, whenever there were large numbers of slaves in any society, "those who are free, are by far the most proud and jealous of their freedom. Freedom is to them not only an enjoyment, but a kind of rank and privilege. Not seeing there, that freedom, as in countries where it is a common blessing, and as broad and general as the air ... liberty looks amongst them, like something that is more noble and liberal." Hence, in "such a people" as slaveholding societies, "the haughtiness of domination combines with the spirit of freedom, fortifies it, and renders it invincible."[34]

That is to say, in the American South the existential experience of freedom juxtaposed against its lived antipode made those in possession of liberty all the more zealous to guard it, because they were daily engaged in brutally dominating others and denying it to them in ways that made them feel superior and painted the principle of liberty itself with a purity it lacked elsewhere. According to Burke, the plantation society of the American South, with its informal landed aristocracy built on slavery—unlike other landed aristocracies in Europe—tended more toward rebellion than social stability, so much so that it could overwhelm the obedience to empire that might otherwise have been inculcated by organized religion and the strength of the Church of England. This made the southern colonies potentially even more rebellious than those in the North.

It has been argued that the most fascinating aspect of Burke's *Speech on Conciliation with America* "is its attempt to mobilize the philosophical history of society in demonstrating that the Americans were already a distinctive people who could be governed only in ways suited to their distinctive character."[35] From the standpoint of Burke's understanding of history as a civilizing process being defended here, we can clearly endorse such a claim. On Burke's view, the American people were descendants of the English people and, as such, shared the broad institutional elements definitional of civilization. The Americans had both organized religion and (although lacking formal titles of nobility) a landed aristocracy of sorts, especially in the South. However, the idiosyncratic and historically contingent elements of American civilization weakened it in Burke's eyes. The Americans gave too much weight to popular democratic forms of representation in their legislative bodies, and insufficient power to those drawn from the "natural aristocracy" who were fully capable of acting as "trustees" or even "virtually" representing the masses, as in the British Parliament. Furthermore, the character of both religion and aristocracy in America worked not to temper the excessive claims of liberty in the name of "habitual social discipline" and obedience, as in Britain (and all civilized societies), but rather fed a ferocious spirit of liberty in both the masses and their representatives. By possessing these distinctive features, the Americans as a people seriously threatened Britain with rebellion should the British fail to comprehend them.[36]

Conciliation and Sympathy

Given Burke's Ornamentalist understanding of the Americans as a civilized people, descended but in important ways distinct from English civilization, we can more easily understand the actual policies that his conservative logic of empire dictated with respect to the thirteen colonies during the American crisis. The fierce, excessive spirit of American liberty, in conjunction with the furious disagreement between the imperial center and periphery over the legal status of the colonies—whether the colonies were an extension of the "realm" subject to absolute sovereignty or coequal states within a confederacy—led Burke to defend the long-standing informal relationships that had defined British rule over the colonies until the end of the Seven Years' War, but which had subsequently eroded. Burke's defense of "informal" empire stressed that the roots of the American crisis lay in the attempt to provide precise legalistic definitions of the relationship between Crown and colonies in place of hewing to the old path and sticking to the long-established set of benign customary bonds that had obtained between Britain and America.[37] In the first speech on conciliation, Burke described his preferred approach to the American colonies as the long-standing one of "a wise and salutary neglect."[38]

Traditionally, this had meant that Britain controlled the American colonies' external affairs through the Navigation Acts and also benefited from the long-standing forms of indirect taxation and subsidization embedded in them.[39] Burke supported the Navigation Acts and considered colonial trade one of the principal sources of Britain's national prosperity, pointing to its scope and rate of increase and analogizing such trade to food that nourished the entire body of empire.[40] While he was influenced by the free trade arguments of his friend Adam Smith and of David Hume, Burke resisted the ultimate conclusion of their arguments, which was to give up the colonies entirely, together with their mercantile systems of preferential trade, in favor of free trade agreements knit together by no more than material self-interest.[41] However, the American colonists had been essentially left alone when it came to issues of self-government and internal taxation, and Burke believed that these policies ought to have remained in place.[42] For this reason, Burke resolutely rejected the Stamp Act.

In short, Burke counseled Parliament that relations with the Americans should be left as they had "anciently stood.... Be content to bind America by laws of trade; you have always done it. Let this be your reason for binding their trade. Do not burthen them by taxes; you were not used to do so from the beginning." Historical precedent mattered far more than abstract metaphysical arguments about rights. However accurate the deductions and consequences drawn "from the unlimited and illimitable nature of supreme sovereignty" were in theory, they should not form the sole basis of practical policy. Pressing for more than was warranted by "the good old mode" of governance, such as by adding new taxes, would have predictably disastrous consequences given the civilizational character of the American colonists. As Burke warned Parliament presciently in his *Speech on American Taxation* (1774), such moves meant that in the end the Americans would "cast your sovereignty in your face."[43] Burke thus argued for a very cautious and reticent invocation of absolute imperial sovereignty, one that followed the old distinction between internal and external modes of governance, as had had historically been applied to the American colonies.[44] This did not mean that Burke rejected imperial sovereignty, merely that he resisted its reflexive invocation as a form of unnecessary provocation directed against the colonists.

For a similar reason, Burke also heatedly protested the subsequent range of measures aimed at controlling internal American affairs and constraining the power of the colonial legislatures known collectively as the Coercive (or "Intolerable") Acts (1774). He also opposed the Quebec Act of that same year, a piece of legislation for governing that province which would have also redrawn some borders in the colonies in ways that were inimical to American interests. Ironically, this was meant to punish the colonies for the Boston Tea Party, by attempting to reassert the principle of "external" rather than "internal" taxation, and by preserving a portion of the Townshend Acts.[45]

However, as farsighted observers of the American crisis such as Benjamin Franklin observed, the problem was that lurking beneath the issue of internal versus external taxation lay a much deeper one. It was, quite simply, the question of whether in the absence of colonial representation in Parliament, and thus a direct say in all matters that affected them, the colonists should pay either sort of tax or allow the British to legislate for them in any fashion whatsoever.[46]

On these larger issues, however, Burke steadfastly rejected measures such as American representation in the British Parliament, approaches that might have prevented the slide toward a "confederate" notion of empire composed of a coequal number of sovereign states. This was in part because of logistical reasons related to geography but also, more importantly, because such a concession would undermine the Declaratory Act and wreak havoc on Burke's cherished notion of "virtual representation."

In fact, Burke's position on American colonists voting in the British Parliament was actually more extreme than a simple defense of virtual representation, which was, after all, a mainstay of metropolitan argument.[47] In responding to William Knox's pamphlet against the Rockingham Whigs, with its claim that the Americans should be represented in Parliament, Burke asserted that such proposals were really nefarious schemes intended to stir up trouble at home by suggesting that too few people were allowed to vote in Britain. In response, Burke argued that, notwithstanding the large number of Britons without the suffrage, there were nevertheless still too many with that capability, and the number actually ought to be reduced rather than increased. He maintained that, owing to the "venality," "corruption of manners," and "idleness and profligacy of the lower sort of voters, no prudent man would propose to increase such an evil." To the contrary, Burke argued, "I believe that most sober thinkers on this subject are rather of opinion, that our fault is on the other side; and that it would be more in the spirit of our constitution, and more agreeable to the pattern of our best laws, *by lessening the number*, to add to the weight and independency of our voters."[48] Obviously, since Burke wanted to lower the number of eligible voters in

England, that made him even less given to accepting arguments about direct American representation in Parliament than he was to accepting arguments about free trade.[49] These substantive conservative beliefs about the role of the natural aristocracy and the evil habits and characterological incapacities of the lower orders thus precluded Burke from arguing for a solution to the American crisis tethered to the expansion of democracy. This made him a good deal more conservative than even American thinkers such as John Adams, who argued early on for colonial representation in the British Parliament as one possible method of preserving the connection between the colonies and the mother country.

Instead, Burke was left in the position of arguing repeatedly for a range of smaller concessions meant to conciliate the American colonists during the period from 1775 to 1778 as the best means to keep them within the empire. Nevertheless, some might argue that the lengths Burke was willing to go to in order to keep the colonies within the imperial fold were extraordinary: In his two 1775 "Conciliation" speeches, Burke argued for the repeal of the North ministry's 1774 "Coercive Acts" and the Quebec Act, both of which the colonists bitterly resented. He also argued that Britain should renounce all future taxation aimed at raising revenue from the colonies through internal taxation, revoke any and all external forms of taxation they disliked (cutting against the principle of the Navigation Acts), and substitute in their place the policy that the Americans should decide how much—or even if—they should voluntarily grant taxes to Britain. By 1778 (after the Declaration of Independence and well into the war) Burke went even further and actually renounced the Declaratory Act, the Rockingham Whigs' signal legislative achievement and the quintessential statement of the absolute sovereignty of king in Parliament over the American colonies.[50]

How should we understand Burke's willingness to concede so much to the American colonists from within the framework of a conservative logic of empire built on a view of civilization that ruled out the expansion of democratic representation as a means of holding the empire together? At the deepest level, Burke's reasons for pursuing the strategy of conciliation and concession regarding the American colonies reflect his understanding of moral psychology, especially the emphasis he placed on "sympathy," or empathetic fellow feeling, in human interaction for developing shared sentiments. This was a position that Burke had in common with many of the thinkers of the Scottish Enlightenment, most notably his friend Adam Smith, and it was foundational for his moral and political theory.[51]

In the American case, Burke believed that the only thing that could keep the intimately related, even if now distinct, civilized "people" of the American colonies within the bosom of the British Empire was shared blood, shared history, and shared institutions. Channeling Shakespeare, Burke claimed, "My hold of the Colonies is in the close affection which grows from common names, from kindred blood, from similar privileges, and equal protection. These are ties, which, though light as air, are as strong as links of iron." His hope was that these commonalities could keep "the chosen race and sons of England" firmly attached to the mother country. Burke told his colleagues in Parliament that he considered the bonds formed from these civilizational similarities "the true act of navigation, which binds you to the commerce of the Colonies, and through them secures you to the wealth of the world" and preserves "the unity of the empire." As compared, all of the legalistic trappings of empire were nothing more than "dead instruments, passive tools.... It is the spirit of English communion that gives all their life and efficacy to them."[52]

Later, in giving up on the notion of demanding tax revenues from the Americans in favor of a system of voluntary grants, Burke told the colonists directly, in 1777: "We know of no road to your coffers, but through your affections."[53] Burke freely admitted that there were those who would dismiss such an approach to empire as "wild and chimerical," but he depicted such naysayers as "vulgar and mechanical politicians... a sort of people who think that nothing exists but what is gross and material; and who therefore, far from being qualified to be directors of the great movement of empire, are not fit to turn a wheel in the machine." On Burke's view, this failure to cultivate the "love of the people," based on "their attachment to their government from the sense of the deep stake they have in such a glorious institution," spelled the doom of all government, whether in England or over the colonies.[54]

Burke's argument thus stressed the affective bonds rooted in Ornamentalist depictions of civilizational similarity, or what we might call civilizational solidarity between the British and the American colonists, as the principal means of holding the British Empire in the New World together. As a result, he framed his defense of increasingly large concessions to the American colonists as akin to cutting off a limb, "but as with a limb to save the body; and I would have parted with more, if more had been necessary. Anything rather than a fruitless, hopeless, unnatural civil war."[55]

This latter sentiment—that the Americans' war for independence from the empire was in fact a "civil war" in which "British blood was spilled by British hands"—became one of Burke's most consistent themes in the latter stages of the crisis.⁵⁶ For this reason, Burke said, American independence "made him sick at heart; it struck him to the soul," and he lamented the loss of the colonies like few other events in his political career.⁵⁷ Indeed, as late as 1782, Burke still hoped that with British recognition of American independence, perhaps a deeper rift between the two kindred peoples might be repaired, even though the Americans had tragically departed from the empire. In writing to Benjamin Franklin regarding a parliamentary motion finally recognizing American independence, a motion that Burke supported, he conveyed to the American statesman his hope that such a measure would "lead to a speedy peace between the two branches of the English nation."⁵⁸ Thus, despite the persistent popular myth that Burke was in favor of American independence, he actually saw it as the colossal, avoidable loss of a civilized if somewhat unruly people from the family fold of empire.

BURKE AND THE NEW WORLD'S "OTHERS": ORIENTALISM, SAVAGERY, AND THE BRITISH EMPIRE AS A CIVILIZING MISSION

Burke stressed the Ornamentalist bonds of civilizational similarity with Britain's colonial settler population as a means of creating imperial unity, but as the American crisis progressed he would also increasingly seek to bind the colonists to Britain in a very different way, through the construction of an absolute Other against which the imperial metropole and periphery could make common cause. In the New World, Burke's conservative logic of empire therefore also relied upon an Orientalist strategy of depicting Native Americans and African slaves as inhabiting a theoretical space of radical alterity, or "savagery." In this regard, Burke's defense of empire rested on a process of Othering no less stark and dramatic than anything that would succeed it in nineteenth- and twentieth-century imperial discourse, even while the differences he focused on were not principally those of race and gender. Instead, Burke concluded that since neither the Native Americans nor the African slaves had either organized religion or a hierarchical society with a landed aristocratic nobility, they consequently lacked the definitional markers of a "civilization" according to his definition of the term. For this reason, Burke argued, the British, together with their colonial American brethren, should stay united in empire in a joint mission to "civilize" the indigenous Americans and African slaves in the New World, whom he understood as profoundly different and inferior beings. To understand Burke's use of Orientalism in the West, we must turn directly to his views on these two groups.

Native Americans

In 1777, William Robertson, the most famous Scottish Enlightenment historian, sent a copy of his recent book, *A History of America,* to Burke. In a letter pursuant to this gift, Robertson praised Burke as one of the best possible judges in Britain on the subject of history. For his part, Burke, whose own understanding of moral philosophy and history were deeply influenced by the Scottish Enlightenment,[59] responded with glowing praise for Robertson's earlier works and then turned to an assessment of Robertson's history, noting,

> The part which I read with the greatest pleasure is the discussion on the Manners and character of the Inhabitants of that new World. I have always thought with you, that we possess at this time very great advantages towards the knowledge of human Nature ... now the Great Map of Mankind is unrolled at once; and there is no state or Gradation of barbarism, and no mode of refinement which we have not at the same instant under our View. The very different Civility of Europe and of China; The barbarism of Persia and Abyssinia. The erratic manners of Tartary, and of Arabia. The Savage State of North America, and of New Zealand.[60]

Like the Scottish Enlightenment thinkers who were among his friends and greatest intellectual influences, Burke was deeply interested in the comparative analysis of cultures and societies and sought to use this knowledge to develop a "science of man." And, as with the Scots, Burke also believed that his own historical moment was a great boon to this endeavor. Unlike in previous eras, the great voyages of discovery and settlement, especially to the New World, had provided a previously unknown wealth of empirical data that unfurled the "Great Map of Mankind" as never before.[61]

There is little doubt that the reason why Robertson held Burke in such regard as a potential judge of his *History of America,* and why Burke in turn lauded this specific aspect of Robertson's book, was Burke's own earlier endeavor, *An Account of the European Settlements in America* (1757),[62] which provides the necessary starting point for any discussion of his views on the New World's "other" inhabitants. Scholars agree that this two-volume work of compilation, abridgment, paraphrase, revision, and general commentary was jointly produced by Edmund and his close friend (and perhaps distant relation), Will Burke, and can clearly be seen as an expression of Edmund Burke's views.[63] In particular, the extraordinary depiction of the "The Manners of the Americans," in part 2 of the *Account,* is worth lingering on because it illuminates Burke's understanding of what he later described, concurring with Robertson, as "the Savage State of North America."[64]

The Burkes focused an extended portion of their narrative on the Amerindians' behavior in war, and particularly their treatment of prisoners, describing in depth various forms of torture, including assertions of cannibalism, after which the scalps of the victims were said to become the "trophies of their bravery" with which "they adorn their houses." However, on the Burkes' rendering of it, one of the most notable markers of Amerindian savagery was the behavior of their women, who "transformed into something worse than furies, act their parts, and even outdo the men, in this scene of horror."[65]

Of course, careful readers of Edmund Burke will recognize that both of these descriptions of savagery, down to the very use of the term *furies* to describe the transformation in female character, would be repeated nearly verbatim in Burke's delineation of Parisian ferocity in the *Reflections on the Revolution in France,* as a means of supporting his fundamental claim that the Revolution was literally reducing the civilized French to the level of "American savages." In the *Reflections,* Burke depicts the forced march of the royal family from Versailles to Paris as "a procession of American savages, entering into Onondaga, after some of their murders called victories, and leading into hovels hung round with scalps, their captives, overpowered with the scoffs and buffets of women as ferocious as themselves, much more than it resembled the triumphal pomp of a civilized martial nation." Shortly thereafter, Burke describes the royal captives as being "slowly moved along, amidst the horrid yells, and shrilling screams, and frantic dances, and infamous contumelies, and all the unutterable abominations of the furies of hell, in the abused shape of the vilest of women."[66] Critically for Burke's view of the Amerindians, the *Account* explains the reason for their behavior as a function of their lack of the institutional components of true civilization, organized religion and aristocracy, arguing that is was the absences of these institutions that explained Native Americans' "savagery."

Combining an early stadial theory of economic development with a view of religious belief as essential to the civilizing process, the *Account* argued that the Native Americans were bereft of organized religion proper: "A people who live by hunting, who inhabit mean cottages, and are given to change the place of their habitation, are seldom very religious.... Though without religion, they abound in superstitions."[67] Against this backdrop, the Burkes declared that they lingered in lurid detail on Native American violence not for sensational effect but rather to make a broader theoretical point about the civilizing effects of organized religion in general and of Christianity in particular. The aim of their descriptions was to "give a true idea of their character" and to show in the strongest possible terms "to what an inconceivable degree of barbarity the passions of men let loose will carry them. It will point out to us the advantages of a religion that teaches a compassion to our enemies, which is neither known nor practiced in other religions."[68] Unlike the compassionate Christians, the Burkes argued, the Native Americans' lack of organized religion deprived them of the habitual social discipline inculcated by religious institutions, with the correspondingly shocking results in their mode of warfare just described.

However, in the *Account* as throughout his work as a whole, Burke does not reduce Native American (or African) "savagery" to a form of racial (and racist) essentialism. Later, in passionately arguing against the British use of Native American troops in the Revolutionary War, Burke claimed that "the fault of employing them did not consist in their being of one color or another" but rather "in their way of making war,"[69] which was tightly tied to their lack of religion. In fact, Burke's work is a clear example of an earlier notion of what constitutes "ethnicity." Only over time did the meaning of this concept shift from a notion of religious to secular "otherness" understood in terms of racial, national, or cultural distinctiveness.[70] Burke's views on Amerindians (and as we shall see shortly, Africans) are evidence of this earlier view. Burke certainly regarded the Native Americans in Orientalist terms as uncivilized and savage Others, but he did so because they lacked organized religion, not because they were nonwhite.

Likewise, and consistent with Burke's overarching notion of the constitutive components of civilization—or its absence—the *Account* explains Native American savagery as resulting from the lack of a stratified hierarchy of social ranks, governed by a landed nobility that could serve as a natural aristocracy:

> The whole fashion of their lives is of a piece; hardy, poor, and squalid; and their education from their infancy is solely directed to fit their bodies for this mode of life, and to form their minds to inflict and to endure the greatest evils. Their only occupations are hunting and war. Agriculture is left to the woman. Merchandise they condemn. When their hunting season is past . . . they pass the rest of their time in an entire indolence. They sleep half the day

in their huts, they loiter and jest among their friends, and they observe no bounds or decency in their eating and drinking."[71]

For Burke, equality in poverty and economic underdevelopment (relishing hunting, holding commerce in contempt, and seeing agriculture as the province of women) were the supposed hallmarks of savage societies. So, too, was the commitment to a form of unbridled, intemperate, uncivilized liberty, a principle that the Burkes describe as definitional of "the government of the Americans": "Liberty, in its fullest extent, is the darling passion of the [Native] Americans. To this they sacrifice everything[,] ... and their education is directed in such a manner as to cherish this disposition to the utmost." Consequently, when their children are grown, "they experience nothing like command, dependence, or subordination."[72] In short, for the Burkes what made Amerindian life savage was in large part that it was marked by equality of poor condition and a concomitant love of unbridled liberty.[73] On Burke's understanding of it, as with religion the lack of a landed aristocracy undermined the habitual social discipline necessary for civilization to flourish. Such views demonstrate clearly that Burke was not an unqualified supporter of liberty, writ large, but rather of one historically narrow and culturally specific instantiation of it. Indeed, for Burke, Amerindian life was marked by an excess of irreligious liberty and equality of rank—the same features that he would later depict as definitional of the French Revolution—and this is exactly what made the Native Americans "savages" (as it would later make the French).

Burke's negative depiction of the Native Americans in the *Account* also links it to Robertson's *History of America*, a text whose author saw the Amerindian "savages" as ripe for a civilizing imperial mission.[74] As in the *History of America*, the *Account*'s assessment of what Burke would later describe in his letter to Robertson as "the Savage State of North America," was unsparing. Like Robertson, the Burkes frequently use the term *savage* pejoratively in the text to describe the Amerindians, as when they refer to "these savage nations" and "the ferocity of their nature." Elsewhere, the Burkes claim that "the Pennsylvanians have suffered severely by the incursions of the savage Americans." While discussing the character of Native American warfare, the Burkes similarly argue that "the conquerors satiate their savage fury with the most shocking insults and barbarities to the dead, biting their flesh, tearing the scalp from their heads, and wallowing in their blood like beasts."[75]

Tellingly, in the second volume of the *Account*, the Burkes place the blame for the tragic violence between these "savages" and the American colonists squarely on the uncivilized Amerindians:

> This savage people commence hostilities against us without any previous notice; and often, without any provocation, they commit the most horrid ravages for a long time with impunity. But when at last their barbarities have roused the sleeping strength of our people, at the same time too that they have considerably lessened it, they are not ashamed to beg a peace; they know we always grant it readily; they promise it shall endure as long as the sun and moon; and then all is quiet, till the French intrigues, co-operating with our indolence, give them once more an opportunity of ravaging our Colonies, and of once more renewing a peace to be broken like all the former.[76]

This is a revealing passage, not simply because it describes the Native Americans in negative terms as "savages," but also because it places the blame for imperial violence in the New World principally on its indigenous inhabitants, who are depicted in stereotypical terms as duplicitous and vicious, both unrelentingly aggressive and entirely unwilling to keep peace with the gentle and pacific American colonists.

At the same time, the Burkes' reference in the preceding passage to "French intrigues" in rousing the Native Americans to violence reminds us that the *Account* was written at the beginning of the Seven Years' War, a fact that highlights the broader imperial context in which this text and Burke's subsequent writings on North America's indigenous peoples were articulated. When placed in the context of the British Empire in the New World in the aftermath of the French and Indian Wars, it becomes clear that Burke, no less than Robertson, was also interested in a mission to civilize the "savages" of North America. In fact, during the American crisis Burke would come to believe that such a civilizing mission against the Amerindian Other was an essential mechanism for holding the British Empire in the New World together. To understand why this was the case, we need to consider Burke's writings on the Native Americans against their appropriate imperial backdrop.

Burke on the British Empire as a Mission to Civilize the Native Americans

Recent scholarship has helped us to understand the American crisis anew, by considering it as posing a number of dilemmas for the British after 1763, and by examining the ways in which these created extraordinary tension between London and the colonists.[77] These problems emerged from the empire's increasingly polyethnic composition in the wake of the territorial acquisitions that were the spoils of the Seven Years' War. Worldwide, the British Empire was about five times bigger than it had been before the war, and among its new members were perhaps a hundred thousand Native Americans in the lands wrested from the French between the Appalachian Mountains and the Mississippi River, and from the Spanish in Florida.[78]

As Linda Colley has shown, this created new difficulties for Britain in terms of how to govern such vast, ethnically diverse territories, owing to Britain's relatively small size, limited natural resources, and small population and standing army. These limitations meant that those charged with directing the empire could not afford to be simply exclusionary with respect to its new subjects; hence the British developed a hybrid vision of empire in the New World after the Seven Years' War. Driven in large part by necessity, Britain sought policies that would not alienate—and potentially raise to arms—the new inhabitants of their empire. To this end, with the Royal Proclamation of 1763, they sought to close off the American West and its Amerindian population beyond the Appalachians from the colonists, who saw it as ripe for expansion, by prohibiting them from settling there. Later, they also introduced the Quebec Act of 1774, which offered special legal and religious privileges to the largely Francophone and Catholic population in Canada. For London, these moves were not merely pragmatic concessions driven by necessity; they were also a means of keeping the American colonists in check. However, for the latter, who still saw themselves in some ways as fellow Britons deserving of special treatment, they smacked of betrayal.[79] Nevertheless, for the British the example of Native American rebellions like Pontiac's War (1763–1764) pressed home the need for implementing the provisions of the proclamation of 1763, and by 1768 Britain had gone a long way toward making it acceptable to Indian leaders.[80]

Aziz Rana has made clear why these British maneuvers should come as such an affront to the American colonists. From the beginning, America was a settler colonial society whose inhabitants linked liberty and subordination so tightly that the colonists' substantive definition of freedom proved unthinkable without the simultaneous suppression and denial of liberty to subject communities such as the Native Americans and African slaves. Over time, the British policy of allowing for broad local autonomy had enabled this conception of colonial liberty to become the status quo, together with its implicit special privileging of colonial subjectivity.[81]

However, after 1763, as the empire became increasingly differentiated and polyglot, British moves toward more meaningful cultural inclusion of its Others threatened the settlers' sense of supremacy and freedom in ways that they believed reduced them to the level of their supposed inferiors. British attempts at restructuring their empire in the New World through judicial and administrative action to expand the rights of Native Americans, Canadian Catholics, and even to some extent African slaves thus upended the stratified hierarchy of imperial subjectivity. In this sense, by reserving lands west of the Appalachians for the Native Americans, the Royal Proclamation of 1763—an act that also required a standing army to enforce it, financed by the Stamp Act—deprived the colonists of their privileged status. At the same time, such legislative enactments seemingly rejected both *terra nullius* and conquest/Christianizing arguments for expansion and ultimately ignored the necessity of native dispossession, which many colonists regarded as the precondition for meaningful self-rule. Britain's apparent willingness to strike a balance between the goals of settlers and natives with respect to liberty was thus perceived by the colonists as a fundamental threat to their superior social standing and power, a threat against which they offered defiance and a reiteration of their status as the empire's only authentic free subjects.[82]

What erupted during the American crisis after the French and Indian War was therefore nothing short of a fundamental disagreement about the nature and purpose of empire itself. For Burke, who was deeply sympathetic to America, the colonists were indeed a privileged, civilized brethren who deserved special treatment by the empire because they were effectively the overseas branch of the British nation. For others in Britain, however, the colonists were imperial subjects, at bottom no different than the French Canadians or Native Americans. As the crisis deepened, this latter view won out in official Britain, with the consequence that the British were increasingly willing to make common cause with both the Native Americans and the African slaves during the Revolutionary War. Thus, partly for theoretical reasons and partly from necessity, Britain's war-fighting machine relied on native American and African auxiliaries, groups who fought overwhelmingly on the British side rather than that of the colonists.[83] Thus, while violence dominated the imperial relationship with Native Americans from the close of the Seven Years' War down to 1815, after 1776 that violence generally pitted the British, in common cause with the Native Americans, against the newly independent colonies and later United States.[84]

Burke's position in this debate was extraordinarily clear. As we have seen, he repeatedly described the American colonists as Britain's civilized brethren and described the Native Americans as brutal savages. As the crisis unfolded, and hostilities between Britain and America commenced, Burke sided wholeheartedly with the "civilized" settler colonists' notion of liberty as appropriately granting them special status within the empire, status that he believed justified their territorial expansion. In making this case, Burke would plead for imperial unity by starkly contrasting the "civilized" world of the colonies with the radical alterity of the "savages" beyond it, whom he described as ripe for a civilizing mission. Burke's recourse to such Orientalist arguments in defense of the British Empire in the New World—and its expansion—is abundantly clear, especially in his writings and speeches about the American Revolution.

For example, in his 1775 *Speech on Conciliation with America*, Burke imagined a scene during the early years of the eighteenth century in which an angel from above might have pointed out the New World to a young Lord Bathurst (who was in attendance for the speech) and said to him: "'Young man, There is America—which at this day serves for little more than to amuse you with stories of savage men, and uncouth manners.... Whatever England has been growing to by a progressive increase of improvement, brought in by varieties of people, by succession of civilizing conquest and civilizing settlements in a series of Seventeen Hundred years, you shall see as much added to her by America in the course of a single life!" Strange as this would have appeared at the time, Burke insisted, the seemingly outlandish prediction by the imaginary angel had in fact come to pass by the mid-1770s, and such great acts of "civilizing conquest and civilizing settlements" had occurred. Burke rejoiced at this felicitous turn of events, saying of Bathurst: "Fortunate man, he has lived to see it! Fortunate indeed, if he lives to see nothing that shall vary the prospect, and cloud the setting of his day!"[85]

Far from retreating from such putatively civilizing acts of settlement and conquest, Burke instead adamantly rejected any "project of hedging-in population" in the American colonies, as "attempting to forbid as a crime, and to suppress as an evil, the Command and Blessing of Providence, 'Encrease and Multiply.'"[86] But Burke goes even further in linking the expansion of the British Empire—understood as a civilizing mission—with God's will, and urging his fellow members of Parliament to take up the imperial burden: "We ought to elevate our minds to the greatness of that trust to which the order of Providence has called us. By adverting to the dignity of this high calling, our ancestors have turned a savage wilderness into a glorious empire; and have made the most extensive, and the only honorable conquests; not by destroying, but by promoting, the wealth, the number, the happiness, of the human race."[87] Here, we see Burke's true understanding of the relationship between providence and empire, not as an onerous burden but rather as a glorious calling. Burke tightly knits together providence, imperial conquest, and territorial expansion with the spreading of civilization's blessings in a way that would make both William Robertson and later nineteenth-century proponents of empire proud. Furthermore, placed in context, Burke touts a civilizing imperial mission as one of the best methods of conciliating Britain's settler colonial brethren.

In fact, throughout the conflict, Burke sought to forge a tight Ornamentalist bond between the British and the American colonists, one centered on the shared Orientalist goal of expanding the civilizing blessings of empire into "savage" new lands. To this end, he implored the colonists to understand Britain's intentions:

> You will not, we trust, believe, that born in a civilized country, formed to gentle manners, trained in a merciful religion . . . we could have thought of letting loose upon you, our late beloved Brethren, these fierce tribes of Savages and Cannibals, in whom the traces of human nature are effaced by ignorance and barbarity. We rather wished to have joined with you, in bringing gradually that unhappy part of mankind into civility, order, piety, and virtuous discipline, than to have confirmed their evil habits, and increased their natural ferocity, by fleshing them in the slaughter of you, whom our wiser and better ancestors had sent into the Wilderness, with the express view of introducing, along with our holy religion, its humane and charitable manners.[88]

While reiterating the long-standing distinction he had drawn in the *Account* between British and colonial "civilization" and Native American "savagery," in this passage Burke takes the further remarkable step of arguing that the two branches of Britain should refrain from fighting each other and should instead make common cause in a civilizing mission aimed at *expanding* the British Empire westward, into the lands of the Native Americans not subdued by the colonists, beyond the lines set by the Royal Proclamation of 1763. This point should definitively put to rest the notion that Edmund Burke was merely interested in the conservation of empire where it already existed and clarify that he also advocated supporting a radical territorial expansion of empire where such aggression could be framed as a providential mission in which the forces of "civilization" were blessed with the opportunity to subdue those of "savagery." The latter view relies on a substantive notion of conservatism derived from Burke's understanding of history as a civilizing process, rather than being reducible to a positional commitment to preserving the status quo.

Similarly, when the American Revolution broke out, Burke argued passionately against arming the Native Americans to fight against Britain's colonial brethren and resolutely rejected the use of such "savage" auxiliary troops in conducting a war against the "civilized" American colonists. He regarded recourse to such uncivilized allies as one of the most surefire methods of alienating the colonists and driving them to an implacable hatred of the British. For this reason, in his "Address to the King" of January 1777, Burke rejected British attempts to bring upon the colonists the wrath of the Native Americans by instigating "an irruption of those fierce and cruel Tribes of Savages."[89] This view is an elaboration of Burke's 1775 "Draft Petition on Use of Indians," in which he condemned

> the means by which this War has been attempted—to call from that Wilderness, which is not yet reclaimed [by] the spirited Enterprise of our American brethren and which they looked to as the present [provision] [object] for the growing industry of future generations, every Class of savages and Cannibals the most cruel and ferocious ever [known] to lay Waste with fire hatchets with Murders, and Sanguinary Tortures of the Inhabitants, the most beautiful Work of Skill and Labor by which the creation and name of God was ever glorified by his Creatures.[90]

From an evidentiary standpoint, it would be difficult to find clearer proof of Burke's Ornamentalist theoretical strategy of attempting to fuse the colonies to Britain through an appeal to civilizational solidarity while simultaneously drawing an indelible Orientalist line between these civilized peoples and the "savage and cannibal" Others of the New World.

Perhaps the most striking public expression of Burke's views on the impropriety of relying on Native American allies in the war against Britain's colonial brethren came in his 1778 "Speech on the Use of Indians," as reported in the *Parliamentary Register* and taken from various drafts of the speech in his hand. In that performance, Burke flatly rejected the use of "savage allies" because he claimed that their method of warfare "was so horrible, that it shocked not only the manners of all civilized people, but far exceeded the ferocity of all barbarians mentioned in history."[91] Taken as a whole, Burke concluded, the Native Americans were not "a *people* in any proper acceptation of the Word—but several gangs of Banditti scattered along a wild of a great civilized empire—a Banditti of the most cruel and atrocious kind such as infest many such empires."[92] This speech was reportedly given to an audience in Parliament that was noticeably laughing when Burke went on to analogize this infestation of ferocious Native American savages to the menagerie of wild animals in the Tower of London.[93]

However, according to contemporaneous reports, when Burke turned to a moving description of the death of Jane McCrea, a woman from New York who was en route to wed a Loyalist officer serving under General Burgoyne, laughter transformed to such sadness that it "drew iron tears" from even the most hardened of listeners. McCrea was allegedly killed and scalped on her wedding day by Native Americans who were in the service of the British military. Burke seized on the event to demonstrate "that the savages, did in effect, indiscriminately murder men, women, and children, friends and foes." In this regard, Burke declared that Burgoyne's attempt to prevent the savage Indians from their vicious mode of war, while "rational and proper," was hopeless and unintelligible "as applied to savages" and "might as well have been applied to the wild beasts of the forest."[94]

In a draft of this speech, Burke drove home this point by describing the death of the civilized maiden McCrea in terms that sound remarkably similar to his later depiction of the assault on that female embodiment of civilization, Marie Antoinette, in her boudoir, during the French Revolution:

> In that moment of blessing that God who meant the union relation and continuance of his Creatures has made the highest point of human felicity and is indeed a part of pleasure and innocence which Angels might look down on and Envy, when this poor Creature dressed up in those pretty little ornaments ... surrounded with tender parents, and sympathizing kindred, and holy Priests and happy Lovers just in that moment [of momentary] anxiety of love—and those with that hair dressed for other purposes that morning torn from her head to decorate the infernal habitation of cruelty and barbarism and there left a naked and [foul scale] her body a mangled ghastly spectacle of blood and horror, crying through an hundred mouths to that whose image was defaced for Vengeance. Is it to be wondered that the whole Country with a general insurrection rose to exterminate the [savages]?[95]

The implications of this incident for Burke's theoretical position are clear: The only approach to take with such savages was not to employ them in fighting the colonists but rather for the British to join with their colonial brethren to either civilize the savages or—failing that—to "exterminate" them and, in so doing, to hold together (and expand) the British Empire in the New World. Burke's great goal in writing about the Native Americans at such length was thus to forge a sympathetic transatlantic bond between civilizations, in large part by Othering the Native American savages in Orientalist terms.[96]

African Slaves

I turn now to ask what Burke made of that second great group of Others in Britain's New World empire, the millions of slaves imported from Africa to provide the underpopulated colonies with the manpower necessary for intensive forms of agricultural production such as sugarcane and tobacco growing. It has been estimated that in the period from 1662 to 1807, the British "empire of liberty" carried roughly 3.4 million Africans into slavery in the New World. This figure means that Britain was the foremost slave-trading power in the Western Hemisphere during this period, bringing as many slaves to America as all of the other nations engaged in the slave trade combined.[97] More than three times the number of Africans left their homeland for America and the Caribbean in British ships than did Europeans, ensuring that, in sheer numbers, in this time frame the British Empire in the New World was in fact more black than white.[98]

What was Burke's position regarding African slavery and the slave trade as the crucial engine enabling empire in the New World? The newer literature on Burke and empire basically avoids this question. Nevertheless, a number of scholars have insisted upon Burke's deep hostility to slavery in a fashion that would seem to support the view of Burke as an anti-imperial thinker.[99] However, a close reading of the evidence drawn from Burke's writings on the subject of slavery over the course of his career yields a very different conclusion.

In their *Account of the European Settlements in America,* the Burkes accepted slavery and made a purely economic case for treating slaves more humanely, concluding that if slaves were less brutally treated, they would be happier and more productive.[100] In this vein, the *Account* defends British imperial slavery in the New World while relieving the British of moral culpability: "Nothing could excuse the slave trade at all, but the necessity we are under of peopling our colonies, and the consideration that the slaves we buy were in the same condition in Africa, either hereditary or taken in war."[101]

That is to say, the inhumanity of slavery was justified by material considerations, an argument that is buttressed with the soothing assurance that the human beings the British traded for were already slaves anyway. But the Burkes in fact go a good deal further than this in arguing for slavery.

The *Account* actually presses for a massive expansion of the British imperial slave trade, and the Burkes lament the fact that British traders confine themselves to portions of the Gold Coast, Sierra Leone, and Gambia.[102] The authors write, "I own, I have often been surprised, that our African traders should choose so contracted an object for their slave trade." The Burkes argued that the British faced too much competition from other European nations for relatively fewer slaves in these regions, who therefore cost too much. Indeed, they tell their readers in the 1750s that such competition has "raised the price of slaves within these few years above thirty percent. Nor is it to be wondered; as in the tract, in which they trade, they have many rivals; the people are grown too expert, by the constant habit of European commerce; and the slaves in that part are in a good measure exhausted."[103] As scholars have noted, this was in fact a very real difficulty faced by British slave traders in the eighteenth century.[104] To counteract the difficulties of dwindling supply and high price, the Burkes consequently recommend going past the Cape of Good Hope into East Africa and pursuing slaves in the largely undefended Portuguese claim of Madagascar and elsewhere. If this path were taken, they insisted, "our African trade might then be considerably enlarged, our own manufactures extended, and our colonies supplied at an easier rate than they are at present, or are likely to be for the future, whilst we confine ourselves to two or three places, which we exhaust, and where we shall find the market dearer every day."[105]

The real problem for the Burkes was therefore not slavery—an institution they not only defended but also sought to enlarge by expanding the slave trade into East Africa—but rather how to handle the large (and hopefully larger) number of African slaves in the British colonies of the New World once they arrived. In writing about Georgia, for example, the Burkes argued that the trustees of that colony correctly worried about settler safety in a society with so many slaves. However, because they saw the civilized colonists as poorly suited to do the type of labor required by plantation agriculture, the Burkes maintained that despite the potential threat of slave rebellions it would be a grave mistake to ban slavery in Georgia or any other southern colony.[106]

Instead, the Burkes framed the real problem posed by slavery as one of how to achieve what the *Account* referred to as "that grand desideratum in politics, of uniting a perfect subjection to an entire content and satisfaction of the people."[107] Unsurprisingly, given Edmund Burke's view of the civilizing process, religion was the key to this endeavor of marrying lack of liberty with happiness. As with the Amerindians, so too with the African slaves: it was Christianity that Burke believed should play the crucial role in disciplining and channeling the untamed and dangerous savage commitment to liberty and equality by shaping it in a civilized fashion.

To this end, the *Account* points to the behavior of the Jesuits in the Spanish colonies as particularly worthy of emulation. The Jesuits "bring the Indians and blacks into some knowledge of religion," they write, which has "a good political effect"—namely: "Those slaves are more faithful than ours, and, though indulged with greater liberty, are far less dangerous. I do not remember that any insurrection has been ever attempted by them; and the Indians are reduced to a more civilized life, than they are in the colonies of any other European nation."[108] Here, the Burkes actually link suitably chastened liberty and slavery, arguing that relatively freer slaves, having been made good Christians, would be more committed to their slave masters. In this regard, the *Account* singled out Jesuit policy in Spain's South American colony of Paraguay as a model for the British colonies in North America and the Caribbean, because it "mollified the minds of the most savage nations; fixed the most rambling; and subdued the most averse to government," adding to human society "three hundred thousand families in a well-regulated community, in the room of a few vagabond untaught savages."[109]

Burke believed that the British were faced with an analogous problem when it came to the management of their slaves in North America and Barbados—that is, the task of achieving perfect subjection and perfect contentment. The *Account*'s answer to this conundrum was to follow the Jesuits' lead. The Burkes insisted, "I know that they are stubborn and intractable for the most part, and that they must be ruled with the rod of iron. I would have them ruled, but not crushed with it.... And I think it clear from the whole course of history, that those nations which have behaved with the greatest humanity to their slaves, were always best served, and ran the least hazard from their rebellions."[110] The *Account* argues that a similar deployment of religion by British slave masters in their colonies—that is, a mixture of "humanity" and the psychological "rod of iron"—would likewise civilize Britain's African slaves while disciplining them to docility and humble obedience.

This could be done, for example, by guaranteeing that the slaves received instruction "in the principles of religion and virtue, and especially in the humility, submission, and honesty, which become their condition." The Burkes believed that the salutary effects of Christian religious instruction would be great. The masters would behave in a more humane fashion toward their slaves, and the slaves would of course "grow more honest, tractable, and less of eye-servants."[111] In other words, the slaves' transformed "manners" and newly internalized sense of humble obedience would ensure their correct and beneficial behavior even when they were not under the watchful gaze of their masters. A more poignant anticipation of the goals of Jeremy Bentham's "panopticon"—a role played for Burke by Christianity rather than the jailor's tower—could hardly be imagined.

Hence it is clear that, at least in 1757, Edmund Burke supported slavery for economic considerations that led him to argue for a massive expansion of the slave trade, together with the maintenance of a firm commitment to spreading the Europeans' putative gift of Christianity to the African slaves as a means of civilizing them. The real question thus becomes: did Burke develop a clear opposition to slavery in his later writings, as a number of scholars insist? The answer to that query is not nearly so simple as some have declared, as is evidenced by a wide range of texts and speeches whose sole author is Edmund Burke.

Lord Dunmore's Proclamation and Fear of Rebellion by the "Other". One of the reasons Burke's interpreters have misunderstood his views on slavery is that at times one runs across arresting depictions of slavery and the slave trade that might lead inattentive readers to miss his broader arguments. For example, in his 1775 *Speech on Conciliation with America,* Burke refers to the slave trade as an "inhuman traffick." However, here as elsewhere, one must ask: what is the broader context for this remark? Upon inspection, one sees that it occurs in the course of Burke's argument *against* a "general enfranchisement," or grant of general emancipation to the slaves in the southern colonies under the control of Loyalists at that time. Burke does point out that one reason for opposing such a proclamation was that the British were in no moral position to convince African slaves that they would be acting in good faith, because the British remained entangled in the trade carrying slaves to America.[112]

However, he also developed two other lines of argument against freeing African slaves in the American South. One was prudential: in the event of an ensuing conflict, American rebels might likewise free and arm their slaves against the British. But Burke's second claim was that emancipating the slaves was impracticable for an entirely different reason. "It is sometimes as hard to persuade slaves to be free, as it is to compel freemen to be slaves," he wrote. This is because "slaves are often much attached to their masters." This is an argument similar to those made later by antebellum thinkers such as George Fitzhugh, John C. Calhoun, and other defenders of slavery who romanticized plantation society as a happy family that the slaves would be loath to leave, given their contentment. It is for this mix of prudential and paternalistic reasons that in the *Speech on Conciliation with America* Burke insists, "I never could argue myself into" a position in favor of emancipating slaves in the southern colonies.[113] Burke's position in 1775 was therefore firmly against the abolition of slavery.

Later, when the war between Britain and America had begun, Burke again took up the problems posed by the question of a "general enfranchisement" of African slaves, but in the face of more pressing circumstances. These were occasioned specifically by the 1775 proclamation of Lord Dunmore, governor of Virginia, promising to grant freedom to all slaves who would take the British side in the conflict.

Dunmore's proclamation took on added meaning in the wake of Lord Mansfield's ruling in the 1772 case of *Somerset v. Stewart,* which pertained to the legal status of slavery in England. While Mansfield was careful to avoid claiming that slavery was illegal on English soil, his decision that it could not be supported by English common law created a number of thorny theoretical difficulties concerning the ultimate legal basis of chattel slavery in both Britain and the colonies. Moreover, irrespective of legal niceties and the actual narrowness of Mansfield's holding, public opinion on both sides of the Atlantic generally concluded that his decision had freed all of the slaves in England. The *Somerset* case thus appeared as a practical threat to colonial life. In particular, it was seen as indicative of British willingness to deny the special status of the settler colonists' liberty and social supremacy, and even to do so by potentially allowing the arming of Africans themselves to this end. For the colonists, Dunmore's promise to free slaves who agreed to fight for the British was seen as especially tangible proof of the latter point.[114] Of course, for slaves the general popular understanding that the *Somerset* decision meant they would be free in England, a view bolstered by Dunmore's proclamation, gave them a measure of hope, just as the proclamation of 1763 had done earlier for the Native Americans.[115]

From Burke's standpoint, Dunmore's proclamation was a horrifying mistake that threatened to alienate Britain's colonial brethren irrevocably from the empire, by effectively treating the savages as the equals of the civilized. It raised for Burke the great fear of rebellion by the African Other. This was a theme he addressed repeatedly in his speeches during the American crisis. As reported in the *Parliamentary Register*, in his "Address to the Colonists" (1777) Burke expressed his "shame" to the Americans that "the African slaves, who had been sold to you on public faith, and under the sanction of Acts of Parliament, to be your servants and your guards, [were] employed to cut the throats of their masters."[116]

As the war unfolded, Burke increasingly paired the "savage" Native Americans and Africans together as enemies of the civilized colonial settlers and, therefore, as wholly unworthy of serving as British allies, as he did in the 1778 "Speech on the Use of Indians" mentioned above. In that speech, according to the *Parliamentary Register*, Burke also invoked Providence in expressing thanks for the temporary failure of Dunmore's proclamation: "Providentially the English white civilized inhabitants had so strengthened themselves, as to keep under his Majesty's negro allies; that not above one thousand or thereabouts were able to escape, and put themselves under the banners of Lord Dunmore." However, Burke feared that Dunmore's strategy was spreading among British governors, and he argued that there was good reason to believe that it would be used in both the Carolinas and parts of Florida. He insisted further that the British threat to free the slaves was in fact "the grand cause of the greater resentment which appeared in the southern, than in many of the northern Colonies." On his view, the southerners quite rightly asked "what security could they receive, that if they admitted an English governor, he would not raise their negroes on them, whenever he thought it good to assert any given disturbances should amount to a rebellion, and declare martial law."[117]

Burke also railed against Dunmore's strategy by again invoking the dangers of demography, pointing to the growing number of Africans in the New World, whom he warned would be uncontrollable once the rage at their "civilized" white slave owners was tapped. Regarding Burke's speech, the *Parliamentary Register* records:

> He appealed to all who knew the southern colonies, and the West Indies, what murders, rapes, and enormities of all kinds, were in the contemplation of all negroes who meditated an insurrection. He lastly asked what means were proposed for governing these negroes, who were 100,000 at least; when they had reduced the province to their obedience, and made themselves masters of the houses, goods, wives and daughters of their murdered lords?[118]

In this way, Burke played on the basest fears of colonial American slave society, warning that the African "savages" would erupt in violence, not only killing them and stealing their property but also raping their wives and daughters. This, then, was another dimension of the starkly negative flip side of Burke's Ornamentalist strategy of civilizational solidarity: binding Britain and colonial America together by contrasting them once again in Orientalist fashion with radical alterity, in this case the ferociously rebellious slave savages. In notes for a draft of this speech, Burke fretted about the combined effect of Lord Dunmore's proclamation and legal decisions like the *Somerset* case. The effect of the former was that the slave "was to have liberty—arms, pay, and to become a Lord over those he had served—the condition of a Soldier is no great dignity to a freeman but to a Slave is the greatest advancement which can be conceived." With respect to the latter, Burke declared that "the ferocity of a wild African [was] to judge of the Law and Liberty of England," and he warned of "the ferocity, the revenge, the fear of returning to servitude of an emancipated Slave."[119] Burke also mourned for the American colonists' "alienation of affections, and distrust and terror of our government, brought on by these measures."[120] In this way, Burke juxtaposed his Ornamentalist concern for those he perceived as civilized colonial brethren with Orientalist fears of a savage slave rebellion. In so doing, he defended a very specific conception of liberty for the "civilized" while passionately decrying its extension to the "savage."

Burke's Later Views on Slavery: Gradual Emancipation, Disciplinarity, and Reenslavement. Throughout his parliamentary career, Burke had a number of opportunities to weigh in on the topic of slavery beyond the issue of the American Revolution, given that from 1774 to 1780 he was MP for Bristol, the second-largest city in England at the time and (together with Liverpool) the one most heavily involved in the slave trade. However, Burke's writings and speeches during this period do not suggest any opposition to the slave trade or bolster his credential as an abolitionist. Indeed, the evidence seems to cut in a very different direction.

For example, on June 5, 1777, Burke made speeches in the House of Commons concerning that body's proposed inquiry into charges that the Company of Merchant Adventurers Trading to Africa, represented by businessmen from London, Liverpool, and Bristol, was using its annual grants from Parliament to maintain a monopoly on the slave trade.[121] Before this, on May 31, John Schoolbred, a merchant in the Company, had written Burke to thank him for his earlier defense of it. On June 2, according to the *Parliamentary History*, Burke subsequently had spoken "against revising the state of the trade to Africa in general, for fear of doing more harm than good." And early on the day of June 5, Burke wrote a letter to Lord North, the prime minister, appealing to him to drop the charges against the Company.[122]

Later on the day of June 5, when the Africa Company was criticized, according to the *Parliamentary History*, Burke "defended the Company's affairs in general, and the necessity of granting them a still farther parliamentary aid." That is to say, Burke argued for an *increase* in the sum awarded to the Africa Company by Parliament for purposes of enabling it to cover its debts. In the course of this debate, the radical MP David Hartley rose to condemn the cruelties of slavery, produced a pair of handcuffs to illustrate his case, and urged some means of mitigating the trade. Burke rose, observed that Hartley had brought convincing proof of slavery's hardships, but reiterated a claim he had made in 1757, that "Africa, time out of mind, had been in a state of slavery, therefore the inhabitants only changed one species of slavery for another." Burke did admit that European slavery seemed rather harsher, which he noted "certainly was a matter of reproach somewhere, and deserved serious consideration,"[123] but none was forthcoming from him.

In fact, at this point in his career Burke stood deeply opposed to legal barriers that limited the number of participants in the slave trade. In 1779, he received a letter from Michael Miller, an influential merchant who would briefly become mayor of Bristol, asking him to oppose the transformation of the Africa Company into a joint-stock company. As it was, any merchant for a small fee could join the Company, whereas a joint-stock venture would have greatly restricted the number of retailers in human beings. Burke wrote to Miller that of course he would oppose such a move as contrary to the principles of free trade and evincing "the grossest ignorance of every commercial principle." He concluded his letter to Miller by insisting that when it came to such a radical notion as transforming the Africa Company, "I, for one, upon these general Ideas, or upon any mere Speculation whatsoever am an Enemy to a change in any Establishment."[124] From one angle, this is of course Burke's oft-remarked love of prescriptive institutions and practices— although not discussed as an abstract principle but deployed here in the service of upholding a wider rather than a narrower field for the slave trade.

However, in this case Burke's endorsement of free trade appears to have been circumscribed and to have applied only to companies internal to the British Empire. In his 1780 *Speech at Bristol Previous to the Election*, he railed against the British loss of "the exclusive commerce of America, of Africa, of the West Indies" through the course of the imperial struggles with France and Spain.[125] This was a long-standing concern. In a draft of his 1775 "Second Speech on Conciliation," Burke enumerated the dreadful consequences "if this unfortunate War should be continued" and the French should get involved, among which was the inestimable damage to "African Trade—West Indian. And thus the whole Fabrick of British Commerce would tumble to the Ground."[126] Indeed, in a fit of pique in 1779, Burke even drew up draft articles of impeachment against Lord North, the nineteenth of which charged that under North's leadership "no measures have been taken for the protections of the Trade to the Coast of Africa or for the annoyance of the Enemy there; by which the said most valuable Branch of Commerce has been wholly lost."[127]

Thus, as MP for the slave-trading city of Bristol, Burke vigorously *defended* the Africa Company, argued for an increase in its annual stipend from Parliament, took steps to keep the playing field for the slave trade as wide open as possible, and greatly fretted over the economic impact of its decline in the global struggle of empires. He did make reference to the admitted hardships of slavery; however, these were clearly secondary to the economic concerns of his constituents and the weight of history and custom—Africans had always been slaves; the best the British could do was to meliorate their condition as such.

So, what are we to make of the claim that abolition of slavery and the slave trade should rank as one of Burke's great causes? This assertion rests chiefly on the fact that, years later, in 1792, Burke sent the influential MP Henry Dundas a preliminary set of regulations titled "Sketch of a Negro Code."[128] Earlier, in 1789, Burke had delivered two brief speeches in Parliament critical of slavery and the slave trade in response to the abolitionist William Wilberforce, but only subsequently did he detail specific policy prescriptions on these issues. Burke acted in response to a popular movement led by the Quakers and other evangelicals, who had presented 519 petitions to the House of Commons from across Britain calling for the abolition of slavery, the largest number ever submitted in a single parliamentary session.[129] In this context, Dundas sought to broker a compromise between the widespread popular forces pushing for the immediate abolition of slavery and the antiabolitionists, one that envisioned gradual emancipation as the goal. Burke had penned his "Sketch" some twelve years earlier, while he was still MP for Bristol. But more than a decade later, Burke had long since ceased to represent Bristol, and the American colonies were no more. It was against this backdrop that he reintroduced his plan, which in careful detail suggests more humane rules to govern the slave trade in West Africa, the ships taking part in it, the treatment of slaves during the middle passage, and their management in the West Indies after arriving and throughout the duration of their new life. But is this plan for regulating the slave trade, introduced in a context in which there was widespread popular sentiment for putting an *immediate* end to the trade altogether, sufficient to establish Burke's credentials as an antislavery thinker, at least late in his life? Ultimately, that depends on how one defines the term *abolitionism* and how one understands its purposes.

In a cover letter explaining his own purposes in the "Sketch" and his reasons for introducing it into the debate in the 1790s, Burke informed Dundas that he rejected immediate abolition of the slave trade as "but a single act," agitated by a "popular spirit, which seldom calls for, and indeed very rarely relishes, a system made up of a great variety of parts, and which is to operate its effect in a great length of time. The people like short methods; the consequences of which they sometimes have reason to repent of." He goes on to inform Dundas: "It is not, that my plan does not lead to the extinction of the slave trade; but it is through a very slow progress"; moreover, Burke insists, whenever "we take our *point of departure* from a state of slavery, we must precede the donation of freedom by disposing the minds of the objects to a disposition to receive it without danger to themselves or to us." Here, Burke maintained that the process of civilizing slaves was "very different" from "the process of bringing *free* savages [like the Native Americans] to order and civilization." Because the minds of the slaves were "crippled," they could "do nothing for themselves . . . everything must be the creature of power. Hence it is, that regulations must be multiplied," and such "regulations can owe little to consent." Indeed, under such circumstances as slavery, Burke maintains, "the very means which lead to liberty must partake of compulsion."[130]

Here, Burke once again depicts "civilized" liberty as a future goal for the slaves, one that necessarily requires power and compulsion to be visited upon them by the British. Of course, we might regard such remarks as simply evincing Burke's well-known reverence for prescriptive institutions, as well as his oft-cited reluctance to destroy any long-standing social practices at one fell swoop. At one level, this is no doubt the case; however, this conventional reading misses the deeper and more disturbing level of Burke's argument.

If we unpack his formulation further, we clearly see something more at work—namely, a plea for reforming the slave trade *as a means of using it to civilize the Africans* both in Africa and in the New World, before emancipation. Only then, Burke believed, would it be safe—not only for the British but also for the Africans themselves—to abolish slavery and the trade at some unspecified future point, after a process that was admittedly "very slow."

"It was my wish," Burke writes of the "Sketch," "whilst the slavery continued, and the consequent commerce, to take such measures as to civilize the coast of Africa by the trade." To this end, his proposed "Sketch of a Negro Code" aimed at inculcating "principles upon which I proceeded in every regulation, which I have proposed towards the civilization and gradual manumission of negroes in the two hemispheres." In 1792, Burke expressed to Dundas and Pitt a view that he had described in the 1757 *Account of the European Settlements in America,* that he trusted "infinitely more" to the happy "effect and influence of religion, than to all the rest of the regulations put together."[131] To that end, a great deal of the code is concerned with Christianizing the Africans, who, Burke says, "are to be led by all due means into a respect for our holy Religion, and a desire of partaking of the benefits thereof."[132] However, Burke stated, until such time as religion and other forms of education could fulfill their civilizing function on the African slaves, he remained "fully convinced that the cause of humanity would be far more benefited by the continuance of the trade and servitude, regulated and reformed, than by the total destruction of both or either."[133]

David Brion Davis has argued that a greater determination to end the slave trade immediately in the 1790s could have won the day. In this light, Davis concludes that Burke's predilection for prescriptive institutions clearly had the effect of helping prolong the traffic in human beings.[134] Additionally, from the perspective set forth here, we can view Burke's last word on slavery as a logical extension of the position that the *Account* had articulated in the 1750s: When slaves could be taught by the British Empire to exhibit the appropriate level of internal self-control, self-discipline, docility, and chastened liberty—in a word, when they were appropriately "civilized"—then (and only then) were they prepared for freedom. Until then, slavery was only prudent.

In this vein, recent work has insightfully grouped Burke's "Sketch of a Negro Code" alongside a number of similar tracts written by British thinkers in the late eighteenth century who were concerned with questions of empire. Taken together, these arguments actually "described the ways that gradual emancipation might serve the broader end of enhancing state power," such that "emancipation could sustain, and even advance, colonial enterprise." However, for the slaves themselves, according to the various plans devised by these thinkers, "compliance with prescribed cultural norms would be the price of the ticket to self-possession."[135]

We can see the force of this argument by juxtaposing the last few of Burke's substantive proposals in his "Sketch of a Negro Code," which deal specifically with slavery in the West Indies, against one another. The first proposal details the preconditions under which slaves would be able to purchase their freedom from slaveholders:

> And in order to [achieve] a gradual manumission of Slaves, as they shall seem fitted to fill the Offices of Freeman, be it enacted that every Negro Slave being thirty years of age and upwards, and who has had three Children born to him in lawful Matrimony and who hath received a Certificate from the Minister of his District, or any other Christian Teacher of his regularity in the duties of Religion, and of his orderly and good behavior, may purchase at rates to be fixed by two Justices of peace the freedom of himself or his Wife, or Children, or of any of them separately, valuing the Wife and Children if purchased into liberty by the Father of the Family, at half only of their marketable value.[136]

There is, to be sure, the expression of a certain sort of "family values" ethos in this proposal, insofar as the father of the family could buy the liberty of his wife and children at half the going rate on the open slave market. However, even that opportunity came with steep behavioral preconditions: only a legally married male slave over thirty, who had fathered three children and whose religious convictions and observations as well as his "orderly and good behavior" were vouched for by a Christian teacher—via "Certificate" no less—was eligible to make any purchase of freedom, whether his own or others'. If one were to describe this in the idiom of contemporary political theory, we might say that Burke was only interested in the slaves' liberty once they had internalized the disciplinary gaze and could act with the necessary degree of chastened subjectivity. If one prefers Burke's own eighteenth-century idiom, we might simply say that on his view slaves were eligible for freedom only if and when they were no longer "eye-servants."

Conversely, Burke argues that Africans' failure to exhibit such chastened subjectivity upon their manumission was cause for an extraordinary punishment—reenslavement. This was to be the case should former slaves fail to meet the disciplinary norms prescribed by the (unintentionally ironic-sounding) "Protector of Negroes," the official magistrate Burke's proposal would create. Along these lines, sections 38 and 39 of the last portion of the code, pertaining to the West Indies, read,

38. And be it enacted that the Protector of Negroes shall be and is authorized and required to act as a Magistrate for the coercion of all idle, dissolute, or disorderly free Negroes, and he shall by office prosecute them for the offences of idleness, drunkenness, quarreling, gaming or vagrancy, in the supreme Court, or cause them to be prosecuted before one Justice of peace, as the Case may require.

39. *And be it enacted that if any free Negro hath been twice convicted for any of the said Misdemeanors and is judged by the said Protector of Negroes, calling to his assistance, two Justices of the peace, that the said twice convicted free Negro is incorrigibly idle, dissolute, and vicious, it shall be lawful by the order of the said Protector and two Justices of peace, to sell the said free Negro into Slavery—* the purchase money to be paid to the person so remanded into servitude, or kept in trust by the Protector and Governor, for the benefit of his Family.[137]

In the end, Burke's great claim to abolitionist fame, the "Sketch of a Negro Code," thus concludes by authorizing reenslavement for free blacks who were twice convicted of being lazy, drunk, quarrelsome, given to games of chance, or finding themselves homeless and jobless. Said assessments were, of course, to be made by privileged whites themselves—the "Protector of Negroes" and two judges. The upshot of such a proposal is to rival the notorious "Black Codes" used to deny freedom to African Americans in the South after the Civil War, legislation that became central to the Jim Crow era. Indeed, while Burke's proposals include "vagrancy," which was key to the Black Codes, they go well beyond the vast majority of the latter in spelling out a broader range of behaviors that would make former slaves forfeit their liberty. Moreover—and despite all of its immense shortcomings from the standpoint of African Americans—at least the Civil War outlawed chattel slavery, which could not be legally reinstituted as a form of punishment for violating the Black Codes. However, legal reenslavement for a wide range of behaviors that showed blacks to be "incorrigibly idle, dissolute, and vicious" was at the very heart of Burke's proposal for gradual emancipation, as written in 1780 and distributed in 1792 during the height of the French Revolution and in the face of claims for the immediate abolition of slavery and the slave trade.

BURKE ON THE "OTHER" REVOLUTION IN THE WEST INDIES

As matters unfolded, Burke's proposal for gradually emancipating and "civilizing" the African slaves in the West Indies would be overtaken by events.

One of the most important of these was the slave rebellions in the Caribbean inspired by the French Revolution's principles of liberty and equality, as enshrined in the Declaration of the Rights of Man. Such ideals as universal rights animated freedom-hungry Africans, leading them to act against the wishes of, in fact, the majority of the revolutionaries in Paris. The most famous of these uprisings was of course the slave revolt in the French colony of Saint-Domingue that began in 1791 and was eventually led by Toussaint Louverture, which culminated in a full-scale revolution and the creation of an independent Haiti free from colonial rule in 1804.

Scholars rarely make reference to Burke's discussion of these events in their depiction of his position on empire.[138] This is unfortunate, because Burke's pronouncements on Britain's struggles to maintain its empire in the Caribbean occur simultaneously with his critique of the French Revolution and the globalization of its theoretical principles. As such, they afford interpreters an outstanding opportunity to consider, with respect to the New World, what Burke thought about the direct relationship between empire and revolution, just as he would later contemplate the nexus of these phenomena in the cases of India and Ireland.

And it is not as if Burke was silent on this score. In 1791, just as the unrest in Saint-Domingue began, he had occasion to consider the West Indies in the course of a debate about what form a new constitution for Quebec should take. According to the *Parliamentary History,* Burke asked what would happen if a French constitution based on the rights of man should be put in place in Canada. He remarked,

> Let this constitution be examined by its practical effects in the French West India colonies. These, notwithstanding three disastrous wars, were most happy and flourishing till they heard of the rights of man. As soon as this system arrived among them, Pandora's box, replete with every mortal evil, seemed to fly open, hell itself to yawn, and every demon of mischief to overspread the face of the earth. Blacks rose against whites, whites against blacks, and each against one another in murderous hostility; subordination was destroyed, the bonds of society torn asunder, and every man seemed to thirst for the blood of his neighbor. . . . All was toil and trouble, discord and blood, from the moment that this doctrine was promulgated among them; and he verily believed that wherever the rights of man were preached, such ever had been and ever would be the consequences.[139]

Even by the standards of Burke's apocalyptic rhetoric, this is an astounding passage, so it is important to get clear on the claims its speaker adduces. The first is that a sugar plantation society governed by an aristocratic minority and defined by the sheer brutality of chattel slavery was—without qualification—"happy and flourishing" before hearing of a doctrine that preached universal human liberty and equal rights. Indeed, for Burke it was precisely the operation of this latter doctrine—and not the viciousness of slavery itself—that led to the slaves' discontent in the first place. That is, "blacks rose against whites" only because of the manifestly ludicrous doctrine of freedom and equality, not because they were human cogs in a system that broke them body and soul. To the contrary, in Burke's rendering of matters the real tragedy was that the slaves' "subordination was destroyed" and the supposedly harmonious "bonds of society torn asunder."

Based on this delineation of the dynamics at work in the West Indies, Burke regarded the French constitution "not with approbation but with horror, as involving every principle to be detested, and pregnant with every consequence to be dreaded and abominated." He asked incredulously of his colleagues in Parliament, as it pertained to Quebec: "Ought this example induce us to send to our colonies a cargo of the rights of man? As soon would he send them a bale of infected cotton from Marseilles."[140] During the French Revolution, one of Burke's favorite metaphors for the spread of the principles of liberty and equality espoused by the revolutionaries was to compare the rights of man to an infectious disease that would obliterate all of the social hierarchies definitional of civilized society in Europe—between nobles and commoners, men and women, rich and poor, parents and children.[141] Here, he uses the same metaphor in a colonial context to suggest that the export of the infectious doctrine across the ocean would have equally baleful effects.

For this reason, Burke later supported a total war by the British against the forces of the French Revolution in the West Indies, just as he did in Europe. In the colonial context, this meant potentially battling the combined enemies of the French army and the freed slaves and other blacks under the leadership of Toussaint Louverture. This alliance was feared after the French, following Georges-Jacques Danton's impassioned arguments, dramatically declared the abolition of slavery in all of their colonies, in 1794.

In response, in his *Letters on a Regicide Peace* (1795–1797), Burke argued at length against a premature peace treaty with the French, in part by holding out the specter of its egalitarian principles making Africans, whom he regarded as savages, the legitimate political emissaries to the British colonies in the West Indies, right alongside other "Regicide" representatives in London. Such a peace with France, Burke wrote,

> immediately gives a right for the residence of a Consul (in all likelihood some Negro or Man of Color) in every one of your Islands; a Regicide Ambassador in London will be at all your meetings of West India Merchants and Planters, and, in effect, in all our Colonial Councils. Not one Order of Council can hereafter be made, or any one Act of Parliament relative to the West India Colonies even be agitated, which will not always afford reasons for protests and perpetual interference; the Regicide Republic will become an integral part of the Colonial Legislature; and, so far as the Colonies are concerned, of the British too.[142]

In the face of this possibility, Burke expressed dismay that in Saint-Domingue the British had failed to take the side of the French plantation aristocracy sooner and, thus, lost the opportunity to make common cause with them against the egalitarian armies of the Revolution and their former slaves. Instead, the British were "spilling the blood of those [French] planters whom we had refused to protect, until they had become our subjects, as well as the best blood of our own, and of the royalists of Europe, to make this a more savory morsel for the regicides."[143]

Such passages show that one of Burke's greatest fears was the unruly democratic consciousness of the uncivilized, acutely emblematized by the image of former French slaves as diplomats in the British slave colonies of the West Indies. Against this "horror," which he saw as brought about directly by the spread of the infectious doctrine of the rights of man, Burke could only lament the fact that the civilized British, led by their landed aristocracy, had not made common cause with the French colonial planter aristocracy earlier to fend off the assault of the egalitarian savage forces that confronted them.[144] Regarding the West Indies, Burke thus sought Ornamentalist solidarity with the British Empire's privileged "civilized" subjects—the West Indian planter aristocracy—as a means of preserving empire and fending off the demotic masses of Others, whom he cast in Orientalist terms as "savage" African slaves revolting from below based on the principles of the rights of man.[145]

Alas, for Burke, Haiti would prove a lost cause, no less than the American colonies had earlier. Instead, with the advances of the French Revolution and the general imperial "swing to the east" after the American Revolution, Burke would come to spend an enormous amount of intellectual energy on the new great site of the British Empire, India. With respect to India, however, Burke's conservative logic of empire was wholly Ornamentalist. In looking east, Burke saw no Orientalist Others, but rather a civilization that was the mirror image of Europe's own, and he sought to defend it on that basis. That is to say, what Burke sought to justify in India was a vision of empire that would protect India's ancien régime as he understood it, a world under dire assault by Warren Hastings.

CHAPTER 3

India

AS WE SAW IN CHAPTER 1, Edmund Burke was a lifelong proponent and defender of the British Empire in India. For Burke, empire on the subcontinent was an extraordinary providential gift and a source of national glory and global envy as well as immense commercial wealth. Furthermore, given his belief in the necessarily bloody and corrupt nature of all founding periods, Burke willingly drew a "secret veil" over the Bengal Revolution led by Robert Clive and its immediate aftermath, which established Britain's territorial empire in India. The effect of this move was the occlusion if not erasure of British malfeasance in the crucial years that concluded with the extraction of the Bengal *diwani* from the Great Mughal. Burke thereby also effectively exculpated the East India Company in general and Clive and his immediate successors in particular for the horrors of the subsequent Bengal famine, a massive human catastrophe that British imperial policies had done so much to bring about. In fact, Burke continued to praise Clive and the empire of conquest he had established in India until the end of Burke's life, notwithstanding the fact that historians now regard the period of Clive's influence as the high-water mark of the Company's corrupt and despotic practices in the eighteenth century.

We also saw that Burke did not actually become an advocate of increased parliamentary oversight of the East India Company until after his service on a House of Commons Select Committee in 1781–1782. Before this period, Burke argued that claims of Company malfeasance were being exaggerated, that the Company was more than capable of policing itself, and that any increased parliamentary control would constitute an unacceptable infringement on its property and other chartered rights, as well as an unjust attempt at extending ministerial power.

However, Burke dramatically altered his views on this issue after serving on the Select Committee in the early 1780s and steeping himself in the study of Indian affairs, so that he became perhaps the most zealous advocate of maximal control of the Company in the name of parliamentary sovereignty and the national interest. In the process, Burke also became undoubtedly one of the most strident critics of East India Company behavior in the late eighteenth century. Of course, it is crucial to note that, given his adherence to the remarkable—and remarkably fast-acting—doctrine of "prescription," with its ability to transform violence, corruption, and despotism into political legitimacy and a just social order, Burke never extended his later critique of the Company back to the period from 1757 to 1772. Consequently, this time frame constituted the "state of exception" in Burke's thought, a period in which he believed that admittedly brutal behavior was best left unexamined. Burke's uncritical acceptance of the first fifteen years of Britain's territorial empire in India was therefore predicated on a willful act of imperial amnesia, one that he justified in the name of prudence, decorum, and consequentialism. Burke's unrelenting criticism of Company behavior in India—which commenced only after 1782—would instead be focused principally on one individual, the first governor general of Bengal, Warren Hastings, and centered exclusively on the period after Hastings took power, in 1772. Burke's criticism, therefore, neither extended back to the most brutal period of British rule in India during the eighteenth century, nor remotely advocated British withdrawal from empire an India, which he continued to regard as a great gift from God until the end of his life.

Against this backdrop, the important questions that concern us in this chapter focus on the *nature* of Burke's criticisms of British imperial practice from 1772 to the conclusion of Hastings's impeachment trial in 1794. What was the basis of Burke's critique of Hastings and the Company over this period? In addition, how do his severe criticisms of imperial practice on the subcontinent comport with Burke's overarching conservative logic of empire as a whole, including in India? To answer these questions, we must first unpack Burke's Ornamentalist understanding of Indian civilization as directly analogous to European civilization. It would be Burke's understanding of India as another Europe that would structure his critique of Hastings and the Company, a critique that was in no way, shape, or form anti-imperial but was instead the contrary.

ORNAMENTALISM IN THE EAST; OR, BURKE ON INDIA AS ANOTHER EUROPE

Burke's critique of empire in India cannot be disassociated from his understanding of the *kind* of harm he accused Hastings of having inflicted there, such that the former governor general should be impeached. And in order to understand this, we must come to grips with Burke's representation of Indian society.[1] To foreground my argument, it is that Burke did indeed seek to forge what Uday Mehta has called a "cosmopolitanism of sentiments" between the British and Indians (or at least between certain sorts of British people and certain sorts of Indians) predicated on sympathetic fellow feeling. However, the method whereby he sought to enlist the affective attachment of his British audience for India was the polar opposite of what Mehta describes. That is, Burke's argument was in no way predicated on respect for cultural pluralism and the opacity of difference, because Burke did not present India as a stranger with whom the British were engaged in a mutually illuminating conversation. To the contrary, Burke sought to accommodate India to British sympathies and affections precisely by analogizing Indian civilization with European civilization in a deeply Ornamentalist fashion.

Specifically, Burke assimilated India to Britain and France and defended the anciens régimes in both these locales as synonymous exemplars of civilization as he understood it. Consequently, when Burke defended India and criticized imperial practice in general and the East India Company and Warren Hastings in particular (which he surely did at great length), he was actually taking up the cudgels on behalf of what he saw as "another Europe."[2]

This can be observed most clearly in four areas: First, at a general level, we see it in Burke's institutional, cultural, and even material and geographical mapping of Indian civilization onto European civilization through a series of analogies that stresses the central importance of India's religions and its landed nobility or aristocracy, the hallmarks of Burkean civilization. Second, Burke emphasizes the functional importance of the Hindu religion in India and compares its theoretical and practical effects favorably with Christianity. Third, we see Burke's remarkable contraction of the conceptual distance between Europe and the subcontinent in his rendering of Muslim India, and specifically in his rejection of the Orientalist tradition of "Oriental despotism" as a means of describing Islam in favor of an Ornamentalist insistence on the importance of the Mughal version of Britain's "ancient constitution." Finally, as a central trope in his political theory, Burke used the moral psychology of "sympathy"—a theoretical strategy predicated on similarity rather than difference—to link Indian and European civilizations in an attempt to convince his parliamentary audience of Hastings's turpitude and need for punishment.

Mapping Indian Civilization onto European Civilization

As we know, for Burke all civilization was marked by the twin institutional pillars of organized religion and a landed nobility, whereas on his view "savage" societies like those in North America and among the African slaves were utterly lacking in these features. The crucial point for understanding Burke's approach to empire in India—and indeed why it was so different from the one he took with respect to the Amerindians and Africans—-is that he perceived India as the quintessence of a civilization defined exactly according to his understanding of the term.

Burke never visited either the New World or India, hence in both instances his Orientalist and Ornamentalist depictions of these places were wholly conceptual and secondhand. He therefore relied on his overarching theoretical understanding of history as a civilizing process, and the conservative logic of empire derived from it, and fit his armchair observations of these locales into his preexisting historiographical narrative.

One of the clearest examples of Burke's doing this to analogize European and Indian civilization arises in his well-known *Speech on Fox's India Bill* (1783), regarding a piece of legislation masterminded by Burke and introduced by his (then) close friend and Whig ally Charles James Fox. By 1783, after his service on the Select Committee, Burke had been fully won over to the idea that parliamentary sovereignty had to be invoked in the strongest possible terms, and the Company brought to heel, in the name of Britain's national and imperial interest. To this end, the purpose of the ill-fated bill, which ultimately brought down the Fox-North coalition owing to the king's opposition, was to set up two commissions under parliamentary control to tightly oversee the East India Company's administration and all of its commercial dealings in India.

In order to make the case that such oversight was necessary to rein in the Company, Burke's speech drew a mental map of India, a map sketched in the unmistakable colors that he used to identify European civilization—and all civilization—in contrast to the lesser, alien worlds of savagery and barbarism in the New World. With regard to India, Burke argued,

This multitude of men does not consist of an abject and barbarous populace; much less of gangs of savages, like the Guaranies and Chiquitos, who wander on the waste borders of the river of Amazons, or the Plate; but a people for ages civilized and cultivated; cultivated by all the arts of polished life, whilst we were yet in the woods. There, have been (and still the skeletons remain) princes once of great dignity, authority, and opulence. There, are to be found the chiefs of tribes and nations. There is to be found an ancient and venerable priesthood, the depository of their laws, learning, and history, the guides of the people whilst living, and their consolation in death; a nobility of great antiquity and renown; a multitude of cities, not exceeded in population and trade by those of the first class in Europe; merchants and bankers, individual houses of whom have once vied in capital with the Bank of England ... millions of ingenious manufacturers and mechanics; millions of the most diligent, and not the least intelligent, tillers of the earth. Here are to be found almost all the religions professed by men, the Braminical, the Mussulmen, the Eastern and the Western Christians.[3]

India, like Europe, possessed the essential components defining Burkean civilization: a landed aristocracy and hierarchy of ranks, including princes and nobles and ranging downward to merchants, mechanics, and farmers; an ancient religion (actually several) described as having a powerful and highly influential institutional infrastructure; and great cities and a flourishing economy, which were the result of this steeply demarcated social tapestry.[4] At the same time, in this passage Burke explicitly and unmistakably juxtaposes India's possession of these facets of civilization with the "savage" Amerindians in South America, in terms that are identical to his depiction of the Amerindians as far back as his *Account of the European Settlements in America*.[5]

Burke then goes on in the speech to directly compare British imperial possessions in India with those of the Holy Roman Empire, "as the nearest parallel I can find." He analogizes the British holdings to those of Austria similarly: "The Nabob of Oude might stand for the King of Prussia; the Nabob of Arcot I would compare, as superior in territory, and equal in revenue, to the Elector of Saxony. Cheyt Sing, the Rajah of Benares, might well rank with the Prince of Hesse at least; and the Rajah of Tanjore ... to the Elector of Bavaria." As in Europe, so in India: there was a well-established nobility and hierarchy of ranks, with recognized kings and princes that even had clear European counterparts. So, too, in India there was a deeply entrenched landed aristocracy, just as in Europe: "The Polygars and the northern Zemindars, and other great chiefs, might well class with the rest of the Princes, Dukes, Counts, Marquisses, and Bishops in the empire."[6]

Later, in his *Speech on the Nabob of Arcot's Debts* (1785), Burke actually did bring in a very large map of the East India Company's landholdings in the Carnatic, in southeastern India, to help make his argument about the similarity between Britain, in particular, and India. Its scale (two inches to five miles) was such that one could see not only villages and roads but also extensive irrigation work and reservoirs. It has been argued that the very style of this map (and the others Burke used for information about India) effaced the distance between England and the subcontinent, insofar as it stressed human-made boundaries over natural phenomena, thereby emphasizing the extent to which India, like England, had been transformed by human effort and, thus, civilized.[7]

In the early 1780s, Hyder Ali, the ruler of Mysore, had waged a war in the Carnatic, a land that Burke described as "not much inferior in extent to England." Burke depicted this war as one of utter devastation of the landscape that made recovery extremely difficult. When it came to the future of this region, Burke thought, it would be wholly unjust if the local nawab of the Carnatic (or nabob of Arcot) were to have his fraudulent "debts," which were really corrupt bargains struck with speculative British investors to fund his wars of aggression against the nearby rajah of Tanjore, accepted as legitimate and paid from the public coffers. To make his case, Burke asserted that such a faulty policy would be akin to subsequently saddling a war-ravaged England with draconian taxation. He asked his parliamentary audience to

> figure to yourself the form and fashion of your sweet and cheerful country from Thames to Trent, north and south, and from the Irish to the German sea east and west, emptied and emboweled ... by so accomplished a desolation. Extend your imagination a little further, and then suppose your ministers taking a survey of this scene of waste and desolation.... What would be your thoughts if you should be informed, that they were computing how much had been the amount of the excises, how much the customs, how much the land and malt tax, in order that they should charge (take it in the most favorable light) for public service, upon the relics of the satiated vengeance of relentless enemies, the whole of what England had yielded in the most exuberant seasons of peace and abundance?[8]

Geographically as well as conceptually, then, Burke mapped India onto Europe in general and sometimes even England in particular. In so doing, he was indeed asking his auditors to engage in an act of theoretical imagination, but not one that compelled them to confront the experience of difference, as Mehta would have it. Rather, his goal was just the reverse: to cut down the conceptual distance between the two locales and to show that, despite their seeming differences, Europe and India were essentially the same in all the ways that mattered. Both places were "civilized" according to Burke's deeply conservative definition of the term: deeply stratified and hierarchical social orders, governed by aristocratic and religious establishments that enabled extensive material and cultural cultivation, and marked by the development of a complex institutional infrastructure. The Company's misdeeds at Hastings's hands were thus inflicted on an Old Regime civilization analogous to Europe's own.[9] By extension this meant that, for Burke, the destruction of Indian civilization would effectively prove similar to the destruction of European civilization with the coming of the French Revolution.

The Role of Hinduism and the Caste System

Religion, of course, was one of the two forces Burke saw as driving the civilizing process in Europe. If possible, he viewed religion, especially Hinduism, as even more important in guiding and safeguarding India's civilizing process. From the time of his first theoretical encounter with it in the 1770s while defending the Hindu rajah of Tanjore against the Muslim nawab of the Carnatic, Burke become possessed by what his longtime political ally and friend Charles James Fox was later to call an "awe bordering on devotion" for Hinduism.[10] Burke's veneration of Hinduism is perfectly consistent with his broader political theory about the requirements for true "civilization" (as opposed to "savagery").

For Burke, Hinduism had "two great principles which ought to be respected, that is to say, great force and stability, and great, glorious and excellent effects." Hindu "Laws and Institutions" had

> been proved by their holding on for a time and duration commensurate to all the Empires which History has made us acquainted with. And still they exist in a green old age, with all the reverence of antiquity and with all the affection to their own institutions that other people have to novelty and change.... That form of Religious Institution connected with Government and Policy that makes a people happy and a Government flourishing[,] ... these are undoubtedly the test of any government; and I must appeal to the whole force of the observation that, whatsoever wherever the Hindoo Religion has been established, that Country has been flourishing.[11]

Burke insisted that the Hindu religion could not be severed from the primordial form of rule in India, and that together these institutions elegantly demonstrated what "the paternal, lenient, protecting arm of a native government does for people."[12] On Burke's account, Indians exhibited a healthy prejudice in favor of the prescriptive inheritance of antiquity, and the deeply hierarchical religious, political, and social institutions bequeathed to them, as much as their very soil.

Along these lines, the key to Burke's reading of Hinduism was his insistence on the central importance and beneficence of the caste system, which he believed guaranteed the peaceful transmission and continuity of India's stratified social order. As he explained it to the House of Lords in his opening speech on Hastings's impeachment,

> In that Country the laws of religion, the laws of the land and the laws of honor, are all united and consolidated in one, and bind a man eternally to the rules of what is called his *caste*.... These people from the oldest times have been distributed into the various orders, all hereditary, which are called castes. These castes are the fundamental part of the constitution of that Commonwealth, both in their Church and in their State. Your Lordships are born to hereditary honors in the chief of your Houses; the rest mix with the people. But in the case of the Hindoos those who were born noble can never fall into any second rank.... These people [are] bound by all laws, human and divine, to those principles of caste and which inveterate usage has grafted in them.... Speak to an Indian of his caste, and you speak to him of his all; when they lose that caste they lose everything.[13]

In this way Burke analogized the caste system to European aristocracy in deeply Ornamentalist fashion, stressing their essential similarity. However, Burke also maintained that the Hindu caste system had deeper, more widespread, and (arguably) even better results than its European counterpart. He concluded that where the Hindu social order and caste system had survived intact, they ensured the material and cultural flourishing of India's various ranks. By fusing religion, politics, and society, Hinduism gave individual acts social meaning and imbued the social order itself with metaphysical purpose and holy sanction. In this sense, for Burke the Indian caste system, with its enduring commitment to social stratification and hierarchy, was perhaps the ultimate conservative device. As P. J. Marshall notes, for Burke, "Hindus were the most conservative people in the world."[14]

Thus, the carefully and laboriously built reservoirs and irrigation systems in the beautiful land of Tanjore, referenced earlier, were, for Burke, far more than simple material objects. Rather, they were testaments to a society imbued with the civilizing force of an ancient religion that provided intergenerational meaning to its hierarchically structured, habitually disciplined, component parts:

> These are the monuments of real kings, who were the fathers of their people; testators to a posterity which they embraced as their own. These are the grand sepulchers built by ambition; but by the ambition of an insatiable benevolence, which, not contented with reigning in the dispensation of happiness during the contracted term of human life, had strained, with all the reachings and graspings of a vivacious mind, to extend the dominion of their bounty beyond the limits of nature, and to perpetuating themselves through generations of generations, the guardians, the protectors, the nourishers of mankind.[15]

This passage sounds strikingly similar to numerous ones from the *Reflections on the Revolution in France,* but it is not a depiction of the European Old Regime. It is a glimpse of Burke's India: a deeply hierarchical society held together in large measure by the Hindu caste system, which specified duties and obligations in ways that enabled civilization to flourish and to maintain intergenerational stability over very long stretches of time. Accordingly, Burke viewed the Hindu world as Indian civilization par excellence and directly analogized it to ancien régime European civilization.

Burke's approach, nevertheless, left him with the problem of how to encompass Islam and the long history of Muslim incursion, settlement, and rule within his understanding of India. This was an especially thorny issue because Islamic rule was stereotyped in the eighteenth century as the paradigmatic instance of Orientalism, or radical difference from Europe: "Oriental despotism." Such a view posed a significant problem for Burke in his attempt to analogize and thereby assimilate India to Europe. However, it was a theoretical conundrum he confronted head on, and he surmounted it in a profoundly Ornamentalist fashion that stressed the similarities between European and Muslim societies. In doing so, Burke completed his project of theoretically assimilating Indian civilization into his conceptual framework of European civilization.

Muslim India: The Ancient Mughal Constitution and Burke's Ornamentalist Rejection of Oriental Despotism

In his *Speech on Fox's India Bill,* Burke asked the House of Commons to consider for a moment the extraordinary circumstances surrounding the British accession to territorial empire in India: "Could it be believed, when I entered into existence[,] ... we should be employed in discussing the conduct of those British subjects who had disposed of the power and person of the Grand Mogul?"[16] In this fashion, Burke situated Warren Hastings and the East India Company as successors to the Mughal emperor, Shah Alam II, in the wake of the Bengal Revolution instituted by Robert Clive.

Since the eighteenth century, many observers—like Burke himself—have regarded the fall of the Mughal Empire as a crucial moment enabling British success in India. Until recently, however, the Mughals' decline was conventionally seen as a complete collapse, after they had been severely weakened by the Maratha Empire of the Hindus. This was said to have created a power vacuum that enabled the British to seize effective control of the subcontinent with combined European and native sepoy forces under Company command and to run together a string of victories that put paid to the Mughals in all but name. By 1765, when the Bengal Revolution was complete, Britain ruled Bengal in the north but also had taken the nearby territory of Oudh (Awadh) under its protection. In the southeast, its tight control over the so-called nabob of Arcot gave it effective control over the Carnatic. To this extent the British had achieved a large territorial empire.[17]

However, this description masks the drastic differences distinguishing the British Empire in the East from that in the West. Unlike in North America, India was not a settler colony; and Company servants, unlike colonists, had no intention of planting themselves in country. Nevertheless, it is still often easy to overlook the extremely skeletal nature of the Company's forces relative to the area and population it had to control. For example, between 1707 and 1775, only 645 white male civilians worked for the East India Company in Bengal.[18] The small number of Company agents was one reason it had to employ an army composed in large part of native troops in order to control such far-flung places as Bengal, Madras, and Bombay. In turn, this required a serious commitment to raising revenue to fund such armies.[19] Working within the inherited institutional structure of the Mughals enabled the Company's (and by extension, Britain's) extractive imperial enterprise in India while also giving it a measure of political legitimacy.

In this regard, recent historians of British imperialism in India have stressed the continued power and relevance of the Mughal successor states with whom the British had to contend and cooperate. These scholars now see the British inheritance of the Mughal Empire's institutional and infrastructural framework as a crucial component in Britain's successful rise to effective control of a land containing more than one-fifth of the world's population by the end of the eighteenth century, an endeavor that may well have proved impossible otherwise.[20] These arguments are vital for understanding the backdrop of Burke's interpretation of the Islamic world in India and, ultimately, his approach to imperial policy concerning it.

It has been argued that the long transformation of Mughal provincial governments that culminated in the rise of autonomous kingdoms, including those in Bengal, Oudh (Awadh), and Hyderabad (in Nizam), was the most striking political change in India during the eighteenth century.[21] The rise of these powerful successor states meant that the East India Company had to accommodate itself and work within the preexisting framework of Mughal legitimacy and power.[22] The Mughals had demonstrated a striking ability to tax the lands under their control and so extract enormous wealth in a relatively peaceful fashion.[23] Given the paucity of its servants in India, the Company required just such an extractive infrastructure to raise and fund its mixed European and sepoy armies.

While there was a good deal of resistance to the Company and its armies in Madras and Bombay, which did much to prevent British imperial expansion after 1765, the granting of the *diwani* nevertheless enabled a more secure territorial empire to arise quickly in Bengal. This was done largely with the aid of the inherited Mughal networks and institutions of wealth extraction. The British relied on the expertise of Indian administrators who had earlier worked for the Mughals. From this standpoint, the empire did not rise from the ashes of Indian weakness but was instead built on the highly developed economic and administrative system of one particular region, Bengal. Furthermore, it arose in part through the cooptation of important sectors of Indian society, including bankers and other merchants, investors, and scholars. In short, important segments of Indian society cooperated with the British, especially in Bengal. The story of the empire's spread there was thus less one of simple despotic imposition than it was of despotism combined with collusion, or what scholars have taken to calling "negotiated empire."[24]

Rather than radical difference, it was in fact the commercial complexity of Indian society, or the real and increasing similarities between India and Europe, that the British sought to exploit. However, in order to achieve this end the British also had to provide services that important strata of Indian society found useful for their own purposes.[25] All of which is to say that, in order for Britain to achieve its aims of commercial gain, military supremacy, and unquestioned authority, local allies had to be found. And they were. Such native collusion was in fact the concomitant of the rule of Clive and his immediate successors, and native Indian partners thereby facilitated the spread of British imperialism.

In this context, as Robert Travers has shown, Burke's vision of Muslim India was profoundly shaped by the continuance of Mughal power on the subcontinent. Influenced by his (then) friend Philip Francis, who had served as a member of the Supreme Council overseeing affairs in Bengal after the passage of the Regulating Act in 1773, Burke in effect overlaid the British theory of the ancient constitution on Mughal India. Burke and Francis developed a Whiggish view of the ancient Mughal Empire as a limited monarchy governed by the rule of law that also applied to private property, such that it preserved the ancient rights of the large Hindu landowners (or zamindars) in Bengal. While the zamindars could be either Hindu or Muslim, Burke focused on the former as a kind of landed aristocracy with historically preexisting property rights that had been protected under the aegis of wise Mughal governors, whose power they also helped to limit.[26]

In developing this position, Burke argued that when the Company acquired the *diwani* from Shah Alam II in 1765, they therefore necessarily stepped into the framework of rule laid down under the Mughal Empire and its ancient constitution. As he told Parliament at the opening of Hastings's impeachment trial: "For when the Company acquired that office in India, an English Corporation became an integral part of the Mogul Empire. When Great Britain assented to that grant virtually, and afterwards took advantage of it, Great Britain made a virtual act of union with that country, by which they bound themselves as securities for their subjects, to preserve the people in all rights, laws and liberties, which their natural original Sovereign was bound to enforce, if he had been in a condition to enforce it."[27]

Burke thus analogized Britain's ancient constitution—with its protections of historically derived rights (including property rights), the rule of law, and a set of individual liberties—to Mughal India. He depicted the British as the inheritors of a Muslim constitutional framework in India much like their own, which they were duty bound to protect. Indeed, Parliament had to act as a trustee that virtually represented its Indian subjects, who had previously been governed by their own ancient constitution. In this fashion, Burke countered Warren Hastings's claims to be acting justly albeit despotically in India by recourse to the eighteenth century (Orientalist) notion of Oriental despotism.[28] In taking this approach, Burke was also further elaborating his rival vision of an Ornamentalist similarity between Indian and British civilization, and doing so in striking terms.

In eighteenth-century Western political thought, the view that (unlike in Europe) all "Oriental" governments were marked by arbitrary and absolute rule, excessive opulence, sensuality, and lack of development—and that Muslim governments were particularly egregious instances of this general trend—was pervasive.[29] Burke's writings and speeches on India flatly denied this view, which was influentially articulated by Montesquieu. This was an important argumentative move because, in his defense, Hastings had excused his excessively authoritarian measures by asserting in part that he was simply hewing to local custom and tradition, governing India in the way that people in that part of world had always governed. As Hastings infamously put it in his opening speech: "The whole history of Asia is nothing more than precedents to prove the invariable exercise of arbitrary power."[30] In his long, nine-day "Speech in Reply" at the end of Hastings's impeachment trial in 1794, Burke reiterated at length one of the prosecution's main lines of argument— namely, that a close examination of the historical record demonstrated no such tradition of Oriental despotism in India, particularly in Mughal India. Burke declared the contrary: "In short, that every word that Montesquieu has taken from idle and inconsiderate Travellers is absolutely false."[31]

Together with many of his contemporaries, Burke did view Islam as an alien incursion into India. Nevertheless, in keeping with his views of the Mughals' ancient constitution, he argued that the hallmark of this "Oriental" people was in fact their commitment to the rule of law as embodied in the Qur'an, in contrast to arbitrary power. In his response to Hastings's self-defense in his opening speech on the impeachment in 1788, Burke asserted,

> I am to speak of Oriental Governments, and I do insist upon it that Oriental Governments know nothing of this arbitrary power.... I do challenge the whole race of man to show me any of the Oriental Governors claiming to themselves a right to act by arbitrary will. My Lords, the greatest part of Asia is under Mahometan Governments. To name a Mahometan Government is to name a Government by law.... The law is given by God, and it has the double sanction of law and of religion.... And, if any man will produce the Khoran to me, and will but show me one text in it that authorizes in any degree an arbitrary power in the Government, I will declare that I have read that book and been conversant in the affairs of Asia to a degree in vain.[32]

This remarkable statement shows that when it came to Islam, the exemplar of Orientalism for many European defenders of empire from the late eighteenth-century onward, Burke's position was the reverse. He described Muslim governments in India instead in deeply Ornamentalist terms as profoundly similar to European societies in general and Britain in particular. Burke's was in fact a view of Ornamentalism rather than Orientalism in the East, just as he held an Orientalist view of Native Americans and African slaves in the West.

In fact, despite his great passion for Hindu society, Burke notably extended this depiction of Muslim societies as defined by the rule of law to the "Garden of Eden" known as Rohilkhand, a land governed by former Afghan Muslim mercenaries who had migrated to northern India in the 1720s.[33] Burke referred to this Muslim region as a "Nation" akin to a "Paradise," with "its populous and splendid towns, its beautiful villas, and its rich vineyards." He went so far as to call Rohilkhand "the most orderly and well regulated Government that had hitherto been seen in India."[34] Hastings, however, had authorized the Company's troops to combine with those of the *wazir* of Oudh, Shuja-ud-Daula, in a war to annex Rohilkhand to Oudh, which did in fact occur shortly after the British slaughtered a large number of Rohillas in battle. This became the basis for one of the early draft articles of impeachment against Hastings, the so-called Rohilla War Charge, which Burke presented and spoke on behalf of in 1786, but which was ultimately rejected by the House of Commons.[35]

The upshot of all this was to encompass the later Muslim as well as the original Hindu civilizations in India within the ambit of the rule of law,[36] and thus to make them both amenable to the same sorts of moral and legal rules that governed European civilization in general and the ancient British constitution in particular. To reject Oriental despotism was to deprive Hastings of a defense that Burke referred to as one of "Geographical morality."[37] In the "Speech in Reply," Burke claims that Hastings simply "made up this volume and code of arbitrary power [which] is not supported by the Laws of the Moguls, by the laws of the Gentoos, by the Laws of the Mahometans, that he is not supported by any Law, custom, or usage whatever, recognized as legal and valid."[38] Because Oriental despotism did not exist, Burke says of Hastings: "Let him fly where he will; from law to law. Law[,] thank God[,] meets him everywhere.... I would as willingly have him tried upon the law of the Koran, or the Institutes of Tamerlane, as upon the Common Law or the State Law of this Kingdom." Whether one lets Hastings have "Eastern or Western Law," Burke argues, the codes are sufficiently similar in Christian, Hindu, and Islamic civilization for him to be condemned.[39]

Burke argued further that Hastings could not find a defensible basis for his claims to absolutism based on some misbegotten understanding of the relation between parliamentary sovereignty and Company prerogative. "In delegating great power to the India Company," Burke argued, "this kingdom has not released its sovereignty" as spelled out in successive charters authorized by Crown and Parliament.[40] Hence, Hastings's power as a Company servant was strictly limited, governed by king in Parliament, and ultimately underwritten by Britain's ancient constitution. Similarly, since the Mughal Empire had an analogous ancient constitution in Bengal, Hastings could find no justification for absolutist rule through the ruse of nonexistent Oriental despotism.

What did such an approach entail for Burke's understanding of the appropriate mode of imperial governance in India? Obviously Burke had no intention of arguing for British repatriation of Indian lands to the Mughals following the Bengal Revolution.[41] Rather, because Burke believed that there was a credible and viable ancient constitution in Bengal resting on Hindu landed property and wise Mughal governance, his ultimate goal was at least to preserve—or even better, restore—something like the Indian ancien régime, with its "natural" system of hierarchy and subordination, such that the Indian aristocracy would be protected from Company predation. As Robert Travers has argued, Burke's "goal was to restore what he saw as the natural channels of authority and subordination within Indian society, protecting the Indian rajahs, sultans, and landholders from the company's interference, and governing them within a loose imperial federation analogous to the Mughal empire itself."[42]

In terms of imperial policy, then, Burke's conception of India as an equivalent civilization governed by an ancient constitution required the British to respect the independence and rights of the Indian rulers and landowners allied to them. On Burke's view, the purpose of the British Empire's agents and forces in India was to guarantee the protection of Indian society, while the function of Parliament was chiefly a judicial one, ensuring that such protection was dispensed fairly. It was, in short, a policy of nonintervention. In fact, Burke's main goal was to restore as much as possible of the old Indian world that had been in the process of eroding subsequent to British imperial intervention. And once that social hierarchy had been restored, Burke hoped, it would remain inviolate. This did not mean, for Burke, that the British Empire in India was not about massive wealth extraction, any less than for other defenders of the project. However, as P. J. Marshall has argued, Burke "believed that the British should imitate the Mughals, who, he thought, had ruled Bengal without disturbing the way of life of the Hindu population. So long as local authority was given to the *zamindars,* the natural rulers of the country, rather than to the agents of the Europeans such as Ganga Gobinda Sinha and Devi Singh, it should remain in Indian hands."[43] However, Warren Hastings proceeded in just the opposite fashion, thereby destroying the ancien régime in India as the Jacobins would later do in France.[44]

Similarity and Sympathy

Burke's contention was that India's Hindu and Muslim populations were defined by the markers of religion and landed aristocracy and governed by the rule of law under an ancient constitution rather than arbitrary power. This was an Ornamentalist theoretical move with extraordinary consequences. It enabled Burke to treat India as another Europe, an equivalent civilization defined by analogous features. In turn, creating this relation of equivalence on the basis of similarity rather than strangeness opened the theoretical door for Burke to seek the fellow feeling of shared sympathetic response from the British elites in his parliamentary audience for those in India, just as he had earlier done with respect to colonial America.

As in his Ornamentalist approach to the American colonies, such a rhetorical strategy is perfectly consistent with the broader presuppositions of Burke's moral theory. On the vision of moral psychology that Burke had articulated in his treatise on aesthetics *A Philosophical Enquiry into the Origin of our Ideas of the Sublime and Beautiful* (1757), "sympathy" was predicated on one's ability to imaginatively inhabit the affective and mental space of the other, to feel as the other feels and to judge his or her actions in response to those feelings, by considering what one would have done under similar circumstances. Like the argument of his friend Adam Smith in *The Theory of Moral Sentiments* (a book that Burke warmly reviewed), Burke's required the *erasure* of difference for fellow feeling to occur. Both Burke and Smith were clear that this could never be done completely—difference could never be eradicated entirely; however, both men were also equally clear that the extent to which fellow feeling and compassion could be evoked was directly linked to the diminishing of difference between actor and observer, and the substitution of similarity in its stead.[45]

During Hastings's impeachment trial, after having spent years equating European and Indian civilization to the greatest extent possible, Burke proceeded to seek the House of Lords' sympathy on the basis of shared feelings for a similar people, to convict Hastings for inflicting suffering on a civilization—and specifically an aristocracy—like their own. This was the clear argumentative strategy in Burke's last monumental statement on India in 1794.

Burke contended that it was necessary to disprove Montesquieu on every point relative to the theory of Oriental despotism, because if one viewed Mughal India with its civilization and ancient constitution as fundamentally different in essence from Britain, then sympathetic fellow feeling would be impossible. He told the aristocratic House of Lords that a belief in the ineradicable difference between Indian and British culture and institutions would mean to fall prey to the notion that the Indians were "confounded in a common servitude, that they have no descendible lands, no inheritance, nothing that makes man proud in himself, that gives him honor and distinction, those things will take from you that kind of sympathy which naturally attaches you to men feeling like yourselves, that have hereditary dignities to support, as you peers have, who have lands of inheritance to maintain, that you will no longer have that feeling that you ought to have for the sufferings of a people whom use has habituated to such suffering."[46] That is to say, in order for the House of Lords to be willing to convict Hastings, Burke believed that they first had to see a body of suffering aristocrats in India not unlike themselves, so that they would be moved to punish the perpetrator of such crimes as if he had committed similar outrages against them.

Only when the lords were armed with fellow feeling for their own kind, or viewed suffering in India as inflicted on a class of people that could just as easily have been them if circumstances had been different, would they be moved to action. Hence Burke's theoretical goal was to create sympathy by erasing difference between the British and Indian landed aristocracies: "I wish to reinstate them in your sympathy. I wish you to respect a people as respectable as yourselves, who know as well as you what is rank, what is Law, what is property, who know how to feel disgrace, who know what equity, what reason, what proportion in punishments, what security of property is, just as well as any of your Lordships, which they have secured by Laws of all their religions, by declarations of all their Sovereigns."[47]

But of course, this had always been Burke's narrative strategy. The express purpose of the imaginary map he had drawn in his *Speech on Fox's India Bill*, with its variegated tapestry of kings, nobles, and duchies, was likewise to use the European successor states to the Roman Empire in Germany as the closest analogy to the Mughal successor states in India. The aim was to consider them "not for an exact resemblance, but as a sort of middle term, by which

India might be approximated to our understandings, and if possible to our feelings; in order to awaken something of sympathy for the unfortunate natives, of which I am afraid we are not perfectly susceptible, whilst we look at this very remote object through a false and cloudy medium."[48]

Again, the complete erasure of difference was impossible, but Burke's Ornamentalist representations of India consistently obliterated as much of it as possible by first constructing Indian civilization in the mold of European civilization, then subsequently urging his listeners and readers to understand violations of Indian civilization in the same terms they would view violations of European civilization. Burke maintains that, conversely, without attempting to create such relationships of similarity, "it is very difficult for our sympathy to fix upon these objects."[49] That is to say, the "false and cloudy" medium is the one which assumes that India and Britain are different, whereas Burke attempts to clear matters up by showing that in all the ways that truly matter they are not. Burke's stress on the deep similarity between Europe and India as the basis for creating sympathy in Parliament for punishing Hastings has been recognized by perceptive scholars, particularly Regina Janes and Frederick Whelan.[50]

In this regard, it is deeply curious that recent commentators, such as Mehta, maintain that Burke wanted to forge a "cosmopolitanism of sentiments" between Britain and India at the same time that he supposedly wanted to recognize, and in fact valorize, the strangeness—indeed, the "utter opacity"—of difference. Burke certainly sought the former, but only by denying the latter. Moreover, the strategy of flattening and diminishing difference, given that it could not be entirely effaced, is entirely in keeping with Burkean (and Smithian) moral theory, wherein sympathy is granted specifically on the basis of felt similarity, not incomprehensible strangeness.[51] For Burke, radical difference undermines the creation of sympathy; it never facilitates it.

What all of this means is that Burke's mental construction of India was not, pace Mehta, predicated on the equality of difference but rather was based on the equality of sameness. Burke's defense of India was the celebration of the known and familiar, not the unknown and unfamiliar. In fact, on Burke's understanding of it—and much unlike the cases of the Amerindians and Africans in the New World—India was not an Other at all; rather, Europe and India were essentially identical. However, this led Burke, not to retreat from the British imperial project of conquest and wealth extraction in India, but rather to defend a version of it much closer to the Mughal model, where earlier hierarchical and religious institutions of the sort that constituted civilization on his schema would remain. Furthermore, the consequence of Burke's assimilating Indian to European civilization, and then seeking sympathy for India on that basis, led to remarkable similarities in his writings and speeches on the dissolution of the Old Regimes in India and France. Burke would criticize both imperial excess in India and later revolutionary excess in France as similar assaults on their respective ancien régime civilizations.

BURKE'S CRITIQUE OF THE BRITISH EMPIRE IN INDIA: OR, THE DESTRUCTION OF INDIAN CIVILIZATION'S ANCIEN RÉGIME

Burke's critique of the British Empire in India bears strong similarities to his analysis of the French Revolution in three areas. The first is in his description of the assault on the Indian nobility and landed aristocracy. The second pertains to his numerous depictions of the downfall of aristocratic Indian women, which are every bit as arresting and important for his narrative of events in India as his depiction of the demise of Marie Antoinette in the *Reflections* is to his narrative of events in France. The third area of similarity centers on Burke's final attempt to conjoin the animating spirits of illegitimate imperial excess and illegitimate political resistance, or tyranny and rebellion, and thus to argue that Indianism and Jacobinism were essentially flip sides of the same theoretical coin. Here, I briefly describe each of these arguments because they tightly link Burke's analysis of France with his analysis of India, as similar conservative dirges in the face of the destruction of analogous civilizations.

The Destruction of the Landed Aristocracy and Nobility

Interpreters of Burke's work on the French Revolution have long noted the central importance he placed on the revolutionaries' attack on the nobility and landed aristocracy as one of the signal events in Western civilization's collapse.[52] However, his account of this phenomenon as part of an attack by the East India Company and Warren Hastings on *Indian* civilization has received relatively little attention by scholars of empire. Yet it is one of the most dominant and important themes in Burke's indictment of British imperial practice in India.⁵³ However, some few scholars have rightly stressed that Burke's critique of Hastings and of Company behavior in India is structurally similar to his view of the French Revolution.⁵⁴ In fact, there is little doubt that the former events predisposed him to view the latter in the same fashion.⁵⁵

Indeed, in an extraordinary passage in the *Speech on Fox's India Bill* of 1783, Burke contrasted the destructive effects of Hastings's ravaging of the Bengali zamindars, whom he described as a landed aristocracy, with the (then flourishing) aristocratic landed order of France before the French Revolution: "Bengal, and the provinces that are united to it, are larger than the kingdom of France; and once contained, as France does contain, a great and independent landed interest, composed of princes, of great lords, of a numerous nobility and gentry, of freeholders, of lower tenants, of religious communities, and public foundations." However, after Hastings became governor general, "the landed interest of a whole kingdom, of a kingdom to be compared to France, was set up to public auction!"⁵⁶

Burke had looked on, amazed and horrified: "I was in a manner stupefied by the desperate boldness of a few obscure young men, who having obtained, by ways which they could not comprehend, a power of which they saw neither the purposes nor the limits, tossed about, subverted, and tore to pieces, as if it were in the gambols of a boyish unluckiness and malice, the most established rights, and the most ancient and revered institutions, of ages and nations.... The country sustains, almost every year, the miseries of a revolution."⁵⁷

In these lines, Burke defines events in Bengal since the advent of Hastings's accession to power as a series of terrible "revolutions." But unlike the suitably veiled decade of marauding by Clive and his immediate successors, a period Burke celebrated, the Company's actions under Hastings were an occasion for looking on in stupefaction—a characteristic response to the sublime.⁵⁸ It is against this backdrop that Burke contrasts the appropriately structured hierarchical world that Bengal had been previously with that which France still was in 1783.⁵⁹ And, as in the *Reflections* and his later writings on the French Revolution, Burke describes the initiators of the second series of revolutions in Bengal after 1772 as wild, upstart schoolboys, mock legislators rashly ripping apart the prescriptive inheritance passed on by their aristocratic forefathers in the form of ancient institutions and rights.

In nearby passages in the very same speech, Burke describes the East India Company's agents, those "destroyers of the nobility and gentry of a whole kingdom," as "birds of prey and passage, with appetites continually renewing for a food that is continually wasting."[60] Later, Burke would use this exact phrase, "birds of prey"—initially applied in 1783 to the Company's destruction of the Indian aristocracy—in his impassioned final public letter to the Duke of Bedford as a means of describing the "Revolution harpies of France," who were engaged in the very same kind of destruction.[61]

Burke avers that other conquerors of India, such as Akbar and Tamerlane, had left the landed aristocracy intact, and that such policies continued until the British took control. Because this was so, the Hindus still "preserved their rank, their dignity, their castles, their houses, their seignories. All the insignias of their situations, and the power and means of subordinating their people.... So here I state that, through all these revolutions and changes of circumstances, a Hindoo policy and a Hindoo government existed in that Country, till given up finally to be destroyed by Mr. Hastings."[62] What Hastings did, that is, was specifically to target and destroy the ancient landed Hindu aristocracy, or zamindars, thereby obliterating the ancient constitution and effecting a social revolution, robbing them of their "castles" and other marks of nobility.[63]

In his "Speech on the Opening of Impeachment" (1788), Burke sought to engage the House of Lords' sympathy for these displaced aristocratic zamindars by directly analogizing the British lords to their besieged Indian brethren. The zamindars, too, were "the ancient nobility, the great princes (for such I may call them), a nobility perhaps as ancient as that of your Lordships (and a more truly noble body never existed in that character)." Then, as if to bring the threat home to them concretely, Burke warned, "I need not tell your Lordships that an attempt to set up the whole landed interest of a Kingdom to auction must be attended not only in that act but every consequential act, with most grievous and terrible consequences." But of course Burke does go on to tell the lords of the dreadful consequences that followed from the confiscation and auctioning off of the lands of the Indian aristocracy, and he does so in terms that he would soon repeat tirelessly in his writings on the French Revolution: "Servants were put in power over their Estates, their persons and their families by Mr. Hastings for a shameful price.... The selling offices of Justice, the selling Masters to their Servants and to the Attornies whom they employed to defend themselves, were all parts of the same system."[64] The confiscation of the landed aristocracy's estates, the dreadful inversion of master and servant, and even the role of attorneys in achieving these ends, would soon become hallmarks of Burke's analysis of the French Revolution.[65]

Nor was Burke's indictment of Hastings's attack on the Indian aristocracy limited only to a defense of its Hindu variant. In his speech before the Commons while attempting to get the "Rohilla War Charge" (1786) accepted as one of the articles of impeachment, Burke defended those Rohillas whom he cast as displaced Islamic aristocrats: "He requested Gentlemen to consider how the people of England would feel, or how the fact would be regarded in Europe, were all the principal men of property among their constituents to be driven from the country, to the amount of sixty thousand. It was not the negroes or peasantry in any country who were immediately affected by conquest or extirpation. It was the chief land-holders, the principal manufacturers, the nobles, the superior clergy, and the men of property among all ranks, who were the sacrifices of ambition."[66] The true sin, for Burke, was that the landed Rohilla aristocrats, men of property, and high-ranking clergy (so to speak)—not the functional equivalent of its New World negro slaves or European peasants—had been displaced by Hastings. In much the same way, the French aristocracy, men of property, and clergy would soon be driven from their lands, an event to be described by Burke in remarkably similar terms.

This is perhaps the best context in which to consider another of Burke's remarks from the same year, 1786, made in correspondence with Mary Palmer. Burke tells her, regarding India: "I have no party in this Business, my dear Miss Palmer, but among a set of people, who have none of your Lilies and Roses in their faces; but who are the images of the great Pattern as well as you and I. I know what I am doing; whether the white people like it or not."[67] These lines have been taken as evidence of Burke's deep and abiding commitment to justice for all Indians, as well as proof of his racial sensitivity and lack of prejudice.[68] However, from the standpoint of the argument being advanced here, such a claim fundamentally misrepresents Burke's theoretical and practical commitments with respect to empire, as well as his understanding of just exactly what the "great Pattern" of human society actually was, or at least should be. As we have seen, Burke's views on empire had little to do with race per se, but rather were guided by an understanding of the civilizing process sorted by the institutional markers of organized religion and aristocracy. In the New World, when Burke deployed that institutional understanding of civilization, he ultimately described two nonwhite peoples—Native Americans and Africans—as "savages" and declared them ripe for a civilizing mission. Similarly, in the case of "civilized" India, Burke was not concerned with the fate of all Indians any more than he was with the plight of all people in "civilized" France. In these cases Burke was distraught not about the fate of the lower orders—those like the "negroes or peasantry," so to speak—but about the fall of the aristocracy, be they in Europe or on the subcontinent and irrespective of their color. In this way, Burke's views on empire were driven far more by class than by racial exclusion—or racial inclusion. In both cases, they were underpinned instead by a deeply hierarchical and religious view of civilization and the civilizing process.

Interestingly, however, Burke did not always lay responsibility for the downfall of the Indian aristocracy at Hastings's feet after 1772. In fact, Burke's critique sometimes encompassed southern as well as northern India, but in both analyses he consistently lamented the fate of Hindu and Muslim aristocrats. For example, as early as 1779, concerning the Carnatic, Burke could speak of "a system of conquest by English arms, in favor of the Nabob of Arcot" a system that "has brought innumerable and unspeakable calamities on all the southern part of Hindostan."[69] Four years later, Burke could say of the Carnatic (which was not under Hastings's control) that it was "the scene, if possible, of greater disorder than the northern provinces." At that time, Burke referred to southern India as the "center and metropolis of abuse," a place in which, "it may be affirmed universally, . . . not one person of substance or property, landed, commercial, or monied, excepting two or three bankers," who were needed to distribute the general spoil, were left in the entire region.[70]

In short, from Hindu to Muslim India, from north to south, and from territories within to those outside Hastings's control, Burke isolated one consistent theme in his narrative, the destruction of the Indian nobility and landed aristocracy, as the key element in the British Empire's failed policy. Consequently, he could conclude of India, in April 1789, six months before the French Revolution broke out: "You have had before you the ruin and expulsion of great and illustrious families, the breach of solemn public Treaties, the merciless pillage and total subversion of the first houses in Asia."[71] Again, it seems clear that Burke could—and in fact did—easily shift this set of theoretical concerns to revolutionary France half a year later.

There were, of course, deep philosophical reasons why Burke would fixate on the fall of the aristocracy. He viewed the vivid description of this fall as an essential mechanism whereby the sympathy of his audience in Parliament could be most easily engaged. Again, this makes good sense within the parameters of Burke's work taken as a whole. It was a fundamental axiom of the moral theory he had developed in the *Philosophical Enquiry* and his other early writings that sympathetic fellow feeling was an affective disposition more naturally activated by the sight (or arresting narrative depiction) of the great falling from their perches atop the hierarchy of social ranks. Obviously, this was an argument Burke put to extraordinary effect in describing the demise of the French royal family and the French aristocracy in the *Reflections*.

As we have already seen, however, Burke also closely described the fall of the aristocracy extensively in his writings and speeches on India, and for the very same purpose of forging a sympathetic bond between his listeners and readers and the aristocrats he cared so deeply about. Burke summed up the moral theory underlying this approach in the "Speech in Reply":

> It is wisely established in the constitution of our heart that mankind interests itself most in the fall and the fate of great personages. They are the objects of tragedy every where, which is addressed to our passions and our feelings, and why? Because men of great place, men of great rank, men of great, allowed, hereditary authority cannot fall without an horrible crash upon all the others that are about them. Such Towers cannot tumble without the ruin of the Cottages. When the principal men who long governed in a Country are cruelly destroyed, that Country can hardly ever be re-established again.[72]

Elsewhere in the same speech, Burke noted that "when persons are reduced from great and opulent situations to low and miserable ones they naturally excite in the mind a greater degree of compassion by comparing the circumstances in which they once stood with those into which they are fallen."[73] Burke's rhetorical strategy here, in focusing on the downfall of the great, was thus deliberate, wholly consistent with his earlier moral theory, and in keeping with his broader principles, as Wollstonecraft, Paine, and later interpreters insisted. In that sense, it was profoundly reflective of Burke's own deepest concerns, which lay not principally with the common people but rather with their social and economic superiors, in India no less than in France. In both cases, Burke's attempt at creating sympathy for the sufferings of the fallen great was ultimately an endeavor that illustrated his abiding conservative commitments to the hierarchy of classes and the disciplining role of religion.

In contrast, passages in Burke's writings and speeches that focus on the sufferings of the common people in India are few and far between. More to the point, even in the instances where Burke describes such suffering, he depicts it as inflicted by the sort of nouveaux riches that Hastings and the

Company put into power as a result of practices of corruption and bribery to replace the old landed Hindu and Muslim aristocracy they had destroyed.

This is clearly the case in the single example from the impeachment trial in which Burke focused at any length on the pain of ordinary Indians, suffered at the hands of the Company's surrogate Devi Singh in Rangpur. Burke's set piece in the opening of the impeachment trial, in which he lingered in lurid and voyeuristic detail on the tortures inflicted by Devi Singh as a means of revenue extraction from poor people as well as zamindars, fits easily within the framework of Burke's argument sketched here. By destroying the ancient Indian constitution and obliterating its landed aristocracy for his own corrupt purposes, Burke argued, Hastings had come to rely on men like Singh, who, unlike their predecessors, were wholly unconstrained by the moral norms of the Mughal Old Regime and therefore acted in predictably excessive fashion. Once again, this clearly mirrored Burke's later description of events in France.[74] On Burke's view, if the Old Regimes in India and France, with their landed aristocracies and organized religions, had been preserved inviolate, the peasants never would have suffered in the first place (a view that obviously overlooks or denies the suffering of the lower orders in both locales as a result of the Old Regimes). Of course, this also did not make Burke any less of a defender of empire in India, because the Mughals provided the imperial model Burke endorsed and hoped the British would become heir to on the subcontinent.

The Assault on India's Female Aristocracy: Or, the Begams of Oudh as the Marie Antoinettes of India, and Munni Begum as the "Vilest of Women"

Burke's concern for the plight of India's aristocratic women, who were understood as a signifier of civilization's peril, was wide-ranging and long-standing.[75] However, he devoted the vast majority of his attention on this subject to one example in particular, the case of the aristocratic Indian women known as the "Begams of Oudh," who were the subjects of one of only four specific articles of impeachment actually brought before the House of Lords by the prosecutors in their endeavor to convict Hastings. Two of the remaining three—the so-called "Presents" and "Contracts" charges—-dealt specifically with corrupt Company practices. The former, as we have seen, pertained to what were effectively unsolicited bribes paid by Indians to Company official for preferential treatment; while the latter concerned the Company's awarding of contracts on dubious terms, unduly increasing the salaries of its employees, and unnecessarily creating new offices that functioned like sinecures for their recipients. In short, these two charges were mainly about British greed. Beyond the "Begams" charge, then, the only other formal indictment of Hastings that pertained to the suffering of the Indian people directly regarded Hastings's "despotic" behavior in first provoking the ruler of Benares, Raja Chait Singh, to engage in a rebellion that was violently crushed by Company forces, after which Benares was absorbed into the new territorial empire of northern India.[76]

This is to say that the sheer volume of pages in Burke's speeches devoted to the anguished depiction of the Begams' fate, understood as one of only two formal charges that directly focused on the damage done to the Indian people, was central to Burke's brief against Hastings in the trial before the House of Lords between 1788 and his acquittal in 1795. This makes it all the more important to unfold Burke's narrative tale over this long period, a tale that effectively transforms the Begams of Oudh into the Marie Antoinettes of India.

The facts of the Begams' story can be recapitulated briefly. In 1775, Asaf-ud-Daula succeeded his father, Shuja-ud-Daula, as the Muslim *wazir*, or effective ruler, of Oudh (Awadh). He inherited a large debt to the British and also had to fund a significant number of British troops quartered in his territory owing to the long-standing relationship between the Company and Oudh (it was Company troops that had enabled Oudh to annex the Rohillas in 1774, and for their part the British very much wanted Oudh to serve as a buffer state for Bengal).

However, the British feared that the ineffectual Asaf-ud-Daula would not be able to pay his debt and placed him under tight British supervision to ensure compliance. The Company's agents in Oudh, led by the British Resident at the *wazir*'s court and at Hastings's urging, pressured the increasingly subservient *wazir* to search his lands for additional potential sources of cash to pay up. One such source was found in the revenues derived from the *jagirs* (or grants of revenue affixed to certain geographical areas) of his mother and grandmother, the so-called Begams of Oudh. The Begams also had access to considerable treasure the *wazir*'s father had left in their palaces and a nearby town. Under pressure from Hastings, the *wazir* extracted a significant amount of wealth from his mother and grandmother and confiscated their lands for a time, a process that involved some violence and the physical accosting of the Begams themselves, along with a search of their private quarters for treasure. The managers of the prosecution insisted that in taking these steps Hastings violated an earlier Company guarantee of the sanctity of the lands held as *jagirs* by the Begams.[77]

For Burke, however, such an assault on aristocratic Indian womanhood was something far more nefarious. In his richly detailed retailing of these events over more than a decade, Burke came to describe them as the ultimate signifier of a wholesale assault upon Indian civilization.

For example, in 1783, Burke noted with horror that "the *instrument* chosen by Mr. Hastings to despoil the relict of Sujah Dowlah was *her own son*, the reigning nabob of Oude. It was the pious hand of a son that was selected to tear from his mother and grandmother the provision of their age, the maintenance of his brethren, and of all the ancient household of his father." Then, he pointed out that Hastings encouraged a "rapacious and licentious soldiery to the personal search of women, lest these unhappy creatures should avail themselves of the protection of their sex" to hide any treasure. In this way, the Begams were "completely despoiled" and deprived of all their wealth, while their eunuchs were imprisoned and tortured.[78]

In referring to this episode in his "Speech on Almas Ali Khan" of 1784, before the impeachment articles had even been drafted, Burke demanded of his colleagues in the Commons: "Could the House, without horror and indignation, recollect the barbarous usage which two unfortunate princesses had experienced? . . . Were they not stripped of their all, and reduced, from the first situations which the country afforded, to a state of penury and beggary? . . . They were bereaved even of their jewels: their toilets, those altars of beauty, were sacrilegiously invaded, and the very ornaments of the sex foully purloined! No place, no presence, not even that of Majesty, was proof against the severe inquisition of the mercenary and the merciless."[79]

The parallels between this description and the rhetorical and argumentative heart of Burke's later *Reflections on the Revolution in France*—the attack on Marie Antoinette's boudoir during October 1789—are profound, as some interpreters have recognized. In both cases, Burke depicted the invasion and violation of female nobility while their male protectors (either eunuchs or royal guards) were torn from them or killed. In this sense, the Begams' violation was for Burke a precursor to Marie's own.[80]

The extent to which the two cases were linked in Burke's mind might best be shown by the fact that in 1794, long after the *Reflections* was written, in the final "Speech in Reply," Burke mistakenly refers to the attackers of the Begams as perpetrating an assault on "the sanctuary of the first women in

Europe," as opposed to Asia, a most revealing slip, given that a few short pages later he does in fact refer to the Begams as "the first women in Asia"! Later in the speech, Burke similarly decries "the sufferings and disgraces of women of the first distinction in Asia, protected by their rank, protected by their sex, protected by their near relation to the prince of the Country, protected by two guarantees of the representatives of the British Government in India."[81]

On Burke's rendering of it, the violation of the inner sanctum of the Begams' boudoir (like the violation of Marie's) in an eventually successful search for treasure was also a thoroughly masculine endeavor. It was commemorated in correspondence between two men Burke saw as Hastings's lackeys, Sir Elijah Impey, chief justice of Bengal, and the Resident at Oudh, Nathaniel Middleton. Burke presents the correspondence between these two as an admixture of unrelenting greed and barely sublimated homoerotic longing. This can be seen in his description of portions of an impassioned letter between Impey and Middleton, in which Burke juxtaposes these outrages against the perfunctory and leaden assertion that "a few severities" were required to pacify the eunuchs. Burke said of this letter: "You cannot help observing the soft language they use. You could imagine they were making love."[82]

Likewise, in words that could have been taken directly from the *Reflections*, Burke urged the House of Lords to convict Hastings for having attacked the Begams of Oudh and, by extension, all the aristocratic women of India, on a scale that was nearly apocalyptic in scope. Hastings, or so Burke argued, had sent soldiers to beat and starve the noble mothers and their children. Such was the fate of the "first women of Asia," a fate that Burke believed could not but compel the sympathy of his auditors, no less than his description of Marie's fate was meant to spur his readers to her defense against the savages who assaulted her. Burke says of the Begams:

> My Lords, if there is a spark of manhood, if there is in your breasts the least feeling for our common humanity, if the least feeling in your Lordships' breasts for the sufferings and distresses of that part of human nature which is made by its peculiar constitution to feel, if there is a trace of this in your breasts, if you are alive to those feelings, it is impossible you can bear or tolerate that wicked Tyrant who is the cause of the whole of it. It is impossible that you should not join with the Commons of Great Britain in feeling the least degree of indignation. You see women who have been proved to be in a most respectable situation exposed, which is held to be the last of indignities, to the view of a base, insulting, ridiculing, or perhaps vainly pitying, populace.[83]

Again, the similarities between the cases of India and France to Burke's views on the importance of hierarchy/class point clearly to his overriding concerns and constitute a significant impediment to any sympathetic readings of him as anti-imperialist or an unqualified defender of liberty irrespective of rank. Burke was concerned not with the freedom of the Indian peasants but with the freedom of their rulers.

However, just in case the reduction of female nobility to the level of spectacle before the base and insulting populace was not reason enough to convict Hastings, Burke presented the lords at length with one other particular example of what he took to be the overwhelming evidence of the colossal inversion of rank, and an unjust attack on civilization, that Hastings had perpetrated in India: the case of Munni Begum.[84]

In 1772, on orders from London, Hastings had relieved Muhammad Reza Khan of his office of *naib,* or effective Indian administrator and head of government, in Bengal. In the reorganization that followed, Hastings appointed Munni Begum as the new young nawab's guardian. Burke subsequently argued incessantly, for over a decade, that only gross corruption or bribery could have accounted for this appointment—because Munni Begum's character was such as to make her totally unfit for this office. For Burke, this was true notwithstanding the fact that she was the wife of a previous nawab: Munni Begum was of unacceptably humble social origins, which led him to engage in a degree of vitriol against her that, when juxtaposed against his panegyrics for the Begams of Oudh, is as striking and similar as his juxtaposition of Marie Antoinette against the revolutionary women of low origin who led her in procession from Versailles to Paris. The latter were women whom Burke did not celebrate for expressing their newfound political and social liberty but, rather, memorably damned as "the furies of hell, in the abused shape of the vilest of women," a phrase that would subsequently earn Mary Wollstonecraft's scorn.[85]

Burke repeatedly condemned Munni Begum as a mere "slave," a despicable "dancing-girl," and a disgusting "prostitute" who had been unduly elevated to aristocratic rank.[86] This occurred while aristocratic women like the Begams of Oudh were simultaneously abused and deprived of all status: "Mr. Hastings deposed the Nabob's own mother, turns her out of the employment and puts at the head of the Seraglio this prostitute . . . . She was born a slave, bred a dancing girl. . . . Your Lordships are to suppose the lowest degree of infamy in occupation and situation when I tell you that Munny Begum was a slave and a dancing girl."[87]

But Hasting went even beyond this. Unconscionably, "in a country where no woman can be seen," Hastings

> made her Guardian. He made her Regent. He made her Viceroy. He made her the Representative of the native Government of the Country in the eyes of Strangers. There was not a trust, not a dignity in the Country which he did not in the minority of this unhappy person (her stepson) put into the hands of this woman.... Here is such an arrangement as I believe never was heard of, a secluded woman in the place of a man of the world, a fantastic dancing girl in the place of a grave magistrate, a Slave in the place of a woman of quality, a Common prostitute made to superintend the education of a young prince, and a stepmother, a name of horror in all countries, made to supersede the natural mother from whose body the nabob had sprung. These are circumstances that leave no doubt of the grossest and most flagrant corruption.[88]

In Burke's world, nothing but complete perfidy and corruption, or a man's inexplicable love for prostitutes, could explain such a lowly woman's elevation to political rank and power. For this reason, while there is absolutely no evidence for the assertion, Burke repeatedly referred to "the lover, Warren Hastings Esqre., and the object of his passion and flame, Munny Begum," and insisted, "It is possible Mr. Hastings might be in love with Munny Begum. Be it so. Many great men have played the fool for Prostitutes from Mark Anthony's days downwards."[89] In any event, Burke considered the demotion of aristocratic women to the status of mere prostitutes, and the elevation of those he described as mere prostitutes to the ranks of political agency and power, as both a moral abomination and a leading signifier of the breakdown of the civilized order in India, no less than in France.

Indianism and Jacobinism

The third and final way in which Burke linked the French Revolution and British imperial excess in India as similar assaults on analogous civilizations was by coupling the animating spirits behind both phenomena—that is, by treating what he called Jacobinism and Indianism as flip sides of the same coin.[90] In Burke's vocabulary, the former represented "rebellion" and the latter "tyranny," both of which were closely connected in his mind. In the "Speech in Reply," Burke declared,

> I must observe always the close connection between crimes of every kind. He that is a Tyrant will be a Rebel. They are things that originate exactly

from the same source. They originate from the wild, unbridled lewdness of arbitrary power. They arise from a contempt of the laws and institutions that bridle mankind. They arise from a contempt of public order. They arise from a harsh, cruel and ferocious disposition, impatient of the rules of law, order and morality. And according as their relation varies, the man is a Tyrant if superior, a Rebel if inferior.[91]

Burke thus invented the term *Indianism* to describe the direct destruction of hierarchical social order from outside and above, while he used the broad term *Jacobinism* to describe the indirect phenomenon whereby the *philosophes* goaded the masses to implement their destructive leveling plans, thereby subverting hierarchy from inside and below. Burke argued that both Indianism and Jacobinism destroyed the laws and institutions, aristocratic and religious, that appropriately "bridled" humankind, or kept it within a putatively beneficent hierarchical order, appropriately infused with habitual social discipline, that was, for him, definitional of all civilization. Thus, in his "Speech in Reply," when considering the issue of Hastings's confiscation of the *jagirs* of the Begams of Oudh, Burke would "venture to say that *Jacobinism* never has or can strike a more deadly blow to property, ranks and dignity than if your Lordships were to acquit this man of this confiscation for the purposes of raising a revenue."[92]

Like Jacobinism, which Burke frequently described as a disease that amounted to a revolt by the duped masses in order to break apart civilization from below, Indianism was an equally dangerous disease, one that threatened to break it apart tyrannically from above. And Burke painted Indianism, like Jacobinism, as a contagious, infectious disease. It may have operated differently, he argued, but it likewise had to be resisted by all available means lest it prove fatal to civilization itself. Hence, he told the House of Lords:

> The House of Commons considered what might be the state of the Country when the persons who came from that school of pride, insolence, corruption and tyranny came to mix themselves with the pure morals of this country; that nothing but contamination, that nothing but corruption, unless we expunge this out of their very hearts and souls, can possibly exist in this country. It is not those criminals, those Robbers that I say he is at the head of the gang of, but every man in Great Britain will be corrupted and must be contaminated, if you let out whole legions of people, generation after generation, tainted with those abominable vices.[93]

The figure invoked in this passage is of course the British "nabob," that bastardized English term for *nawab,* or regional leader under the Mughal

Empire.[94] It was feared that these men, accustomed to exercising arbitrary or despotic powers in India, would bring this same approach to ruling back to Parliament with them, wrecking the fabric of the ancient constitution and ultimately civilization itself. However, as has recently been argued, it is important to recognize that on Burke's account of the nabobs and the fundamental threat they posed in metropolitan Britain, it was not so much that India had corrupted them, but vice versa. Many believed differently at the time—that India had corrupted Hastings and other members of the Company, that this proved that empire in India was doomed to failure, and that withdrawal from the entire enterprise was the only means to national self-preservation.

However, as we know, Burke was firmly opposed to imperial retreat and fervently sought to reform the empire in India rather than dismantle it. His solution was therefore to argue the opposite: India had not infected the nabobs; to the contrary, Hastings represented the lowest and most corrupt type of Briton long before he left for India. British imperialism could be faulted, therefore, only because it had failed to eradicate this particular subset of naturally corrupted Britons before they could do damage abroad. By extension, Burke's position held that if the right imperial ambassadors were sent to India, then the providential gift of empire in South Asia could be preserved for futurity.[95] For Burke, Indianism was thus a plague of naturally corrupt, despotic, and therefore failed human beings that threatened ancien régime civilization in Britain—and hence India—from the top down. Alternatively, Jacobinism was a revolt of the democratic masses spreading outward from France that threatened civilization from the bottom up. Nowhere was this latter threat clearer than in the place of Burke's birth and the third great nodal point of the British Empire in the eighteenth century, Ireland.

CHAPTER 4

Ireland

EDMUND BURKE WAS IRISH. All interpreters agree on this, although almost everything else about Burke's origins, not to mention the ideological and political commitments they might be supposed to entail, has been the subject of intense scholarly debate. Most of Burke's biographers maintain that he was born in Dublin of a mixed marriage between a lifelong Protestant father (Richard Burke) and a mother from a long-standing Catholic family (Mary Nagle). However, some have opined that Burke was born in County Cork and spent an early formative period among his Catholic Nagle relations in the Blackwater country there. It has likewise been suggested that his attorney father had only recently converted to the Anglican established Church of Ireland and had done so purely for strategic reasons (since among numerous other discriminatory provisions, the eighteenth-century penal laws barred Catholics from practicing as lawyers).[1]

In any event, Burke remained formally committed to Anglican Protestantism throughout his life, a fact that allowed him to attend Trinity College, Dublin, the educational epicenter of establishment Ireland, which enabled his entire subsequent political career in England. In fact, after he left Ireland at the age of twenty, Burke settled in England and returned to his homeland only four times over the course of his life, all for relatively short periods of time. And, as we saw unmistakably in chapter 1, Burke firmly rejected anything like Irish nationalism, fervently insisting throughout his life that in order to flourish Ireland must forever remain a subordinate part of the British Empire. Indeed, Burke consistently looked on the prospect of Irish independence with nothing short of horror, a horror that grew more pronounced in his later years with the advent of the French Revolution, for reasons to be explored in the latter half of this chapter. However, throughout his life Burke was also deeply sympathetic to the plight of Irish Catholics, a group who, after all, included his close relatives. He was sharply critical of the so-called Protestant Ascendancy in Ireland that severely discriminated against Catholics, so much so that throughout his time in Parliament he was constantly accused of crypto-Catholicism by his political enemies.[2]

As in his views on both the New World and India, then, Burke's views on Ireland combined a sharp critique of empire's practical implementation with an unwavering devotion to it in principle. Likewise, Burke's specific proposals for how best to maintain the empire in Ireland, as in the New World and India, were driven by a conservative logic of empire that ultimately rested on his understanding of the civilizing process. The latter point becomes especially evident when one considers Burke's Ornamentalist approach to the issues that came to define Britain's imperial connection to Ireland in the 1790s during the time of the French Revolution—the twin questions of "Catholic relief" from the penal laws, and political enfranchisement, or the right of Catholics to vote and hold political office in the Irish Parliament and elsewhere.

I take up the particulars of how Burke wed a fervent Ornamentalist defense of empire in Ireland to an equally unwavering defense of Irish Catholics, in the final section of this chapter. Before doing so, however, I wish to establish that Burke's entire approach to Ireland was one that prioritized the preservation of empire as his foremost consideration. This is best done by considering Burke's views on three issues that did so much to define imperial politics relating to Ireland from the 1760s through the 1780s: the debates over the absentee tax, Irish free trade, and the so-called legislative independence of Ireland from Britain. In order to understand Burke's position on these issues, however, we must gain some purchase on the complex place of Ireland within the context of the eighteenth-century British Empire.

EIGHTEENTH-CENTURY IRELAND: KINGDOM AND COLONY

Disagreements over Burke's biography—that is, whether his was an essentially Protestant or Catholic upbringing—point to the fundamental divide in eighteenth-century Irish society. Of course, England's experience in Ireland dates back much further, to the Anglo-Norman invasions of the twelfth and thirteenth centuries, which established the "Old English" settlements on the island. Nevertheless, the pre-Reformation Old English were obviously Catholic, and, after centuries of intermixing with their coreligionists (the native Gaelic Irish), they had, by the sixteenth century, seen their area of effective control reduced to the small strip of land on the east coast near Dublin known as the Pale. However, all of this changed shortly after 1541, when in the wake of the Reformation the aggressively Protestant founder of the Anglican Church, Henry VIII, formally declared Ireland a sister "Kingdom" (one without a crown, but with its own long-standing Parliament, consisting as in England of a House of Lords and House of Commons). The Protestant "New English" settlement of Ireland commenced shortly thereafter, in the 1560s, and was to alter fundamentally the tenor of Ireland's internal dynamics as well as its relationship to England, although the nature of those changes has been hotly disputed.[3]

On the one side, there are those who stress the colonial nature of Ireland's status with respect to England. This argument focuses on the pronouncements and mind-set of the English officials charged with actually developing policy toward Ireland from the late sixteenth century onward. British officials thought of and repeatedly referred to Ireland as a colony and urged that it be treated as such. What this entailed, as Nicholas Canny has argued, is that the native Celtic or Gaelic Irish (and if necessary the increasingly Hibernian Old English who mixed with them) were to be understood and treated as savage or barbarian heathens lacking in "true" religion—despite their Catholicism. They were also deemed bereft of economic and cultural development and often even of civil society writ large. Accordingly, the Irish were viewed as appropriately subject to legitimate missions of English conquest aimed at civilizing them or, failing that, at extirpating or even eradicating them should they resist. This "Atlanticist" approach to Ireland emphasizes its place as a colonial beachhead for a British Empire moving swiftly westward, an empire that would employ the same tactics in the New World and often even the same personnel, as in the cases of Sir Walter Raleigh and the Winthrop, Calvert, and Penn families. On this score, it has been argued that colonial Ireland ought to be understood as a training ground for ideas readily deployed in the expansion of the British Empire throughout North America and the Caribbean in the seventeenth century.[4] In Ireland itself, the most important consequences of this sort of policy, before Cromwell, came with the colonization, or "planting," of Ulster by large numbers of English and Scottish Protestants under James I, and the confiscation and subsequent reallocation of massive tracts of Catholic land deemed forfeit to the Crown after the Gaelic aristocracy left Ireland for mainland Europe in the notorious "Flight of Earls" in 1607.

The other conceptual framework for understanding Ireland focuses on its place as a kingdom within a "composite" or "multiple" European monarchy. This perspective stresses the similarity between England's incorporation of Wales in 1536 and the uniting of the English and Scottish crowns in 1603, and it highlights the similarity between these acts of absorbing nearby territories and the broader pattern of European state formation, in which multiple titles were often claimed by a single monarch as the result of either voluntary negotiation or violent imposition.[5] On this view, England is regarded like numerous other European states in the early modern period, as a similar instance of a single sovereign combining diverse territories variously acquired through inheritance, conquest, cession, or incorporation, under one ruling body. Nevertheless, the English monarchy, like other European monarchies, also allowed these subordinate entities to retain separate representative institutions, laws, immunities, and even ecclesiastical institutions.[6] From this standpoint, Ireland looks less like the leading edge of a colonial model of imperial expansion into the New World, and more like a long-standing provincial entity common to early modernity. This reading dovetails with the idea that in many ways the Ireland that emerged from the Restoration through the reign of George III is better understood as a typical ancien régime society with a "confessional state," or an established church, than as a new kind of settler colony. It has in fact been claimed that many features of eighteenth-century Hanoverian Ireland that are often regarded as "colonialist," like the existence of large-scale social inequalities, the restriction of political power to a relatively small propertied elite, and the use of legal penalties to quell religious dissent, were in fact common in many parts of eighteenth-century Europe.[7]

As is often the case with such ideal types, however, there is now general agreement that the colonial and "multiple monarchy"/ancien régime frameworks are far from mutually exclusive. For example, some have maintained that the key to understanding early modern Ireland lies in Ireland's ambiguous status—legally a kingdom but practically a colony. As such, Ireland combined elements of both the New World and the Old, and consequently European imperial and colonial expansion and European state building were carried out simultaneously under the auspices of multiple monarchies.[8]

More recently, both sides in this debate have also given some interpretive ground. Postcolonialist and Atlanticist authors have come to agree that the languages of political resistance in Ireland that emerged during this period

(Jacobitism, republicanism, and "patriotism") were not anticolonial ones aimed at independence (at least until the end of the eighteenth century, and the rise of the United Irishmen). Nor can it be said that the Irish identified with other colonized natives in the New World, Africa, or Asia; indeed, many Irish were busily involved in helping colonize those very places and people, from early on in the story. For their part, supporters of the ancien-régime or kingdom position have recognized that nothing like the large-scale expropriation of native Irish lands or the plantation settlements of the sixteenth and seventeenth centuries occurred anywhere else in Europe. Similarly, it is now accepted that while all "confessional states" in Europe discriminated against nonadherents to the official religion, the depth of discrimination and exclusion practiced against the Irish Catholics went much further and fundamentally eroded the lines of "vertical" attachment between landlords and tenants and, hence, social stability in Ireland, in unprecedented ways.[9]

The fraught nature of its status meant that Ireland was simultaneously akin to an ancien régime kingdom and a New World colony at the end of the seventeenth century. This is captured by the claim that Ireland was not so much a *terra Florida,* or a model colony derived from an official blueprint, as it was a kind of "unruly palimpsest, on which, though much rewritten and scored out, could be discerned in an untidy jumble 'kingdom', 'colony', 'dependency', and, faintly, 'nation.'"[10] This mélange was the backdrop against which the central issues confronting Ireland in the eighteenth century, and hence confronting Edmund Burke, would unfold.

The theoretical questions underpinning Ireland's ambiguous status as both kingdom and colony from the late sixteenth to the end of the eighteenth century have been well described by J. G. A. Pocock. Over the course of a number of essays,[11] Pocock has developed a narrative that helps us think about the history of Ireland from 1541 to 1800—or from the time that Ireland was declared a kingdom to the time that this kingdom was joined to Great Britain through the Act of Union—as having deeply contested meanings. For this reason, ideologically freighted names such as the "English Civil War" and the "Glorious Revolution" might be better understood as the "Wars of the Three Kingdoms" so as to foreground the meaning of those conflicts for the Irish as well as the English. Indeed, from the standpoint of the vast majority of Irish, the latter portion of the period from 1637 to 1651 and that of 1688 to 1691 were indeed taken up by wars of "conquest" and "colonization."[12]

The first of these wars came about as a result of the long-simmering animosities generated by the various Elizabethan and Jacobean expropriations of Catholic lands, especially the planting of Ulster in the early seventeenth century and the continued confiscation and push for new plantations carried out by Charles I's lord deputy, Thomas Wentworth. These events contributed greatly to the Catholic rebellion of 1641, which can be understood as an attempt by the Old English and Gaelic Irish aristocrats who led the rebellion to reassert their particular understanding of Ireland's place as an autonomous sister kingdom, although one subject to the British Crown (but not the British Parliament), within the structure of multiple monarchy.[13] Of course, their rebellion, which killed an estimated twelve thousand Protestants—though it was widely believed at the time and long after to have been many more—was ruthlessly avenged by Cromwell and led to a still further confiscation of land and a further planting of colonists.

Similarly, the period from 1688 to 1691 in Ireland saw the last attempt by the Catholic Old English and the native Gaelic Irish to define for themselves the nature of their subordination to England by rebelling against William of Orange, in support of the deposed English king, James II. However, the Jacobite rebellion that turned at the Battle of the Boyne and culminated in the Treaty of Limerick actually demonstrated the very great extent to which even the Catholic Old English found themselves with a colonial status.[14] This was because the Old English were pursuing an older brand of Catholic "settler nationalism," thus making claims against the very state that had sent them to Ireland in the first place.[15] As a consequence, the Old English goal of maintaining an independent Irish Parliament subservient only to the Crown (or essentially a "federative" union) ran smack up against the "incorporative" tendencies of an aggressively Protestant England. After the Treaty of Limerick, however, the Old English and Gaelic Irish ruling class were definitively finished, and the period of the Protestant Ascendancy commenced in Ireland, an era in which the Anglo-Protestant landed and middle classes exerted hegemony over the majority population, Ireland's Catholics, as well as its nonconforming Protestant Dissenters, especially the Scottish Presbyterians.[16]

By this point, at the end of the seventeenth century, both the large-scale colonization of Ireland by England and Scotland and the expropriation of Catholic lands on an extraordinary scale had been achieved. While Catholics comprised roughly 80 percent of Ireland's population in the 1800s, already by the beginning of that century 86 percent of the country's land was in Protestant hands.[17] This was the settlement upheld by the penal, or "popery," laws, and despite the recent search for analogs in early modern Europe, the discriminatory depth of those laws was unprecedented and unparalleled.[18]

Over the course of the eighteenth century, Ascendancy Ireland would go on to create its own theoretical conundrums, problems that played out with profound practical consequences in the latter half of the 1700s. Chief among these were, first, a range of questions about Ireland's commercial place within the British Empire, crystallized in the debates over the absentee tax and Irish free trade. The second set of problems emerged with the rise of a new form of Protestant, rather than Catholic, "settler nationalism" in the 1770s and 1780s, which culminated in the push by the "patriot" party for the legislative independence of the Irish Parliament. And, of course, the third and most far-reaching debate centered on the exclusion of Catholics (and to an important if lesser extent, Dissenters) from political and economic power.

This third debate, focused on Catholic relief or emancipation from the penal laws and the issue of Catholic political enfranchisement, went to the heart of the Protestant Ascendancy's power. The failure to resolve it peacefully would lead to the rise of the United Irishmen, a group greatly influenced by the principles of the French Revolution and committed to wholesale Irish independence. Edmund Burke was to be highly involved in all of these debates and would frame all of them from the standpoint of his overarching conservative logic of empire and his view of history as a civilizing process.

BURKE ON TAXATION, COMMERCE, AND EMPIRE

Ireland's ambiguous imperial status, as a kingdom possessed of its own legislature but also as an economically dependent colony, generated many eighteenth-century political debates in Britain about the status of Irish commerce and the place of Ireland within the broader Atlantic economy.[19] Two of the most important of these concerned the desirability of an absentee tax and Irish free trade. Taken together, Burke's views on these two issues demonstrate his lifelong commitment to the British Empire in his homeland, and his prioritizing of the empire's survival over and above all other considerations related to Ireland.

The Absentee Tax and the Unity of Global Empire

The idea of a tax on those who owned landed estates in Ireland but resided elsewhere, many of whom were English, was a long-standing plank of the Irish patriot party agenda. Jonathan Swift had raised it as far back as 1729 in his text *A Modest Proposal,* a satirical work written the year before Burke was born. The idea behind the tax was either to convince holders of estates in Ireland to live there and become integral parts of the community, or, failing that unlikely prospect, to oblige them to contribute financially to the Irish, whose lands often provided a significant source of income for the absentees. In 1773, the idea of an absentee tax was actually brought to the North administration by its own chief secretary to the lord lieutenant of Ireland, John Blaquiere, who convinced North that the measure should be brought to a vote before the Irish Parliament. Blaquiere told the British Parliament in London that the proceeds from such a tax could also be used to pay down the Irish national debt to England.[20]

Like his political patron at the time, Rockingham—though on a much smaller scale—Burke was one such absentee landowner whose rents were threatened by the proposed tax. Not only did both men vigorously oppose the measure, but also Burke did so in ways that explicitly stressed the tendency of the absentee tax to weaken the British Empire. In a letter to the Irish MP Sir Charles Bingham, who later deployed some of Burke's arguments when he spoke against the legislation on the floor of the Irish House of Commons,[21] Burke first rejected the authority of the Irish Parliament to assume, independently of English wishes, the mantle of imperial legislative authority. In a crucial formulation, he put the problem this way:

> If it be true, that the several bodies, which make up this complicated mass, are to be preserved as one Empire, an authority sufficient to preserve that unity, and by its equal weight and pressure to consolidate the various parts that compose it, must reside somewhere: that somewhere can only be in England.... If all this be admitted, then without question this Country must have the sole right to the Imperial Legislation. By which I mean, that law, which regulates the polity and economy of the several parts, as they relate to one another and to the whole. But if any of the parts, which (not for oppression but for order) are placed in a subordinate situation, will assume to themselves the power of hindering or checking the resort of their municipal subjects to the center, or even to any other part, of the Empire, they arrogate to themselves the imperial rights, which do not, which cannot belong to them, and, so far as in them lies, destroy the happy arrangement of the entire Empire.[22]

On Burke's account, imperial harmony was all-important, and it required the unquestioned supremacy of England over Ireland in all matters that pertained to the imperial connection between the two neighbors. Empire was not a form of "oppression" but a vehicle for a proper global "order," one productive of a "happy arrangement" between England and Ireland. From this standpoint, the overriding problem of the proposed tax on absentees could be found in its very presumptuousness—that is, in its assumption that such a subordinate entity as the Irish Parliament could ever possibly believe it was within its purview to formulate policy that in any way bound the metropole. Such an arrogation of power would threaten the very basis of empire itself, which for Burke was ultimately predicated on the unquestioned authority of London.

In the same fashion, Burke also firmly rejected the idea that the Irish Parliament, the legislative organ of a "subordinate country," had the authority to inhibit the free movement of Britain's imperial citizens from one site of empire to another. Such a measure would inhibit "a free communication, by *discretionary residence,*" which was "necessary to all the other purposes of communication." At a deeper level, Burke contended that such a view was mistakenly built on the assumption "that England is a foreign country" to Ireland and was, therefore, a rejection of the empire's appropriate tendencies toward assimilation; it was, in effect, an unacceptable "renunciation ... of *common naturalization,* which runs through this whole empire."[23]

In his letter to Bingham, Burke considered the plight of a hypothetical member of the British imperial elite if such an onerous tax should be enacted. He pointed out that "a man may have property in more parts than two of this empire. He may have property in Jamaica and in North America, as well as in England and Ireland. I know some that have property in all of them. What shall we say to this case?" Burke insisted that his "poor distracted citizen of the whole empire" would be caught in the "*ricochet* cross-firing of so many opposite batteries of police and regulation" that "he is likely to be more of a citizen of the Atlantic Ocean and the Irish Sea, than any of these countries." In short, the unity of empire necessitated the free flow of its elites from one set of their properties to another, subject to minimal regulation, bureaucratic red tape, and onerous taxation. Burke admitted that the tendency of such deregulation and minimal taxation ensured that the financial ledger between core and periphery would never be balanced, and "that a great proportion of the money of every subordinate country will flow towards the metropolis." Nevertheless, he considered this "unavoidable" and "perhaps more than balanced, by the united strength of a great and compact body."[24] That is to say, Ireland's impoverishment relative to England was compensated for by the safety the empire provided to his native land, on Burke's rendering of matters. Thus, when Burke wrote to Rockingham about the absentee tax in 1773, he fulminated against the proposition: "There never surely was a Scheme of such preposterous Policy; nor that tends more in its principle and example to the separation and derangement of the whole contexture of this Empire considered as a well ordered, connected, and proportioned body."[25]

Burke's opposition to the absentee tax in Ireland cannot merely be reduced to issues of naked self-interest, his friendship with Rockingham, or Whig party politics; rather, it expresses his deep and principled concern for maintaining the unity and order of empire.[26] This is not to say that Burke hovered above self-interest or was incapably of crassly expressing it. In 1781, for example, he rejected a subsequent attempt to resuscitate the absentee tax after it had failed to pass the first time, by rejecting new arguments that it might be used as a means of providing support for Ireland's poor. He maintained that it "seems indifferent to a Man, whose property is confiscated in the whole or in any part, whether the confiscation is applied to Parochial concerns or to those of the State—or whether it goes to the support of a Poor house or of a Barrack."[27] Nevertheless, there are two additional compelling reasons for refusing to simply reduce Burke's views to the low level urged by Namierite historiography, which sees ideas as unimportant in motivating political behavior.

The first is that Burke's position on the absentee tax in Ireland during the 1770s is wholly consistent with his earlier articulation and defense of the Declaratory Act of 1766, as applied to America, which was central to his notions of imperial superiority and subordination. And of course, that legislation was explicitly based on the earlier Declaratory Act for Ireland of 1720, which Burke likewise wholeheartedly endorsed. Thus, Burke's constitutional arguments about empire in the case of the absentee tax in Ireland are of a piece with his arguments about imperial unity and imperial subordination earlier developed with respect to the American colonies.[28]

The second reason to insist on the priority of Burke's ideas over other potential motives as they concern the absentee tax comes from letters written in the last year of his life. In one of these, to his later political patron, Lord Fitzwilliam, Burke reiterated his strong dissatisfaction with those among his allies in the Irish opposition who confronted the Protestant Ascendancy Burke otherwise loathed. Burke complained to Fitzwilliam, himself the holder of large landed estates in Ireland: "You are branded by the odious Name of Absentees, as if you were bound to be present in Ireland at every roll call as if you were Soldiers, and the very people, a great part of the power and consideration of whose families has arisen from English Matches, as their

Estates have arisen from English grants, have endeavored to make English intermarriages impracticable, and the inheritance of Irish property by Englishmen odious and precarious."[29]

For Burke, the very notion that the Irish opposition to the Protestant Ascendancy would agree to treat fellow citizens of the empire as soldiers stationed in an alien territory, prevent marriages between the English and the Irish, or deny the inheritance of Irish land by Englishmen was an abomination that threatened to undo the empire by fraying its unity and harmony, by treating England as a foreign country. That this was a very real concern for Burke is clear also from an extraordinary letter he wrote to his protégé French Laurence some six week before Burke's death. In that letter, Burke derides the idea being pushed by the Irish opposition of reintroducing calls for an absentee tax in the politically charged climate of the French Revolution, which had inspired the rise of Irish republican nationalism. In such circumstances, Burke railed against "an absentee tax, which in its principle goes more to the disconnection of the two kingdoms than anything which is proposed by the United Irishmen."[30] Thus, Burke's final statement on the issue of the absentee tax—which rhetorically depicted it as more of a force for the dissolution of empire than the first Irish independence movement—was actually entirely in keeping with those throughout his career.[31]

Irish Free Trade: Sweet Commerce and the Sinews of Empire

Throughout his career in Parliament, Burke was a staunch advocate of increased free trade for Ireland.[32] His arguments on this subject are important to consider, especially in the wake of recent attempts to depict what Montesquieu called *doux commerce,* or "sweet commerce," as the eighteenth-century antidote to empire.[33] Viewed superficially, Burke's commitment to an appreciable dose of laissez-faire for Ireland might seem to speak to his credentials as an anti-imperialist. But drawing this conclusion would be a mistake. Whereas one can arguably make the case that thinkers such as Smith, Diderot, and Kant saw empire and commerce as theoretical antipodes, Burke's views were in fact very different. In the Irish case, he argued that trade liberalization could and would act as a crucial imperial glue, and that free trade would reinforce Ireland's commitment to the empire in the wake of Britain's loss of the American colonies.

Interestingly, Burke's position on Irish free trade itself developed from what he perceived as his native countrymen's unwillingness to act their part in preventing war with America and, thus, failing to keep the transatlantic British Empire intact.[34] In 1775, Burke argued that Ireland had "the Balance of the Empire and perhaps its fate forever, in her hands." If the Irish Parliament could be convinced to vote against supplying British troops, or making other grants to aid the war effort in North America, through such "friendly *mediation*" Ireland might defuse the impending conflict between England and America and "preserve the whole Empire from a ruinous War."[35] When the Irish Parliament failed to do this, Burke upbraided his political connections there for failing to play the "part assigned you by providence to act, that rarely, if ever happens to a nation, rarely indeed to mankind; you were in the situation, in which you might act as the Guardian Angels of the whole Empire." Irish dithering in this regard was "a species of Turpitude not decent to name."[36] Far from taking on an anti-imperial hue, then, Burke lamented that the Irish had missed a unique providential chance to play the part of keeping the empire together by preserving the American colonies within it: "Ireland has missed the most glorious opportunity ever indulged by heaven to a subordinate State, that of being the safe and certain mediator in the quarrels of a great Empire."[37]

In subsequent debates during 1778 to 1780, however, Burke came to recognize that his native countrymen had themselves drawn rather different lessons from the American revolt. Chief among these, Burke maintained, was the Irish belief that it was through the very process of rebellion that the American colonists had achieved the offer of unfettered free trade from Britain. Burke saw that many in Ireland, both Protestants and Catholics (since the trade restrictions affected both sides of the religious divide) drew the obvious conclusion: "Ireland, now, will not be satisfied with anything short of a free trade. America has pointed out to her, not the rule of her conduct, but her just claim upon this country. The people of Ireland have reasoned fairly and justly: the colonies they know have been offered the most that their own most sanguine expectations could aspire to—a free trade with all the world. America, in her revolt, has had a choice of favors held out to her. This is the reward of rebellion."[38]

Of course, this is not to say that Burke was necessarily opposed to the theoretical principles of free trade per se, or that his advocacy of it in the Irish case was merely to mollify his countrymen lest they follow the path of the Americans. In a letter of 1780 to the Irish MP Thomas Burgh, Burke asserted that his goal was "to fix the principle of a free trade in all the parts of these islands, as founded in justice, and beneficial to the whole, but principally to this seat of the supreme power [England]."[39] However, as we have already seen, Burke's commitment to free trade, unlike that of Adam Smith, was not sacrosanct beyond the British Isles, whether in the New World or India, and it did not imply the renunciation of colonies.

Rather, in Ireland as in America, Burke came to advocate free trade most strongly when the failure to grant it most seriously threatened the unity and integrity of the empire (hence, he did not make the same offer to India). In fact, it was "the mad, cruel, and accursed American war" that had done so much "to call forth the spirit, the resentments, and resolution of the Irish nation, whether already in actual existence, or in embryo, ready to burst forth with tenfold mischief, or in a storm strike this nation, and shake it to its lowest foundations."[40] In short, Burke feared that the same mistakes that had been made in America with respect to denying free trade, mistakes that fomented the American Revolution, were also being made in Ireland and risked the same results. Those opposed to free trade in all instances constantly described protectionism as a boon to empire, but Burke pointed out that through the pursuit of *purely* mercantilist policies the British had "lost already *one third* of the empire past redemption."[41]

Burke's commitment to empire thus drove his position on free trade, so much so that it went a long way toward finally costing him his seat in the Commons for Bristol, England's second-largest city. Bristol was heavily involved in the colonial trade, and its powerful constituents were very displeased with their representative's pro-free-trade stance on Ireland, which they perceived as undercutting their economic well-being. Nevertheless, in a private letter of 1778 to one of those constituents, Samuel Span, master of Merchants Hall in Bristol, Burke did not waver on his commitment to free trade, understood as one of the sinews of empire: "It is found absolutely necessary to improve the portion of this Empire which is left so as to enable every part to contribute in some degree to the strength and welfare of the whole.... These opinions I am satisfied will be relished by the clear understanding of the Merchants of Bristol who will discern that a great Empire cannot at this time be supported upon a narrow and restrictive scheme either of commerce or government."[42]

In the public letter to Span that followed, Burke likewise explicitly cast his defense of Irish free trade as a means of preserving the British Empire in the wake of the loss of the American colonies: "There is a dreadful schism in the British nation. Since we are not able to reunite the empire, it is our business to give all possible vigor and soundness to those parts of it which are still content to be governed by our councils."[43]

Burke was equally forthright to his constituents about the issue of Irish free trade in his *Speech at Bristol Previous to the Election* (1780), which he gave just one day before he withdrew his name from consideration for reelection. By then, his position on Irish free trade in combination with his arguments in favor of Catholic relief from the penal laws had cost him the support of the electorate. Burke nevertheless told those whom he had represented that, in the wake of the American war, "my only thought was how to conform to our situation in such a manner as to unite to this kingdom, in prosperity and in affection, whatever remained of the empire."[44]

Hence, from first to last Burke's position on Irish free trade was inseparable from his unswerving commitment to empire, a point Thomas Mahoney long ago recognized.[45] Yet Mahoney also argues that Burke's subsequent about-face on this subject, evident in his opposition to Pitt's renewed plan for Irish free trade in 1785, was the greatest betrayal of political principle by Burke in his entire career, one that was both shocking and inexcusable, since Pitt's plan would most certainly have benefited the commercial and mercantile classes in Ireland, which included many Catholics as well as Protestants, rather than the Ascendancy, which relied on landed interests and control of the Irish Parliament.[46] However, from the perspective outlined here, which stresses Burke's prioritization of empire *over* his commitment to free trade, one might suggest another conclusion: In 1785, the American Revolution was over and the colonies had become independent, so the pressing circumstances that necessitated the concession of free trade as a mechanism to induce Ireland to stay within the empire had sufficiently dissipated, to the extent that such demands could be resisted without fear that Ireland would sever the imperial connection as a result. Such a suggestion takes on added strength in view of the aftermath of 1782, the year in which the Protestant Irish Parliament was granted "legislative independence" by Great Britain.

IRELAND'S LEGISLATIVE "INDEPENDENCE"

The issues of an absentee tax and Irish free trade were already a vibrant part of British politics at the beginning of the eighteenth century, but they would take on added urgency during the era of the American Revolution with the rise of the Irish Volunteers, who sought Ireland's legislative independence from England. The Irish Parliament dated back to the fourteenth century. However, from very early on it was a parliament subservient to England.

Subsequent to the enactment of Poynings' Law (1494) under Henry VIII, it could meet only when authorized to do so by the English monarch, and all legislation put before it had to have the prior approval of the English as well as the Irish Privy Council. A decade after the Glorious Revolution of 1688 in England, and with the ascent of the Protestant "New English" to power in Ireland complete, the stage was set for a clash of views about the nature of sovereignty within a multiple monarchy, a clash that would last well into the eighteenth century. This struggle pitted an aggressive Protestant Irish Parliament, which increasingly sought more autonomy as a sister kingdom, against English politicians who regarded Ireland as everything from a wholly dependent kingdom to a foreign country like any other to an ordinary colony. In no case, however, did the policy makers in London think of Ireland as an equal partner, much less a sovereign entity.[47]

The Irish patriot position, then, is best seen as a sort of Protestant settler nationalism, and it was advocated from the turn of the century by figures like William Molyneux. His pamphlet *The Case of Ireland Stated* (1698) argued that Irish Protestants were born with all of the same rights and privileges of free and equal Englishman but were being unduly denied them by the mother country.[48] In the later *Drapier's Letters* (1724–1725), Jonathan Swift summarized the patriot complaint in the eighteenth century by arguing that English legislative interference with Ireland's affairs, and its ultimate control over the Irish Parliament, had reduced the Irish to "slaves," since they were bound by laws to which they had not consented.[49]

The English responded to these types of arguments with the Declaratory Act of 1720, which made it clear by statute that the Irish Parliament was subordinate to the British king in Parliament. Later in the century—shortly before the American Revolution—a decision was made to have all future chief English executives, or lord lieutenants, reside in Ireland, where they were supported by a "Castle party" in the Irish Parliament. At that time, a choice was also made to strongly reaffirm Poynings' Law.[50]

However, Irish patriot leaders saw in the American Revolution a chance to go beyond mere free trade concessions from England. Under the leadership of Henry Grattan and Henry Flood, and backed by the Earl of Charlemont and a new Protestant military association known as the Volunteers, which came to number roughly eighty thousand armed men, Ireland's Protestant political elites were in a position to demand a good deal more. The Volunteers were ostensibly formed to fend off a possible invasion from America's ally in the War of Independence, Catholic France, but by bringing the gun into Irish politics they had given the opposition in the Irish Parliament political leverage against England and its Protestant "Ascendancy" allies in the Irish Parliament and executive, especially during wartime. Narrowly, Grattan, Charlemont, and the other leaders of the movement used this leverage to press for trade concessions (which also benefited middle-class Presbyterian Dissenters in the north, who were a driving force in the Volunteers, as well as Catholics, who could engage in trade). More broadly, however, the Patriot opposition won for the Irish Parliament the ability to craft legislation that was formally free from English interference and direction. This was granted with the repeal of the Declaratory Act by England in 1782 and by significant amendments to Poynings' law. This so-called Revolution of 1782 thereby achieved a limited but important formal degree of "legislative independence" for Protestant Ireland and was a significant victory for its particular brand of settler nationalism or settler colonialism.[51]

What was Burke's position on Protestant settler nationalism and the Revolution of 1782? The short answer is that he did not approve of it, but the real question is, why? There are basically two dimensions to Burke's theoretical opposition to Irish legislative independence, both of which point strongly to the idea that, when it came to Ireland, Burke's prime directive was to keep his homeland firmly within the empire and wholly subordinate to England.

The first aspect of Burke's position had everything to do with his notion of Ireland's subordinate place within the empire. As we have seen this was a consistent position throughout Burke's career. Early on, he had opposed the Octennial Act of 1768, which had limited the duration of Irish parliaments to eight years, thereby making them more answerable to the Irish electorate. This made the Octennial Act a favorite measure of the Irish parliamentary opposition. On Burke's view, however, such a move dangerously undermined Poynings' Law. As he put it to his friend, the Irish MP Charles O'Hara, in a letter of 1768:

> The madness of the Government here [in England] which passed the Octennial Act is to be equaled only by the Phrensy of your Country [Ireland] which desired it, and the tameness of this country [England] which bore it. I consider that act as a virtual repeal of one of the most essential parts of Poyning's Law; and I think it will necessarily draw on a change in other parts; and indeed many material alterations in the State of your Country, as it stands by itself, and as it is related to England. However, you have your day of Joy, and your drunken Bout for the present.[52]

As both R. B. McDowell and Eamon O'Flaherty have pointed out, by accepting Poynings' Law and opposing the Octennial Act, which would weaken it, Burke clung tight to the notion of Ireland as a subordinate kingdom and undercut one of the central planks of the patriot opposition.[53]

However, Burke's view of both pieces of legislation is fully in keeping with his staunch support of the Declaratory Act for Ireland of 1720, which was the inspiration for the Declaratory Act of 1766, which applied to America. As we have seen, the latter Declaratory Act was one of the Rockingham Whigs' signal achievements and the subject of Burke's first major speech in Parliament. Thus, while he did not speak against legislative independence for Ireland and "Grattan's Parliament" at the time, and even grudgingly accepted Irish "legislative independence" as part of the newly developed Whig position in the wake of the American Revolution, he never liked it. In 1782, he wrote to his friend John Hely Hutchinson, an Irish MP, that the repeal of the Declaratory Act for Ireland "could only serve to disgrace the British Legislature, without serving that of Ireland in any degree."[54]

A few years later Burke would clearly express his view that England and Ireland were not equals in the imperial project, and that the latter nation was still appropriately subordinate to the former. Burke's views, set forth in 1785, are worth quoting at length, since they directly contravene any "anticolonial" or "anti-imperial" reading of his thought and express incontrovertibly his notion of Ireland as a subordinate imperial entity. In the wake of the "Revolution of 1782," a moderate move that established at best a limited legislative independence for his place of birth, Burke argued,

> To Ireland, independence of legislature had been given; she was now a coordinate, though less powerful state; but pre-eminence and dignity were due to England. It was she alone that must bear the weight and burden of empire; she alone must pour out the ocean of wealth necessary for the defense of it; Ireland and other parts might empty their little urns to swell the tide; they might wield their little puny tridents; but the great trident that was to move the world, must be grasped by England alone and dearly it cost her to hold it. Independence of legislature had been granted to Ireland; but no other independence could Great Britain give her without reversing the order and decree of nature: Ireland could not be separated from England; she could not exist without her; she must for ever remain under the protection of England, her guardian angel.[55]

Burke thus regarded true Irish independence as a shocking affront to the natural order of things, a suicide pact made in ignorance of how Ireland's very existence was owed to imperial England. It was for these reasons that, in 1796, long after the Revolution of 1782, Burke could claim, "I never liked, as it is well known, that total [legislative] independence of Ireland which, without, in my opinion adding any security to its Liberty, took it out of the common constitutional protection of the Empire."[56] In the last year of his life Burke declared likewise that "the whole of the Superior, and, what I should call, *Imperial* politics, ought to have its residence here [in England]." For Ireland this meant a position of permanent subordination to England in all questions of common concern; it meant for, the Irish, "in a word with her to live and die."[57] In this respect, even partial legislative autonomy from England—which in the end was all the revolution amounted to—was a step in exactly the wrong direction as far as Burke was concerned.

These conclusions make a great deal of sense when one understands that, for Burke, England was not a colonial power to be fought by the Irish in the name of gaining independence, but rather England was Ireland's "guardian angel," one under whose imperial "protection" the Irish should remain under "forever." Burke expressed similar sentiments near the end of his life to the Irish Catholic political leader John Keogh, who had praised Burke as a "true Irishman." Burke thanked him for the compliment, especially, he wrote, "considering as I do England as my Country, of long habit, of long obligation and of establishment, and that my primary duties are here. I cannot conceive how a Man can be a genuine Englishman without being at the same time a true Irishman."[58] For Burke, Ireland's best interests were generally synonymous with England's and inseparable from Ireland's subordinate place within the empire. However, as Burke also made clear at least as far back as 1779, early in his parliamentary career: "If ever any concessions on the part of his native country should be insisted upon, derogatory to the interest and prosperity of this country [England], he would be one of the first men in that House, in the character of a British senator, to rise and oppose [in] the most peremptory and decisive manner, any proposition tending directly or indirectly to any such point."[59] These twin maxims—a belief in the shared interests of England and Ireland within the framework of the British Empire, and a willingness to support the former should he ever interpret those interests as clashing—consistently informed Burke's political thought and action.[60]

Given that Burke's most fervent wish was for Ireland to remain an integral and subordinate part of the British Empire, we can now turn to unraveling the reasons for his long-standing support of the Irish Catholics. This support took the shape of arguments for repeal of the discriminatory penal laws, and partial political enfranchisement of Catholic elites. But neither of these positions was remotely anti-imperial; actually, both were made in defense of the imperial connection between Britain and Ireland. Burke thought that the best way to hold the empire together in harmony in Ireland was to find a way of peacefully integrating the Catholics within it. Burke made this argument from within the framework of his conservative logic of empire and his understanding of history as a civilizing process. Specifically, his whole approach should be understood as an Ornamentalist appeal to the Protestant Ascendancy in Ireland and political elites in England asking them to see the Catholics as part of one shared people and civilization rather than as alien and hostile savages.

CATHOLIC EMANCIPATION, CATHOLIC ENFRANCHISEMENT, AND THE CIVILIZING PROCESS

The Revolution of 1782 highlighted the limits of Protestant settler nationalism and colonialism, because it pointed to the fundamental contradiction inherent in the New English argument. It was logically incoherent for the Protestant patriots to build their case for legislative independence on the notion that all government without consent is slavery, when in fact Protestants themselves were the architects of laws that had deprived 80 percent of Ireland's population of civil and political rights and liberties. In this respect, an extension of the patriot argument led to the question: If the Protestants were slaves, then what of the Catholics whose "enslavement" under the popery laws was surely far more complete and had been produced in large part by New English Protestants themselves? The history of eighteenth-century Ireland was one in which the denial of liberty had led to a brand of settler nationalism that had, in turn, led to claims for the extension of liberty to Irish Protestants, but these positions highlighted a still deeper exclusionary divide that was traceable to Ireland's unsettled history of conquest.[61]

While Protestant patriots thus deployed older civic humanist or republican languages of political argument whose provenance could be traced back to antiquity, they pointedly did not rely on emerging democratic discourses in demanding the Irish Parliament's relative autonomy to go along with commercial concessions from Britain, and were content to halt the process of making demands when they had achieved these limited goals.[62] However, other groups were subsequently keener to draw out the logical implications of arguments about the relationship between consent and slavery.

The real problem for Ascendancy Ireland and the British Empire therefore came in the 1790s, when Protestant elites were confronted by a range of dissenting middle classes, including Presbyterians, who were also to a great extent locked out of the Irish political process. These Dissenters were willing to make common cause with the disenfranchised Catholics, who comprised four-fifths of Ireland's population, and this alliance changed matters radically. Together these groups would form the United Irishmen, a body that drew on the democratic principles of the French Revolution to seek total emancipation from the penal laws, complete Catholic and Dissenter enfranchisement—and ultimately true independence from England and an end to the British Empire in Ireland. By the end of the eighteenth century, then, two very different and competing notions of liberty had appeared: one was born of the Reformation and tied to the Protestant Ascendancy, and it denied liberty to Catholics and Dissenters; the other was based on the liberal democratic principles of the French Revolution, and it provided the theoretical basis for Ireland's first nonsectarian, ant-imperialist nationalist movement.[63]

By the 1790s, the United Irishmen's platform of total emancipation from the penal laws, universal male enfranchisement, and Irish national independence from England and the empire would create profound theoretical difficulties for Burke. This was because the United Irishmen combined what Burke forever desired to keep separate: Catholic relief from the penal laws, which he fervently sought, and a vastly expanded suffrage and Irish independence, which horrified him. Moreover, the United Irishmen pursued this program animated by the egalitarian, democratizing principles of the French Revolution, with its discourse of universal rights, a language of politics that Burke believed spelled the end of Western civilization.

On all three of these fronts, Burke would respond by relying on the Ornamentalist strand of his conservative logic of empire. The results would be an impassioned defense of Catholic relief and the acceptance of a limited franchise for the Catholic aristocracy and gentry, all with the express aim of keeping Ireland firmly within the familial embrace of the British Empire and away from the waiting clutches of the French Revolution, widespread democracy, and Irish national independence. On Burke's view, however, the Protestant Ascendancy in Ireland was failing to take the steps necessary to mollify Catholics in a timely fashion, because they were incapable of seeing Catholics as members of a shared civilization. At the end of his days, Burke came to believe that this failure of the Ornamentalist imagination on the part of the Protestant Ascendancy was driving the Catholics and Dissenters into the arms of the atheist, democratic French revolutionaries, who, in turn, were fomenting Irish independence. For Burke, this pointed to the necessity of a union between Britain and Ireland in order to save the Irish and, ultimately, British and Western civilization as a whole.

The Popery Laws: Discrimination, Conquest, and the Obliteration of Ireland's Native "Natural Aristocracy" and Religion

Burke's Opposition to the Penal Laws. While Ireland was in many ways a typical European-style ancien régime with a confessional state and political power in the hands of a small propertied elite, it was also unique. Unlike elsewhere in Europe, the established church and political and economic power in Ireland were under the tight control of a distinct demographic minority, which systematically discriminated against the vast majority of the country's population in order to maintain its position. The Protestant Ascendancy that ruled eighteenth-century Ireland was largely the product of the Cromwellian and Williamite conquests and confiscations of the 1640s and 1690s. In turn, the penal, or popery, laws protected its privileged status against the Catholics and Dissenters. By the mid-eighteenth century, these laws prevented all Catholics from voting and holding seats in the Irish Parliament and excluded them from most other public offices, the legal profession, and the judiciary; from attending Trinity College and universities in Europe; and from bearing arms and serving in the military. Catholic bishops were also banished from Ireland, and Catholics were legally barred from intermarrying with Protestants. Other penal laws devastated Catholics economically. For example, upon their owner's death, Catholic lands were not eligible for primogeniture, but rather were equally subdivided between the remaining sons unless the eldest son converted to Protestantism, in which case he would become the sole heir regardless of paternal wishes. Thus, Catholics faced a true dilemma: convert to the Protestant-established Church of Ireland or watch their landed estates be broken down into progressively smaller and poorer plots of land over time. At the same time, if any Protestant converted to Catholicism, he or she thereby forfeited all landed property and could be thrown in jail indefinitely without further cause.[64]

With reason, Burke has been seen as one of the most important advocates of Catholic emancipation from the penal laws in the late eighteenth century. Burke was committed to Catholic relief over the entire course of his political life, dating to the early 1760s, when he served as secretary to William Gerard Hamilton in Dublin Castle, himself the chief secretary to the lord lieutenant of Ireland. At that time, there was widespread agrarian unrest led by the Catholic "Whiteboys" in Munster, who were resisting the tithe and the enclosure of common lands. It was against this backdrop that Burke drafted and circulated (even if he never published) his careful description of the discriminatory effects of the penal laws, known as the *Tracts Relating to Popery Laws*.[65]

In the *Tracts,* Burke argues unabashedly that "a Law against the majority of the people, is in substance a Law against the people itself. . . . It is not particular injustice, but general oppression"; and likewise declares that "a Constitution against the interest of the many, is rather of the nature of a grievance than a Law."[66] This uncompromising view of the penal laws was a position Burke maintained throughout his time in Parliament, where he repeatedly circulated the *Tracts* to political allies throughout his career. Burke was also a major force pushing for the various Catholic relief bills of 1778, 1782,[67] and 1793, bills that slowly but progressively repealed the most onerous aspects of the Irish penal laws.

Nor were these positions without political consequence for Burke. Along with his views on Irish free trade, Burke's support for Catholic relief in 1778 was responsible for him losing his seat for Bristol, and he was one of the major targets of the anti-Catholic Gordon Riots (1780). Burke's commitment to his Catholic countrymen also provided mounds of ammunition for political enemies who wished to indict him as a closet papist. However, Burke never wavered in his support for Catholic relief. While pushing for the repeal of the remaining aspects of the penal laws in 1792, he memorably described the entire system as "a machine of wise and elaborate contrivance; and as well fitted for the oppression, impoverishment and degradation of a people, and the debasement, in them, of human nature itself, as ever proceeded from the perverted ingenuity of man."[68] In fact, during the early 1790s, Burke's only son, Richard, acted as agent for the Irish Catholic Committee in Dublin, a group whose aims included the repeal of the penal laws in their entirety.

Nevertheless, it is important to go beyond registering the mere fact of Burke's opposition to the penal laws, to consider what it was about them that he objected to so strenuously from the standpoint of his broader theoretical commitments. We know that at no point did Burke's opposition to the popery laws lead him to advocate Irish independence as a means of overturning them, for example. However, one might still be tempted—as many of his most influential interpreters have—to attribute his hostility to the penal laws to Burke's supposedly general commitment to liberty, and his equally general opposition to oppression.[69] But such views fail to capture Burke's position in Ireland, as elsewhere.

After all, while the penal laws were indeed brutal, they were nothing like African chattel slavery. Yet Burke defended slavery for an extended period of time (including the expansion of the slave trade at one point). Although he eventually supported the gradual abolition of slavery, he demanded that the freed Africans be required to prove they could be suitably "civilized" or face being reenslaved. Similarly, while the conquest of Ireland was violent, it had nothing on the conquest of America, which, as we have seen, Burke wholeheartedly supported and wished to extend as part of a broad mission to civilize the Native Americans. Likewise, while Burke's vaunted writings and speeches on India certainly express a concern for the liberty of upper-caste Indians, whom he believed should be free from Hastings's depredations, that commitment did not extend to a general argument on behalf of the liberty of the Indian lower orders, whom he was content to leave as they had anciently stood, most notably in the caste system he lauded, just as he was willing to leave the French lower orders bereft of individual liberty under Bourbon absolutism. In short, we find no general commitment to liberty *simpliciter* and no universal opposition to oppression in Burke's conception of empire, or anywhere else in his political thought for that matter, so we cannot deploy such a conceptual nonstarter as a shorthand explanation for his opposition to the penal laws in Ireland. Instead, we must look deeper, to Burke's understanding of history as a civilizing process, to understand both his career-long push for Catholic relief, or emancipation from the penal laws, and his related views on Catholic enfranchisement.

Conquest and Prescription: Burke's Irish History. As has been stressed recently by Seán Patrick Donlan in particular, the crucial features of Burke's understanding of Irish history revolve around the theme of conquest.[70] In the *Tracts,* Burke rejected the arguments of "those miserable performances which go about under the names of Histories of Ireland," with their absurd claims that it was "indulgence and moderation in Governors" that had led to Irish Catholic resistance such as the rebellion of 1641. For Burke, such rebellions were not produced by English toleration and leniency of government in Ireland; rather, when viewed aright, from the standpoint of the "interior

History of Ireland," they could be apprehended as resulting "from the most unparalleled persecution."[71]

Central to Burke's understanding of Irish history was his rejection of the sort of "settler nationalist" or Protestant settler colonial narrative of history presented by William Molyneux and the New English, which stressed the consensual nature of Anglo-Irish historical relations. Rather, Burke considered England as having engaged in a long history of conquest in Ireland, a view more in keeping with later Catholic historiography.[72]

This was an interpretation Burke pressed right through to the 1790s and, most extensively, in his public *Letter to Sir Hercules Langrishe* (1792). Therein, Burke told his friend the Irish MP that the "Glorious Revolution" in Ireland "was, to say the truth, not a revolution, but a conquest, which is not to say a great deal in its favor." In this respect, Burke maintained, the penal laws enacted in the wake of Limerick merely amplified upon the spirit of the Statutes of Kilkenny in the fourteenth century, which forbad intermixing between the Gaelic Irish and the Old English, an animus that pervaded English policy through the Elizabethan, Cromwellian, and Williamite periods. Burke therefore rejected as hollow a boast by the English historian Sir John Davies in the early seventeenth century, that the enlightened liberty of English law had been extended to Ireland. Rather, Burke wrote, "the original scheme was never deviated from for a single hour." Instead, "all the penal laws of that unparalleled code of oppression, which were made after the last event [Limerick in 1691], were manifestly the effects of national hatred and scorn towards a conquered people; whom the victors delighted to trample upon, and were not at all afraid to provoke." Thus, whereas "in all other places and periods" known in history the passage of time had eventually "blended and coalited the conquered with the conquerors," this had failed to occur in Ireland. Consequently, the spirit that prevailed after 1691, like that which preceded it, was not the spirit of liberty but rather "was that of not the mildest conqueror." It was a spirit wherein "the Protestants, settled in Ireland, considered themselves in no other light than that of a sort of a colonial garrison, to keep the natives in subjection to the other state of Great Britain."[73]

However, as keen observers have recognized, such views did not mean that Burke believed the English history of conquest in Ireland was ultimately illegitimate—far from it.[74] Similarly, notwithstanding his extensive criticism of the penal laws, Burke's commitment to the doctrine of prescription prevented him from making a broader argument for the wholesale redistribution of Irish lands that were acquired as part of the seventeenth-century conquests and confiscations. Rather, Burke came to see those acts of confiscation and conquest in Ireland as sacrosanct and inviolable, no less so than in the rest of Europe or in India.[75] Burke maintained that, regarding the Protestant Ascendancy in Ireland, too, one should "let Time draw his oblivious veil over the unpleasant modes by which lordships and demesnes have been acquired in their, and almost all countries upon earth."[76] Indeed, in the face of Burke's extraordinarily deep commitment to prescriptive property arrangements, even some scholars attempting to make the anachronistic argument that Burke's position in the *Tracts* expresses a "postcolonial" viewpoint are compelled to accept that, at the end of the day, like the Protestants Molyneux and Swift, Burke accepted the prescriptive validity of English conquest in Ireland, and accepted as legitimate the world of radical property inequality such conquests had created.[77]

Burke's problem with the conquest of Ireland was therefore not that it had happened, and certainly not that it needed to be overturned by radical land redistribution and Irish independence from England. Rather, for Burke, the great difficulty was that the peculiarities of Ireland's conquest had warped and transmogrified Ireland's "natural aristocracy" and destroyed the appropriate relationship between landed wealth and political power that it should ideally embody. The effect of England's history of conquest in Ireland, and the penal laws that accompanied it, had been to distort Irish civilization and to stunt the civilizing process on the island in fundamental ways.

The Penal Laws and the Perversion of Ireland's "Natural Aristocracy" into a "Plebeian Oligarchy". In Burke's narrative, the pattern of Irish conquest since the beginning of the seventeenth century, with its various waves of colonization and confiscation, meant the creation of an overbroad and unacceptably diluted Protestant aristocracy unworthy of the name and unable to perform its necessary functions. In an early letter to Charles O'Hara, written in 1762 against the backdrop of the Whiteboy disturbances in Munster, Burke referred to the problem underlying Catholic disaffection as "the unfeeling Tyranny of a mungril Irish Landlord."[78]

Thirty years later, in writing to Langrishe, Burke described this mongrelized would-be Protestant aristocracy as a "plebeian oligarchy" that was "a monster in itself." It was a stratum of leadership which no people unaccustomed to slavery would long endure. For Burke, the Protestant Ascendancy was too narrowly defined to be truly democratic (no solution on his account, in any event) and too broadly configured to be a true natural aristocracy:

"The Protestants of Ireland are not *alone* sufficiently the people to form a democracy; and they are *too numerous* to answer the ends and purposes of *an aristocracy*." The exclusion of all Catholics from the vote and from the ability to hold public office created the Protestants as a ruling class far too large to yield "admiration, that first source of obedience" from the Catholics. In a rightly constituted natural aristocracy, Burke argued, political power was appropriately vested in "the few," who alone could be afforded such deference from the masses. But the Catholics did not see this among their Protestant overlords and, hence, would not defer where they could not admire: "I hold it to be absolutely impossible for two millions of plebeians, composing certainly, a very clear and decided majority in that class, to become so far in love with six or seven hundred thousand of their fellow citizens (to all outward appearances plebeians like themselves, and many of them tradesmen, servants, and otherwise inferior to some of them) as to see with satisfaction, or even with patience, an exclusive power vested in them, by which *constitutionally* they become the absolute masters."[79] The effect of the popery laws was the legal enshrinement of nondissenting Protestants in their entirety as a misbegotten aristocracy too large to fulfill its civilizing mission, one populated by plebeians who had no business ruling in the first place.

The converse was also true, according to Burke: Those members of the Catholic landed nobility who should have been part of any natural aristocracy, rightly understood, were wholly excluded from political power by the very same legacy of conquest and penal laws that had inappropriately empowered too broad a swath of Protestants. As McBride has astutely observed, for Burke, under the Protestant Ascendancy: "The natural relationship between property and authority ... had been contorted by ethnic and religious antagonisms resulting from the Elizabethan, Jacobean, and Cromwellian plantations, so that Protestant tradesmen and servants were raised above Catholic noblemen."[80]

The Penal Laws and the Assault on Ireland's Native Religion. Burke saw the same stunting of the Irish civilizing process when he considered the effects of English conquest and the penal laws on its other great institutional engine, organized religion. As we know, Burke stressed the crucial role of Christianity in the European civilizing process. In this respect, perhaps the most important feature of Burke's emphasis on religion in Ireland was to stress the role of Catholicism in the civilizing process, including even those aspects of the Catholic Church that his contemporaries most disliked, such as the monasteries.[81] The problem with the penal laws was that they undercut the role of the

Catholic Church as an institution crucially important to the civilizing process.

Burke emphasized this in his 1795 follow-up letter to Sir Hercules Langrishe. He did so in the course of driving home one of this favorites themes—that the Protestant Ascendancy was virtually inviting the infectious disease, or "epidemical distemper," of revolutionary principles into Ireland by its ham-handed treatment of the Catholic majority there. Rather than fortifying the Catholic "dyke" against the French Revolution, Burke insisted, the Ascendancy was dynamiting it and depriving themselves of a vital ally in the Catholic population. The consequences of this from the standpoint of the civilizing process were crystal clear to him, and he warned Langrishe: "The worst of the matter is this: you are partly leading, partly driving, into Jacobinism that description of your people, whose religious principles,—Church polity, and habitual discipline,—might make them an invincible dyke against the inundation."[82] In this passage, Burke reiterated the central role of organized religion—and perhaps especially the Catholic Church, with it layers of hierarchy and obedience—in creating the "habitual social discipline" necessary for the masses to defer to the natural aristocracy. Without the discipline and obedience inculcated by religion, Burke believed, the Irish (as all people) would devolve into an aimless gaggle of egalitarian savages.

Elite Catholic Enfranchisement and the Creation of a True "Natural Aristocracy"

Burke's efforts at Catholic enfranchisement in the 1790s were thus underpinned by his conservative understanding of the civilizing process in Ireland. His goal in pushing for limited enfranchisement for Catholic elites was to counteract the effects of the monstrous "plebeian oligarchy" of the Protestant Ascendancy, with its narrowly self-interested leaders, by creating a true "natural aristocracy." This was the explicit goal of Burke's *Letter to Sir Hercules Langrishe,* a Protestant aristocrat and member of the Irish ruling class whose fears of Catholic empowerment Burke was keen to quell. As a result, Burke's letter deserves the closest attention.

At stake were two issues concerning Catholic enfranchisement, as Burke explained them to Langrishe. The first concerned whether Catholics were fit to hold the highest offices of the *"State"* or *"Supreme Government."* Here, Burke maintained "that to exclude whole classes of men entirely from this *part* of government cannot be considered *absolute slavery,*" but rather "only implies a lower and degraded state of citizenship" and "may be no bad mode of government," depending on the circumstance. Burke cajoles Langrishe on this point: "Between the extreme of *a total exclusion,* to which your maxim goes, and *an universal unmodified capacity,* to which the fanatics pretend, there are many different degrees and stages" that accord with "prudence."[83]

Burke is at pains to insist that in "our constitution" (meaning that of the British), "there has always been a difference made between *a franchise* and *an office,* and between the capacity for the one and for the other. Franchises were supposed to belong to the *subject,* as *a subject,* and not *as a member of the governing part of the state."* However, while giving ground to the Ascendancy on this point, Burke insists that "our constitution is not made for great, general, and proscriptive exclusions; sooner or later, it will destroy them, or they will destroy the constitution.... They who are excluded from votes (under proper qualifications inherent in the constitution that gives them) are excluded, not from the *state,* but from *the British Constitution."* According to Burke, such citizens do not even have a *"virtual* representation" based on a sympathetic feeling for their interests, let alone *"an actual."*[84]

Burke's argument is thus that gradations of citizenship that preclude certain categories of citizens from the highest offices of the state, as well as from the vote, are perfectly acceptable within a rightly constituted polity. However, he maintains that the universal proscription of Catholics, as such, from political office and the suffrage would eventually have disastrous consequences for the cohesion of any civilized society based on principles like those of the British constitution.

Obviously, this raises the question of what, on Burke's understanding, were the "proper qualifications" for being able to vote or hold political office. And, here, Burke is unmistakably clear—and in ways that are completely in keeping with his antidemocratic response to the French Revolution and his overall conservative understanding of the civilizing process. Burke agrees wholeheartedly with Langrishe that the only Catholics who should be allowed to vote or hold any kind of office are "persons of consideration, property, and character: and firmly attached to the king and constitution." But he goes much further, declaring, "As to the low, thoughtless, wild and profligate, who have joined themselves with those of other professions, but of the same character; you are not to imagine, that, for a moment, I can suppose them to be met, with any thing else than the manly and enlightened energy of a firm government, supported by the united efforts of all virtuous men, if ever their proceedings should become so considerable as to demand its notice.

I really think that such associations should be crushed in their very commencement."[85]

It is vitally important to be clear on what Burke is saying here, because it runs directly counter to the way he is depicted by an ever-increasing array of contemporary scholars. Burke insists that any attempt to agitate for the extension of the suffrage or a share of political power by citizens without sizable amounts of property, through social mobilization, for example, should be "crushed" in the cradle by the state. However, Burke tells Langrishe that just because these "wicked men" from the Catholic lower orders engage in such "seditious courses" as agitating for full citizenship rights and the vote does not mean that their "rational, sober, and valuable" countrymen from the Catholic aristocracy "should not be indulged in their sober and rational expectations." He warns Langrishe, ominously, of the alternative: If "better people" from the Catholic aristocracy are prevented from reaping some benefits from the constitution as it stands, a far worse outcome could ensue: namely, "the absurd persons" from the Catholic lower orders might go about "overturning this happy constitution" and "introducing a frantic democracy." In other words, Burke's concern was not for the Catholics en masse, any more than it was for all Indians (or all Frenchmen), but rather for the aristocracy in all these locales, whom he defends as standing at the apex of a reified social hierarchy. Thus, Burke's solution to ameliorating the plight of the Irish Catholics was to "raise an aristocratic interest; that is, an interest of property and education amongst them: and to strengthen by every prudent means, the authority and influence of men of that description."[86] In this respect, Burke's position on Ireland is no less conservative than his concern for the plight of the Indian aristocracy under Hastings's rule, or the plight of the French aristocracy during the Revolution.

Nor is Burke's circumscription of the political privileges of the franchise and political-office-holding to the Catholic elite, or "natural aristocracy," as a means of avoiding a "frantic democracy" in Ireland an isolated sentiment. A few short pages later, he tells Langrishe and, by extension the public, concerning the Irish:

> You separate very properly the sober, rational, and substantial part of their description from the rest. You give, as you ought to do, weight only to the former. What I have always thought of the matter is this—that the most poor, illiterate, and uninformed creatures upon the earth, are judges of a *practical* oppression. It is a matter of feeling; and as such persons generally have felt most of it, and are not of an over-lively sensibility, they are the best judges

of it. But for the *real cause,* or the *appropriate remedy,* they ought never to be called into council about the one or the other. They ought to be totally shut out; because their reason is weak; because when once roused, their passions are ungoverned; because they want information; because the smallness of the property which individually they possess, renders them less attentive to the consequence of the measures they adopt in affairs of the moment.[87]

Such passages have proven all too easy to ignore by many Burke scholars, but they are not particularly difficult to interpret. Burke's claim is straightforwardly that the "poor, illiterate, and uninformed" ought to be "totally shut out" from any real political power, including the vote, because of their weak reason, proneness to passion, and lack of property. Such sentiments are fully in accord with an interpretation of Burke as the defender of a consistently conservative ideological position underpinned by a particular understanding of the civilizing process. And it would be this hierarchical world that Burke fought so hard to defend and reform in Ireland, as well as everywhere else his vision turned, that he feared was ending apocalyptically with the coming of the French Revolution. For Burke, the Revolution would threaten the very existence of the British Empire and Western civilization itself. This is especially clear when we consider Burke's conservative logic of empire as applied to Ireland against the contextual backdrop of the French Revolution in the 1790s.

BURKE'S NIGHTMARE; OR, HOW THE PROTESTANT ASCENDANCY'S FAILURE OF ORNAMENTALIST IMAGINATION LOST IRISH CIVILIZATION

Burke versus the United Irishmen

In the 1790s, France's revolutionary armies were overrunning Europe and, from 1793 until Burke's death in 1797, Britain and France were at war. Burke feared, as many did at the time, that France would invade Ireland. These fears were not idle. In 1796 the French under General Lazare Hoche assembled a large armada with exactly this aim. This force attempted to land at Bantry Bay in County Cork but was forced to turn back owing to bad weather. Accompanying the French invasion force as one of the chief military aides to General Hoche was the well known revolutionary leader of the United Irishmen, Theobald Wolfe Tone.

Wolf Tone, himself nominally affiliated with the Church of Ireland and thus a Protestant (as were all of the United Irishmen's founders), had helped establish the group in 1791. Initially, its official aims were to transcend religious differences between Protestants and Catholics with the goal of ending the penal laws and, crucially, of achieving universal manhood suffrage. The former goal was largely achieved by 1793, but the latter—which would necessarily empower those Wolfe Tone called the "men of no property"—was a political dead letter in both Dublin and London. As events unfolded, however, it became clear that even such an unprecedented level of parliamentary reform would have proved insufficient to satisfy the United Irishmen, who eventually decided to stop short of nothing less than Irish independence from England.[88]

The United Irishmen's guiding theoretical light was Burke's archenemy, Thomas Paine, the man whose writings had sparked American independence and who defended the French Revolution in the wake of Burke's attack on it. Paine was made an honorary member of the group, his ideas infused their statement of principles and subsequent pamphlets, and they distributed large numbers of the *Rights of Man,* Paine's impassioned reply to Burke's *Reflections,* free of charge. Speaking about the fierce debate unleashed by the clash between Burke and Paine over the French Revolution, Wolfe Tone himself remarked, "This controversy and the gigantic event which gave rise to it, changed in an instant the politics of Ireland.... In a little time the French revolution became the test of every man's political creed and the nation was fairly divided into two great parties, the aristocrats and the democrats (epithets borrowed from France)."[89] With Wolfe Tone at the helm, and with the example of the French Revolution and Citizen Paine before them, the United Irishmen chose the side of democracy and, in doing so, also emerged as Ireland's first nationalist movement. Ultimately, in 1798, they would engage in armed rebellion against England with the aid of the French, whose military assistance for an invasion of Ireland Paine himself had urged while he was in France.[90] The goal of this uprising was to achieve complete independence from the British Empire and create a democratic republic in Ireland based on universal manhood suffrage and the rights of man, the principles at the heart of the French Revolution as they understood it.

Burke's relation to the United Irishmen would seem unproblematic. Like them, he sought to repeal the penal laws, although for very different reasons: For Burke, dismantling the popery laws was a way to ensure Catholic loyalty to the empire, whereas for the United Irishmen and Wolf Tone it was the first salvo in the battle for democracy and independence. However, on all of the other crucial issues, Burke was diametrically opposed to the group, even if, for a brief moment, on the question of Catholic relief politics had, indeed, made for the strangest of bedfellows. As we have already seen, Burke despised the notion of radical parliamentary reform and found the push toward universal manhood suffrage a shocking and disturbing turn of events in Ireland that went well beyond allowing a Catholic "natural aristocracy" a degree of political power. And the only position Burke found as troubling as the United Irishmen's commitment to democracy was their commitment to independence, a threat that took on added intensity in the ferment of the 1790s. Finally, that the United Irishmen took Paine as their theoretical inspiration—Burke's nemesis and a man whom he excoriated in *An Appeal from the New to the Old Whigs* as a drunkard and degenerate who should be hung from a lamppost for his views—-simply added insult to injury.

Unfortunately, however, these facts have not prevented contemporary scholars from developing a range of implausible alternative descriptions of Burke's views on the United Irishmen that unnecessarily muddy the waters concerning his approach to his homeland. Rather than confronting Burke's own claims to intellectual consistency and his commitments to empire in Ireland, and trying to reckon Burke's antipathy to the United Irishmen from that standpoint, these interpreters have instead read their own commitments into those of their intellectual hero in a misleading fashion.[91]

The sum of such views is that Burke was supposedly a thinker deeply divided against himself. That is to say, he was in his heart of hearts an Irish nationalist opposed to empire who secretly wished he were Theobald Wolfe Tone, and was effectively complicit with the United Irishmen's political project of universal manhood suffrage and independence, the position to which his theoretical views are said to logically lead. He never managed to say any of this anywhere in the vast corpus of his published work or private correspondence, but that doesn't mean it wasn't true. This view of Burke as a closet Irish nationalist is meant to be convincing notwithstanding the fact that the United Irishmen's program was built almost entirely on the ideas of Burke's greatest adversary, Thomas Paine, whose own views and actions in fact helped lead the United Irishmen to join forces with the French revolutionaries in an attempt to invade Ireland and decouple it from the British Empire. Apparently this does not matter, however, because Burke's most widely recognized contribution to the history of ideas, the *Reflections on the Revolution in France,* was itself really the greatest inconsistency of his intellectual life. But, surely, once we have reached this point, matters have come to a strange interpretive pass, indeed.[92]

The problem with all of these claims is not simply that they ignore the wide range of textual and contextual evidence that creates an unbridgeable gulf between Burke and the United Irishmen, but also that they simply ignore Burke's own stated reason for opposing the group: during the 1790s, in the aftermath of Irish "legislative independence" in the previous decade, Burke simply blamed Catholic persecution in its entirety on the Protestant Ascendancy and the narrow "Junto" faction of Protestant Irish political operatives that he saw as controlling the English executive at Dublin Castle. Conversely, he placed *none of the blame* for Ireland's problems on England. In other words, on Burke's account, after 1782 there was no reason to blame England for any oppression of the Catholics whatsoever; hence, he saw incipient Irish nationalism with its push for independence as a wholly inapt response to the nonexistent problem of English imperial domination and control of Irish affairs.

If one were given to psychoanalytic interpretations, or the parlor game of filling in the substance of a given thinker's argument in the absence of evidence, the reasons for this particular bit of psychological self-deception—which works on the extraordinary assumption that England had no influence on what happened in Ireland—would be a ripe field for speculation. However, here I simply wish to establish that this was, in fact, Burke's stated position, one that he repeated time and again in the last decade of his life. It was a view that essentially placed the entire blame for Ireland's woes on a portion of the Protestant Ascendancy that he treated as if it had no connection to, and was in fact beyond the reach of, political power in the imperial metropole of London.[93]

For example, in a letter to his son, Richard, who was employed by the Catholic Committee in the early 1790s, Burke argued that since "Independency" (i.e., 1782), when it came to Ireland the "government" was "almost wholly in their own [Irish] hands." No one in England seriously wanted to "keep down the Catholics, in order to keep the whole Mass of Ireland feeble"; rather, all the English wanted from the Irish was silence, and if that was not forthcoming it was entirely the fault of the "Junto of Jobbers" within the Ascendancy that ran the country, all on their own. Speaking of their associates on the Catholic Committee, Burke told his son: "Our friends are greatly, radically, and, to themselves, most dangerously, mistaken if they do not know, that the whole of what they suffer is from Cabals purely Irish."[94]

Burke made this case in even more striking terms to his Irish Catholic correspondents, like the Reverend Thomas Hussey. In one letter to Hussey,

Burke castigated the United Irishmen directly for mistakenly blaming the plight of the Irish on the English. After 1782, Burke found that sort of claim absurd:

> It is a foolish Language adopted from the united Irishmen, that their Grievances originate from England. The direct contrary. It is an ascendancy, which some of their own factions have obtained here; that has hurt the Catholics with this Government.... For, in the name of God, what Grievance has Ireland, as Ireland, to complain of with regard to Great Britain? Unless the protection of the most powerful Country upon Earth, giving all her privileges without exception in common to Ireland, and reserving to her self only the painful preeminence of tenfold Burdens be a matter of complaint.

Burke thus rejects the notion that the Irish, qua Irish, or as "Member[s] of the Empire," have any complaint about their colonial status during the 1790s. The "Catholics as Catholics" had grievances, but these were entirely the result of the Irish Protestant Ascendancy's own policies and had nothing to do with England.[95] According to Burke, empire in Ireland was instead an asymmetrical bargain in which the Irish received all the benefits of security and special privileges and the British suffered all of the imperial burdens. If it was a raw deal, it was a raw deal for the English, on Burke's account, not the Irish.

In a later letter to Hussey, Burke repeated this argument, directly indicting the United Irishmen for what he saw as their faulty premise: that England was ultimately to blame for Ireland's plight. Burke tells Hussey that "all the evils of Ireland originate within itself. That unwise body, the United Irishmen, have had the folly to represent those Evils as owing to this Country [England]," when in reality the most London could be accused of was "total neglect" of Ireland. The English had "farmed out" Irish affairs "to the little Faction that Domineers there...; nor do they any way interfere that I know of, except in giving their countenance and the sanction of their Names to whatever is done by that *Junto.*"[96] Bizarrely, Burke thus seemed to have believed that by sanctioning what the Protestant Ascendancy did in Ireland, England was actually demonstrating its *lack* of power over and concern for what happened there, rather than the contrary. This strange understanding of the relationship between the colonizer and the colonized, which in Ireland effectively denied that there was anything like a general "suffering under the Yoke of a British Dominion" worthy of a unified fight for independence that transcended religious differences, is surely one of the most compelling demonstrations of Burke's fidelity to the British Empire. It also speaks to his blindness (willful or otherwise) when it came to England's role in ultimately creating and countenancing Irish suffering, if not his remarkable capacity for self-deception.[97]

The Protestant Ascendancy's Failure of Ornamentalist Imagination: Missing the Rise of Jacobinism and the Threat to Irish Civilization

The problem for Burke was thus not that England was oppressing Ireland, which he categorically denied to be a feature of the imperial relationship between the two countries after 1782, but rather that a faction within the Irish Protestant Ascendancy acting wholly on its own was pushing a wide body of Irish people into the waiting arms of the French revolutionaries. For Burke, to paraphrase Yeats, Ireland was slouching towards the rough beast whose hour had come round at last in Paris. In this sense, Burke's great fear was that the Ascendancy's misbegotten policies, which failed to recognize Ireland's Catholics and Dissenters as coeval components of a shared Irish civilization, would lead these groups to embrace "Jacobinism," the sum of all evil in Burke's lexicon. In short, the Protestant Ascendancy suffered from a failure of Ornamentalist imagination, and saw the Other where they should have seen a similar civilized people and a natural ally.

Burke's views on Ireland in the last decade of his life centered on the concept of Jacobinism, as he defined it, and its dangers. Interestingly, Burke's most extended attempt to define Jacobinism as a general phenomenon occurs not in a discussion of France but rather of Ireland, in the course of a 1795 letter to an Irish MP, William Smith. This gives us some sense of how entwined the related problems of France and Ireland, and thus of revolution and empire, were for Burke, and how he attempted to provide a theoretically consistent response to both phenomena from his standpoint as a conservative who viewed history as a civilizing process driven by the church and nobility. In a passage worth quoting at some length, owing to its importance to both Burke himself and the argument put forth here, Burke asks rhetorically:

> What is Jacobinism? It is an attempt (hitherto but too successful) to eradicate prejudice out of the minds of men, for the purposes of putting all power and authority into the hands of the persons capable of occasionally enlightening the minds of the people. For this purpose the Jacobins have resolved to destroy the whole frame and fabric of the old Societies of the world, and to regenerate them after their fashion: To obtain an army for this purpose, they

every where engage the poor by holding out to them as a bribe, the spoils of the Rich. This I take to be a fair description of the principles and leading maxims of the enlightened of our day, who are commonly called Jacobins. As the grand prejudice, and that which holds all the other prejudices together, the first, last, and middle Object of their Hostility, is Religion. With that they are at inexpiable war. They make no distinction of Sects. A Christian as such, is to them an Enemy. What then is left to a real Christian, (Christian as a believer and as a Statesman) but to make a league between all the grand divisions of that name, to protect and to cherish them all; and by no means to proscribe in any manner, more or less, any member of our common party. The divisions which formerly prevailed in the Church, with all their overdone Zeal, only purified and ventilated, our common faith; because there was no common Enemy arrayed and embattled to take advantage of their dissensions: But now nothing but inevitable ruin will be the consequence of our Quarrels.[98]

Jacobinism for Burke was thus foremost a brand of revolutionary secularism whose principal target was organized Christianity, understood as the single most important institution driving the Western civilizing process. Christianity was the institution that naturalized and sanctified the deep hierarchical inequalities, social practices, and received beliefs (or prejudices) that Burke was so concerned to defend. To achieve the destruction of organized religion the Jacobins engaged in a form of duplicitous class warfare, on Burke's account, by bribing the poor with the promise of property redistribution from the landed aristocratic few to the many. Let us examine how this argument played out specifically in Burke's later writings on Ireland.

Burke tells Smith that religion is "the most effectual Barrier, if not the sole Barrier, against Jacobinism," and this is especially important in the case of the Irish Catholics, because "the Catholics form the great body of the lower Ranks" in Ireland, and "no small part of those Classes of the middling that come nearest to them." And, Burke warns the Irish MP, "the seduction of that part of mankind from the principles of religion, morality, subordination, and social order, is the great Object of the Jacobins." Burke points out that two centuries' worth of religious experiments had been tried in an effort to talk the Irish people out of their overwhelming commitment to Catholicism, and had failed. That made the options clear-cut: "You have now your choice for full four fifths of your people, the Catholic religion or Jacobinism."[99]

Given this state of affairs, Burke stood absolutely flabbergasted at what he understood as the Protestant Ascendancy's unrelenting war on the wrong enemy, its fellow Christians, rather than on the "grand Evil of our time,"[100] revolutionary secularism:

> I imagined that at this time no one was weak enough to believe, or impudent enough to pretend, that questions of Popish and Protestant opinions or interest are the things by which men are at present menaced with crusades by foreign invasion, or with seditions which shake the foundations of the State at home.... On the contrary, all these Churches are menaced, and menaced alike. It is the new fanatical Religion, now in the heat of its first ferment, of the Rights of Man, which rejects all Establishments, all discipline, all Ecclesiastical, and in truth all Civil order, which will triumph, and which will lay prostrate your Church; which will destroy your distinctions, and which will put all your properties to auction, and disperse you over the Earth. If the present Establishment should fall, it is this Religion which will triumph in Ireland and in England, as it has triumphed in France. This Religion, which laughs at creeds and dogmas and confessions of faith, may be fomented equally among all descriptions, and all sects.... Against this new, this growing, this exterminatory system, all these Churches have a common concern to defend themselves. How the enthusiasts of this rising sect rejoice to see you of the old Churches play their game, and stir and rake the cinders of animosities sunk in their ashes, in order to keep up the execution of their plan for your common ruin![101]

On Burke's reading, the Protestant Ascendancy thus went on ignorantly fighting the old wars of religion occasioned by the Reformation, while the new leveling secular enthusiasm of revolutionary atheism threatened the obliteration of Western civilization, in Ireland as elsewhere. For Burke, the Protestant Ascendancy stubbornly refused to extend civilizational solidarity to Irish Catholics, thereby driving them into the waiting arms of the fanatical Jacobins. As has been recently argued, on Burke's reading the Ascendancy's version of Protestantism had become "so emptied of positive content that the doctrinal core necessary to motivate a pan-Christian defensive action against atheism" was effectively "reduced to nothing." This wholly negative form of Protestant religious belief produced an "indifference" that made the Ascendancy insensate to "the threat of a permanent enthusiasm" posed by the secular atheism of the French Revolution, a form of enthusiasm that would dwarf the dangers posed by earlier religious manifestations of the phenomenon.[102]

Such a view helps us better understand Burke's feverish arguments relative to Catholic relief and limited Catholic enfranchisement in the 1790s. As some interpreters have noted, Burke's goal in vigorously pressing for these policies in the face of the French Revolution was to eliminate remaining legal oppression against the Catholics, as well as enfranchising their aristocratic elites, precisely to remove grievances that could be exploited by the Jacobins to rally the Catholics to their cause. It was for this latter reason that Burke warned the secretary at war, William Windham, that what was done in Ireland "vitally affects the whole System of Europe, whether you regard it offensively or defensively. Ireland is known in France; Communications have been opened and more will be opened. Ireland will be a strong Dyke to keep out Jacobinism; or a broken bank to let it in."[103] Burke strongly warned William Smith of the grave danger of continuing to treat Irish Catholics "as no better than half Citizens." In such a case, Burke insisted, "they will be made whole Jacobins. Against this Grand and dreadful Evil of our time (I do not love to cheat myself or others) I do not know any solid Security whatsoever. But I am quite certain, that what will come nearest to it, is to interest as many as you can in the present order of things, religiously, civilly, politically—by all the ties and principles by which mankind are held."[104]

Because Burke understood Jacobinism as the principal danger to empire and civilization in Ireland posed by the threat of revolution, in his last years he vented his spleen again and again at the failure of Ornamentalist imagination exhibited by the Protestant rulers in Ireland. He saw the Protestant Ascendancy as ridiculously conducting a crusade against "Papists" and, all the while, driving them into an unholy alliance with the secular, atheistic Jacobins. While the Revolutionaries, in "a full Cry of The Dogs of War," were busy hunting down the pontiff himself, Burke sneered that only in Ireland was the pope still "terrible to somebody. I am glad to know that your minds are in every other respect so much at Ease in Ireland, that you can entertain yourselves with this Species of apprehension."[105] "Poor souls they are to be pitied," he observed, "who think of nothing but dangers long past by; and but little of the perils that actually surrounded them." Burke feared that it would take an invasion of Ireland by those nominal Protestants Napoleon and General Hoche to shake the Ascendancy out of its sectarian religious hatred and make it realize that the old paradigm of animosities no longer held in the brave new world ushered in by the French Revolution. But, by then, of course, it would be too late.[106] So it was, Burke wrote sarcastically, that "the little wise men of the West, with every hazard of this Evil, are resolved to persevere" in their absurd aim of a "Western Crusade against Popery."[107]

Burke was perplexed and infuriated by the Protestant Ascendancy's failure of Ornamentalist imagination: rather than seeing the Catholics and

Dissenters as broad coreligionists in a shared civilization, and potential allies in a war against Revolutionary atheism and secularism, the Ascendancy in Ireland was acting in the opposite fashion. By its unrelenting discrimination against the Irish Catholics, the Ascendancy was threatening to destroy the imperial connection between Britain and Ireland and to open the door to the catastrophic spread of revolutionary principles, culminating in the end of Western civilization itself. Nearing death, Burke increasingly came to worry about a broad-based alliance of Protestant *and* Catholic lower orders in Ireland jointly clamoring for French egalitarianism. In this vein, he warned Henry Grattan about "the mutinous Spirit which is in the very constitution of the lower part of our compatriots of every description, and now begins to ferment with tenfold force by the leaven of republicanism."[108]

In 1794, when his close political ally Fitzwilliam was briefly appointed lord lieutenant of Ireland, Burke had held out hope that the Ascendancy could be stopped from exacerbating this alliance by changing its policies. But Fitzwilliam alienated the Ascendancy by his push for further reform on behalf of the Catholics and was recalled by Pitt, leading Burke to bemoan the failure "in Ireland to stop the lamentable Flux of blood, under which the Empire is expiring."[109]

At his most insightful (and despite blaming it all on the Ascendancy), Burke seemed to recognize that Ireland was in fact ripe for rebellion, and not just from the Catholic lower orders but from the dissenting Protestant middling and lower classes as well, groups who had also had their fill of Ireland's massive socioeconomic inequality. The popery laws, after all, had also affected the Dissenters, and the Presbyterians in particular, albeit to a more limited extent than the Catholics.[110] In addition, Presbyterianism was institutionally democratic in important ways, a fact that made it more amenable to radical politics.[111]

In his most honest moments, Burke seemed to recognize that popular discontent among the poor ran deep among the Irish, whether Catholic or Protestant. He understood that poverty and political exclusion had the power to unify the lower orders in ways that transcended religious differences, leading them to rebel not just against the Ascendancy but also against those whom they saw as its puppet masters in London, and thus to challenge the very existence of the British Empire in Ireland. At the end of the eighteenth century, as Burke saw with gathering dread, the Protestants and Catholics were unifying. The United Irishmen were a "strong Republican, Protestant Faction in Ireland" headed by Wolfe Tone, who led a group of like-minded men that Burke unhesitatingly called "Conspirators and Traitors."[112] Thus it seemed to him that the Protestants outside the Ascendancy were rapidly becoming as much of a lost cause as the Catholic majority: "The government is losing the hearts of the people, if it has not quite lost them. . . . I know very well that when they disarm a whole province, they think that all is well; but to take away arms, is not to destroy disaffection. It has cast deep roots in the principles and habits of the majority amongst the lower and middle classes of the whole Protestant part of Ireland."[113]

Burke's awareness of the growing alliance between Catholics and Protestants is abundantly evident in a letter he wrote to Fitzwilliam after the latter had been recalled as lord lieutenant. In it, Burke concurred with Grattan's overall negative assessment of the situation in Ireland, even if he disagreed about who was ultimately to blame for it:

> It is plainly in Ireland little less than a war declared between property and no property—between the high and the Low, the rich and the poor, brought on, partly by the Circumstances of the Country; but, I may say, much more by the fault of Government [the Ascendancy], which has fomented the Evil, and widened the Breach between the parties. The nature of this War, now being made between Wealth and want, renders it almost above human Wisdom, to tell what Course ought to be taken. As long as Government Stands, and sides with that property (which it must do or it will not long be Government) it must be victorious; being possessed of all the Revenues and all the forces of the State. *The other party can do nothing at all but aggravate the Tyranny by provoking it, unless by the aid of a foreign Jacobin force and in that Case their Victory would be the utter subversion of human Society itself, of all religion, all Law, all order, all humanity, as well as of all property.*[114]

As the italicized portion of this revealing passage indicates, Burke realized that the only way the "poor," or those with "no property," could win the war they were engaged in was with the assistance of the Jacobins. However, it was precisely due to his deeply consistent conservative defense of empire and the view of civilization it was built upon that Burke could not accept this solution. Obviously, it meant Irish independence and the end of the British Empire in Ireland, which he had fought to preserve there just as much as in the New World and India. But the spread of Jacobinism to Ireland also meant the obliteration of the ancien régime in his homeland, rather than its reform. Instead of opening up the Protestant Ascendancy to the rightful claims of the Catholic Church and Catholic aristocracy, a rebellion inspired by the French Revolution would have dreadful consequences: It would secularize the society, throw open Irish political institutions to the unfit masses, and, by instituting universal manhood suffrage, destroy any hope of re-creating the natural aristocracy. The resulting democracy would, in turn, upend all hierarchy and social order and raze all existing prescriptive property relationships. Burke considered such transformations tantamount to "the utter subversion of human Society itself," as much in Ireland as in France.[115]

Burke therefore spent his last days warning that the various forms of economic, legal, social, and cultural leveling promised by an alliance between the French revolutionaries and Irish radicals would be inevitably accompanied by a "wild democratic representation" in the public sphere of high politics.[116] He warned of the spread of this democratic revolution from France to Ireland, and thence from Ireland to England. He speculated that this might simply be the result of his onetime political ally Charles James Fox—the "new Whig" with whom he had broken irrevocably over the French Revolution—becoming prime minister. Burke maintained that if this happened Fox would sign a truce with the French in order "to make the influence of what He calls the People *every thing*, and that of the Crown—*Nothing*, which I conceive to be the definition of a complete Democracy, or I do not know what a Democracy is. It is for this end, he proposes that kind of Peace which he recommends and is one of the chief advantages which he expects and very rationally expects at some period or other from such an arrangement."[117]

However, Burke believed that, even if Fox did not take power, the spread of French democratic principles from Ireland to England was inevitable if such principles should ever take root firmly in the soil of his homeland. He expressed his fear that there would be nothing short of a "Revolution" in Ireland with the aim of just such a radical democratic "alteration in the constitution of Parliament," under the guidance of French leveling maxims. If this came to pass, Burke declared, "It would be impossible long to resist an alteration of the same kind on this [English] side of the Water; and I never doubted, since I have come to the Years of discretion, nor ever can doubt, that such changes in this Kingdom would be preliminary steps to our utter ruin: But if I considered them as such, at all times, what must they appear to me at a moment like the present."[118] At the end of his life, then, Burke's greatest fear was the promise of a democratic revolution overtaking Ireland, and he declared it impossible to look upon such events as were occurring without being "shocked with the monstrous wickedness of the Jacobin Agitators in

Ireland, and not to be frightened at the regularity, the order, and the combined movement of which so many persons, low and illiterate in appearance, are capable."[119]

BURKE AND THE ORNAMENTALIST UNION FOR EMPIRE

In 1798, the year after Edmund Burke's death, there was a major rebellion against British rule in Ireland. It was led by the United Irishmen based on their understanding of the principles of Thomas Paine and the French Revolution, and its goal was to win complete Irish independence from England. At least in this respect, Burke's death was a timely one, since witnessing an Irish rebellion against the British Empire would surely have been one of the saddest moments of his entire life. In 1795, he had contemplated early moves in that direction thusly:

> The Language of the day went plainly to a separation of the two Kingdoms. God forbid, that anything like it should ever happen. They would be both ruined by it; But Ireland would suffer most and first ... *she*, most assuredly, never would obtain that independent glory, but would certainly lose all her Tranquility, all her prosperity, and even that large degree of Lustre which she has by the very free and very honorable connection she enjoys with a Nation the most splendid and the most powerful upon Earth. Ireland *constitutionally* is independent—*Politically* she never can be so. It is a struggle against Nature.[120]

Such a position reifies Ireland's colonial dependence upon England. Indeed, Burke's views on all acts of rebellion in Irish history depict them consistently as crimes against nature, even if provoked. For example, in discussing the uprising of 1641, Burke mentions "the enormity of this unnatural rebellion, in favor of the independence of Ireland."[121] In the face of imperialism's injustices, Burke counseled the Irish lower and middling orders to instead exhibit "a still discontented passive obedience."[122] True, Burke did seek to increase the aristocratic representation of Irish society nominally responsible for governing his homeland in the wake of "legislative independence" by including elite Catholics within it, and he did oppose the harsh popery laws. Nevertheless, in the end, Burke suggested, the best that the vast majority of Irish people could do was to satisfy themselves with humble expressions of unhappiness. He believed that such supplicating remonstrances should aim at the incremental transformation of an empire, an antidemocratic polity, a sharply stratified economic world, and a Christian culture that Burke could not imagine otherwise without casting it as the end of civilization and human society. If, however, Paineite groups like the United Irishmen dared to go beyond such measures, Burke declared, he would fully endorse all "Measures of Rigor and Coercion used to repress and punish the Excesses of an impatient disorderly or misguided multitude."[123]

Of course, just such measures were ultimately taken in the name of preserving the British Empire. French help arrived too late to save the United Irishmen, and the rebellion of 1798 was ruthlessly put down. Subsequently, in 1800, the English government demonstrated the true principles of its empire, and the true balance of power between Britain and Ireland: It dispensed entirely with the pretense of Irish legislative "independence" achieved in 1782, which Burke had clung to so desperately in the 1790s as a means of absolving England for the troubles in Ireland and blaming them all on a small portion of the Protestant Ascendancy in his homeland. With the Act of Union, England legally subsumed its fractious neighbor within the new "United Kingdom of Great Britain and Ireland." Further Catholic emancipation was denied, and the empire was preserved. The dream of an independent, nonsectarian (let alone secular), democratic Ireland had died—not with Edmund Burke in 1797 but rather with Theobald Wolfe Tone, who committed suicide in prison after his capture aboard a French warship in 1798.[124] Of course, Ireland's troubles, far from ending with the union, began a new phase that would last for two centuries and, in some ways, still continues.

Hence we come to the final query concerning Edmund Burke's conservative logic of empire as applied to Ireland. That question is not whether Burke supported the idea of Irish independence but whether he would have supported the Act of Union. The possibility of a formal legal incorporation of Ireland into Britain was one that Burke touched upon at a number of points in his career,[125] but never answered definitively, since it was not an immediate, concrete problem confronting him. The closest he came to taking a position on the matter was in a 1794 letter to Fitzwilliam, in which he stated that he "always looked upon an Union" as "a bold experimental remedy, justified, perhaps called for, in some nearly desperate Crisis of the whole Empire."[126] Would 1798 have constituted such a crisis for Burke? While we do not have a definitive answer to that question, R. B. McDowell is surely right in claiming "that Burke would have exerted all his powers in support of any policy" that would "preserve and tighten all the links between Great Britain and

Ireland" and aid in the "maintenance of the Empire."[127] Other scholars have likewise noted that union was the logical culmination of Burke's position.[128] We are now in a position to fully understand why this would be the case: for Burke, Ireland—rightly understood and appropriately reformed—was imperial England's closest civilizational relative. Thus Burke's position on a potential union between Ireland and England was built on his Ornamentalist understanding of the relationship between his native and adopted homelands, one that reveals for a final time his consistent commitment to preserving the British Empire and to doing so on the basis of deeply held conservative principles concerning civilization and the civilizing process.

Conclusion

ORNAMENTALISM, ORIENTALISM, AND THE LEGACY OF BURKE'S CONSERVATIVE LOGIC OF EMPIRE

The British exported and projected vernacular sociological visions from the metropolis to the periphery, and they imported and analogized them from the empire back to Britain, thereby constructing comforting and familiar resemblances and equivalencies and affinities. The result was, indeed, "one vast interconnected world"; and the phrase that best describes this remarkable transoceanic construct of substance and sentiment is *imperialism as ornamentalism*. . . . The British created their imperial society, bound it together, comprehended it and imagined it from the middle of the nineteenth century to the middle of the twentieth in an essentially ornamental mode. For ornamentalism was hierarchy made visible, immanent and actual. And since the British conceived and understood their metropolis hierarchically, it was scarcely surprising that they conceived and understood their periphery in the same way. . . . As such, hierarchy was the conventional vehicle of organization and perception in both the metropole and the periphery: it provided the prevailing ideology of empire, and it underpinned the prevailing spectacle of empire. Thus envisaged, the British Empire was, like the British nation and the British people, a quintessentially Burkeian enterprise.

DAVID CANNADINE, *Ornamentalism: How the British Saw Their Empire*

EDMUND BURKE DEVELOPED A THEORETICAL defense of the British imperial project wholly outside the theoretical parameters and assumptions of liberalism. Indeed, Burke adhered to a view of history as a civilizing process that stressed the fundamental importance of the landed aristocracy and organized religion for human progress and development. Conversely, he rejected as philosophically absurd and politically disastrous basic liberal notions such as natural human equality and declarations of universal individual rights, and he consistently lampooned any notion of political and social equality between the sexes or between the higher and lower orders. Similarly, Burke despised any notion of democracy and even argued for the diminution of the franchise in England, so that the aristocracy could more effectively do their job of ruling the country and "virtually" representing those who were, to his mind, appropriately locked out of "actual" representation or any active role in politics.

In this book, I have argued that Burke relied on this conservative understanding of civilization and the civilizing process as the basis for providing specific policy prescriptions for the various sites of the eighteenth-century British Empire. Specifically, drawing on terms associated with the work of both David Cannadine and Edward Said, respectively, I have argued that Burke alternately defended empire on the basis of Ornamentalism, when he sought to stress sociological similarities between the imperial core and its periphery, and Orientalism when he aimed to emphasize radical differences between them. Here, I wish to draw out some of the broader implications of this analysis.

One important point to emerge from a careful engagement with Burke's arguments concerning empire is that the contemporary scholarly focus on the theoretical relationship between liberalism and empire has prevented interpreters from seeing the full range of ways that modern empires have been conceptualized, justified, and defended. My argument is not that Burke developed *the* (only) conservative logic of empire. Rather, the aim has been to show that he did develop one such illiberal defense of the British imperial project in the New World, India, and Ireland, and did so along lines that were intellectually coherent and deeply consistent with his critique of the French Revolution. However, to the extent that Cannadine's influential revisionist argument (highlighted in the epigraph) is accurate, a conservative logic of empire would subsequently prove crucial to British imperialism in its heyday, in the years after the Indian Mutiny down to postwar decolonization (1857–1953).

Cannadine has argued that throughout the nineteenth and well into the twentieth century, Britain was only superficially a liberal society. Rather, it was "deeply conservative in its social attitude and in its political culture. The social structure was generally believed to be layered, individualistic, traditional, hierarchical and providentially sanctioned.... It was in practice a nation emphatically *not* dedicated to the proposition that all men (let alone women) were created equal."[1] In short, since conservative assumptions pervaded the British self-understanding throughout this period, it was natural for the architects of Britain's empire to envisage the world they were to govern "in traditional, Burkeian terms."[2] Imperialism as Ornamentalism was thus the process of theoretically assimilating the unknown and potentially alien world of the colonial periphery into the conservative, hierarchical social world that prevailed at the imperial core, and ruling on the basis of that conception. "Understood in this way, as a conservative, traditional, ordered phenomenon, the British Empire was not exclusively about race or color, but was also about class and status." What this entailed as a practical matter of imperial governance was the identification and cooptation of collaborators from indigenous social hierarchies—at least as the British understood them—in order to run the empire.[3] In this fashion, the British Empire was often predicated on the theoretical act of Saming those people in its dependencies in order to rule the periphery more effectively. As we have seen throughout this book, this Ornamentalist strategy began with Edmund Burke, as is evident in his arguments about colonial America, Ireland, and— especially—India. Thus, Burke's arguments prefigure one of the dominant imperial strategies utilized by the architects of British imperialism from the mid-nineteenth to the mid-twentieth century.

As I have shown, Burke read India in profoundly Ornamentalist terms, as another Europe—that is, as a "civilization" possessed of organized religions and landed aristocracies. For Burke, India was a highly stratified world of social ranks exemplified by the Hindu caste system that he lauded. Thus, after the necessary act of willful imperial amnesia in which he overlooked Clive's conquest of Bengal and the devastating famine it helped unleash on the Indian people, Burke hoped that the British Empire would be conducted on the model of the Mughal Empire it had replaced. That is, he sought to preserve the capacities for material extraction established by the Mughals, while leaving intact ancient Indian civilization as he depicted it. Ultimately, this is why Burke railed against Hastings and "Indianism"—for assaulting Indian civilization from outside and above, especially by attacking its landed aristocracy and caste system, thereby threatening the hierarchical Indian Old Regime. In this respect, my argument is similar to that of Thomas Metcalf, who sees Burke as a central figure in the articulation of one strand of imperial justification used by the British from the mid-eighteenth to the twentieth century—namely, the elaboration of essential characteristics that the Indians shared with themselves. As Metcalf notes, "Such views were of course part of Burke's larger conservative conception of human nature and his veneration of the past. For Burke, as for most Englishmen, private property in land lay at the heart of an enduring social order. Hence, to bring about a justly ruled India, property, above all else, had to be made secure."[4]

However, whereas Metcalf and subsequent scholarship have stressed the eclipse of this theoretical approach of focusing on similarities in India by liberals' various strategies of stressing differences as a means of justifying imperial rule, especially after 1857,[5] Cannadine reminds us of the persistence of a substantively conservative, illiberal argument predicated on drawing hierarchical analogies between Britain and the subcontinent, arguments for which the notion of caste was key. This was Burke's legacy: "It was atop this layered, Burkeian agrarian image of Indian society," Cannadine argues, that the British created a system of rule during the Raj that was by turns direct, indirect, authoritarian, and collaborationist but, in the end, "always took for granted the reinforcement and preservation of tradition and hierarchy." In many ways this image of South Asia as a world of gentry leaders governing a society dominated by caste would prevail until the end of the British Empire in India.[6] P. J. Marshall has found largely convincing the claim that British officials during the hundred-year period after 1857 were committed to the conservative ideals of preserving tradition and hierarchy in India. Indeed, as Marshall notes, historical research has shown this was largely because the agents of the British Empire in India were themselves the carriers of conservative values and ideals.[7]

Of course, nothing about my argument denies the various Orientalist theoretical strategies focused on difference that were pressed in the case of India by James and J. S. Mill, Henry Maine, and other liberals. However, it would likewise be a mistake to ignore the Ornamentalist strand of imperial argument concerning India inaugurated by Burke. Unfortunately, most scholars of empire have done just that; in fact, they have made the more egregious error of assuming that Burke's arguments on India—the original Ornamentalist mode of imperial justification—were somehow anti-imperial or anticolonial, when nothing could be further from the truth.

Furthermore, Cannadine argues that these same "conventional Burkeian wisdoms and customary conservative modes" would guide the British approach to governance as the "scramble for Africa" and other parts of Asia unfolded during the period after 1857. That is, in Africa and elsewhere, Britain's strategy for governing its empire was one of indirect rule through the reliance on native aristocrats perched atop their social hierarchies. In this way, it can be argued, the British understanding of traditional India became the model for the new imperial system of indirect rule, predicated on the cooperation of indigenous elites. The British understood these societies as paternalistic, rural, and hierarchical, with layers and gradations of status, an idealized image of their own homeland that they clung to even as it was being eroded in the metropole.[8] Subsequently, it would arguably also be this view of societies at the empire's periphery—as "traditional, royal, layered, Burkeian organism[s]"— that would guide British imperial policy in the Near and Middle Eastern Mandates set up by the League of Nations after World War I and overseen by such social conservatives as Winston Churchill.[9] On this score, P.J. Marshall contends that Cannadine "proves convincingly for most, if not perhaps for all, of his hundred years," that the British aspired to theoretically remodel the world according to their own hierarchical self-understanding.[10] Isaac Kramnick was correct when he argued, some forty years ago, that "India was a vast stage upon which Burke could parade his conservative defense of tradition and custom."[11] Moreover, Burke's powerful version of Ornamentalism, particularly as applied to India, would long outlive him.

However, as we have also seen in this book, Burke's arguments were not always Ornamentalist. To the contrary, sometimes they were deeply Orientalist in Edward Said's (and Metcalf's) sense of that term: that is, they focused on the theoretical construction of radical difference as a justificatory strategy for imperial domination.[12] This was clearly Burke's approach to the Native Americans and African slaves in the New World. In this sense there is a side of Burke's arguments that looks a good deal more like the arguments of James and J.S. Mill and later defenders of empire as a "civilizing mission" than Burke's hagiographical interpreters have recognized. A number of points need to be made on this score.

First, Burke's version of Orientalism was not a geographically defined one. In fact, he came to locate the Other not in the "Orient," or East, but rather in the West. In fact, his Ornamentalist understanding of India enabled him to reject the tradition of "Oriental despotism," while he clearly saw radical difference in North America and the Caribbean. The second and related point is that, for

Burke, unlike for Said and his followers, the Other was constituted not by race or gender but by the presence or absence of aristocracy and religion, the markers of civilization, on his understanding of the term. Thus Burke could simultaneously defend Indian civilization and urge an expansionary "civilizing" mission against the Native Americans and the continued enslavement of Africans, those groups he depicted as "savages," throughout the period of the American Revolution. The latter groups were understood as lacking the institutional markers that defined civilization, and their continued Orientalist domination and forfeiture of liberty were thus urged by Burke specifically as a means of forging a further Ornamentalist bond of civilizational solidarity between the British and the North American colonists in order to hold the empire together.

Recently, Duncan Bell has perceptively argued that one of the reasons why some theoretical defenses of empire are so frequently missed altogether or misunderstood is because so few interpreters have grappled sufficiently with the phenomenon of "settler colonialism."[13] This is clearly the case with Burke. In fact, the entire enterprise of defining Burke as an "anti-imperial" thinker would prove incapable of getting off the ground if the vast majority of interpreters did not focus exclusively on his writings about India and would turn west to discover his Orientalist defense of settler colonialism against the "savages" in America and the Caribbean. It is also worth remarking that in later phases of the British Empire, it was especially in the large-scale settler colonies of Canada, Australia, New Zealand, and South Africa that the Orientalist strategy of Othering the indigenous populations was most fully pursued, with disastrous and tragic results. Thus, later instantiations of British imperialism would evince the same animus toward difference that Burke expressed toward the Others who confronted settler colonists in America and the Caribbean, even as the bases of demarcating "civilization" changed from social rank and religion to race and gender.

Of course, the one "settler colony" that has been discussed at any length with respect to Burke is Ireland, although it is rarely framed in those terms. In this instance, despite his repeated criticisms of British imperial practice in Ireland, we have seen the extraordinary extent of Burke's commitment to colonization and empire in his homeland, as well as his lifelong hostility to the notion that Ireland should ever become a truly independent nation. Against this backdrop, Burke's arguments regarding Ireland also display other important features of future imperial arguments.

For example, despite the fact that Britain retained control of Ireland after the half measure of "legislative independence" in 1782, Burke nonetheless used this legislation as the occasion for drawing a bright line of distinction between what happened in the kingdom/colony before and after that date. Thus, for Burke, the real "alibi of empire" occurred in Ireland, where he laid all the blame for imperial mismanagement at the feet of the Protestant Ascendancy in his homeland and none of it at the doorstep of England. The result was to conveniently exculpate the British architects of empire in Ireland—including himself—for what occurred there, while railing against Irish independence and floating the notion of union as the solution to Ireland's problems (which of course is what finally happened in 1800). This strategy of blaming the settler colonists and other administrators of empire at the periphery for its failures, rather than the metropole for the scandal of empire itself, would have a very long history, and many would say that it still flourishes in the neo-imperial world of the present.

Burke's arguments relative to Ireland are also informative concerning debates about empire in another way. A number of Enlightenment intellectuals—including Montesquieu, Condorcet, Smith, and Diderot—and a range of contemporary intellectuals have argued for some version of the *doux commerce* thesis, the idea that free trade in goods and ideas serves as the antidote to empire and imperialism. However, this was clearly not Burke's position. In fact, when the British Empire was threatened in Ireland, Burke argued for a policy of Irish free trade specifically as a means of holding it together, just as he had done in the case of the American colonies. Of course, he also argued simultaneously, and vehemently, against a tax on the absentee owners of Irish land (such as himself and his political patron Rockingham) in order to assure the smooth and inexpensive functioning of the global empire in the interest of its elites. In both cases, Burke utilized free trade arguments in the service of empire, not to undermine it.

This last point leads to a still broader question about how Burke's arguments relate to the Enlightenment more generally and, by extension, to the question of the relationship between Enlightenment and empire. Put reductively, the question is: Was the Enlightenment the scourge of empire or its handmaiden?[14] As Burke's arguments show, the answer to this query is effectively that "the Enlightenment" is a monolithic and unwieldy category that does not map in any direct way onto a particular thinker's view of empire or colonialism. That is, nothing at all can be divined about a given thinker's association to some strand of Enlightenment ideas and his or her commitment to empire. Burke's case highlights this point: he was himself a child of the (Scottish) Enlightenment, but he transformed the Scots' historical arguments into a conservative view of the civilizing process that defended settler colonialism in the New World and an empire of conquest in India, both of which his liberal Scottish friend and intellectual fellow traveler, Adam Smith, rejected.

The difficulty that an overbroad understanding of "the Enlightenment," combined with a too narrow focus on some portion of a canonical thinker's work, can have for an understanding of that thinker's relationship to empire is problematic. The perils of such an approach can be seen in an essay that specifically considers Burke's relation to Said's theory of Orientalism. Its author, one of Burke's more skilled interpreters, nevertheless concludes that Burke's attempts to forge bonds of sympathy between the British and Indians on the basis of their civilizational similarity demonstrates his resistance to the discourse of radical alterity and Otherness, largely clearing him of the charge of Orientalism. Instead, it is argued that Burke "can be called a humanist of the Enlightenment, and appears to share Said's normative commitments." Most important among these is said to be "a discourse of universalism," as evidenced by Burke's attack on the East India Company "on behalf of the empire's Indian subjects."[15]

The problem with this view, however, is that while Burke was indeed an Enlightenment thinker, he was no more a humanist given to universalism than he was an anti-imperialist. To the contrary, in India (as in France) Burke's concern was not for individual liberty writ large, let alone a defense of universal individual rights derived from some common notion of humanity, a discourse Burke abhorred. In his writings on both India and France, Burke took up the cudgels not on behalf of all human beings but rather in the service of a very specific conservative, hierarchical understanding of civilization and those who had made it possible, the landed aristocracy and the purveyors of organized religion. Furthermore, painting Burke as a humanist and universalist based on his (misunderstood) views on India fails to account for how his deeply hierarchical and exclusionary worldview underpinned his Orientalist arguments elsewhere.

Burke was, in fact, quite happy to describe the Amerindians and Africans, who fell outside the ambit of his definition of civilization, as "savages"—and to deny them any measure of political or social liberty—and he did so for the very reasons Said has identified with Orientalism. That is, Burke described these groups as the antipode to the "civilized" peoples of Britain and the North American and Caribbean settler colonies, a theoretical move that made them ripe for a civilizing mission. Furthermore, as I have shown, Burke hoped that his Orientalist move of Othering the savages and slaves in the New World would also bring the colonial peoples in America and the Caribbean together in solidarity with the metropole, thus cementing the empire in bonds of civilizational solidarity. By partial engagement and a misreading of the evidence, then, scholars miss the great extent to which Burke was willing to deploy exclusionary Orientalist arguments, albeit in the West rather than the East.

This last argument also challenges one of the central claims of much of Burke scholarship since World War II—namely, that Burke maintained a commitment to universal justice and liberty rooted in a belief in scholastic natural law.[16] This interpretation is unsustainable in light of the evidence. "Natural law," understood as a set of universal, transhistorical, moral principles divined by "right reason" that act as a backstop against certain sorts of inhumane behavior, played no part in Burke's writings on the "savages" of the New World. Burke did not invoke natural law principles to argue against the conquest of the Native Americans or the enslavement of Africans. To the contrary, he argued early in his career for the expansion of empire in America through conquest, as well as expansion of the slave trade; and throughout his life, he argued for the use of the institutional embodiment of "natural law" in the West—organized Christianity—as a means of "civilizing" the Amerindians and African slaves so that they might at some future unspecified date be worthy of the chastened liberty afforded to them on the terms set by the "civilized" Britons and Americans. We also saw that, in the case of freed slaves, Burke believed that the penalty for failure to adhere to Western norms of "civilization" ought to be the complete loss of liberty through reenslavement.

In fact, Burke invoked natural law arguments only in circumstances where the societies were already "civilized" according to his definition of the term: in India and Ireland. But here, as with everything else he ever wrote about religion, Burke was emphatically *not* interested in the metaphysical business of defending one among a number of competing claims to ontological certitude derived from the Christian, Muslim, or Hindu faiths. Rather, Burke argued that the laws derived from any of these faiths could and should have been utilized to condemn Warren Hastings. There is likewise little doubt that, had he ever commented on the matter, Burke would surely have said that Muslim or Hindu law could likewise have served as an argument against the penal laws in Ireland, just as well as laws derived from Christianity. The point here is that throughout his work Burke consistently focused on the *functional* role played by law derived in part from religious institutions operating within "civilized" societies, as a means whereby individuals could be held to account for wantonly immoral acts.

However, for Burke such laws were not universal even in these civilized societies, because he believed they could not and should not be used as a moral basis for condemning (and by extension, punishing) such behaviors as Robert Clive's original conquest of India and his role in the famine it led to, or England's conquest of Ireland and the land confiscations that gave rise to the Protestant Ascendancy and the penal laws in the first instance. Burke accepted as morally and politically legitimate the conquests made in both India and Ireland, just as he accepted the legitimacy of old violence in Europe. Of course, Burke's definition of what constituted "old" and, thus, beyond the pale of rectification was strikingly brief in duration—less than a century in Ireland, and less than a decade in India from the time he first wrote about the subcontinent.

In this respect, as in all others, Burke's defense of empire is tightly linked to his defense of the Old Regime in Europe. This view most conspicuously pervades his writings on Ireland and India but is abundantly evident throughout his work on empire. Occasionally, Burke argued that old hierarchical orders could be threatened from outside and above—as was the case in India. However, as can be seen in his writings on colonial America, and particularly in his work on the Caribbean and Ireland in the 1790s, Burke's greatest fear was that the conservatively ordered British Empire would perish in an assault from within and below. This fear was exacerbated by the French Revolution, whose principles Burke believed acted like a solvent on civilization as he understood it. To be clear, the principles that Burke most hated and feared were those of modern secular liberal democracies. Burke's nightmare was a world in which the British Empire, like the European Old Regime, would largely expire in a revolt of the many against the few, a revolt that he consistently depicted as savagery triumphant over civilization. Here, Burke was perhaps remarkably prescient. It has been argued that what ultimately put paid to the British Empire after World War II was the success of more egalitarian, democratic social movements in combination with nationalist yearnings for independence, or what has been called "the ending of empire as the ending of hierarchy."[17]

All of which leads to a final, cautionary note worth sounding. To the extent that the argument about Burke's conservative logic of empire presented in this book is convincing, it ought to make contemporary readers wary of embracing the founding father of modern conservatism as a philosophical ally in attempts to defend anti-imperialism, individual liberty, democratic equality, and cultural difference. In short, just because a thinker is occasionally the enemy of your enemies does not make him your friend.[18] One can, of course, defend Burke's conservative logic of empire as a normative ideal, but it is important to get clear on what his imperial vision actually was. Debates about Burke's defense of empire are well worth having, but only after we recover and grapple with the actual substance of his positions.

NOTES

INTRODUCTION

1. See Edward Said, *Orientalism* (1978; repr., New York: Vintage Books, 2003); and David Cannadine, *Ornamentalism: How the British Saw Their Empire* (Oxford: Oxford University Press, 2001).

2. For prominent examples of Said's influence on postcolonialism, see Dipesh Chakrabarty, *Provincializing Europe: Postcolonial Thought and Historical Difference* (Princeton, NJ: Princeton University Press, 2007); Homi K. Bhabha, *The Location of Culture* (New York: Routledge, 1994); Enrique Dussel, *The Invention of the Americas: Eclipse of "the Other" and the Myth of Modernity* (New York: Continuum, 1995); and Rosalind Morris, ed., *Can the Subaltern Speak? Reflections on the History of an Idea* (New York: Columbia University Press, 2010), a volume in which Gayatri Chakravorty Spivak and a number of scholars take up themes from Spivak's influential essay from the 1980s.

3. More broadly, Said notes: "The construction of identity ... involves the construction of opposites and 'others' whose actuality is always subject to the continuous interpretation and re-interpretation of their differences from 'us.' Each age and society re-creates its 'Others'" (*Orientalism*, p. 332).

4. For prominent examples of Said's influence on the new imperial history," see Mrinalini Sinha, *Colonial Masculinity: The "Manly Englishman" and the "Effeminate Bengali" in the Late Nineteenth Century* (Manchester, U.K.: Manchester University Press, 1995); Kathleen Wilson, ed., *A New Imperial History: Culture, Identity and Modernity in Britain and the Empire, 1660–1840* (Cambridge: Cambridge University Press, 2004); Catherine Hall and Sonya Rose, eds., *At Home with the Empire: Metropolitan Culture and the Imperial World* (Cambridge: Cambridge University Press, 2006); Antoinette Burton, *Empire in Question: Reading, Writing, and Teaching British Imperialism* (Durham, NC: Duke University Press, 2011); and Tony Ballantyne, *Orientalism and Race: Aryanism in the British Empire* (London: Palgrave Macmillan, 2002).

5. Cannadine, *Ornamentalism,* p. xix. Cannadine explicitly contrasts his view with Said's and, by extension, the strong version of Said's thesis taken up by the devotees of the new imperial history: "*Pace* Edward Said and his 'Orientalist' followers, the British Empire was not exclusively (or even preponderantly) concerned with the creation of 'otherness' on the presumption that the imperial periphery was different from, and inferior to, the imperial metropolis: it was at least as much (perhaps more?) concerned with what has recently been called the 'construction of affinities' on the presumption that society on the periphery was the same as, or even on occasions superior to, society in the metropolis. Thus regarded, the British Empire was about the familiar and domestic, as well as the different and the exotic."

6. For these points and a good overview of this literature, see Jennifer Pitts, "Political Theory of Empire and Imperialism," *Annual Review of Political Science* 13 (2010): 211–235. See also Sankar Muthu's introduction to *Empire and Modern Political Thought,* ed. Sankar Muthu (Cambridge: Cambridge University Press, 2012), pp. 1–6. Much of the best work in this area builds on groundbreaking scholarship associated with the Cambridge school of intellectual history. For examples, see Anthony Pagden, esp. *Lords of All the World: Ideologies of Empire in Spain, Britain and France, c. 1500–c. 1800* (New Haven, CT: Yale University Press, 1995); James Tully, *An Approach to Political Philosophy: Locke in Contexts* (Cambridge: Cambridge University Press, 1993); J. G. A. Pocock, *The Discovery of Islands: Essays in British History* (Cambridge: Cambridge University Press, 2005); Richard Tuck, *The Rights of War and Peace: Political Thought and the International Order from Grotius to Kant* (Oxford: Oxford University Press, 1999); and David Armitage, *The Ideological Origins of the British Empire* (Cambridge: Cambridge University Press, 2000).

7. Muthu, *Empire and Modern Political Thought,* p. 4.

8. On the various liberal arguments in defense of empire, see Uday Singh Mehta, *Liberalism and Empire: A Study in Nineteenth-Century British Liberal Thought* (Chicago: University of Chicago Press, 1999); Jennifer Pitts, *A Turn to Empire: The Rise of Imperial Liberalism in Britain and France* (Princeton, NJ: Princeton University Press, 2005); Jeanne Morefield, *Covenants without Swords: Idealist Liberalism and the Spirit of Empire* (Princeton, NJ: Princeton University Press, 2005); Karuna Mantena, *Alibis of Empire: Henry Maine and the Ends of Liberal Imperialism* (Princeton, NJ: Princeton University Press, 2010); Duncan Bell, *The Idea of Greater Britain: Empire and the Future of World Order, 1860–1900* (Princeton, NJ: Princeton University Press, 2007); Duncan Bell, ed., *Victorian Visions of Global Order: Europe and International Relations in Nineteenth Century Political Thought* (Cambridge: Cambridge University Press, 2007); and Bart Schultz and Georgios Varouxakis, eds., *Utilitarianism and Empire* (Lanham, MD: Lexington Books, 2005).

9. See David Bromwich, *The Intellectual Life of Edmund Burke: From the Sublime and the Beautiful to American Independence* (Cambridge, MA: Harvard University Press, 2014), pp. 19, 9, 6.

10. Pitts, *A Turn to Empire,* p. 278n17. Pitts contends that Burke's criticisms of the British Empire are "not well explained as at root a conservative impulse to preserve traditional societies" (p. 60).

11. See Sankar Muthu, *Enlightenment against Empire* (Princeton, NJ: Princeton University Press, 2003), pp. 4–5.

12. Mehta writes, "The important point is not whether Burke was or was not an imperialist in an explicit or declared sense. In the eighteenth century that question had not surfaced to self-consciousness and had scarcely any of the associations that it has acquired following the nationalist struggles and the decolonization of European empires in this [twentieth] century" (*Liberalism and Empire*, p. 158).

13. Ibid., p. 22.

14. See Sunil Agnani, *Hating Empire Properly: The Two Indies and the Limits of Enlightenment Anticolonialism* (New York: Fordham University Press, 2013). Agnani maintains that even though Burke "rarely argued against empire as such," one can declare that while "there have been many revolutionary books written against colonialism, Burke, however, wrote a conservative book against it" (pp. 70–71).

15. Jacob T. Levy, review of *Enlightenment against Empire*, by Sankar Muthu, *Perspectives on Politics* 2, no. 4 (2004): 829–830, quoted at p. 829.

16. Mehta, *Liberalism and Empire*, pp. 22, 164, 137, 155, 150. For her part, Pitts argues that Burke's work on empire ought to "chasten our tendency to draw from the *Reflections* a broader political philosophy of hierarchy and exclusion." To the contrary, for Pitts, Burke's writings on empire "suggest that what appears to be Burke's remarkable indifference to the sufferings of the French people under the *ancien régime* may be itself a blind spot in his thought, rather than an indication of broader and deeper commitments to aristocratic rule at any cost" (*A Turn to Empire*, pp. 94, 5).

17. See Luke Gibbons, *Edmund Burke and Ireland: Aesthetics, Politics, and the Colonial Sublime* (Cambridge: Cambridge University Press, 2003). Gibbons describes his book "as complementing Mehta's focus on India by integrating Burke's aesthetics and his Irish background more fully into [his] searching critiques of colonialism" (p. xii).

18. See Frederick G. Whelan, *Enlightenment Political Thought and Non-Western Societies: Sultans and Savages* (New York: Routledge, 2009), pp. 167–168 and associated notes.

19. Daniel I. O'Neill, *The Burke-Wollstonecraft Debate: Savagery, Civilization, and Democracy* (University Park: Penn State University Press, 2007).

20. Burke's particular developmental conception of "civilization" was only one of a wide range of possible ways of thinking about the idea. The word itself was coined after his birth and attained popular currency during his lifetime. For an informative conceptual history, see David Cannadine, *The Undivided Past: Humanity beyond Our Differences:* (New York: Alfred A. Knopf, 2013), pp. 219–257.

21. For the view that conservatism is best understood as a political ideology born in hostility to democratic leveling, see especially Don Herzog, *Poisoning the Minds of the Lower Orders* (Princeton, NJ: Princeton University Press, 1998). The book's title is taken from Burke's description of what the French Revolution was bringing about. For the way this hostility manifested itself in Burke's rejection of women's political agency, see Linda M. G. Zerilli, *Signifying Woman: Culture and Chaos in Rousseau, Burke, and Mill* (Ithaca, NY: Cornell University Press, 1994).

22. The first of these approaches is the one taken by Bromwich, who draws a sharp divide between "Whigs" and "Tories" in the eighteenth century and effectively reserves the term *conservative* exclusively for the latter group. For Bromwich, Burke *cannot* be a conservative *because* he was a Whig, meaning (as per Samuel Johnson) "a supporter of the revolution settlement of 1689, a believer in the authority of Parliament as superior to the king, a person who saw frequent causes for alarm at encroachment by the king on parliamentary sovereignty" (*The Intellectual Life of Edmund Burke*, p. 20). Narrowly, the problem with this line of argument is that Burke spent a good portion of his intellectual life defending the claim that the Whigs were the true preservers of the proper, historically rooted conception of the appropriate relationship between king and Parliament, and hence had the better claim to preserving an inheritance that went back at least a century before him. This is one important meaning of the term *conservative*. More broadly, Bromwich fails to grapple with any of the ideological markers of conservatism discussed here and, therefore, can dismiss the idea that Burke was a conservative in this deeper, substantive sense only by avoiding the evidence.

23. Here, I agree with a very serious historian of political thought, who (pace Bromwich) notes, "In his opposition to the French Revolution [Burke] not only became for his time the acknowledged champion of the conservatives then ranged against it, but he put forward a view of human nature and society on which conservatives have drawn and to which they have appealed ever since" (see Iain Hampsher-Monk, *A History of Modern Political Thought* [Oxford: Blackwell, 1992], p. 261).

24. For an interesting discussion of this interpretive tendency, see Isaac Kramnick, "The Left and Edmund Burke," *Political Theory* 11, no. 2 (1983): 189–214.

25. Contemporary scholarship has rightly rejected the "Smith problem" as a false dichotomy predicated on a misreading of Smith's central theoretical terms. For this reappraisal, see Ryan Patrick Hanley, *Adam Smith and the Character of Virtue* (Cambridge: Cambridge University Press, 2011); Dennis Rasmussen, *The Problems and Promise of Commercial Society: Adam Smith's Response to Rousseau* (University Park: Penn State University Press, 2008); and Fonna Forman-Barzilai, *Adam Smith and the Circles of Sympathy: Cosmopolitanism and Moral Theory* (Cambridge: Cambridge University Press, 2010).

26. See Frank O'Gorman, *Edmund Burke: His Political Philosophy* (Bloomington: Indiana University Press, 1973); and Frederick Dreyer, *Burke's Politics: A Study in Whig Orthodoxy* (Waterloo, Ontario: Wilfrid Laurier University Press, 1979).

27. Thus we have had utilitarian, republican, protoromantic, bourgeois, psychoanalytic, aesthetic, and—most influentially—conservative natural law readings of Burke. All of these interpreters maintain that Burke can be understood as a generally consistent exemplar of a particular body of thought or with reference to some overarching framework of analysis. On the profusion of interpretive positions constitutive of the "Burke problem," see O'Neill, *The Burke-Wollstonecraft Debate*, pp. 1–20 and 51–52.

28. For example, while J. G. A. Pocock has written extraordinarily insightful pieces on the political languages of the ancient constitution and political economy as bases for understanding certain of Burke's texts, he has never attempted to synthesize Burke's use of these various languages such that an image of him as a consistent, coherent thinker emerges. In fact, Pocock has steadfastly resisted such attempts, maintaining that he is not concerned with "the possible consistencies and inconsistencies in Burke's text or thought" and noting that "it seems more important to establish that Burke can be read in both of these contexts than to inquire whether he can be read in both of them simultaneously"(see "The Political Economy of Burke's Analysis of the French Revolution," in *Virtue, Commerce, and History: Essays on Political Thought and History, Chiefly in the Eighteenth Century* [Cambridge: Cambridge University Press, 1985], p. 194). At its worst, the search for consistency is a move that creates a pernicious mythology, as Quentin Skinner rightly accused Leo Strauss and his followers of having done by ascribing omniscient qualities to the great political philosophers of yore, whose internal self-contradictions and changes of mind they explained away by recourse to such sleight of hand as the esoteric reading of texts. This is one of the telling blows landed in Skinner's classic piece "Meaning and Understanding in the History of Ideas"; see *Meaning and Context: Quentin Skinner and His Critics,* ed. James Tully (Princeton, NJ: Princeton University Press, 1988).

29. See esp. Mark Bevir, *The Logic of the History of Ideas* (Cambridge: Cambridge University Press, 1999). Bevir argues that historians of ideas should explain the particular views expressed by an author in a text by locating them synchronically within that individual's own wider web of beliefs while also relating that thinker's web of beliefs to the relevant intellectual traditions that she or he has inherited. However, he also maintains that synchronic explanations must be buttressed with diachronic ones in order to account for how beliefs change over time and why an individual author might make a revolutionary break with or transform an intellectual tradition.

30. Ibid., pp. 187–218, 221–264. I find compelling Bevir's claim that figures in the history of political thought sought intellectual consistency, or an internal coherence within their belief system. This is not because those thinkers are exceptional (as per the Straussians) but rather because such a claim jibes with our common experience. In everyday political argument, those who follow one set of statements with another that seemingly contradicts it are usually asked to explain how they see such claims as fitting together in an intellectually consistent—and hence logically defensible—fashion. If they cannot do so, we rightly consider them as holding an untenable or self-defeating position. This is far from saying that the great thinkers of the past never contradicted themselves or changed their minds. However, it is to insist that as a general matter authors who put forward theoretical justifications for their positions in the form of everyday political arguments or theoretical treatises seek equally to integrate them into coherent webs of belief. There are intuitively plausible reasons for this: We generally find it psychologically discomfiting to come to believe, or to be shown by our interlocutors, that our webs of belief are obviously self-contradictory or merely haphazard. Because this is so, we seek intellectual

coherence, or at least to provide a compelling reason why our views are only apparently contradictory, or why and how they have changed in response to some perceived intellectual dilemmas over time. On the features of Bevir's argument that distinguish it from the Cambridge school, see Daniel I. O'Neill, "Revisiting the Middle Way: *The Logic of the History of Ideas* after More Than a Decade," *Journal of the History of Ideas* 73, no. 4 (2012): 583–592.

31. See *The Works of the Right Honourable Edmund Burke* (London: Bell & Daldy, 1872), vol. 3, p. 26.

32. For partial exceptions, see Uday Mehta's essay "Edmund Burke on Empire, Self-Understanding, and Sympathy," in Muthu, *Empire and Modern Political Thought*, pp. 155–183; Conor Cruise O'Brien, *The Great Melody: A Thematic Biography of Edmund Burke* (Chicago: University of Chicago Press, 1992); and Agnani, *Hating Empire Properly*. However, while Agnani attempts to link Burke's writings on the Caribbean and India to those on France, he does not focus at any length on Burke's position on the North American colonies, the Native Americans, or Ireland. Likewise, Mehta largely ignores both the New World and Irish contexts. Moreover, I think that both authors ultimately miss the theoretical thrust of the links between Burke's writings on empire and revolution, for reasons I discuss in chapters 2 and 3. A more comprehensive meditation on these themes is O'Brien's idiosyncratic biography, *The Great Melody*. However, O'Brien does not consider Burke's views on Native Americans or slaves at any length, which I argue are central to Burke's thinking, while O'Brien's deep affection for his subject leads him to make unsupportable claims regarding Burke and Ireland, as I discuss in chapter 4.

33. As per Pocock, *The Discovery of Islands*, p. 87. Small portions of this argument have appeared in embryonic form in previous articles: Daniel I. O'Neill and Margaret Kohn, "A Tale of Two Indias: Burke and Mill on Empire and Slavery in the West Indies and America," *Political Theory* 34, no. 2 (2006): 192–228, for which I wrote all of the material on Burke; Daniel I. O'Neill, "Rethinking Burke and India," *History of Political Thought* 30, no. 3 (2009): 492–523; and Daniel I. O'Neill, "Edmund Burke, the 'Science of Man,' and Statesmanship," in *Scientific Statesmanship, Governance and the History of Political Philosophy*, ed. Kyriakos N. Demetriou and Antis P. Loizides (New York: Routledge, 2015), pp. 174–192. All of this material has been greatly revised and greatly expanded for this book.

34. Richard Bourke, *Empire and Revolution: The Political Life of Edmund Burke* (Princeton, NJ: Princeton University Press, 2015).

35. Ibid., pp. 1, 9, 15, 797. Bourke not only insists that the term *conservatism* is anachronistic as applied to Burke (pp. 678–679) but also describes the attempt to depict Burke as a conservative as underpinned by a "value-laden and a Manichean perspective" (p. 745). The same might be said about the attempt to describe Burke as an unalloyed defender of the "spirit of liberty" against the "spirit of conquest." In chapter 1, I consider one aspect of the argument Bourke makes in *Empire and Revolution*, as well as his earlier work on Burke.

36. See Armitage, *The Ideological Origins of the British Empire*.

CHAPTER 1. BURKE AND EMPIRE IN CONTEXT

1. For the etymology and development of the term, see esp. David Armitage, *The Ideological Origins of the British Empire* (Cambridge: Cambridge University Press, 2000), pp. 1–23, 29–30; and Anthony Pagden, *Lords of All the World: Ideologies of Empire in Spain, Britain and France, c. 1500–c. 1800* (New Haven, CT: Yale University Press, 1995), pp. 12–17. For an excellent overview, see Pagden's *Peoples and Empires: A Short History of European Migration, Exploration, and Conquest, from Greece to the Present* (New York: Modern Library, 2003). See also Daniel I. O'Neill, "Empire," in *SAGE Encyclopedia of Political Theory*, ed. Mark Bevir (Thousand Oaks, CA: SAGE Publications, 2010), pp. 417–423.

2. See Margaret Kohn, "Colonialism," in *Stanford Encyclopedia of Philosophy*, Summer 2012 edition, ed. Edward N. Zalta, http://plato.stanford.edu/archives/sum2012/entries/colonialism/.

3. See esp. Nicholas Canny, *Kingdom and Colony: Ireland in the Atlantic World, 1560–1800* (Baltimore, MD: Johns Hopkins University Press, 1988).

4. On these points, see esp. Sankar Muthu, introduction to *Empire and Modern Political Thought*, ed. Sankar Muthu (Cambridge: Cambridge University Press, 2012), p. 6.

5. David Armitage, "The British Conception of Empire in the Eighteenth Century," in *Imperium/Empire/Reich: An Anglo-German Comparison of a Concept of Rule*, ed. Franz Bosbach and Hermann Hiery (Munich: K. G. Saur, 1999), pp. 91–107, quote at p. 94.

6. J. G. A. Pocock, "British History: A Plea for a New Subject," in *The Discovery of Islands: Essays in British History* (Cambridge: Cambridge University Press, 2005), p. 29. Pocock explains elsewhere in the volume that his use of the term *Atlantic Archipelago* is meant to avoid nationalist histories, especially those wherein "British history" is collapsed into nothing more than "English history" (p. 77).

7. Armitage, *The Ideological Origins of the British Empire*, pp. 170–172.

8. Armitage, "The British Conception of Empire in the Eighteenth Century," p. 104.

9. On this theme, see Jack P. Greene, "Empire and Identity from the Glorious to the American Revolution," in *The Oxford History of the British Empire: The Eighteenth Century*, ed. P. J. Marshall (Oxford: Oxford University Press, 2001), pp. 208–230, at pp. 208–212; and Armitage, *The Ideological Origins of the British Empire*, p. 194. More generally, see J. G. A. Pocock's classic *The Ancient Constitution and the Feudal Law*, 2nd ed. (Cambridge: Cambridge University Press, 1987).

10. On this connection, see Elizabeth Mancke, "The Languages of Liberty in British North America, 1607–1776," in *Exclusionary Empire: English Liberties Overseas, 1600–1900*, ed. Jack P. Greene (Cambridge: Cambridge University Press, 2010), pp. 25–49.

11. On this notion of commerce, see esp. Pagden, *Lords of All the World*, pp. 178–200, and *Peoples and Empires*, pp. 83–98. On Scottish Enlightenment

assumptions about the civilizing effects of commerce, see Christopher J. Berry, *Social Theory of the Scottish Enlightenment* (Edinburgh: Edinburgh University Press, 1997).

12. On the importance of *res nullius* arguments, see Pagden, *Lords of All the World*, pp. 74–86, 128; on Locke in particular, see James Tully, "Rediscovering America: The *Two Treatises* and Aboriginal Rights," in his *An Approach to Political Philosophy: Locke in Contexts* (Cambridge: Cambridge University Press, 1993), pp. 137–176; and Barbara Arneil, *John Locke and America: The Defence of English Colonialism* (Oxford: Oxford University Press, 1996).

13. For the persistence of feudally rooted conquest arguments that stressed the evangelical importance of Christianizing the "heathen" Native Americans, see Aziz Rana, *The Two Faces of American Freedom* (Cambridge, MA: Harvard University Press, 2010), pp. 28–33; and Pagden, *Lords of All the World*, p. 88. For the role of such arguments after 1763, see P. J. Marshall, "A Nation Defined by Empire, 1755–1776," in his magisterial collection of essays *"A Free Though Conquering People": Eighteenth-Century Britain and Its Empire* (Aldershot, U.K.: Ashgate, 2003), pp. 214–215; and P. J. Marshall, *The Making and Unmaking of Empires: Britain, India, and America, c. 1750–1783* (Oxford: Oxford University Press, 2005), p. 185.

14. See Armitage, "Protestantism and Empire: Hakluyt, Purchas and Property," chap. 3 of his *Ideological Origins of the British Empire*, pp. 61–99; and Greene, "Empire and Identity from the Glorious to the American Revolution," pp. 213–214.

15. See Linda Colley's outstanding *Britons: Forging the Nation, 1707–1837* (New Haven, CT: Yale University Press, 1992). Colley is particularly good on the triumphalist nationalism—and the associated blind spots—that such Protestantism engendered.

16. See Pagden, *Peoples and Empires*, p. 86.

17. See Armitage, "The British Conception of Empire in the Eighteenth Century," p. 95; and *Ideological Origins of the British Empire*, p. 9.

18. On this theme, see Greene, "Empire and Identity from the Glorious to the American Revolution," quoted at p. 208.

19. Marshall, introduction to Marshall, *The Oxford History of the British Empire: The Eighteenth Century*, p. 24.

20. Pagden, *Peoples and Empires*, p. 100.

21. See Kathleen Wilson, "Introduction: Histories, Empires, Modernities," in *A New Imperial History: Culture, Identity and Modernity in Britain and the Empire, 1660–1840*, ed. Kathleen Wilson (Cambridge: Cambridge University Press, 2004), pp. 1–26, at p. 11.

22. Kathleen Wilson, *The Sense of the People: Politics, Culture and Imperialism in England, 1715–1785* (Cambridge: Cambridge University Press, 1995), p. 157.

23. See esp. Greene, *Exclusionary Empire*.

24. Both the phrase "swing to the east" and the neat demarcation of "first" and "second" empires go back to V. T. Harlow, *The Founding of the Second British Empire, 1763–1793*, 2 vols. (London: Longmans Green, 1952–1964).

25. See P. J. Marshall, *"A Free Though Conquering People,"* p. x; see also in the same volume "The Eighteenth Century Empire," pp. 184, 186, and "Britain without

America—a Second Empire?" in Marshall, *The Oxford History of the British Empire*, pp. 576–595.

26. Marshall, "Britain without America—a Second Empire?" p. 594.

27. See Marshall, introduction to *The Oxford History of the British Empire*, p. 16; and "Empire and Authority in the Later Eighteenth Century," in *"A Free Though Conquering People,"* p. 115. See also C. A. Bayly, *Imperial Meridian: The British Empire and the World, 1780–1830* (London: Longman, 1989), pp. 8–9; and Armitage, "The British Conception of Empire in the Eighteenth Century," pp. 106–107. Reflexively, of course, the empire also shaped British identity and helped forge the nation and distinguish it from other European countries; see P. J. Marshall, "Imperial Britain," *Journal of Imperial and Commonwealth History* 23, no. 3 (1995): 379–394, at p. 385; Colley, *Britons;* and the work of Kathleen Wilson, including *The Island Race: Englishness, Empire and Gender in the Eighteenth Century* (London: Routledge, 2003).

28. See Marshall, "Britain without America—a Second Empire?" pp. 581, 593.

29. Narrowly, using the term *imperialism* runs the risk of anachronism, because it was coined only in the middle of the nineteenth century. Likewise, one could argue that such a claim fails to distinguish between the imperial and the colonial (or the anti-imperial and anticolonial) in discussing Burke's position.

30. Cited in Burke, *The Writings and Speeches of Edmund Burke,* Paul Langford, general editor, 9 vols. (Oxford: Oxford University Press, 1981–2015), vol. 2, p. 46 (hereafter, *W&S*). References to *The Correspondence of Edmund Burke,* ed. Thomas W. Copeland, 10 vols. (Chicago: University of Chicago Press, 1958–1978), are hereafter *Corr.*

31. Burke, *W&S*, vol. 2, pp. 47–48.

32. Ibid., p. 196.

33. Ibid., p. 460, emphasis original.

34. See Burke's letter to the Committee of Correspondence of the General Assembly of New York, April 6, 1774, in *Corr.*, vol. 2, pp. 528–529, emphasis original. This letter echoes an earlier one Burke wrote to the influential James De Lancey in New York in 1771, in which he tells its recipient: "I have always been and shall ever be earnest to preserve the Constitutional dependence of the Colonies on the Crown, and Legislature of this Kingdom, and a friend to every just and honorable measure that tends to secure it" (pp. 290–291).

35. Burke, *W&S*, vol. 3, pp. 313, 285.

36. See P. J. Marshall, "The British in Asia: Trade to Dominion, 1700–1765," in Marshall, *The Oxford History of the British Empire,* pp. 487–507, at pp. 491–493.

37. See Nick Robins, *The Corporation That Changed the World: How the East India Company Shaped the Modern Multinational* (London: Pluto Press, 2006), pp. 2–3. Robins argues convincingly that the Company's revolution in Bengal "deserves to be placed alongside other better-known revolutions—the American, French and Russian—for the way that it shaped the modern world. In the space of less than a decade, the Company had rerouted the flow of wealth westwards" (p. 80).

38. For example, see Nicholas B. Dirks, *The Scandal of Empire: India and the Creation of Imperial Britain* (Cambridge, MA: Harvard University Press, 2008), p. 10; see also p. 43.

39. Cited in Robins, *The Corporation That Changed the World*, p. 78.

40. Ibid., pp. 90–94; see also, Sushil Chaudhury, *From Prosperity to Decline: 18th Century Bengal* (New Delhi: Manohar Publishers, 1999); and Rajat Kanta Ray, "Indian Society and the Establishment of British Supremacy, 1765–1818," in Marshall, *The Oxford History of the British Empire*, pp. 508–529, at p. 514.

41. One laudable exception to this oversight is Frederick Whelan, *Edmund Burke and India: Political Morality and Empire* (Pittsburgh, PA: University of Pittsburgh Press, 1996), whose argument I take up below.

42. See F.P. Lock, *Edmund Burke*, 2 vols. (Oxford: Oxford University Press, 1998, 2006), vol. 1, p. 485. Dirks, *The Scandal of Empire*, p. 54.

43. Burke, *W&S*, vol. 2, p. 220.

44. Burke, *W&S*, vol. 6, p. 316.

45. Ibid., pp. 340–341.

46. See Robins, *The Corporation That Changed the World*, pp. 92–93; Hastings quoted at p. 93.

47. See Paine, *The Complete Writings of Thomas Paine*, ed. Philip S. Foner (New York: Citadel Press, 1945), vol. 1, pp. 23–24, 20. For India's importance to Paine's arguments about America, see J.M. Opal, "*Common Sense* and Imperial Atrocity: How Tom Paine Saw South Asia in North America," *Common-Place* 9, no. 4 (July 2009), www.common-place.org/vol-09/no-04/forum/opal.shtml; and J.M. Opal, "Thomas Paine and the Revolutionary Enlightenment, 1770s–1790s," in *Common Sense and Other Writings*, edited by J.M. Opal (New York: Norton, 2012), pp. vii–xxxv.

48. Paine, *The Complete Writings of Thomas Paine*, vol. 2, pp. 118–119.

49. Burke, *W&S*, vol. 5, p. 426. For Burke's opposition to the creation of the East India Select Committee in 1772, see *W&S*, vol. 2, pp. 370–374.

50. To his great credit, Frederick Whelan has confronted directly the difficulty that Burke's endorsement of Clive's behavior in the Bengal Revolution poses for any would-be hagiographical interpretation of his overall position on empire in India. As Whelan correctly points out, "Neither in his impeachment speeches nor elsewhere did Burke challenge the 'necessity' or the rightfulness of the diplomacy, battles, tricks, treaties, and other undertakings—notably those of Clive—that created the empire, or the undoubted political ambition involved" (Whelan, *Edmund Burke and India*, p. 66). Unfortunately, in his essay "Burke on India," for *The Cambridge Companion to Edmund Burke* (ed. David Dwan and Christopher J. Insole [Cambridge: Cambridge University Press, 2012], pp. 168–180), Whelan tempers his rather blunt—and accurate—earlier assessment by asserting that for Burke the period from 1756 to 1765 was really a series of "revolution(s)" in which Burke only defended Clive's actions at Plassey in 1757, themselves taken "in retaliation for the Nawab's previous attack on the English" (p. 175). However, we know that this cannot be the case, because Burke gloried in Clive's extraction of the *diwani* from the Mughal

emperor—after military force was used against the latter and he was effectively held captive until he agreed—which did not take place until 1765. This was no doubt the culmination of the Bengal Revolution and by far its single most important act. Furthermore, to support his argument, Whelan references Burke's depiction in the *Fox's India Bill* speech of Bengal as suffering "the miseries of a revolution" (*W&S*, vol. 5, p. 427) on something like a yearly basis (Whelan, "Burke on India," p. 175). However, a close reading of that passage in Burke's speech—which comes right after his brief mention of the famine—clearly shows that it is meant as a criticism of Hastings and his policies, which Burke dates in the speech as commencing in 1772. Hence, the miseries of successive earlier Indian revolutions, and even the horrors of the Bengal famine, are effectively laid by Burke at Hastings's feet, not Clive's. Therefore Whelan's earlier statement, while less flattering to Burke, is far more accurate.

51. Burke, *W&S*, vol. 8, p. 213.

52. Letter to Captain Thomas Mercer of February 26, 1790, in *Corr.*, vol. 6, p. 95, emphasis original. On the general theme, see Daniel I. O'Neill, *The Burke-Wollstonecraft Debate: Savagery, Civilization, and Democracy* (University Park: Penn State University Press, 2007), pp. 150–151, 161–162, 173–174.

53. Burke, *W&S*, vol. 6, p. 462.

54. Ibid., pp. 316–317. Whelan smartly references this passage in Burke's writings and rightly points to his use of the same image of throwing "a politic, well-wrought veil" over the Glorious Revolution of 1688 (*Edmund Burke and India*, p. 37); however, it should be noted that the violence of the Bengal Revolution of 1757–1765 in India dwarfed that of 1688 in England.

55. Burke, *W&S*, vol. 7, p. 568.

56. Dirks, *The Scandal of Empire*, p. 198. Thus, Dirks notes, while Burke "railed against Hastings on virtually every aspect of his rule, he exonerated Clive and drew a veil over the period of conquest" (p. 291). Of course, Dirks is drawing here on the term invented by Carl Schmitt and recently used by Giorgio Agamben. While far more sympathetic to Burke and thus unlikely to endorse Dirks's broad claim, Whelan nevertheless reluctantly agrees with the notion that British India under Clive—whom Burke honors—was more corrupt than it was under Hastings, whom he vilifies: "The abuses that, according to Burke, occurred during Hastings's governorship (1772–1785) were of the sort that probably flourished on an even greater scale during the preceding period (1757–1772), and the attitudes that underlay them were certainly a continuation of a preexisting outlook" (*Edmund Burke and India*, p. 87). This makes Whelan's position on the issue of Burke's attitude toward the period of conquest a curious one. At one point, he argues that Burke believed that "although the East India Company's regime had quickly become corrupt and abusive, its title to rule in Bengal was sound, arising as it did from a combination of conquest in justifiable wars and formal grants of authority from the Mogul emperor, the nominal suzerain" (p. 7). Elsewhere, in speaking of Plassey (1757) and Buxar (1764), Whelan claims, "Both these battles, however, were seen by the British, and evidently by Burke as well, as justifiable responses to previous surprise attacks on the East India Company's outposts, with massacres of civilians, by the notorious nawabs Siraj

al-Daula and Mir Kasim. Such military conquests as there had been, therefore, had consisted of just wars undertaken not in pursuit of an imperial design, but as legitimate defense; in accordance with the eighteenth-century law of nations, Burke recognized the legitimacy of sovereignty acquired through victory in a just war, or through formal cessions accompanying the terminations of wars" (p. 23). While British imperial self-justification such as this obviously strains historical credulity to the extreme—why would we uncritically accept imperialists' claims that they were engaging in just war in territories and on people whom they forcibly imposed themselves in the first instance?—it is of course theoretically possible that Burke could have justified the Bengal Revolution in this fashion. The interpretive problem, however (which Whelan's phrase "evidently by Burke as well" hints at), is that he simply did not defend the origins of Indian empire on the basis of just war theory derived from natural law. Rather, as Whelan rightly argues elsewhere in his book, for Burke, "'sacred veils' had to be drawn over origins . . . as in Bengal, where prescription (even after only a few decades) appears to have supplemented the rather weak argument that the British had received a formal grant of authority from the Mogul emperor as a basis for Burke's willingness to accept the legitimacy of the empire" (p. 268).

57. See Richard Bourke, *Empire and Revolution: The Political Life of Edmund Burke* (Princeton, NJ: Princeton University Press, 2015), p. 366. Bourke quotes Burke from "Proceedings against Clive," May 21, 1773, Cavendish Diary, Eg. MS., 248, fol. 254.

58. See Burke, *W&S*, vol. 2, pp. 390–396.

59. Cited in P. J. Marshall, introduction to Burke, *W&S*, vol. 5, p. 3. Marshall is the editor of volumes 5–7 of Burke's *Writings and Speeches*, which cover his work on India. See also Lock's reference to this line in *Edmund Burke*, vol. 2, p. 33.

60. In *A Turn to Empire: The Rise of Imperial Liberalism in Britain and France* (Princeton, NJ: Princeton University Press, 2005), Jennifer Pitts accepts this point: "Burke's early views on India appear to contradict his later judgments, as historians have noted, for until the late 1770s, Burke tended to defend the Company's independence against efforts by the Crown to bring the Company under greater state control" (p. 63).

61. Burke, *W&S*, vol. 5, p. 145.

62. Ibid., p. 179.

63. Ibid., pp. 386–387.

64. For a discussion of the considerable distance between Burke and Smith on matters of imperial political economy, see Donald Winch, *Riches and Poverty: An Intellectual History of Political Economy in Britain, 1750–1834* (Cambridge: Cambridge University Press, 1996).

65. Burke, *W&S*, vol. 5, p. 404.

66. Burke, *W&S*, vol. 6, p. 351.

67. Ibid., p. 277.

68. Ibid., p. 315.

69. See Edmund Burke to French Laurence, 28 July, 1796, in *Corr.*, vol. 9, p. 62.

70. For his part, Whelan points out that even where Burke criticized the practice of empire most stringently, he nevertheless adhered steadfastly to the notion that it was wholly legitimate, desirable, and providential. Whelan insists that "Burke endorsed both the legitimacy and the beneficial nature of an appropriately organized and governed empire," in India *(Edmund Burke and India*, p. 19). As he notes in a later essay, Burke's views on India were thus consonant with his desire to preserve the British Empire wherever he found it: "As in America and Ireland, Burke's aim in India was to reform the administration of the empire with the intention of preserving it, and he acquired and presented his knowledge of Asia with this end explicitly in view" (see *Enlightenment Political Thought and Non-Western Societies: Sultans and Savages* [New York: Routledge, 2009], pp. 103–109, quoted at p. 106).

Likewise, P. J. Marshall, who in addition to being perhaps the leading authority on the British Empire in the eighteenth century has also written extensively on Burke, stresses the providential origins of the empire as central to Burke's understanding of why it should never be abandoned. Marshall argues that Burke "certainly believed that there could be no turning back or renunciation of empire in India" (introduction to *W&S*, vol. 6, p. 34). Burke "was sure that empire in India had providential origins" (p. 26). Since this was the case, Burke "firmly rejected" the conclusion "that British empire in India was an aberration that should be renounced." To the contrary, "he believed that empire in India was a dispensation of providence that Britain could not shirk"; indeed, Burke was concerned with what he saw as "the inescapable duties that rule imposed" (introduction to *W&S*, vol. 7, p. 13).

F. P. Lock, the author of the definitive biography of Burke, similarly asserts that Burke never suggested British withdrawal from India, principally because "Burke did not regard empire as in itself morally wrong. Conquests and empires were facts of history, and therefore part of the providential plan.... For Burke, there could be a 'good' empire, and he clearly believed that the British Empire was (potentially at least) such." Thus, to the extent that Burke's writings and speeches rejected British withdrawal or Indian self-determination, "they were ultimately complicit with the colonial or imperial project of domination" (*Edmund Burke*, vol. 2, pp. 174, 162).

Nicholas Dirks goes a good deal further, insisting that, in spite of Burke's relentless attempt to prosecute Warren Hastings, by making this an intensely personal attack Burke did not ultimately hold the East India Company (let alone the British nation) responsible for its systematically abusive conduct on the subcontinent. Burke's personalization of the problem turned a blind eye to the real scandal— empire itself—and effectively "ennoble[d] the idea of empire" in India. For Dirks, "Burke's real legacy was the transformation of Company rule into British imperium. Through his role in shaping the reforms and then in impeaching Hastings, he managed to rescue the imperial mission, transforming corruption into virtue, private malfeasance into public good, mercantile disgrace into national triumph" (see *The Scandal of Empire*, pp. 206–207, 296, 313–314).

As discussed in the introduction, it would certainly be appropriate to add Richard Bourke to this list of insightful interpreters who see Burke as a defender of empire in India, as elsewhere. Indeed, this is one of the central themes of Bourke's *Empire and Revolution*.

71. The former is the central theme of Conor Cruise O'Brien, *The Great Melody: A Thematic Biography of Edmund Burke* (Chicago: University of Chicago Press, 1992); the latter is the theme of Luke Gibbons, *Edmund Burke and Ireland: Aesthetics, Politics, and the Colonial Sublime* (Cambridge: Cambridge University Press, 2003); and to a lesser extent, Seamus Deane, *Foreign Affections: Essays on Edmund Burke* (Notre Dame, IN: University of Notre Dame Press, 2005).

72. Burke, *W&S*, vol. 9, p. 591.

73. Ibid., pp. 675–676.

74. Burke, *Corr.*, vol. 9, p. 113.

75. Ibid., p. 277.

76. More than a half century ago, in what remains the most thorough treatment of Burke on Ireland, Thomas Mahoney concluded that Burke's "great devotion to the British Empire" was one of the central hallmarks of his position, and that his "imperialism" made him "entirely unsympathetic" to the goal of Ireland's "full and complete independence" (see Thomas H. D. Mahoney, *Edmund Burke and Ireland* [Cambridge, MA: Harvard University Press, 1960]), pp. 310, 121. More recently, perhaps the most gifted contemporary historian of Ireland has noted "Burke's sincere belief that Ireland could not thrive without the British connection" (Ian McBride, "Burke and Ireland," in Dwan and Insole, *The Cambridge Companion to Edmund Burke,* pp. 181–194, quoted at p. 186). Rather, McBride concludes, Burke's answer to imperial corruption in Ireland, as in India, "was not *less* English government but *more* of it" (see *Eighteenth-Century Ireland: The Isle of Slaves* [Dublin: Gill & Macmillan, 2009], p. 10, emphasis original). Similarly Seán Patrick Donlan, the editor of a recent volume aimed at coming to grips with Burke's "Irish identities," maintains that Burke "was not anti-imperial or anti-colonial." On Burke's view, he argues, "the Irish nations were to be treated fairly, but Ireland was and ought to remain a subordinate kingdom" ("The 'Genuine Voice of Its Records and Monuments'?: Edmund Burke's 'Interior History of Ireland,'" in *Edmund Burke's Irish Identities,* ed. Donlan [Portland, OR: Irish Academic Press, 2007], pp. 69–101, quoted at p. 80). Reflecting on Burke's understanding of the Irish Constitution in the same volume, Eamon O'Flaherty contends that Burke's position was the "combination of a metropolitan, imperial perspective and a concern for Catholic rights rooted in his own personal experience and family connections." However, O'Flaherty maintains that Burke never let the latter half of this perspective trump the former. While Burke accused the British of many acts of oppression in Ireland, for him "neither prudence nor justice suggested that these oppressions warranted a repudiation of the subordination of Ireland within the Empire" (see "Burke and the Irish Constitution," in Donlan, *Edmund Burke's Irish Identities,* pp. 102–116, quoted at pp. 105, 109). J. C. Beckett goes still further, insisting of Burke that "there is nothing national, let alone nationalist about the policies he advocated for Ireland. Indeed, if we are to describe Burke as in any sense 'nationalist' then he was an English (or perhaps one should say British), rather than an Irish nationalist" ("Burke,

Ireland, and the Empire," in *Irish Culture and Nationalism, 1750–1950,* ed. O. Mac-Donagh, W. F. Mandle and P. Travers [London: Macmillan, 1983], pp. 1–13, quoted in Donlan, *Edmund Burke's Irish Identities,* p. 6). One might argue that such a claim is hyperbolic. Nevertheless, even a scholar as sympathetic to Burke as T. O. McLoughlin, who positions Burke with a number of "Irish voices against England in the eighteenth century," accepts that "Edmund Burke was one of the most eloquent advocates of empire in the eighteenth century.... He thought Ireland but a part, and a subservient part, of the British empire, [and] ... he regarded Westminster as the center of that empire and the arbiter of Ireland's best interests" (*Contesting Ireland: Irish Voices against England in the Eighteenth Century* [Dublin: Four Courts Press, 1999], p. 161). Most recently, Richard Bourke has noted that when it came to the British Empire, for Burke "the separation of Ireland was anathema in any imaginable future" (*Empire and Revolution,* p. 9).

77. For example, Jennifer Pitts argues that when Burke called a given state of affairs "providential," he did not necessarily approve of it but merely maintained that it had to be accepted as God's will. As evidence for this reading, she instances Burke's use of providential language in the aftermath of his son Richard's tragic death in the 1790s. On this view, Burke saw providence as fate, whether good or bad, and as likely to be the latter as the former. For Pitts, Burke thus "saw imperial governance as a painful if inevitable duty as much as a glorious or desirable vocation"; hence his commitment to an enlarged empire "was highly qualified" ("Burke and the Ends of Empire," in Dwan and Insole, *The Cambridge Companion to Edmund Burke,* pp. 145–155, quoted at pp. 147–148). There are a number of difficulties with this line of argument. First, while the mere invocation of Providence certainly did not constitute Burke's approval of the phenomenon under consideration, that clearly does not end the story. Why should we assume that Burke automatically perceived the British Empire in India or Ireland as an instance of Providence's negative side, rather than a manifestation of God's blessings? As interpreters, we must ask the additional contextual question of whether Burke rejoiced in or merely grudgingly accepted a given instance of God's mysterious ways. Fortunately, the specific query of how Burke perceived empire can be fleshed out with reference to a wide range of additional available evidence. And as we have seen, when that evidence is taken into account Burke was very far from a grudging acceptance of empire, but rather warmly embraced it. Indeed, it was precisely because Burke relished empire as a providential gift tied to British national glory that he so lamented the ways it had been handled in practice.

78. Lock, *Edmund Burke,* vol. 2, pp. 173–174.

79. See F. P. Lock, "Burke, Ireland and India: Reason, Rhetoric and Empire," in Donlan, *Edmund Burke's Irish Identities,* pp. 154–170, quoted at p. 167. Lock's principal targets in this essay are Luke Gibbons, Uday Mehta, and (to a lesser extent) O'Brien.

80. On this point, see Lock, "Burke, Ireland and India."

81. See Marshall, introduction to *The Oxford History of the British Empire,* pp. 7–8.

82. See Marshall, "The Eighteenth-Century Empire," pp. 182, 192, 194; and "Britain and the World in the Eighteenth Century: I, Reshaping the Empire," p. 10, both of which appear in Marshall, *A Free Though Conquering People.*

83. Marshall, "Empire and Authority in the later Eighteenth Century," pp. 118–119.

84. Marshall, *A Free Though Conquering People,*" p. xi.

85. Marshall, "Britain and the World in the Eighteenth Century, IV: The Turning Outwards of Britain," in Marshall, *A Free Though Conquering People,*" p. 4.

86. For examples of this genre, see Jennifer M. Welsh, *Edmund Burke and International Relations: The Commonwealth of Europe and the Crusade against the French Revolution* (New York: St. Martin's Press, 1995); David Boucher, "Edmund Burke and Historical Reason in International Relations," in his *Political Theories of International Relations: From Thucydides to the Present* (Oxford: Oxford University Press, 1998), pp. 308–329; Boucher, "The Character of the History of the Philosophy of International Relations and the Case of Edmund Burke," *Review of International Studies* 17 (1991): 127–148; R. J. Vincent, "Edmund Burke and the Theory of International Relations," *Review of International Studies* 10 (1984): 205–218; and Vilho Harle, "Burke the International Theorist—or the War of the Sons of Light and the Sons of Darkness," in *European Values in International Relations,* ed. Vilho Harle (New York: Pinter, 1990). Such approaches aim at squaring certain of Burke's utterances with later theories of international relations (such as "realism," "idealism," "liberalism," "constructivism," and the like). For criticisms of this endeavor, see David Armitage, "Edmund Burke and Reason of State," *Journal of the History of Ideas* 61, no. 4 (2000): 617–634.

87. See esp. Iain Hampsher-Monk, "Edmund Burke and Empire," in *Lineages of Empire: The Historical Roots of British Imperial Thought,* ed. Duncan Kelly (Oxford: Oxford University Press, 2009), pp. 117–136; P. J. Marshall, "Burke and Empire," in *Hanoverian Britain and Empire: Essays in Memory of Philip Lawson,* ed. Stephen Taylor, Richard Connors, and Clyve Jones (Rochester, NY: Boydell Press, 1998), pp. 288–298; and Richard Bourke, "Liberty, Authority, and Trust in Burke's Idea of Empire," *Journal of the History of Ideas* 61, no. 3 (2000): 453–471. See also Whelan, *Edmund Burke and India,* pp. 19–23.

88. See Marshall, "Burke and Empire," p. 290; see also his "Britain and the World in the Eighteenth Century: I, Reshaping the Empire," p. 11; and Hampsher-Monk, "Edmund Burke and Empire," p. 119.

89. Marshall, "The Eighteenth-Century Empire," pp. 192–193.

90. Burke, *W&S,* vol. 3, p. 70, emphasis original. Marshall makes reference to this passage in "Burke and Empire," p. 290.

91. On this point, see Marshall, "Burke and Empire," pp. 290–291.

92. Hampsher-Monk, "Edmund Burke and Empire," p. 120.

93. Bourke, "Liberty, Authority, and Trust in Burke's Idea of Empire," pp. 457, 455. See also Richard Bourke, "Sovereignty, Opinion and Revolution in Edmund Burke," *History of European Ideas* 25 (1999): 99–120.

94. Burke, *W&S,* vol. 9, pp. 488–489.

95. Burke, *W&S*, vol. 3, p. 132. The importance of this passage for comprehending Burke's overall view of empire is highlighted by both Bourke ("Liberty, Authority, and Trust in Burke's Idea of Empire," p. 457), and Hampsher-Monk ("Edmund Burke and Empire," p. 119).

96. Hampsher-Monk, "Edmund Burke and Empire," p. 118–119, emphasis original.

97. Burke, *W&S*, vol. 3, pp. 316–317, emphasis original. The importance of this passage is noted by Hampsher-Monk ("Edmund Burke and Empire," p. 119); and Marshall ("Burke and Empire," p. 292). In his book *The Making and Unmaking of Empires*, P. J. Marshall notes of this passage: "For Burke, an empire based on ideological propositions about Protestantism, commerce, maritime power and freedom had given way to an empire based on the practical needs of the very diverse peoples who were now the king's subjects" (p. 204).

98. See Bourke, "Liberty, Authority, and Trust in Burke's Idea of Empire."

99. Burke, "Ryder Diaries" (1766), in *W&S*, vol. 2, p. 50. The importance of this passage is noted by Bourke ("Liberty, Authority, and Trust in Burke's Idea of Empire," by Marshall ("Burke and Empire"), and by Armitage, "The British Conception of Empire in the Eighteenth Century," p. 104. On the broad theoretical point, see Hampsher-Monk, "Edmund Burke and Empire," p. 123.

100. Burke, *W&S*, vol. 6, p. 277; on the importance of this passage see Marshall, "Burke and Empire," p. 290.

101. For example, Bourke has turned to one of the most famous concepts in Burkean political theory, "prudence," in an attempt to delineate Burke's rationale for treating peoples differently within the imperial context ("Liberty, Authority, and Trust in Burke's Idea of Empire," pp. 455–456). However, this merely pushes the questions posed here to a different level of abstraction: namely, what counts as prudential action for Burke? Put differently, on what basis did Burke distinguish a prudent from an imprudent imperial policy? Absent a substantive answer to this question, prudence becomes an endlessly elastic category. Similarly, while Marshall has accurately suggested "that a body of underlying principle can be found in Burke's responses to imperial problems over a long period," his attempt to identify the leading thread of Burke's argument—"doing justice" under parliamentary sovereignty—is less helpful ("Burke and Empire," pp. 289, 292). As in the case of *prudence*, so, too, we can ask with such a vague term as *justice*—what does it mean for Burke? What would it mean, on Burke's view, for example to render "justice" to the Native Americans as opposed to the natives of India? As we shall see, two very different things, to be sure, but why? That is the question the present book is concerned to answer.

CHAPTER 2. THE NEW WORLD

1. On these issues, see esp. J. G. A. Pocock, "Political Thought in the English-Speaking Atlantic, 1760–1790: (I) The Imperial Crisis," and "Political Thought in

the English-Speaking Atlantic, 1760–1790: (II) Empire, Revolution, and an End of Early Modernity," in *The Varieties of British Political Thought, 1500–1800,* ed. J. G. A. Pocock (Cambridge: Cambridge University Press, 1993), pp. 246–317. See also his "Archipelago, Europe and Atlantic after 1688," in *The Discovery of Islands: Essays in British History,* by J. G. A. Pocock (Cambridge: Cambridge University Press, 2005), p. 111. On the Act of Union between England and Scotland as an "incorporating" rather than a "federating" one, see John Robertson, ed., *A Union for Empire: Political Thought and the British Union of 1707* (Cambridge: Cambridge University Press, 1995).

2. See Jack P. Greene, *Peripheries and Center: Constitutional Development in the Extended Polities of the British Empire and the United States, 1607–1788* (New York: W. W. Norton, 1990), pp. 79–80, 149–150. See also Eliga Gould, "Liberty and Modernity: The American Revolution and the Making of Parliament's Imperial History," in *Exclusionary Empire: English Liberty Overseas, 1600–1900,* ed. Jack P. Greene (Cambridge: Cambridge University Press, 2010), pp. 112–131.

3. On the importance of this fear for metropolitan arguments, see Greene, *Peripheries and Center,* pp. 118–119; and P. J. Marshall, "The Case for Coercing America before the Revolution," in *"A Free Though Conquering People": Eighteenth-Century Britain and Its Empire* (Aldershot, U.K.: Ashgate, 2003), pp. 9–22, at p. 16; and P. J. Marshall, *The Making and Unmaking of Empires: Britain, India, and America, c. 1750–1783* (Oxford: Oxford University Press, 2005), p. 167. For British arguments more generally, see Eliga Gould, *The Persistence of Empire: British Political Culture in the Age of the American Revolution* (Chapel Hill: University of North Carolina Press, 2000), esp. pp. 134–136.

4. Pocock, "Political Thought in the English-Speaking Atlantic, 1760–1790: (II)," pp. 261–265, 280–282. On the Lockean origins of the confederacy argument, see also Anthony Pagden, *Lords of All the World: Ideologies of Empire in Spain, Britain and France, c. 1500–c. 1800* (New Haven, CT: Yale University Press, 1995), pp. 128–130. For the colonists' assumptions that their legislative assemblies functioned as substitutes for Parliament, see Gould, "Liberty and Modernity," pp. 113–116.

5. See J. G. A. Pocock, "Empire, State and Confederation: The War of American Independence as a Crisis in Multiple Monarchy," in Pocock, *The Discovery of Islands,* pp. 146, 152–153.

6. See esp. Harry T. Dickinson, "Burke and the American Crisis," in *The Cambridge Companion to Edmund Burke,* ed. David Dwan and Christopher J. Insole (Cambridge: Cambridge University Press, 2012), pp. 156–167.

7. One prominent scholar has even surmised that the specific language of the Declaratory Act was suggested by Burke, given his familiarity with Irish affairs, because the wording of the legislation was modeled specifically on the Dependency of Ireland Act (Conor Cruise O'Brien, *The Great Melody: A Thematic Biography of Edmund Burke* [Chicago: University of Chicago Press, 1992], p. 112n1). O'Brien claims that Burke was "more likely than any other Rockingham to have been familiar with that precedent." However, in discussing O'Brien's hypothesis, John

Faulkner points out that Attorney General Charles Yorke, credited by other scholars with proposing the Declaratory Act, is also like to have known the precedent ("Burke's First Encounter with Richard Price: The Chathamites and North America," in *An Imaginative Whig: Reassessing the Life and Thought of Edmund Burke*, ed. Ian Crowe [Columbia: University of Missouri Press, 2005], pp. 93–126, at p. 95n3).

8. Edmund Burke, *The Writings and Speeches of Edmund Burke*, Paul Langford, general editor, 9 vols. (Oxford: Oxford University Press, 1981–2015), vol. 3, p. 314, hereafter *W&S*.

9. On this point, see Dickinson, "Burke and the American Crisis," p. 159. For an argument that the theoretical view of metropolitan sovereignty held by Burke and the Rockingham Whigs was therefore at bottom no different than that of George Grenville, who pushed through the Stamp Act, see Stephen Conway, "Britain and the Revolutionary Crisis, 1763–1791," in *The Oxford History of the British Empire: The Eighteenth Century*, ed. P. J. Marshall (Oxford: Oxford University Press, 2001), pp. 325–346, at pp. 329–330.

10. Burke, *W&S*, vol. 2, pp. 47, 49.

11. Ibid., p. 49, 50 (second quotation is from the Ryder Diaries).

12. Ibid., p. 194.

13. Ibid., p. 194. For Burke's claims that the colonists are the "descendants of Englishmen," see also *W&S*, vol. 3, p. 120.

14. See Burke, "Second Speech on Conciliation" (as per the *Parliamentary Register*), in *W&S*, vol. 3, p. 193, emphasis original.

15. See Burke, *The Correspondence of Edmund Burke*, ed. Thomas W. Copeland (Chicago: University of Chicago Press, 1958–1978), vol. 3, pp. 181–182, emphasis original; hereafter, Corr.

16. Burke, *W&S*, vol. 3, p. 119, emphasis original.

17. For an expansion of the themes in the next few paragraphs, see Daniel I. O'Neill, *The Burke-Wollstonecraft Debate: Savagery, Civilization, and Democracy* (University Park: Penn State University Press, 2007), esp. chap. 4. For the ways in which this historical understanding of civilization went back to Burke's *Philosophical Enquiry into the Origin Our Ideas of the Sublime and Beautiful* (1757) and *An Essay Towards an Abridgment of the English History* (1757), see *The Burke-Wollstonecraft Debate*, chap. 2.

18. See *An Appeal from the New to the Old Whigs*, in *The Works of the Right Honourable Edmund Burke*, Bohn's British Classics (London: Bell & Daldy, 1872), vol. 3, p. 85 (hereafter, *Works*).

19. Burke, *W&S*, vol. 8, p. 147.

20. Burke, *Works*, vol. 3, p. 87.

21. Burke, *W&S*, vol. 3, pp. 64–70.

22. For passionate rejections of both, see Burke's "Speech on a Committee to Inquire into the State of the Representation of the Commons in Parliament" (1782), in *The Portable Edmund Burke*, ed. Isaac Kramnick (New York: Penguin Books, 1999), pp. 174–182.

23. As Burke later put it in his *Letter to Sir Hercules Langrishe* (1792): "Virtual representation is that in which there is a communion of interests, and a sympathy in feelings and desires between those who act in the name of any description of people, and the people in whose name they act, though the trustees are not actually chosen by them. This is virtual representation. Such a representation I think to be, in many cases, even better than the actual" (*W&S*, vol. 9, p. 629). I discuss this portion of Burke's position as it relates to Ireland in chapter 4. For a general overview of Burke on representation, see James Conniff, *The Useful Cobbler: Edmund Burke and the Politics of Progress* (Albany: State University of New York Press, 1994).

24. Burke, *W&S*, vol. 8, pp. 143–146.
25. Ibid., pp. 128–129.
26. Burke, *Works*, vol. 3, p 85.
27. Burke, *W&S*, vol. 3, p. 120.
28. Ibid., p. 121.
29. Ibid., p. 125.
30. Ibid., p. 121.
31. The quote is from ibid., p. 125.
32. Ibid., p. 121.
33. Burke, *W&S*, vol. 3, pp. 121–122, 124, 130. For a perceptive reading of these passages in Burke along similar lines, see J. C. D. Clark, "Edmund Burke's *Reflections on the Revolution in America* (1777): Or, How Did the American Revolution Relate to the French?" in Crowe, *An Imaginative Whig*, pp. 71–92, at pp. 82–84.

34. Burke, *W&S*, vol. 3, pp. 122–123, 130.
35. Pocock, "Political Thought in the English-Speaking Atlantic, 1760–1790," p. 277. Likewise, P. J. Marshall asserts that Burke was a rare exception in that he did not share in the general inability of metropolitan Britons "to envisage colonial America in concrete terms as a distinct society rather than as an abstract problem of governance and economic regulation" ("Britain and the World in the Eighteenth Century, II: Britons and Americans," in Marshall, *"A Free Though Conquering People,"* p. 3n3).

36. Burke's view of the Americans as a people defined by a "high and free spirit" went back at least to his 1769 *Observations on a Late State of the Nation,* where he noted, "People must be governed in a manner agreeable to their temper and disposition; and men of free character and spirit must be ruled with, at least, some condescension to this spirit and this character. The British colonist must see something which will distinguish him from the colonists of other nations" (*W&S*, vol. 2, p. 194).

37. See Pocock, "Empire, State and Confederation," p. 150. In the same essay, Pocock succinctly describes Burke's position as one which held that, in the absence of a clearly articulated and jointly shared definition of the legal status of the American colonies, "there were no debatable issues and the mistake lay in trying to debate them" (p. 155). Elsewhere, Pocock describes Burke's belief "that all that was necessary was a return to the system of informal empire which had benignly ruled by a series of customary understandings" ("Political Thought in the English-Speaking Atlantic, 1760–1790," p. 266).

38. Burke, *W&S*, vol. 3, p. 118. For the importance of this phrase for understanding Burke's approach to empire in the American colonies, see Gould, "Liberty and Modernity," p. 117; and Faulkner, "Burke's First Encounter with Richard Price," pp. 96–97.

39. On the centrality of the Navigation Acts, see Stephen Conway, "Britain and the Revolutionary Crisis, 1763–1791," pp. 325–326. For broad American acceptance of them, see Gould, *The Persistence of Empire,* pp. 123–125.

40. Burke, *W&S*, vol. 3, p. 114.

41. Ibid., pp. 137–138. Warren Elofson and John Woods, the editors of vol. 3 of Burke's *Writings and Speeches,* do a fine job of explicating his simultaneous commitment to increased trade between Britain and America, and his unwillingness to give up on the fundamental premises of mercantilism and colonialism, at pp. 44, and 138nn1–2. For the differences between Burke and the "free trade" school, see Donald Winch, *Riches and Poverty: An Intellectual History of Political Economy in Britain, 1750–1834* (Cambridge: Cambridge University Press, 1996).

42. On this internal/external distinction, see esp. Greene, *Peripheries and Center,* pp. 114–115, 120–122.

43. Burke, *W&S*, vol. 2, p. 458; see also pp. 429–430.

44. See Dickinson, "Burke and the American Crisis," pp. 161–164.

45. On subsequent taxes, see Conway, "Britain and the Revolutionary Crisis, 1763–1791," pp. 331–336.

46. See Greene, *Peripheries and Center,* pp. 82–113.

47. See ibid., pp. 79–82.

48. Burke, *Observations on a Late State of the Nation* (1769), in *W&S*, vol. 2, p. 177; emphasis added.

49. For Burke's dismissal of American representation in Parliament, see also *W&S*, vol. 3, pp. 145–146; and his 1776 letter to Francis Maséres, the former attorney general of Quebec, who was a noted defender of American representation, in *The Correspondence of Edmund Burke,* in *Corr.*, vol. 3, pp. 306–308.

50. Burke, *W&S*, vol. 3, pp. 146, 373–374.

51. See O'Neill, *The Burke-Wollstonecraft Debate,* esp. chap. 2.

52. Burke, *W&S*, vol. 3, pp. 164–165.

53. Ibid., p. 280. On the importance of "affection" for Burke's imperial strategy with respect to the colonies, see Clark, "Edmund Burke's *Reflections on the Revolution in America* (1777)," p. 83.

54. Burke, *W&S*, vol. 3, p. 165.

55. Ibid., pp. 323.

56. Ibid., pp. 182, 266; see also *Corr.*, vol. 3, pp. 181, 230.

57. Ibid., p. 394. Also see Dickinson, "Burke and the American Crisis," pp. 164–165.

58. Burke, *Corr.*, vol. 4, pp. 418–419, at p. 419 (letter of 28 February 1782). P. J. Marshall directs us to this letter in *The Making and Unmaking of Empires,* p. 356n12.

59. See O'Neill, *The Burke-Wollstonecraft Debate,* esp. chap. 2.

60. Burke, *Corr.*, vol. 3, pp. 350–351.

61. Burke's depiction of this ethnographic and comparative endeavor has become well known to scholars, as seen in P. J. Marshall and Glyndwr Williams's *The Great Map of Mankind: Perceptions of New Worlds in the Age of Enlightenment*, which takes its title from Burke's turn of phrase in this letter (Cambridge, MA: Harvard University Press, 1982).

62. Edmund and Will Burke, *An Account of the European Settlements in America*, 2 vols. (1757; repr., New York: Arno Press, 1972), hereafter, *Account*.

63. For the book's provenance, see F. P. Lock, *Edmund Burke*, vol. 1: *1730–1784* (Oxford: Oxford University Press, 1998), pp. 127–130. Lock notes that, since Edmund's was the superior intellect, there is some justification for attributing to him "any remark of superior insight" to be found in the text; at any rate, the work as a whole "owes much to his mind" (pp. 127, 130). At the time, James Boswell recorded in his journal that Burke had admitted to him that he had contributed to and, more important, "revised" the book. For his part, Boswell believed "it is every where evident that [Edmund] Burke himself has contributed a great deal to it." A similar view was held by one of Burke's earliest biographers, James Prior (see Lock, *Edmund Burke*, vol. 1, p. 127). Lock also makes the connection between the *Account* and Burke's affinity for Robertson's book as expressed in Burke's letter, and he describes both texts as kindred attempts at "mapping mankind" (p. 136).

64. Of this section, Lock concludes, "Given the different outlooks of Edmund and Will, the one philosophical, the other preoccupied with economic exploitation, it can confidently be ascribed to Edmund" (*Edmund Burke*, vol. 1, p. 136).

65. *Account*, vol. 1, pp. 201, 198.

66. Burke, *W&S*, vol. 8, pp. 117, 122. On the connection between the first passage and the *Account*, see Luke Gibbons, *Edmund Burke and Ireland: Aesthetics, Politics, and the Colonial Sublime* (Cambridge: Cambridge University Press, 2003), pp. 183–185, 204–207. However, Gibbons's interpretation of this passage's meaning is highly problematic (as I discuss shortly). On the theme of the second, see Linda M. G. Zerilli, "'The Furies of Hell': Woman in Burke's 'French Revolution,'" in her *Signifying Woman: Culture and Chaos in Rousseau, Burke, and Mill* (Ithaca, NY: Cornell University Press, 1994), pp. 60–94. Of course, Burke's depiction of the French revolutionaries as "cannibals"—a term he often used figuratively but occasionally literally to describe them—was one of his favorite tropes. On these themes generally, see O'Neill, *The Burke-Wollstonecraft Debate*, chaps. 4 and 6.

67. *Account*, vol. 1, pp. 173–174.

68. Ibid., pp. 199–200.

69. Burke, *W&S*, vol. 3, p. 356.

70. See esp. Colin Kidd, "Ethnicity in the British Atlantic World, 1688–1830," in *A New Imperial History: Culture, Identity, and Modernity in Britain and the Empire, 1660–1840*, ed. Kathleen Wilson (Cambridge: Cambridge University Press, 2004), pp. 260–277. Kidd argues that, "despite the undoubted reality of racism, slavery, and xenophobia," in fact, "ethnicity was first and foremost a theological issue throughout the early modern period" (pp. 261–262). See also Kathleen Wilson, *The*

Island Race: Englishness, Empire and Gender in the Eighteenth Century (London: Routledge, 2003), pp. 7–8.

71. *Account*, vol. 1, pp. 168–169.

72. Ibid., pp. 175–176.

73. To some extent, these views link Burke's position to that of Scottish Enlightenment modernists, specifically Adam Smith and William Robertson. As Frederick Whelan argues, for Smith, Robertson, and later John Millar, "equality is a product of extreme primitivism, while stable subordination, like other aspects of a differentiated social structure, is both a sign of civilization and a necessary support for orderly economic and political life"("Scottish Theorists, French Jesuits, and the 'Rude Nations' of North America," in his *Enlightenment Political Thought and Non-Western Societies: Sultans and Savages* [New York: Routledge, 2009], pp. 48–77, quoted at p. 60). Whelan insightfully goes on to remark that for thinkers like Smith and Robertson, "democratic governance may be deduced from social equality" (p. 61).

74. Whelan notes that among this group of thinkers, Robertson "offers perhaps the most negative view of the savagery and vices of the Indians, including those of North America," and mentions that "Robertson's (uncompleted) aspiration to write a narrative of European empires presupposed a view of the American natives as savages in need of civilization" ("Scottish Theorists, French Jesuits, and the 'Rude Nations' of North America," pp. 53, 76). A number of other scholars have arrived at the same conclusion. For general overviews, see the essays of N. T. Phillipson, "Providence and Progress: An Introduction to the Historical Thought of William Robertson," and Karen O'Brien, "Robertson's Place in the Development of Eighteenth-Century Narrative History," in *William Robertson and the Expansion of Empire*, ed. Stewart J. Brown (Cambridge: Cambridge University Press, 1997), pp. 55–73, and 74–91. Robertson's linking of stadial history to providence and commercial expansion, a narrative in which supposedly superior European minds were spreading their blessings across the globe to the uncivilized, meant that the Native Americans faced a tragic choice between assimilating and perishing (see Bruce P. Lenman, "'From Savage to Scot' via the French and the Spaniards: Principal Robertson's Spanish Sources," in Brown, *William Robertson and the Expansion of Empire*, p. 209). Such evidence has led J. G. A. Pocock to assert, "It is necessary, therefore, to read the *History of America* as a classical text in what we used to call 'imperialism' and presently call 'colonialism'" (see *Barbarism and Religion*, vol. 4: *Barbarians, Savages, and Empires* [Cambridge: Cambridge University Press, 2005], p. 190).

Nevertheless, Whelan has resisted linking Burke's stance with Robertson's, arguing instead that the *Account* was heavily influenced by Joseph-François Lafitau's more positive assessment of the Amerindians and was thus "surprisingly favorable" in its views of the Native Americans. This is particularly evident, Whelan claims, in that the text "notably does not refer to the Indians as 'savages,' thus avoiding the various (often negative) connotations of that word" (afterword to *Enlightenment Political Thought and Non-Western Societies*, pp. 167–168, quoted at 168). However, it is simply not true that Burke refrained from referring to the natives of North America by the pejorative term *savage* in the *Account*, as I show presently.

75. *Account*, vol. 1, p. 186; vol. 2, p. 202; vol. 1, p. 194.

76. *Account*, vol. 2, pp. 31–32.

77. See esp. Linda Colley, *Captives* (New York: Pantheon Books, 2002); and Aziz Rana, *The Two Faces of American Freedom* (Cambridge, MA: Harvard University Press, 2010).

78. See Colley, *Captives*, p. 171; and Rana, *The Two Faces of American Freedom*, p. 27.

79. See Colley, *Captives*, pp. 200–237. For the problems posed by Quebec in particular, see esp. Peter Marshall, "British North America, 1760–1815," in Marshall, *The Oxford History of the British Empire: The Eighteenth Century*, pp. 372–393.

80. On this theme, see Daniel K. Richter, "Native Peoples of North America and the Eighteenth-Century British Empire," in Marshall, *The Oxford History of the British Empire: The Eighteenth Century*, pp. 347–371, esp. pp. 364–365. See also Marshall and Williams, *The Great Map of Mankind*, pp. 209–210, and Marshall, *The Making and Unmaking of Empires*, p. 280.

81. See Rana, *The Two Faces of American Freedom*, pp. 1–79;

82. See ibid., esp. pp. 3–8, 21–25, 48, 65–66, 68. See also C. A. Bayly, "The British and Indigenous Peoples, 1760–1860: Power, Perception and Identity," in *Empire and Others: British Encounters with Indigenous Peoples, 1600–1850*, ed. Martin Daunton and Rick Halpern (Philadelphia: University of Pennsylvania Press, 1999), pp. 19–41.

83. See Colley, *Captives*, pp. 202, 207, 232–233.

84. Richter, "Native Peoples of North America and the Eighteenth-Century British Empire," p. 347.

85. Burke, *W&S*, vol. 3, pp. 115–116.

86. Ibid., p. 129.

87. Ibid., p. 166.

88. Ibid., pp. 281–282.

89. Ibid., pp. 267–268.

90. Ibid., p. 180.

91. Ibid., pp. 355–356.

92. Ibid., p. 365, emphasis original.

93. Ibid., p. 361.

94. Ibid., pp. 361, 357–358. On the importance of the McCrea incident and Burke's utilization of it, see Colley, *Captives*, pp. 228–232. In a draft of the speech at Sheffield, Burke's notes read, "Their mode of War can be no other.—proved not to be altered or alterable mode of War—not from Henepin and Lahontan but authors of the first Magnitude and Credit—Lafitau—Charlevoix—Governor Colden" (*W&S*, vol. 3, p. 366). Once again, this demonstrates that the conclusions about Native American "savagery" that Burke drew from his sources run counter to those described by Whelan, irrespective of how sympathetically those sources themselves might read their Amerindian subjects.

95. Burke, *W&S*, vol. 3, pp. 363–364.

96. In *Edmund Burke and Ireland*, Luke Gibbons considers some of Burke's writings on Native Americans and follows Colley in drawing attention to the McC-

rea incident. However, his conclusions are diametrically opposed to those drawn here (and by Colley, for that matter). Gibbons argues that, for Burke, "The Indians' savagery was not entirely of their own making, but may have been one of the consequences of their succumbing to white civilization." That is, Gibbons argues, savagery or barbarism "for Burke is not so much an inherent characteristic of Indian life as a state into which they have fallen due to historical circumstances, which in their case meant the corrosive influence of colonization" (pp. 187–188). The implausible conclusion Gibbons draws from this reading is that, for Burke, "the ultimate responsibility for the 'natural' ferocity of the Indians lay not with the savages themselves but with their civilizing masters" (p. 207; see also pp. 200–203). The problem with this conclusion should be clear: By neglecting not only large amounts of textual evidence but also Burke's own theory of history—not to mention the broader imperial context in which that theory was articulated—Gibbons gets Burke's position exactly the wrong way around, by failing to understand that for Burke the Amerindians were savages precisely because they lacked the defining institutional features of civilization. For Burke, this was what led the Native American "savages" to such reprehensible behavior, not British or colonial civilization and commerce. Furthermore, Gibbons misses Burke's intentions in invoking such examples as the McCrea incident and others in the first place, which was not to castigate the colonists or the British but rather to bind them closer together by depicting the Amerindians as lesser beings in need of civilization by them.

97. See David Richardson, "The British Empire and the Atlantic Slave Trade, 1660–1807," in Marshall, *The Oxford History of the British Empire: The Eighteenth Century*, pp. 440–464, at pp. 440–441.

98. See Philip D. Morgan, "The Black Experience in the British Empire, 1680–1810," in Marshall, *The Oxford History of the British Empire: The Eighteenth Century*, pp. 465–486, at p. 465.

99. For example, one of Burke's early biographers argues that the campaign for the abolition of the slave trade should be given honorary mention as one of Burke's great causes (see Carl B. Cone, *Burke and the Nature of Politics: The Age of the French Revolution* [Lexington: University of Kentucky Press, 1964], p. 385). Likewise, Conor Cruise O'Brien has asserted unequivocally that "Burke hated slavery" (*The Great Melody*, p. 91). Luke Gibbons claims simply that Burke was "among the foremost opponents of slavery at this early period" (*Edmund Burke and Ireland*, p. 167).

100. On this theme, see Lock, *Edmund Burke*, vol. 1, p. 133.

101. *Account*, vol. 2, pp. 128–129.

102. For an exceptional (in both senses of that term) reading of the *Account*'s argument on slavery, see Michel Fuchs, *Edmund Burke, Ireland, and the Fashioning of the Self* (Oxford: Voltaire Foundation, 1996), pp. 99–103, to which the following paragraphs are indebted.

103. *Account*, vol. 1, p. 309.

104. Richardson, "The British Empire and the Atlantic Slave Trade," p. 453.

105. *Account*, vol. 1, pp. 309–310; quoted at p. 310.

106. *Account*, vol. 2, pp. 265–266.

107. *Account*, vol. 1, pp. 285–286.
108. Ibid., p. 241.
109. Ibid., pp. 279, 285.
110. *Account*, vol. 2, p. 128.
111. Ibid., pp. 129–130. The online *Oxford English Dictionary* defines an "eye-servant" in part as "one who does his duty only when under the eye of his master or employer."
112. Burke, *W&S*, vol. 3, pp. 130–131.
113. Ibid.
114. See Rana, *The Two Faces of American Freedom*, pp. 79–89.
115. See Colley, *Captives*, pp. 233–235.
116. Burke, *W&S*, vol. 3, p. 281.
117. Ibid., p. 360.
118. Ibid., p. 359. On Lord Dunmore's Proclamation, see pp. 267–268.
119. Ibid., p. 360n1.
120. Ibid., p. 360.
121. Ibid., pp. 340–341.
122. See Burke, *Corr.*, vol. 3, pp. 345–346; see also pp. 340–342 for Burke's direct correspondence with John Bourke dated May 21, 1777. Bourke was a member of the committee running the Africa Company and had also appealed for help to Burke as a powerful MP sympathetic to the Company's plight.
123. Burke, *W&S*, vol. 3, pp. 340–341.
124. Burke, *Corr.*, vol. 4, pp. 60, 62.
125. Burke, *W&S*, vol. 3, p. 631.
126. Ibid., p. 210.
127. Ibid., p. 462.
128. Ibid., pp. 562–581.
129. On this movement, see John Oldenfield, *Popular Politics and British Anti-Slavery: The Mobilisation of Public Opinion against the Slave Trade, 1787–1807* (Manchester, U.K.: Manchester University Press, 1995).
130. Burke, *Corr.*, vol. 7, pp. 122, 124, emphasis original.
131. Ibid., p. 124.
132. *W&S*, vol. 3, pp. 567–568.
133. Burke, *Corr.*, vol. 7, p. 124.
134. See David Brion Davis, *The Problem of Slavery in Western Culture* (Ithaca, NY: Cornell University Press, 1966), pp. 396–399.
135. See Christopher L. Brown, "From Slaves to Subjects: Envisioning an Empire without Slavery, 1772–1834," in *Black Experience and the Empire*, ed. Philip D. Morgan and Sean Hawkins (Oxford: Oxford University Press, 2004), pp. 111–140, quoted at pp. 111–112, 123, 125.
136. Burke, *W&S*, vol. 3, p. 580.
137. Ibid., pp. 580–581; emphasis added.
138. Burke's lengthiest intervention on the topic is mentioned by O'Brien, *The Great Melody*, pp. 418–419. The most thorough discussion is Sunil M. Agnani's *Hat-*

ing Empire Properly: The Two Indies and the Limits of Enlightenment Anticolonialism (New York: Fordham University Press, 2013), pp. 133–161. However, my interpretation of these passages is very different from Agnani's, for reasons I make clear here.

139. William Cobbett, ed., *Cobbett's Parliamentary History of England* (London: T. C. Hansard, 1806), vol. 29, pp. 366–367.

140. Ibid., p. 367.

141. See O'Neill, *The Burke-Wollstonecraft Debate,* chaps. 4 and 6.

142. Burke, *W&S*, vol. 9, p. 99.

143. See letter of December 24, 1796, in Burke, *Corr.*, vol. 9, pp. 198–202, quoted at p. 202.

144. Recently, it has been argued that Burke's position on the slave rebellions in the West Indies during the 1790s points to the "limits of Enlightenment anticolonialism." Sunil Agnani maintains that Burke's responses to black violence display a "fear" that seems incongruous "in a writer otherwise sympathetic to movements for justice in Europe's colonies." Specifically, they "seem in tension with his passionate denunciations of fellow Briton Warren Hastings for the abuses he oversaw at the East India Company in Bengal." Similarly, Burke's defense of the West Indian planter aristocracy is said to demonstrate "the pressures put on Burke's thought by the events in St. Domingue"; while Burke's denunciation of black political representatives prompts the claim that interpreters "must supplement the more sympathetic reading of his fear on behalf of the vulnerable elements in a body politic with a troubled reflection upon what does not earn his sympathy" (*Hating Empire Properly,* pp. 134, 144, 150). Although Agnani's recognition that there are deeply troubling dimensions of Burke's position on empire is a welcome advance over the usual paeans to his thinking on the subject, it is nevertheless problematic from the perspective of the argument I am advancing here, for a number of reasons. First, as we have already seen, it is misleading to see Burke as fundamentally "anticolonial" or "anti-imperial" in any sense, whether in the West Indies, America, India, or Ireland. In the West Indies, as everywhere else, Burke remained deeply committed to maintaining the colonies as an integral part of the British Empire. Therefore, the case study of Burke's views on the West Indies cannot demonstrate the "limits" of a position ("anticolonialism") that he never in fact held. Second, Agnani does not engage with Burke's broader position on African slavery, the Native Americans, or the American colonies in any depth. Consequently, he fails to come to grips with Burke's overall view of empire in the New World and to situate his views on the West Indies within it. However, as I have tried to show, if one takes all of this evidence into account, and especially if one situates Burke's approach to empire in the New World within the framework of his particular understanding of history as a civilizing process, then his views on the West Indies are not "in tension" with his positions on imperial governance elsewhere but, rather, deeply consistent with his overarching conservative logic of empire. Finally, like those of many other scholars, Agnani's conclusion—that Burke was "otherwise sympathetic to movements for justice in Europe's colonies"—is ultimately derived from an implausible reading of Burke's writings and speeches on India.

145. This conclusion also differs from that of Guido Abbattista, "Edmund Burke, the Atlantic American War and the 'Poor Jews at St. Eustatius,'" *Cromohs*, no. 13 (2008): 1–39. Abbattista focuses on Burke's criticism of the treatment of the minority Jewish merchant community on the small West Indian island of Saint Eustatius early in the so-called fourth Anglo-Dutch War of 1780–1784, which was part of the broader imperial conflict precipitated by the American Revolution. Abbattista argues that Burke's criticisms "undoubtedly stand out for their noble, liberal and, we may confidently say, enlightened stature" (p. 3). However, and strikingly, Abbattista makes this unvarnished assertion about Burke's "enlightened" position even as Burke himself ignored entirely the island's majority population, African slaves, who did not merit his consideration. The "civilized" Jews earn Burke's empathy, while the Africans do not even make it meaningfully into Burke's speech. As such, the sufferings of the "savages" are effectively effaced from Burke's narrative.

CHAPTER 3. INDIA

1. In this respect, if in no other, my approach is similar to that of Uday S. Mehta's *Liberalism and Empire: A Study in Nineteenth-Century British Liberal Thought* (Chicago: University of Chicago Press, 1999). For his part, Mehta argues that Burke's view of India was marked by a profound humility in the face of a world that he did not understand. He writes, "Burke exposes himself and enters a dialogue with the unfamiliar and accepts the possible risks of that encounter. Those risks include the possibility of being confronted with utter opacity—an intransigent strangeness, an unfamiliarity that remains so, an experience that cannot be shared, prejudices that do not readily fuse with a cosmopolitan horizon, a difference that cannot be assimilated. In accepting these risks and not settling them in advance of the encounter, Burke, I believe, shatters the philosophic underpinnings of the project of the empire by making it no more than a conversation between *two* strangers" (p. 22, emphasis original). For Mehta, it is this willingness to engage in a "conversation across boundaries of strangeness" that ultimately produces the "cosmopolitanism of sentiments" he ascribes to Burke (pp. 42, 139; see also pp. 136 and 216).

2. This phrase comes from F. P. Lock, *Edmund Burke* (Oxford: Oxford University Press, 1998, 2006), vol. 2, pp. 161–176, and vol. 1, pp. 529–532. On Lock's specific claim that, for Burke, India was "another Europe," see vol. 2, pp. 164, 173. See also P. J. Marshall, "Burke and India," in *The Enduring Edmund Burke*, ed. Ian Crowe (Wilmington, DE: Intercollegiate Studies Institute, 1997), pp. 39–47.

3. Edmund Burke, *The Writings and Speeches of Edmund Burke*, Paul Langford, general editor, 9 vols. (Oxford: Oxford University Press, 1981–2015), vol. 5, pp. 389–390 (hereafter *W&S*).

4. Of this passage Frederick Whelan rightly notes, "India contains all the ingredients that add up to a thriving civilization as Burke understands this, that is, a

recognized social hierarchy, property, religion, and other institutions, all firmly grounded in long usage" (see *Enlightenment Political Thought and Non-Western Societies: Sultans and Savages* [New York: Routledge, 2009], pp. 103–129, quoted at p. 114; see also Frederick Whelan, *Edmund Burke and India* [Pittsburgh, PA: University of Pittsburgh Press, 1996], p. 5).

5. Of this crucial difference, Regina Janes smartly notes, "Burke's tackling of the Hastings impeachment was predicated on his perception of Indian society. It is extremely unlikely that he would have exerted himself as he did had he thought India to be similar to those societies" that he called gangs of savages. Instead, in India Burke "found a civilized society not identical to, but fully analogous with, the societies of Europe" (see Regina Janes, "At Home Abroad: Edmund Burke in India," *Bulletin of Research in the Humanities* 82, no. 2 [1979]: 160–174, quoted at pp. 163–164).

6. Burke, *W&S*, vol. 5, p. 390.

7. See Lock, *Edmund Burke,* vol. 2, pp. 170–171, 168.

8. Burke, *W&S,* vol. 5, pp. 520–521.

9. In his essay "Burke on India" (*The Cambridge Companion to Edmund Burke,* ed. David Dwan and Christopher J. Insole [Cambridge: Cambridge University Press, 2012], pp. 168–180), Frederick Whelan aptly notes, "Burke's study of India convinced him that the company's misrule was being inflicted on, and disrupting, a stable social order that embodied an ancient and refined civilization, a civilization that was comparable to those of Europe and equally deserving of respect" (p. 172).

10. Quote from Lord Holland, *Memoirs of the Whig Party during My Time,* cited by P. J. Marshall, in his introduction to Burke, *W&S,* vol. 5, p. 13.

11. Burke, *W&S,* vol. 6, pp. 304–305.

12. Ibid., p. 305.

13. Ibid., pp. 302–303, emphasis original.

14. Marshall maintains, "The Hindu religion and the Hindu social order were, Burke thought, impossible to separate. Religion had shaped the social order in the very remote past and had clamped it into a mold which remained unchanging throughout the centuries" (Marshall, introduction to *W&S,* vol. 6, p. 21). Similarly, Whelan notes, "The integration of individuals into a profoundly, even rigidly, customary community seemed especially obvious in Hindu India, where, as Burke explained, the laws of the land, of religion, and of honor, coincided in the ancient rules of the caste system." For Whelan, Burke's view of Hinduism formed a central pillar of his "traditionalism," the key to understanding Burke's overall view on empire in India. As such, it helps underpin Whelan's "substantial agreement with the thesis that Burke's appreciation of Indian traditions made him one of the first to develop a 'conservative theory of Indian society, culture, and government'" (see *Edmund Burke and India,* pp. 262–265, quoted at pp. 262–263).

It bears mention that contemporary scholars of India have largely rejected essentialist interpretations of caste like Burke's. They argue that such views, which have become central to our contemporary understanding of caste, are as much a product of British imperialism in India as they are a depiction of some underlying Indian reality. On this score, see Susan Bayly, *Caste, Society, and Politics in India from the Eighteenth Century to the Modern Age* (Cambridge: Cambridge University Press, 1999); and Nicholas B. Dirks, *Castes of Mind: Colonialism and the Making of Modern India* (Princeton, NJ: Princeton University Press, 2001). The latter book actually opens with an epigraph taken from Burke's depiction of caste, which is itself testament to his role in the creation of the modern understanding of the concept.

15. Burke, *W&S*, vol. 5, p. 522.

16. Ibid., p. 392.

17. P.J. Marshall, "The British in Asia: Trade to Dominion," in *The Oxford History of the British Empire: The Eighteenth Century*, ed. P.J. Marshall (Oxford: Oxford University Press, 2001), pp. 487–507, at p. 503.

18. Cited in Linda Colley, *Captives* (New York: Pantheon Books, 2002), p. 251.

19. P.J. Marshall, *The Making and Unmaking of Empires: Britain, India, and America, c. 1750–1783* (Oxford: Oxford University Press, 2005), p. 185.

20. See esp. C.A. Bayly, *Indian Society and the Making of the British Empire* (Cambridge: Cambridge University Press, 1998); P.J. Marshall, "Britain and the World in the Eighteenth Century: III, Britain and India," and "Britain and the World in the Eighteenth Century, IV: The Turning Outwards of Britain," in *"A Free Though Conquering People": Eighteenth-Century Britain and Its Empire* (Aldershot, U.K.: Ashgate, 2003); Robert Travers, *Ideology and Empire in Eighteenth-Century India* (Cambridge: Cambridge University Press, 2007); Robert Travers, "Contested Despotism: Problems of Liberty in British India," in *Exclusionary Empire: English Liberties Overseas, 1600–1900*, ed. Jack P. Greene (Cambridge: Cambridge University Press, 2010), 191–219; and Rajat Kanta Ray, "Indian Society and the Establishment of British Supremacy, 1765–1818," in Marshall, *The Oxford History of the British Empire*, pp. 508–529. Colley, too, stresses this point, in *Captives*, pp. 251–253.

21. Bayly, *Indian Society and the Making of the British Empire*, p. 18.

22. Ray, "Indian Society and the Establishment of British Supremacy," p. 510.

23. Colley, *Captives*, p. 252.

24. P.J. Marshall, *The Making and Unmaking of Empires*, pp. 271–272.

25. See Marshall, "Britain and the World in the Eighteenth Century: III," pp. 3–6, 9–11, 15–16; see also Marshall, "Britain and the World in the Eighteenth Century: IV," pp. 16–18. For commercial similarities between Britain and India, see Onur Ulas Ince, "Not a Partnership in Pepper, Calico, or Tobacco: Edmund Burke and the Vicissitudes of Colonial Capitalism," *Polity* 44, no. 3 (2012): 340–372.

26. See Travers, *Ideology and Empire in Eighteenth-Century India*, pp. 8–9, 23–24, 27, 228–229, 241.

27. Burke, *W&S*, vol. 6, pp. 281–282. Travers rightly stresses the importance of this crucial passage in *Ideology and Empire*, pp. 220–221.

28. See Travers, *Ideology and Empire*, pp. 217–223.

29. For a general overview, see Michael Curtis, *Orientalism and Islam: European Thinkers on Oriental Despotism in the Middle East and India* (Cambridge: Cambridge University Press, 2009), esp. pp. 67–71; and chap. 5, "Edmund Burke and Despotism in India," pp. 103–138. See also Whelan, *Edmund Burke and India*,

pp. 188–260. Like Travers, Curtis stresses that, for Burke, the Mughals had preserved the deeply hierarchical Hindu world that they had inherited (pp. 119–124).

30. Quoted in Travers, *Ideology and* Empire, p. 218. See esp. *W&S*, vol. 6, pp. 347–349, where Burke references Hastings's remarks to this effect.

31. Burke, *W&S*, vol. 7, p. 265.

32. Burke, *W&S*, vol. 6, p. 353. This is a point Burke makes repeatedly in his writings and speeches on India, as for example in the "Speech in Reply": "Now Mahometans are so far from having no Laws or rights that when you name a Mahometan, you name a man governed by Law, a Prince governed by Law, a people entitled to protection by Law, and by Law only" (*W&S*, vol. 7, p. 273). In general, see *W&S*, vol. 6, pp. 352–360; and *W&S*, vol. 7, pp. 264–286, 570.

33. Burke, *W&S*, vol. 6, p. 110. See Marshall's editorial preface to Burke's "Rohilla War Charge" speech in *W&S*, vol. 6, pp. 80–81.

34. Burke, *W&S*, vol. 6, pp. 84, 110, 100.

35. Ibid., pp. 79–113.

36. Regarding the Hindus, Burke writes, "These people are governed, not by the arbitrary power of any one, but by laws and institutions in which there is the substance of a whole body of equity, diversified by the manners and customs of the people, but having in it that which makes law good for anything, a substantial body of equity and great principles of jurisprudence, both civil and criminal" (*W&S*, vol. 6, pp. 365–366).

37. Burke, *W&S*, vol. 6, p. 346.

38. Burke, *W&S*, vol. 7, p. 276.

39. *W&S*, vol. 6, p. 365–366; see also vol. 7, pp. 282–283.

40. Burke, *W&S*, vol. 6, p. 281.

41. As Nicholas Dirks wryly observes in *The Scandal of Empire: India and the Creation of Imperial Britain* (Cambridge, MA: Harvard University Press, 2006), "Burke's tirades against Hastings might have been the national expression of a bad conscience, but Burke no more offered to give India back to the Mughals than did Hastings offer to return his early winnings to the Company. Indeed, the trial of Warren Hastings was at one level simply the continuation of earlier parliamentary efforts to take control over a rogue English state, to harness imperial power—and wealth—securely to Britain. And once that was accomplished, whatever the particular political, or financial, fortunes of Warren Hastings, empire would no longer be a scandal" (p. 21). For similar points, see also Marouf Hasian Jr., "Nostalgic Longings and Imaginary Indias: Postcolonial Analysis, Collective Memories, and the Impeachment Trial of Warren Hastings," *Western Journal of Communication* 66, no. 2 (2002): 229–255; and Andrew McCann's chapter "Edmund Burke's Immortal Law: Reading the Impeachment of Warren Hastings, 1788," in his *Cultural Politics in the 1790s: Literature, Radicalism and the Public Sphere* (New York: St. Martin's Press, 1999), esp. pp. 43–44.

42. Travers, "Contested Despotism," p. 205.

43. P. J. Marshall, *The Impeachment of Warren Hastings* (Oxford: Oxford University Press, 1965), p. 181; see also Marshall, "Burke and India," pp. 42, 46. On this

point, see further David Musselwhite, "The Trial of Warren Hastings" (in *Literature, Politics, and Theory,* ed. Francis Barker, Peter Hulme, Margaret Iversen, and Diana Loxley [London: Methuen, 1986], pp. 77–103), who writes, "Perhaps the impeachment, with all its ceremonial, its place apart, its studied contrivance, was the greatest folly of the period, an artificial landscape where the institutions collapsing elsewhere—religion, property, chivalry, to recall the *Reflections* once more—might be shored up for a little more time. And in turn does not India, too, emerge as another folly: a place where all that had lost purchase in Europe could be reinscribed and reconstituted?" (p. 103).

44. On this point, see Jeff D. Bass, "The Perversion of Empire: Edmund Burke and the Nature of Imperial Responsibility," *Quarterly Journal of Speech* 81 (1995): 208–227. Bass notes, "The Company had merely succeeded in disrupting the highly ordered socio-political structure of an ancient and refined civilization, a result totally at odds with the professed designs of empire-builders throughout history" (p. 212).

45. For a discussion of these themes, see Daniel I. O'Neill, *The Burke-Wollstonecraft Debate* (University Park: Penn State University Press, 2007), chaps. 1 and 2, and "The Sublime, the Beautiful, and the Political in Burke's Work," in *The Science of Sensibility: Reading Burke's* Philosophical Enquiry, ed. Michael Funk Deckard and Koen Vermeir (New York: Springer, 2012), pp. 193–221.

46. Burke, *W&S,* vol. 7, p. 264.

47. Ibid., p. 279.

48. Burke, *W&S,* vol. 5, p. 390.

49. Ibid., p. 404.

50. For example, Janes astutely argues, "Burke's arguments, both to the Commons and to the Lords, are founded on the premise of sympathetic identification. Against Hastings' plea that India was ruled by despots and that its people possessed no rights and privileges that superseded the will of the sovereign, Burke returns again and again to the assertions that such rights and privileges do exist and that the people and states of India must be regarded and treated as Britons regard and treat themselves.... What is important to Burke himself is the structural similarity between Europe and India, a similarity on behalf of which he used all the devices he used for America; what is important to him in his rhetoric with respect to persuading his audience is expunging the sense of distance and the exotic.... Burke's central problem in the Hastings impeachment was to arouse in his audience the fellow feeling for India that he himself possessed and that he found lacking or inadequately developed in that audience" ("At Home Abroad," pp. 164–166).

Similarly, Frederick Whelan argues that as a means of "arousing their sympathy for Indian sufferings," Burke set about "trying to render [India's] essential features familiar." Among the "striking examples" of this, Whelan lists "Burke's extended comparison of the political geography of India to that of the contemporary German empire, and his portrayal of Indian aristocrats and gentry as equivalent to their English counterparts" ("Burke on India," p. 172). Elsewhere, in speaking specifically of his *Speech on Fox's India Bill*, Whelan notes that Burke's "main intention seems to be to render India as comprehensible as possible by affirming its similarities to familiar things, thus arousing sympathy for their Indian subjects in the minds of his British auditors." All of this was a part, Whelan argues, of Burke's "attempt to de-exoticize" India ("Burke, India and Orientalism," pp. 113, 115).

51. As Manu Samnotra has very helpfully pointed out to me, however, Burke fails to meet at least Smith's criteria for the establishment of sympathy, "to the degree that negotiation of the view is completely absent from his descriptions in Parliament. In other words, he does not really try to discover what the Indians themselves think about all of this."

52. See, J. G. A. Pocock, "The Political Economy of Burke's Analysis of the French Revolution," in *Virtue, Commerce, and History* (Cambridge: Cambridge University Press, 1985), pp. 193–212; and Pocock, introduction to Burke's *Reflections on the Revolution in France (*Indianapolis: Hackett, 1987), pp. vii–lvi.

53. For an important exception, see Isaac Kramnick, *The Rage of Edmund Burke: Portrait of an Ambivalent Conservative* (New York: Basic Books, 1977).

54. For this argument, see esp. Regina Janes, "Edmund Burke's Flying Leap from India to France," *History of European Ideas* 7, no. 5 (1986): 509–527.

55. Janes suggests "that the crusade relative to India accounts for the rapidity, the intensity, and many of the categories of Burke's negative reading of the revolution in the *Reflections* (ibid., p. 509). Similarly, Whelan observes, "Bengal's traditional, differentiated social structure is like that of Europe, which suggests that Bengalis are fundamentally not unlike Europeans. Bengali society, in fact, is like the society of *ancien régime* France, which Burke was to evoke in similar terms a few years later against revolutionaries there—and indeed, his analysis of Hastings' destructive policies in India doubtlessly prepared and predisposed him to see similarly destructive implications in the Revolution" ("Burke, India, and Orientalism," pp. 113–114; see also Whelan, *Burke and India,* pp. 156–159).

56. Burke, *W&S,* vol. 5, pp. 425–426.

57. Ibid., p. 427.

58. On the centrality of Burke's aesthetic theory to his analysis of India, see Sara Suleri, *The Rhetoric of English India* (Chicago: University of Chicago Press, 1992), chap. 2, "Burke and the Indian Sublime," pp. 24–48.

59. On this passage see Janes, "Edmund Burke's Flying Leap," pp. 512–513.

60. Burke, *W&S,* vol. 5, pp. 402–403.

61. In his *Letter to a Noble Lord,* Burke writes of "these obscene harpies, who deck themselves, in I know not what divine attributes, but who in reality are foul and ravenous birds of prey" (*W&S,* vol. 9, p. 156).

62. Burke, *W&S,* vol. 6, pp. 311–312.

63. On this point see Whelan, *Edmund Burke and India,* pp. 154–155.

64. Burke, *W&S,* vol. 6, pp. 382, 385–386.

65. See O'Neill, *The Burke-Wollstonecraft Debate,* chap. 6. Whelan notes, "The similarity of the French to the Indian case is striking; and Burke's sensitivity and heated reaction to the French confiscations were probably in part due to his investigation of Hastings and Bengal, which began before his scrutiny of events in France, and continued simultaneously with it" (*Edmund Burke and India,* p. 158).

66. Burke, *W&S,* vol. 6, p. 111.

67. See Edmund Burke, *The Correspondence of Edmund Burke,* ed. Thomas W. Copeland, 10 vols. (Chicago: University of Chicago Press, 1958–1978), vol. 5, p. 255, hereafter *Corr.*

68. For example, Uday Mehta writes of this remark: "The statement is remarkable both for the capaciousness of Burke's own sympathy and for his brazenly direct way of pointing to the narrowness that informed prevailing prejudices" (*Liberalism and Empire,* p. 167). As Mehta points out, in his footnote to this passage, "David Bromwich has referred to this last sentence as 'one of the most startling and admirable things ever said by a human being'" (p. 167n25, citing Bromwich's review of *The Great Melody,* by Conor Cruise O'Brien, *New Republic,* March 1, 1993, p. 37).

69. Burke, *W&S,* vol. 5, p. 45.

70. Ibid., p. 422.

71. Burke, *W&S,* vol. 7, p. 35.

72. Ibid., p. 340.

73. Ibid., p. 529. Jennifer Pitts cites these passages and links them to Burke's earlier moral theory, his similar arguments about the French royal family and aristocracy in the *Reflections,* and his attempt to inculcate sympathy in his audience in keeping with the principles of the moral psychology he endorsed. However, she concludes from such passages that Burke's speech *misled* his auditors into believing that he was chiefly concerned with the misfortune of the Indian aristocracy. Pitts writes that Burke's "emphasis on the nobility, although deliberate, was perhaps misguided in that it seems to have left many among his audience and later readers convinced of his own restricted sympathies" (*A Turn to Empire,* p. 75). Whelan comes closer to the mark when he writes, in part: "Both in Bengal and France the displacement, and to some extent, the revolutionary destruction of the landed gentry and nobility of the old regime was prominent among Burke's concerns.... This focus reflected the fact that the wealth of the aristocratic class was a principal target of the revolutions, as well as Burke's respect for property and social hierarchy. It is noteworthy that he emphasizes this theme especially in his 'Closing' speech at Hastings's trial, which was delivered to the House of Lords towards the end of the year of Terror in France" ("Burke on India," p. 176). For his part, Marshall points out that at the time of "the closing stages of the impeachment[,] events in France had made Burke even more fervent in his insistence that aristocracy must be cherished in India" ("Burke and India," p. 46).

74. For Burke's description of Devi Singh's brutalities, a performance which required that some of the emotionally overwrought English ladies who heard it be taken from the chamber, see *W&S,* vol. 6, pp. 415–422. Whelan, who is at times given to overstating Burke's sympathy for ordinary Indians as well as uncritically endorsing Burke's depiction of the Old Regimes in both India and France, nonetheless recognizes the logic underpinning Burke's standpoint: "Unlike the old gentry, whose position and conduct were largely determined by the customary moral framework, the new owners of the lands or of tax-farming rights would be uninhibited by traditional norms or a sense of social responsibility. Instead, they would be motivated exclusively by their desire for a lucrative return on their investment, and by the

need to pay off the purchase price and the bribes or kickbacks that Burke assumed they had to pay to their company patrons. The predictable and actual consequence of their pursuit of maximum profits was the oppression of the peasantry through rack renting and coercive extraction of payments. Once again, this was to be Burke's expectation in the case of the new class of landed adventurers in France" (*Edmund Burke and India*, p. 159).

75. For example, as far back as 1779, he had argued that the Hindu "King of Tanjore" had suffered severely at the hands of the Muslim "Nabob of Arcot," who also had "his [the king's] women cruelly stripped of all the ornaments of their persons" (Burke, *W&S*, vol. 5, p. 120).

76. For a detailed overview of all four charges brought by the managers, see Marshall, *The Impeachment of Warren Hastings*, pp. 88–179; see also Geoffrey Carnall and Colin Nicholson, eds., *The Impeachment of Warren Hastings* (Edinburgh: Edinburgh University Press, 1989).

77. See Marshall, *The Impeachment of Warrant Hastings*, pp. 109–129; Marshall's editorial preface to Burke's speeches on the article of impeachment, in *W&S*, vol. 6, pp. 129–133; Marshall's footnote, vol. 5, p. 410n2, and his editorial introduction to vol. 7, p. 2.

78. Burke, *W&S*, vol. 5, pp. 411, 418–419, emphasis original.

79. Ibid., p. 465.

80. Whelan notes, "The emphasis Burke gave to the case of the begams of Oudh illustrates the special solicitude for victims of high rank that recurs in his political writings and speeches." In this regard, he argues that the "famous portrayal of an idealized Marie Antoinette" is in fact "a passage that invites comparison with Burke's description of the mistreated royal ladies of Oudh" (*Edmund Burke and India*, pp. 185–186). Similarly, Janes wishes "to suggest that it is not the Begams who spin on the Queen's orb, but that it is Marie Antoinette who emerges from the zenana" ("Edmund Burke's Flying Leap," p. 524). Andrew McCann similarly argues that Burke "evokes the threat posed by the lawless character of Company mercantilism under Hastings by drawing attention to the violence and cruelty of its assaults on the private space and, ultimately, the bodies of Indian women. The image of Marie Antoinette fleeing Jacobin daggers, for most readers the crux of the *Reflections*, is but an echo of the more exacting violence Burke replayed at the impeachment as a way of illustrating the excesses of what might be called colonial libertinage" (*Cultural Politics in the 1790s*, p. 36). For McCann, this description of the Begams' fate, like Burke's "infamous descriptions" of Devi Singh's behavior in Rangpur, means that "Burke's evocation of public sympathy ... cannot be separated from his portrayal of the violence threatening Indian women" (p. 37).

81. Burke, *W&S*, vol. 7, pp. 463, 474, 525, emphasis added.

82. Ibid. p. 465.

83. Ibid., pp. 537–538. For similar sentiments, see pp. 456–460 of the same volume.

84. Two scholars who have pointed to the theoretical importance of Munni Begum for Burke, while drawing very different conclusions about it, are Kramnick

(*The Rage of Edmund Burke,* chap. 7) and Whelan (*Edmund Burke and India,* pp. 150–154).

85. Burke, *W&S*, vol. 8, p. 122.

86. Burke, *W&S*, vol. 7, pp. 52–53.

87. Ibid., pp. 52–53. Burke's description would appear to be false historically, as well as deeply elitist and sexist. As Marshall points out, "Burke's abuse of Munni Begam . . . was misplaced. The historian Ghulam Husain Khan (1789) described her as, although 'not of virtuous family nor of a noble birth, yet she is a woman of infinite merit' and he commended her 'good sense as well as her steadiness of temper'" (*W&S*, Marshall's footnote, vol. 7, p. 52n1). Regina Janes recognizes this to some extent, arguing, "Burke defends the dignity of the Begams of Oudh and their women from Hastings' scurrilities, but flings 'prostitute' liberally at Munny Begam who, however despicable her origins, had risen to a position of considerable power and respectability" ("At Home Abroad," p. 170). However, one is perplexed why impoverished origins or the occupations they sometimes require should ever be considered "despicable."

88. Burke, *W&S*, vol. 7, pp. 51, 53–54.

89. Ibid., pp. 592, 613; see also pp. 609–610.

90. For Burke's thoughts on what he called Jacobinism, see *Corr.*, vol. 8, p. 432. On "Indianism," see Marshall's editorial preface to Burke's *Speech in Reply, W&S*, vol. 7, p. 229.

91. Burke, *W&S*, vol. 7, p. 339.

92. Ibid., p. 437, emphasis added.

93. Ibid., p. 261.

94. On these fears in England, see H. V. Bowen, "British India, 1765–1813: The Metropolitan Context," in Marshall, *The Oxford History of the British Empire*, pp. 530–551.

95. On this theme, see Tillman W. Nechtman, *Nabobs: Empire and Identity in Eighteenth-Century Britain* (Cambridge: Cambridge University Press, 2010), pp. 96, 103, 106–110.

CHAPTER 4. IRELAND

1. For the generally received view, see F. P. Lock, *Edmund Burke,* vol. 1: *1730–1784* (Oxford: Oxford University Press, 1998), pp. 1–28. For suggestions to the contrary, see Conor Cruise O'Brien, *The Great Melody: A Thematic Biography of Edmund Burke* (Chicago: University of Chicago Press, 1992), pp. 3–23; and Louis Cullen, "Burke, Ireland, and Revolution," *Studies in the Eighteenth Century* 16 (February 1992): 21–42.

2. For an attempt to sift the evidence regarding Burke's commitment to Ireland in a dispassionate fashion, see F. P. Lock, "Burke, Ireland and India: Reason, Rhetoric and Empire," in *Edmund Burke's Irish Identities,* ed. Seán Patrick Donlan (Portland, OR: Irish Academic Press, 2007), pp. 154–170, esp. pp. 155–156.

3. For an excellent overview, see Ian McBride, *Eighteenth-Century Ireland: The Isle of Slaves* (Dublin: Gill & Macmillan, 2009).

4. For this argument, see esp. Nicholas Canny, *Kingdom and Colony: Ireland in the Atlantic World, 1560–1800* (Baltimore, MD: Johns Hopkins University Press, 1988). In stressing the personnel linkages between Ireland and the New World, Canny follows the work of David Beers Quinn (see pp. 6–8 and associated notes).

5. See McBride, *Eighteenth-Century Ireland*, pp. 161–169.

6. For this point, see David Armitage, *The Ideological Origins of the British Empire* (Cambridge: Cambridge University Press, 2000), p. 26.

7. See McBride, *Eighteenth-Century Ireland*, p. 5. The perspective is most closely associated with Sean Connolly, *Religion, Law, and Power: The Making of Protestant Ireland: 1660–1760* (Oxford: Oxford University Press, 1992). McBride assesses the evidence and relative merits of this position at pp. 100–156.

8. See Armitage, *The Ideological Origins*, p. 25.

9. See McBride's discussion of these positions in *Eighteenth-Century Ireland*, p. 102.

10. Thomas Bartlett, "'This Famous Island Set in a Virginian Sea': Ireland in the British Empire, 1690–1801," in *The Oxford History of the British Empire: The Eighteenth Century*, ed. P. J. Marshall (Oxford: Oxford University Press, 2001), pp. 253–275, quoted at p. 254.

11. See esp. "The Atlantic Archipelago and the War of the Three Kingdoms," "The Third Kingdom in Its History," "Archipelago, Europe and Atlantic after 1688," "The Significance of 1688: Some Reflections on Whig History," and "The Union in British History," in *The Discovery of Islands: Essays in British History*, by J. G. A. Pocock (Cambridge: Cambridge University Press, 2005).

12. Pocock, "The Atlantic Archipelago and the War of the Three Kingdoms," p. 93; see also "The Significance of 1688," p. 130. See also Armitage, *The Ideological Origins*, p. 153.

13. Pocock, "The Atlantic Archipelago and the War of the Three Kingdoms," pp. 91, 97, 101.

14. Ibid., p. 99.

15. Pocock, "The Union in British History," p. 171.

16. Pocock, "Archipelago, Europe and Atlantic after 1688," p. 109.

17. Cited in James Kelly, "'Era of Liberty': The Politics of Civil and Political Rights in Eighteenth-Century Ireland," in *Exclusionary Empire: English Liberty Overseas, 1600–1900*, ed. Jack P. Greene (Cambridge: Cambridge University Press, 2010), pp. 77–111, at p. 80.

18. McBride, *Eighteenth-Century Ireland*, p. 112.

19. Armitage, *The Ideological Origins*, pp. 148–149.

20. See Lock, *Edmund Burke*, vol. 1, p. 345.

21. Ibid., p. 346.

22. Burke, *The Writings and Speeches of Edmund Burke*, Paul Langford, general editor, 9 vols. (Oxford: Oxford University Press, 1981–2015), vol. 9, pp. 488–489, hereafter *W&S*.

23. Burke, *W&S,* vol. 9, pp. 493, 489–90, emphasis original.

24. Ibid., pp. 491–493, emphasis original.

25. See Edmund Burke to the Marquess of Rockingham, September 29, 1773, in Burke, *The Correspondence of Edmund Burke,* ed. Thomas W. Copeland (Chicago: University of Chicago Press, 1958–1978), vol. 2, p. 468, hereafter *Corr.*

26. In *Edmund Burke and Ireland* (Cambridge, MA: Harvard University Press, 1960), Thomas H. D. Mahoney argues, "The time and energy which Burke put into the fight against the proposed tax in 1773, the forcefulness and pertinency of the arguments which he advanced, and the fact that these convictions remained as strong with him to the end of his life as in 1773 make it difficult to reach any other conclusion than that Burke sincerely believed in the cause which he espoused and was motivated principally not by party feeling or personal friendship but by his belief that such a tax would be a serious blow to the British Empire which could ultimately weaken it dangerously" (p. 58).

Similarly, O'Brien argues that Burke's position on the absentee tax was "entirely consistent" with his broader views on Ireland, which were "the exact reverse of that of the father of Irish Republicanism, Theobald Wolfe Tone." Wolfe Tone wanted to break the connection with England, O'Brien points out, whereas Burke "thought that what Ireland needed was the removal of existing restraints and penalties, rather than the introduction of new ones; and the strengthening, not the weakening, of relations between the two kingdoms. Burke's writings on the Absentee Tax have the ring of conviction, and are animated by the same spirit as animates the rest of his writing about Ireland" (*The Great Melody,* p. 70). For similar conclusions, see also Michael J. Griffin, "Burke, Goldsmith and the Irish Absentees," in Donlan, *Edmund Burke's Irish Identities,* pp. 117–132, esp. pp. 124–126; and R. B. McDowell, *Ireland in the Age of Imperialism and Revolution, 1760–1801* (Oxford: Oxford University Press, 1991), pp. 234–236.

27. See letter to William Tighe, April 10, 1781, in *Corr.,* vol. 4, p. 349. This expresses an understanding of the relation between taxation and poverty that some of Burke's contemporary conservative followers would no doubt relish.

28. On this point, see Eamon O'Flaherty, "Burke and the Irish Constitution," in Donlan, *Edmund Burke's Irish Identities,* pp. 102–116, at p. 108.

29. See Burke to Fitzwilliam, letter of March 15, 1797, in *Corr.,* vol. 9, pp. 282–284, quoted at p. 284.

30. See Burke to French Laurence, letter of June 1, 1797, in ibid., pp. 364–366, quoted at p. 365.

31. Both of these letters are referenced by Mahoney, in *Edmund Burke and Ireland,* pp. 57–58.

32. I borrow the phrase "sinews of empire" directly from Michael Craton, *Sinews of Empire: A Short History of British Slavery* (Garden City, NY: Anchor Press, 1974).

33. For examples of this sort of argument, see Sankar Muthu, *Enlightenment against Empire* (Princeton, NJ: Princeton University Press, 2003); and Jennifer Pitts, *A Turn to Empire: The Rise of Imperial Liberalism in Britain and France* (Princeton, NJ: Princeton University Press, 2005).

34. For an excellent discussion of this aspect of Burke's thought, see Mahoney, *Edmund Burke and Ireland*, pp. 66–69.

35. See Burke to the Duke of Richmond, September 26, 1775, in *Corr.*, vol. 3, p. 218, emphasis original.

36. See Burke to Charles O'Hara, January 7, 1776, in ibid., p. 244.

37. See Burke to the Earl of Charlemont, June 4, 1776, in ibid., p. 271.

38. See "Speech on Trade Concession with Ireland" (December 6, 1779), in *W&S*, vol. 9, pp. 535–542, quoted at p. 539.

39. Burke, *W&S*, vol. 9, p. 550.

40. Ibid., p. 533.

41. Ibid., p. 527, emphasis original.

42. See Burke to Samuel Span, letter of April 9, 1778, in *Corr.*, vol. 3, p. 426. See also a pair of 1780 letters to two other Bristol businessmen, the sugar refiner John Merlott and the hosier Job Watts, expressing similar points, in *Corr.*, vol. 4, pp. 223–225 and pp. 260–262.

43. Burke, *W&S*, vol. 9, p. 508.

44. Burke, *W&S*, vol. 3, p. 630.

45. See *Edmund Burke and Ireland*, pp. 75–92, 103–111. Mahoney notes accurately of Burke: "His imperial mentality is well brought out in this entire episode since he stressed his conviction throughout the business that the welfare of the British Empire itself required the grant of trade concessions to Ireland at that time" (p. 83).

46. See ibid., pp. 146–151, 315.

47. Bartlett, "This Famous Island Set in a Virginian Sea," p. 259.

48. In addition to Bartlett, see Kelly's "Era of Liberty." For the "patriot" position as a brand of "settler nationalism," see Pocock, "The Significance of 1688."

49. On the centrality of this trope, see McBride, *Eighteenth-Century Ireland*, pp. 125, 274–275.

50. Bartlett, "This Famous Island Set in a Virginian Sea," pp. 262–264; Kelly, "Era of Liberty," pp. 91–92.

51. See McBride, *Eighteenth-Century Ireland*, p. 347; Kelly, "Era of Liberty," p. 100; Bartlett, "This Famous Island Set in a Virginian Sea," pp. 265–268.

52. Burke to Charles O'Hara, letter of February 20, 1768, in *Corr.*, vol. 1, pp. 342–343.

53. On this point, see R. B. McDowell's remarks in Burke, *W&S*, vol. 9, p. 396 (McDowell is the editor of volume 9 of Burke's *W&S*); and O'Flaherty, "Burke and the Irish Constitution," p. 105.

54. Burke, *Corr.*, vol. 4, p. 440.

55. See Burke's "Speech on Irish Commercial Propositions," May 19, 1785, in *W&S*, vol. 9, quoted at p. 591.

56. Burke to Lord Fitzwilliam, November 20, 1796, in *Corr.*, vol. 9, p. 122.

57. See Burke's letter to an unknown Irish correspondent in *W&S*, vol. 9, pp. 675–676, emphasis original.

58. *Corr.*, vol. 9, p. 113.

59. *W&S*, vol. 9, p. 542.

60. Conor Cruise O'Brien has stressed Burke's long-standing concern for Ireland's Catholic majority, which he traces all the way back to Burke's father's potential Catholicism and the time the younger Burke spent as a child with Catholic relatives, to explain Burke's position on Irish legislative independence. On O'Brien's account, Burke was opposed to legislative independence, extracted in large measure by the Volunteers, who were "the armed power of an exclusive, dominant caste," because it would guarantee a monopoly on political power to a wholly Protestant Irish Parliament. Such a grant would allow this self-interested faction to lock in anti-Catholic discrimination by dispensing with Poynings' Law, making it more difficult for England to control Irish legislation and thus help the Catholic majority (see *The Great Melody*, pp. 175–201, and 243–253, quoted at p. 188). O'Brien argues that Burke could nevertheless grudgingly accept Irish legislative independence in 1782 and not speak out against it, because "it was largely a sham, as Burke well knew," and could be obviated in the name of legislating in defense of Irish Catholics from England, if need be. The British could withdraw legislative independence at any time, and meanwhile England "maintained its control over the Irish executive and thus exercised a powerful influence, to say the least, over legislative processes also," through the English-appointed lord-lieutenant of Ireland and support in the Irish Parliament. O'Brien's argument is, thus, that Burke wanted to keep Ireland tightly in the fold of empire and not grant legislative "independence" so as to protect Irish Catholics. If this is so, then it is only in an uncomprehending retrospective nationalist mythology, O'Brien argues, that Burke appears treacherous—like the Irishman siding with England against his home country's push for greater autonomy. However, O'Brien is forced to admit that Burke "never explicitly articulated this distinction in a parliamentary debate" (*The Great Melody*, p. 245, 251, 201; for similar views, see Mahoney, *Edmund Burke and Ireland*, pp. 119–135). Indeed, Burke never made such arguments explicit *anywhere* in his public or private pronouncements, at least those for which we have any record. Thus, the difficulty here as elsewhere with O'Brien's interpretation is that he too often fills in the silences in Burke's speeches and the empty spaces in his texts with his own preferred outcomes in the absence of compelling evidence, even if he stops short of the more untenable claims about Burke and Ireland that have been put forth since *The Great Melody* appeared.

61. On this point, see esp. Kelly, "Era of Liberty," where the author notes that Ireland's history in the eighteenth century serves as a powerful reminder that those seeking liberty for themselves can simultaneously deny it to others (see pp. 108–111).

62. See McBride, *Eighteenth-Century Ireland*, pp. 275–277.

63. Kelly, "Era of Liberty," pp. 78, 102–103, 109–111.

64. For a good overview, see Maureen Wall, *The Penal Laws, 1691–1760* (Dundalk, Ireland: Dun Dealgan Press, 1976).

65. See Ian McBride, "Burke and Ireland," in *The Cambridge Companion to Edmund Burke*, ed. David Dwan and Christopher J. Insole (Cambridge: Cambridge University Press, 2012), pp. 181–194. For a discussion of the argument of the *Tracts*

in historical context, see Michel Fuchs, *Edmund Burke, Ireland, and the Fashioning of the Self* (Oxford: Voltaire Foundation, 1996), pp. 265–297. For Burke's Irish connections in the 1760s, see Cullen, "Burke, Ireland, and Revolution." Whiteboy resistance produced a backlash that culminated in the judicial murder of one of Burke's distant relatives, Father Nicholas Sheehy.

66. Burke, *W&S,* vol. 9, pp. 454, 462.

67. See esp. Burke's *Letter to Lord Kenmare* (1782), in ibid., pp. 564–580.

68. *Letter to Sir Hercules Langrishe,* in Burke, *W&S,* vol. 9, p. 637.

69. For example, in Mahoney's highly sympathetic *Edmund Burke and Ireland,* the author claims that Burke's unmodified "hatred of oppression" clearly stands out as one of the great themes in his work (p. 310). Such a view is the guiding assumption of O'Brien's even more sympathetic *Great Melody.* It also prevails in some of the most influential works on Burke and Ireland that have succeeded these landmark contributions. For example, in *Foreign Affections: Essays on Edmund Burke* (Notre Dame, IN: University of Notre Dame Press, 2005), Seamus Deane writes that "liberty, in Burke's understanding of it, was the essential feature of the civilizing purpose of Empire. Once cleaned of its pollutions in Ireland and India, it could resume the career which had begun in the Glorious Revolution and was then renovated in the American War of Independence" (p. 3; see also p. 8). Similarly, in *Edmund Burke and Ireland: Aesthetics, Politics, and the Colonial Sublime* (Cambridge: Cambridge University Press, 2003), Luke Gibbons argues that "much of Burke's abiding concerns with colonial oppression, whether in Ireland, America, or India, are bound up with his acute awareness of the capacity of the servant to rise up against intolerable abuses of state power" (p. 3). Even the most perceptive readers of Burke are prone to attribute to him a general or unqualified commitment to liberty and an equally universal hostility to oppression or conquest, as in Richard Bourke's essay "Liberty, Authority, and Trust in Burke's Idea of Empire," *Journal of the History of Ideas* 61, no. 3 (2000): 453–471. So, too, F. P. Lock occasionally writes of "Burke's larger-scale efforts on behalf of oppressed peoples, whether in Ireland or India" ("Burke, Ireland and India, p. 156). For an unreconstructed and wholly uncritical expression of the view, see Bruce Frohnen, "An Empire of Peoples: Burke, Government, and National Character," in *The Enduring Edmund Burke,* ed. Ian Crowe (Wilmington, DE: Intercollegiate Studies Institute, 1997), pp. 128–142.

70. See esp. Donlan's outstanding essay "The 'Genuine Voice of Its Records and Monuments'? Edmund Burke's 'Interior History of Ireland,'" in Donlan, *Edmund Burke's Irish Identities,* pp. 69–101, to which this section is indebted. Paralleling Donlan, McBride notes, "What is most striking about Burke's writings on Ireland is that they revolve around the theme of conquest and its legacies" (*Eighteenth-Century Ireland,* p. 98).

71. Burke, *W&S,* vol. 9, pp. 478–479.

72. See Donlan, "Edmund Burke's 'Interior History of Ireland,'" pp. 73–77.

73. Burke, *W&S,* vol. 9, pp. 614–616. This view was consistent with Burke's position on the Ascendancy going back to the 1760s, as expressed in a letter to Charles O'Hara, where Burke noted, of Ireland: "As to the rottenness of the country; if it

was rotten, I attributed it, to the ill policy of the Government towards the body of the Subjects there" (letter of November 27, 1767, in *Corr.*, vol. 1, pp. 335–337, quoted at p. 337).

74. McBride, "Burke and Ireland," p. 191.

75. Donlan notes that Burke "made a similar defense of property, including the Cromwellian and Williamite settlements.... Deeply critical of the seventeenth-century confiscations in Ireland, Burke argued, on the basis of prescription, against radical changes in property ownership" ("Edmund Burke's 'Interior History of Ireland,'" p. 82; see also pp. 94–95). Likewise, Lock notes, "For all his hatred of the Protestant Ascendancy, Burke never contemplated except with horror any suggestion that the lands confiscated in the seventeenth century should be restored to their old owners.... While he might excoriate the 'new' owners ... he never questioned that their titles were now valid, and should not be disturbed" ("Burke, Ireland and India," p. 163).

76. Letter to Richard Burke (post February 19, 1792), in *W&S*, vol. 9, p. 653.

77. For example, see Thomas O. McLoughlin, *Contesting Ireland: Irish Voices against England in the Eighteenth Century* (Dublin: Four Courts Press, 1999), pp. 165, 163, 167.

78. Letter to Charles O'Hara, ante August 23, 1762, *Corr.*, vol. 1, p. 147.

79. Burke, *W&S*, vol. 9, p. 600, emphasis original.

80. McBride, "Burke and Ireland," p. 181; see also his remarks on the same theme in Burke in *Eighteenth-Century Ireland*, pp. 155–156; Donlan, "Edmund Burke's 'Interior History of Ireland,'" pp. 87–91; and Cullen, "Burke, Ireland, and Revolution," which stresses Burke's central "belief in the importance of continuity and especially propertied continuity" in Ireland as elsewhere (p. 36).

81. McBride, "Burke and Ireland," p. 191. This is an important theme in the *Reflections on the Revolution in France*, as well.

82. Burke, *W&S*, vol. 9, p. 668. See also in the same volume the "Letter to Richard Burke," pp. 646–647, and "To Unknown: Letter on Affairs of Ireland," p. 675. Also see Burke's letter to Fitzwilliam of May 15, 1795, in *Corr.*, vol. 8, pp. 242–243.

83. See Burke, *W&S*, vol. 9, pp. 598–600. Emphasis is original throughout my discussion of this essay, unless otherwise noted. In a later letter, Burke wrote, "In the main I approve of keeping the superior offices of the State and of the military in the hands of the conformists to the Church of Ireland as established" (see *Corr.*, vol. 7, p. 350).

84. Burke, *W&S*, vol. 9, p. 601; see also pp. 628–629.

85. Ibid., p. 596.

86. Ibid., pp. 596–597.

87. Ibid., p. 621.

88. For an outstanding discussion of the United Irishmen, see Jim Smyth, *The Men of No Property: Irish Radicals and Popular Politics in the Late Eighteenth Century* (Notre Dame, IN: University of Notre Dame Press, 1998).

89. Quoted in ibid., p. 92.

90. See Eric Foner, *Tom Paine and Revolutionary America* (Oxford: Oxford University Press, 2005), p. 253.

91. Some see in Burke a kind of soothsayer who unfortunately lacked the courage to endorse the policy prescription of Irish independence to which his theoretical logic putatively led. Hence, we are told that despite his astute analysis, Burke unfortunately "flinched from the possibility that the colonial relation was of itself incompatible with any set of principles that could be said to be in accord with universal justice" (Deane, *Foreign Affections*, p. 93). Another purveyor of this view argues that Burke sadly lacked the courage of his convictions, because "Wolf Tone was, after all, what Burke would have liked to be and might perhaps have been had he dared" (Fuchs, *Edmund Burke, Ireland, and the Fashioning of the Self*, p. 312). Luke Gibbons bluntly asserts that Burke "was a man deeply divided against himself" regarding his views on colonialism, because "in an Irish context [his] cultural logic led ultimately to the political project of the United Irishmen." Since this was the case—and despite all evidence to the contrary—Gibbons argues that at important junctures Burke and the United Irishmen were in fact close theoretical allies, not merely strange comrades of momentary political convenience on the issue of Catholic relief. In fact, Gibbons argues, the United Irishmen, by "turning their attention to the rights of endangered, native cultures, can be seen as giving a specific Burkean inflection to what were otherwise Paineite conceptions of the universal rights." Likewise, he contends that, "for Burke, as for the radical cultural currents in the United Irishmen, international solidarity did not consist in the relation of one abstract human being to another, divested of their cultural differences, but in the affiliations between individuals who saw in their own histories and attachments a way of reaching out to others." Therefore, in this instance as in others, for the United Irishmen, "their greatest antagonist, Burke, was indeed their helper" (*Edmund Burke and Ireland*, pp. xi, xiii, 225, 236, 233). The obvious problem with this view is that the specific, concrete form of "international solidarity" chosen by the United Irishmen as a means of protecting "the rights of endangered, native cultures" was to reach out for an alliance with the Jacobins of revolutionary France. This was an alliance that, as we shall see, sent "their helper" Burke into apoplectic claims that the apocalypse was nigh. In its most extreme versions, the thesis that Burke was a "divided Irishman" has led to some extraordinary claims. For example, one interpreter holds that Burke's basic problem stretching back to the 1770s was "how to be a covert Irish nationalist and yet keep his seat in the English parliament" (see McLoughlin, "Edmund Burke: Divided Irishman," in his *Contesting Ireland,* p. 170). Another commentator has argued that if his sympathy for the "terrible hunger, distress, and injustice" that drove "Irish Jacobinism" did not quite "push Burke into becoming a republican revolutionary like Irish Whig counterparts Arthur O'Connor and Wolfe Tone, he verged on complicity" (Iain McCalman, "Popular Constitutionalism and Revolution in England and Ireland," in *Revolution and the Meaning of Freedom in the Nineteenth Century,* ed. Isser Woloch [Stanford, CA: Stanford University Press, 1996], p. 140, quoted in Gibbons, *Edmund Burke and Ireland,* p. 14). Given such representations of Burke's position, it is little wonder that an eminent Irish historian could declare of Burke's *Reflections on the Revolution in France* that it was in fact "the greatest inconsistency of his intellectual life" (Cullen, "Burke, Ireland, and Revolution," p. 22).

92. To his great credit, and despite floating a weaker version of the "divided Burke" thesis, O'Brien rejects any attempt to link Burke and the United Irishmen. Speaking of Wolfe Tone and Burke both supporting Catholic relief in the 1790s, O'Brien notes that "Burke would have been horrified" if he had known of Wolfe Tone's "real sentiments": "As regards longer-term objectives, the two remained utterly opposed. Burke hoped that the removal of all Catholic disabilities would have a tranquilizing effect, diminish the attractions of Jacobinism, and strengthen the connection between Ireland and Great Britain. Wolfe Tone hoped that the struggle of enfranchisement, the resistance to it, and the spread of revolutionary ideas, would destroy sectarian differences, and produce a new Ireland, emancipated both from British rule and from Catholic superstition" (*The Great Melody*, pp. 498, 500).

93. On this point, see Mahoney, *Edmund Burke and Ireland*, pp. 196–197.

94. Letter of November 18, 1792, *Corr.*, vol. 7, p. 290.

95. See letter to Hussey, May 18, 1795, in *Corr.*, vol. 8, 246–247.

96. Letter to Hussey, post December 9, 1796, *Corr.*, vol. 9, p. 165, emphasis original. See also a letter to his son, Richard, of November 2, 1792, in which Burke writes of the "very strange information" believed by the Society of United Irishmen: "They think that the Conduct of the Castle [the British administration in Ireland] is the result of directions from hence [England]; and that here they do nothing but plot some mischief against Ireland. Alas I wish they could be got seriously and with a ruling spirit to think if it at all. But things move in the reverse order from what they imagine. They think the Ministers here instruct the Castle and that the Castle sets the Jobbing ascendancy in motion; whereas it is now, wholly, and has, ever since I remember, been for the greater part, the direct contrary. The Junto in Ireland entirely governs the Castle; the Castle, by its representations of the Country governs the Ministers here—So that the whole Evil has always originated, and does still, originate among ourselves [that is, among the Irish]" (*Corr.*, vol. 7, 283). By this extraordinary rendering of matters, Burke describes a world in which the colonized control the colonizer, not vice versa, and are free to contravene the views of the nearby metropole at will.

97. On this theme, see Burke's letter to John Keogh, a leader of the Catholic Committee, dated November 17, 1796, from which the quote in this sentence is drawn. It reads, in part: "Contrary to all reason; experience and observation, many persons in Ireland have taken it into their heads, that the influence of the Government here has been the cause of the misdemeanors of persons in Power in that Country, and that they are suffering under the Yoke of a British Dominion—I must speak the truth—I must say, that all the evils of Ireland originate within itself; and that it is the boundless credit which is given to an Irish Cabal that produces whatever mischiefs both Countries may feel in their relation. England has hardly anything to do with Irish Government. I heartily wish it were otherwise; but the body of the people of England, even the most active Politicians, take little or no concern in the Affairs of Ireland. They are therefore by the Minister of the Country, who fears, upon that account, no responsibility here, and who shuns all responsibility in

Ireland, Abandoned to the discretion of those who are actually in possession of its internal Government—This has been the case more eminently for these five or six last Years; and it is a System, if it deserves that name, not likely to be altered" (*Corr.*, vol. 9, 114). See also Burke's letters to French Laurence, ibid., 190–191, 244, 270–271). On this point, see also Mahoney, *Edmund Burke and Ireland*, p. 295.

98. Burke, *W&S*, vol. 9, pp. 661–662. See also the "Second Letter to Hercules Langrishe," ibid., p. 669.

99. Burke, *W&S*, vol. 9, p. 663.

100. Burke, *Corr.*, vol. 8, p. 136.

101. Burke, *W&S*, vol. 9, pp. 647–648.

102. See Ross Carroll, "Revisiting Burke's Critique of Enthusiasm," *History of Political Thought* 35, no. 2 (Summer 2014): 317–344, quoted at pp. 341–342.

103. Burke to Windham, October 16, 1794, in *Corr.* vol. 8, pp. 41–42. The editor of Burke's writings and speeches on Ireland, R. B. McDowell, notes, "When, in the early 1790s, Irish Catholic relief again came to the fore in politics, it was for Burke an issue of imperative urgency. The *dies irae* [day of wrath] had opened for Europe. It was all-important to check the spread of French principles, and an obvious way of accomplishing this in Ireland was to remove a major grievance, which the radicals would exploit—the exclusion of the Catholics from political power" (McDowell's editorial preface to Burke, *W&S*, vol. 9, pp. 417–418). See also McDowell, *Ireland in the Age of Imperialism and Revolution*, pp. 392–393. Similarly, O'Brien argues, "Burke saw the stigmatized condition of the Irish Catholics—their not being treated as full and equal citizens—as the factor that laid them most open to the seductions of Jacobin ideology." For this reason, Burke "set out to try to convince Langrishe (and others) that further resistance to Catholic enfranchisement" would "push the Catholics into the arms of the radical Dissenters, the United Irishmen, and so in the direction of revolution" (*The Great Melody*, pp. 472, 477, 482; see also pp. 570–577). Likewise, O'Flaherty maintains, "In ways reminiscent of his attitude to prudent concessions on Irish trade in 1778, Burke believed that a timely grant of political rights to Catholics might cement their loyalty to the state and prevent an alliance of disaffected Catholics and republican radicals" ("Burke and the Irish Constitution," p. 114). F. P. Lock notes, "In the 1790s, Burke became increasingly furious with the Ascendancy for refusing concessions to the Catholics, and therefore (as he thought) driving them into the hands of the Jacobins" ("Burke, Ireland and India," p. 163). The notion that Burke's push for Catholic emancipation and limited Catholic enfranchisement in the 1790s was driven by his fear of the French Revolution's ideas finding an audience in Ireland is also one of the central themes of Mahoney's *Edmund Burke and Ireland* (see pp. 166–167, 180–181, 207–211, 214–215, 219–221, 365).

104. Burke, "Letter to William Smith," in *W&S*, vol. 9, p. 664.

105. See Burke to unknown, February 28, 1793, in *Corr.*, vol. 7, pp. 350–351.

106. Burke, *W&S*, vol. 9, pp. 682, 678.

107. See Burke to the Reverend Thomas Hussey, post December 9, 1796, in *Corr.*, vol. 9, pp. 162, 164, where the example of Napoleon and Hoche is also given.

For the importance of Burke's correspondence with Hussey, and of this letter in particular, see Dáire Keogh, "Thomas Hussey, Edmund Burke, and the Irish Directory," in Donlan, *Edmund Burke's Irish Identities*, pp. 182–200. See also Burke's letter to French Laurence of December 8, 1796, in which he lambastes the Ascendancy as the "Lilliputian Directory in Ireland," which "instead of preparing to resist the French . . . are making war with all might upon Popery" *(Corr.,* vol. 9, 151).

108. See letter to Grattan of March 8, 1793, in *Corr.,* vol. 7, p. 361.

109. See letter to William Elliot, February 24, 1795, in *Corr.,* vol. 8, p. 158.

110. See McBride, *Eighteenth-Century Ireland,* pp. 286–287, 290–294, 311.

111. Smyth, *The Men of No Property,* p. 89.

112. See Burke to John Keogh, November 17, 1796, in *Corr.,* vol. 9, pp. 114–115.

113. See letter to William Windham, March 30, 1797, in *Corr.,* vol. 9, pp. 300–301.

114. See Burke to Lord Fitzwilliam, December 20, 1796, in *Corr.,* vol. 9, pp. 188–189, emphasis added.

115. The antidemocratic thrust of Burke's pronouncements with respect to Ireland in the 1790s renders problematic Seamus Deane's attempt to reduce all of Burke's arguments concerning France, India, America, and Ireland to a critique of "faction" (see his "Factions and Fictions: Burke, Colonialism and Revolution," in Deane, *Foreign Affections,* pp. 86–102). To the contrary, in Ireland, Burke wanted to enlarge and diversify one minority "faction"—the Ascendancy—by admitting a small number of Catholic elites to the ruling class as a means of fending off what he saw as radical secular democracy based on the principles of the French Revolution. We can call Burke's position a general opposition to "faction" only if we are willing to see the vast majority composed of the disenfranchised—those whom Burke feared—as themselves a "faction." Of course, this was precisely James Madison's argument in *The Federalist*. However, while Madison freely admitted that his opposition to "majority faction" was antidemocratic, nowhere does Deane frame the issue in Burke's thought on Ireland in this fashion. However, as I have argued elsewhere (*The Burke-Wollstonecraft Debate: Savagery, Civilization, and Democracy* [University Park: Penn State University Press, 2007]), it was not the problem of a minority faction that Burke objected to in the case of the French Revolution but rather precisely that of a majority faction—or democracy. My view on this point is similar to F. P. Lock's: "There seems, then, every reason to believe that, in justifying British rule in Ireland and India, Burke was expressing deeply held personal convictions. The consistency of the ideas and values to which he appeals is further evidence. In each country, he saw a mass of mankind needing protection, guidance, and control. For this purpose, a hereditary landed elite, respected by the majority and exercising responsibility for (but not responsible to them) was his solution. In Ireland, the gentry class needed to be broadened, by the readmission of Catholics into full membership, and by opening the elite to new Catholic recruits" ("Burke, Ireland and India," p. 167).

116. See Burke to Laurence, June 3, 1797, in *Corr.,* vol. 9, p. 365.

117. See Burke to Laurence, letter of March 1, 1797, in *Corr.,* vol. 9, pp. 265–266, emphasis original.

118. See Burke to Laurence, letter of May 12, 1797, in *Corr.*, vol. 9, pp. 336–337.

119. See Burke to Fitzwilliam, letter of May 21, 1797, in *Corr.*, vol. 9, p. 356. Even on his deathbed Burke bemoaned this democratic transformation and "the bad politics of beginning, continuing, and ending with what is called parliamentary Reform." See French Laurence to Earl Fitzwilliam, letter of July 9, 1797 (the day of Burke's death), in *Corr.*, vol. 9, p. 373. See also Burke's letter to an unknown correspondent in 1797, where he rejects the idea that citizens require actual representation, as an excess of political theory: "If Men have the real Benefit of a *Sympathetic* Representation, none but those who are heated and intoxicated with Theory will look for any other" (*W&S*, vol. 9, p. 674, emphasis original). As McDowell points out, this speaks either to the depth of Burke's wishful thinking or to his willingness to put his head in the sand: "Burke does not seem to have given much thought to how easily the Catholic community, consolidated and hardened by a century or more of severe pressure, once emancipated, would fit into the Irish political and social framework he accepted—the British connection, the predominance of the largely Protestant world. He never suggested in the early 1790s that Catholic enfranchisement should be accompanied by parliamentary reform, and very few Catholics were likely to be returned to the unreformed Parliament" (from McDowell's introduction to part 2, in Burke, *W&S*, vol. 9, p. 418). Mahoney argues that Burke's position on this issue was self-contradictory, because his push to enfranchise Catholic elites and open some offices to them was effectively a brand of parliamentary reform, despite his stated opposition to such moves in England (see *Edmund Burke and Ireland*, pp. 305, 320–322).

120. See letter to the Reverend Thomas Hussey, May 18, 1795, in *Corr.*, vol. 8, pp. 246–247, emphasis original.

121. Burke, *W&S*, vol. 9, p. 655.

122. See letters to Richard Burke of November 6, 7, 10, 1792, in *Corr.*, vol. 7, p. 287.

123. See letter to Edward Hay, June 26, 1795, in *Corr.*, vol. 8, p. 272. Again, to his credit, O'Brien recognizes this fact: "Burke was constrained by his wider commitment, against the French Revolution, not merely to leave that people [the Catholics] to their fate, but actively to side with Pitt, who was ultimately responsible for the continuation and exasperation of their oppression, through the consequences of Fitzwilliam's recall. Burke acknowledged that that people had just cause for rebellion. Yet, whenever the justifiable rebellion should come, he would be obliged, by his wider commitment, to support its repression" (*The Great Melody*, p. 584).

124. Wolfe Tone's extraordinary views on independence, and the form of radicalized Enlightenment that they embodied—and that Burke abhorred—have been captured well by Pocock: "There appeared radicals within the Protestantism that was not presbyterian who aimed to break with both established religion and the executive's control of the Dublin parliament—with 'empire', therefore, in both Tudor senses of the term—and were attracted to American and later French revolutionary models. They came to propound an Enlightened republicanism which offered to include, but at the same time to assimilate, all three confessions." That is,

what Wolfe Tone professed "was not other than a more radical version of Enlightenment. The offer to divorce the state from all recognition of religion, granting equal civil rights to those of all confessions, carried the implication that all were equally in harmony with civil society.... The programmes favoured by Wolfe Tone rested on the assumption that Irish like French Catholics would accept the status offered them by the Civil Constitution of the Clergy; it was the Enlightened, not the Catholic, view of Catholicism" ("The Union in British History," in *The Discovery of Islands*, pp. 174–176).

125. See, for example, the *Two Letters on the Trade of Ireland* (1778), in *W&S*, vol. 9, pp. 510–511; and Burke's letter to Samuel Span of April 23, 1778, in *Corr.*, vol. 3, p. 434.

126. See letter circa September 26, 1794, in *Corr.*, vol. 8, pp. 20–21.

127. McDowell, introduction to part 2, in Burke, *W&S*, vol. 9, p. 428.

128. Writing of the Act of Union, Bartlett argues that "Edmund Burke would surely have approved this concentration on Empire. For him the only true union between Ireland and England was an Imperial one" ("This Famous Island Set in a Virginian Sea," p. 271). That Burke would have approved of union is a view shared by Conor Cruise O'Brien, as per n. 123 above. On this point, see also James Conniff, "Edmund Burke's Reflections on the Coming Revolution in Ireland," *Journal of the History of Ideas* 47, no. 1 (1986): 37–59. For a reading of the *Reflections on the Revolution in France* as a "proleptic" comment on the Union between Great Britain and Ireland, see Claire Connolly, "*Reflections* on the Act of Union," in *Edmund Burke's Reflections on the Revolution in France: New Interdisciplinary Essays*, ed. John Whale (New York: Manchester University Press, 2000), pp. 168–192.

CONCLUSION

1. David Cannadine, *Ornamentalism: How the British Saw Their Empire* (Oxford: Oxford University Press, 2001), p. 121, emphasis original.

2. Ibid., p. 10.

3. Ibid., pp. 126 (quoted), 124.

4. Thomas Metcalf, *Ideologies of the Raj* (Cambridge: Cambridge University Press, 1995), p. 20.

5. For example, see Jennifer Pitts, *A Turn to Empire: The Rise of Imperial Liberalism in Britain and France* (Princeton, NJ: Princeton University Press, 2005); and Karuna Mantena, *Alibis of Empire: Henry Maine and the Ends of Liberal Imperialism* (Princeton, NJ: Princeton University Press, 2010).

6. Cannadine, *Ornamentalism*, pp. 43–44.

7. In a review of *Ornamentalism*, Marshall notes: "Thanks in particular to the indefatigable labours of Anthony Kirk-Greene on the Colonial Service and to numerous studies of the ICS, it seems clear that overseas administrators were overwhelmingly drawn from genteel rural or semi-rural backgrounds, if not usually from directly agrarian ones, that their views about society were likely to be conservative

with a small 'c' and that they tended to vote Conservative. Such generalisations have been substantiated by sophisticated studies of the intellectual assumptions of Indian civil servants, such as those of Clive Dewey. He charts the decline by the 1870s of the utilitarian individualism and free market enthusiasms of the earlier nineteenth century and the rise in their place of an increasing commitment to Indian 'collectivities', such as village communities. The Punjab Land Alienation Act of 1900, intended to protect such communities from the consequences of a free market in land, was a striking example of how such beliefs could be embodied in policy-making." See Marshall's review of *Ornamentalism: How the British Saw Their Empire*, by David Cannadine. *History in Focus* (Institute of Historical Research), no. 6 (June 2001), http://www.history.ac.uk/ihr/Focus/Empire/reviews/marshall2.html.

8. Cannadine, *Ornamentalism,* pp. 58 (quoted), 61, 64–67.

9. Ibid., pp. 132 (quoted), 71–82, 130.

10. P. J. Marshall, review of *Ornamentalism.*

11. Isaac Kramnick, *The Rage of Edmund Burke: Portrait of an Ambivalent Conservative* (New York: Basic Books, 1977), p. 128.

12. Edward Said, *Orientalism* (1978; repr., New York: Vintage Books, 2003).

13. See Duncan Bell, *Remaking the World: Essays on Liberalism and Empire* (Princeton, NJ: Princeton University Press, forthcoming).

14. The literature on this question is vast; for a sample of contrasting views, see Sankar Muthu, *Enlightenment against Empire* (Princeton, NJ: Princeton University Press, 2003); and Thomas McCarthy, *Race, Empire, and the Idea of Human Development* (Cambridge: Cambridge University Press, 2009).

15. Frederick Whelan, "Burke, India, and Orientalism," in his *Enlightenment Political Thought and Non-Western Societies: Sultans and Savages* (New York: Routledge, 2009), pp. 103–129, quoted at pp. 128–129.

16. This reading is traceable to Leo Strauss, *Natural Right and History* (Chicago: University of Chicago Press, 1953). Its most vociferous expression can be found in the work of Peter Stanlis; see *Edmund Burke and the Natural Law* (Ann Arbor: University of Michigan Press, 1958), and *Edmund Burke: The Enlightenment and Revolution* (New Brunswick, NJ: Transaction Publishers, 1991); see also Francis Canavan, *The Political Reason of Edmund Burke.* Durham, NC: Duke University Press, 1960; and *Edmund Burke: Prescription and Providence* (Durham, NC: Carolina Academic Press and Claremont Institute for the Study of Statesmanship and Political Philosophy, 1987). See, among the more recent works, Joseph L. Pappin III, *The Metaphysics of Edmund Burke* (New York: Fordham University Press, 1993); and Bruce Frohnen, *Virtue and the Promise of Conservatism: The Legacy of Burke and Tocqueville* (Lawrence: University Press of Kansas, 1993).

17. Cannadine, *Ornamentalism,* p. 170.

18. I owe credit for the pithy formulation of this point to Kirstie McClure, in conversation.

WORKS CITED

Abbattista, Guido. "Edmund Burke, the Atlantic American War and the 'Poor Jews at St. Eustatius.'" *Cromohs*, no. 13 (2008): 1–39.

Agnani, Sunil. *Hating Empire Properly: The Two Indies and the Limits of Enlightenment Anticolonialism*. New York: Fordham University Press, 2013.

Armitage, David. "The British Conception of Empire in the Eighteenth Century." In *Imperium/Empire/Reich: An Anglo-German Comparison of a Concept of Rule*, edited by Franz Bosbach and Hermann Hiery. Munich: K. G. Saur, 1999.

———. "Edmund Burke and Reason of State." *Journal of the History of Ideas* 61, no. 4 (2000): 617–634.

———. *The Ideological Origins of the British Empire*. Cambridge: Cambridge University Press, 2000.

Arneil, Barbara. *John Locke and America: The Defence of English Colonialism*. Oxford: Oxford University Press, 1996.

Ballantyne, Tony. *Orientalism and Race: Aryanism in the British Empire*. London: Palgrave Macmillan, 2002.

Bartlett, Thomas. "'This Famous Island Set in a Virginian Sea': Ireland in the British Empire, 1690–1801." In *The Oxford History of the British Empire: The Eighteenth Century*, edited by P. J. Marshall. Oxford: Oxford University Press, 2001.

Bass, Jeff D. "The Perversion of Empire: Edmund Burke and the Nature of Imperial Responsibility." *Quarterly Journal of Speech* 81 (1995): 208–227.

Bayly, C. A. "The British and Indigenous Peoples, 1760–1860: Power, Perception and Identity." In *Empire and Others: British Encounters with Indigenous Peoples, 1600–1850*, edited by Martin Daunton and Rick Halpern. Philadelphia: University of Pennsylvania Press, 1999.

———. *Imperial Meridian: The British Empire and the World, 1780–1830*. London: Longman, 1989.

———. *Indian Society and the Making of the British Empire*. Cambridge: Cambridge University Press, 1998.

Bayly, Susan. *Caste, Society and Politics in India from the Eighteenth Century to the Modern Age*. Cambridge: Cambridge University Press, 1999.

Bell, Duncan. *The Idea of Greater Britain: Empire and the Future of World Order, 1860–1900*. Princeton, NJ: Princeton University Press, 2007.

———. *Remaking the World: Essays on Liberalism and Empire*. Princeton, NJ: Princeton University Press, forthcoming.

———, ed. *Victorian Visions of Global Order: Europe and International Relations in Nineteenth Century Political Thought*. Cambridge: Cambridge University Press, 2007.

Berry, Christopher J. *Social Theory of the Scottish Enlightenment*. Edinburgh: Edinburgh University Press, 1997.

Bevir, Mark. *The Logic of the History of Ideas*. Cambridge: Cambridge University Press, 1999.

Bhabha, Homi K. *The Location of Culture*. New York: Routledge, 1994.

Boucher, David. "The Character of the History of the Philosophy of International Relations and the Case of Edmund Burke." *Review of International Studies* 17 (1991): 127–148.

———. *Political Theories of International Relations: From Thucydides to the Present*. Oxford: Oxford University Press, 1998.

Bourke, Richard. *Empire and Revolution: The Political Life of Edmund Burke*. Princeton, NJ: Princeton University Press, 2015.

———. "Liberty, Authority, and Trust in Burke's Idea of Empire." *Journal of the History of Ideas* 61, no. 3 (2000): 453–471.

———. "Sovereignty, Opinion and Revolution in Edmund Burke." *History of European Ideas* 25 (1999): 99–120.

Bowen, H. V. "British India, 1765–1813: The Metropolitan Context." In *The Oxford History of the British Empire: The Eighteenth Century*, edited by P. J. Marshall. Oxford: Oxford University Press, 2001.

Bromwich, David. *The Intellectual Life of Edmund Burke: From the Sublime and the Beautiful to American Independence*. Cambridge, MA: Harvard University Press, 2014.

Brown, Christopher L. "From Slaves to Subjects: Envisioning an Empire without Slavery, 1772–1834." In *Black Experience and the Empire*, edited by Philip D. Morgan and Sean Hawkins. Oxford: Oxford University Press, 2004.

Burke, Edmund. *The Correspondence of Edmund Burke*. 10 vols. Edited by Thomas W. Copeland. Chicago: University of Chicago Press, 1958–1978.

———. *Reflections on the Revolution in France*. Edited by J. G. A. Pocock. Indianapolis: Hackett, 1987.

———. *The Works of the Right Honourable Edmund Burke*. Bohn's British Classics. 8 vols. London: Bell & Daldy, 1872.

———. *The Writings and Speeches of Edmund Burke*. Paul Langford, general editor. 9 vols. Oxford: Oxford University Press, 1981–2015.

Burke, Edmund, and Will Burke. *An Account of the European Settlements in America*. 2 vols. 1757. Reprint, New York: Arno Press, 1972.

Burton, Antoinette. *Empire in Question: Reading, Writing, and Teaching British Imperialism*. Durham, NC: Duke University Press, 2011.

Canavan, Francis. *Edmund Burke: Prescription and Providence*. Durham, NC: Carolina Academic Press and Claremont Institute for the Study of Statesmanship and Political Philosophy, 1987.

———. *The Political Reason of Edmund Burke*. Durham, NC: Duke University Press, 1960.

Cannadine, David. *Ornamentalism: How the British Saw Their Empire*. Oxford: Oxford University Press, 2001.

———. *The Undivided Past: Humanity beyond Our Differences*. New York: Alfred A. Knopf, 2013.

Canny, Nicholas. *Kingdom and Colony: Ireland in the Atlantic World, 1560–1800*. Baltimore, MD: Johns Hopkins University Press, 1988.

Carnall, Geoffrey, and Colin Nicholson, eds. *The Impeachment of Warren Hastings*. Edinburgh: Edinburgh University Press, 1989.

Carroll, Ross. "Revisiting Burke's Critique of Enthusiasm." *History of Political Thought* 35, no. 2 (Summer 2014): 317–344.

Chakrabarty, Dipesh. *Provincializing Europe: Postcolonial Thought and Historical Difference*. Princeton, NJ: Princeton University Press, 2007.

Chaudhury, Sushil. *From Prosperity to Decline: 18th Century Bengal*. New Delhi: Manohar Publishers, 1999.

Clark, J. C. D. "Edmund Burke's *Reflections on the Revolution in America* (1777): Or, How Did the American Revolution Relate to the French?" In *An Imaginative Whig: Reassessing the Life and Thought of Edmund Burke*, edited by Ian Crowe. Columbia: University of Missouri Press, 2005.

Cobbett, William, ed. *Cobbett's Parliamentary History of England*. London: T. C. Hansard, 1806.

Colley, Linda. *Britons: Forging the Nation, 1707–1837*. New Haven, CT: Yale University Press, 1992.

———. *Captives*. New York: Pantheon Books, 2002.

Cone, Carl B. *Burke and the Nature of Politics: The Age of the French Revolution* Lexington: University of Kentucky Press, 1964.

Conniff, James. "Edmund Burke's Reflections on the Coming Revolution in Ireland." *Journal of the History of Ideas* 47, no. 1 (1986): 37–59.

———. *The Useful Cobbler: Edmund Burke and the Politics of Progress*. Albany: State University of New York Press, 1994.

Connolly, Claire. "*Reflections* on the Act of Union." In *Edmund Burke's* Reflections on the Revolution in France: *New Interdisciplinary Essays*, edited by John Whale. New York: Manchester University Press, 2000.

Connolly, Sean. *Religion, Law, and Power: The Making of Protestant Ireland: 1660–1760*. Oxford: Oxford University Press, 1992.

Conway, Stephen. "Britain and the Revolutionary Crisis, 1763–1791." In *The Oxford History of the British Empire: The Eighteenth Century*, edited by P. J. Marshall. Oxford: Oxford University Press, 2001.

Craton, Michael. *Sinews of Empire: A Short History of British Slavery*. Garden City, NY: Anchor Press, 1974.

Crowe, Ian, ed. *The Enduring Edmund Burke: Bicentennial Essays.* Wilmington, DE: Intercollegiate Studies Institute, 1997.
Cullen, Louis. "Burke, Ireland, and Revolution." *Studies in the Eighteenth Century* 16 (February 1992): 21–42.
Curtis, Michael. *Orientalism and Islam: European Thinkers on Oriental Despotism in the Middle East and India.* Cambridge: Cambridge University Press, 2009.
Davis, David Brion. *The Problem of Slavery in Western Culture.* Ithaca, NY: Cornell University Press, 1966.
Deane, Seamus. *Foreign Affections: Essays on Edmund Burke.* Notre Dame, IN: University of Notre Dame Press, 2005.
Dickinson, Harry T. "Burke and the American Crisis." In *The Cambridge Companion to Edmund Burke,* edited by David Dwan and Christopher J. Insole. Cambridge: Cambridge University Press, 2012.
Dirks, Nicholas B. *Castes of Mind: Colonialism and the Making of Modern India.* Princeton, NJ: Princeton University Press, 2001.
———. *The Scandal of Empire: India and the Creation of Imperial Britain.* Cambridge, MA: Harvard University Press, 2008.
Donlan, Seán Patrick, ed. *Edmund Burke's Irish Identities.* Portland, OR: Irish Academic Press, 2007.
Dreyer, Frederick. *Burke's Politics: A Study in Whig Orthodoxy.* Waterloo, Ontario: Wilfrid Laurier University Press, 1979.
Dussel, Enrique. *The Invention of the Americas: Eclipse of "the Other" and the Myth of Modernity.* New York: Continuum, 1995.
Faulkner, John. "Burke's First Encounter with Richard Price: The Chathamites and North America." In *An Imaginative Whig: Reassessing the Life and Thought of Edmund Burke,* edited by Ian Crowe. Columbia: University of Missouri Press, 2005.
Foner, Eric. *Tom Paine and Revolutionary America.* Oxford: Oxford University Press, 2005.
Forman-Barzilai, Fonna. *Adam Smith and the Circles of Sympathy: Cosmopolitanism and Moral Theory.* Cambridge: Cambridge University Press, 2010.
Frohnen, Bruce. "An Empire of Peoples: Burke, Government, and National Character." In *The Enduring Edmund Burke,* edited by Ian Crowe. Wilmington, DE: Intercollegiate Studies Institute, 1997.
———. *Virtue and the Promise of Conservatism: The Legacy of Burke and Tocqueville.* Lawrence: University Press of Kansas, 1993.
Fuchs, Michel. *Edmund Burke, Ireland, and the Fashioning of the Self.* Oxford: Voltaire Foundation, 1996.
Gibbons, Luke. *Edmund Burke and Ireland: Aesthetics, Politics, and the Colonial Sublime.* Cambridge: Cambridge University Press, 2003.
Gould, Eliga. "Liberty and Modernity: The American Revolution and the Making of Parliament's Imperial History." In *Exclusionary Empire: English Liberty Overseas, 1600–1900,* edited by Jack P. Greene. Cambridge: Cambridge University Press, 2010.

———. *The Persistence of Empire: British Political Culture in the Age of the American Revolution*. Chapel Hill: University of North Carolina Press, 2000.
Greene, Jack P. "Empire and Identity from the Glorious to the American Revolution." In *The Oxford History of the British Empire: The Eighteenth Century*, edited by P. J. Marshall. Oxford: Oxford University Press, 2001.
———, ed. *Exclusionary Empire: English Liberties Overseas, 1600–1900*. Cambridge: Cambridge University Press, 2010.
———. *Peripheries and Center: Constitutional Development in the Extended Polities of the British Empire and the United States, 1607–1788*. New York: W. W. Norton, 1990.
Gunn, Simon, and James Vernon, eds. *The Peculiarities of Liberal Modernity in Imperial Britain*. Berkeley: University of California Press, 2011.
Hall, Catherine, and Sonya Rose, eds. *At Home with the Empire: Metropolitan Culture and the Imperial World*. Cambridge: Cambridge University Press, 2006.
Hampsher-Monk, Iain. "Edmund Burke and Empire." In *Lineages of Empire: The Historical Roots of British Imperial Thought*, edited by Duncan Kelly. Oxford: Oxford University Press, 2009.
———. *A History of Modern Political Thought*. Oxford: Blackwell, 1992.
Hanley, Ryan Patrick. *Adam Smith and the Character of Virtue*. Cambridge: Cambridge University Press, 2011.
Harle, Vilho. "Burke the International Theorist—or the War of the Sons of Light and the Sons of Darkness." In *European Values in International Relations*, edited by Vilho Harle. New York: Pinter, 1990.
Harlow, V. T. *The Founding of the Second British Empire, 1763–1793*. 2 vols. London: Longmans Green, 1952–1964.
Hasian, Marouf, Jr. "Nostalgic Longings and Imaginary Indias: Postcolonial Analysis, Collective Memories, and the Impeachment Trial of Warren Hastings." *Western Journal of Communication* 66, no. 2 (2002): 229–255.
Herzog, Don. *Poisoning the Minds of the Lower Orders*. Princeton, NJ: Princeton University Press, 1998.
Ince, Onur Ulas. "Not a Partnership in Pepper, Calico, or Tobacco: Edmund Burke and the Vicissitudes of Colonial Capitalism." *Polity* 44, no. 3 (2012): 340–372.
Janes, Regina. "At Home Abroad: Edmund Burke in India." *Bulletin of Research in the Humanities* 82, no. 2 (1979): 160–174.
———. "Edmund Burke's Flying Leap from India to France." *History of European Ideas* 7, no. 5 (1986): 509–527.
Kelly, James. "'Era of Liberty': The Politics of Civil and Political Rights in Eighteenth-Century Ireland." In *Exclusionary Empire: English Liberty Overseas, 1600–1900*, edited by Jack P. Greene. Cambridge: Cambridge University Press, 2010.
Keogh, Dáire. "Thomas Hussey, Edmund Burke, and the Irish Directory." In *Edmund Burke's Irish Identities*, edited by Seán Patrick Donlan. Portland, OR: Irish Academic Press, 2007.

Kidd, Colin. "Ethnicity in the British Atlantic World, 1688–1830." In *A New Imperial History: Culture, Identity, and Modernity in Britain and the Empire, 1660–1840*, edited by Kathleen Wilson. Cambridge: Cambridge University Press, 2004.

Kohn, Margaret. "Colonialism." In *Stanford Encyclopedia of Philosophy*, Summer 2012 edition. Edited by Edward N. Zalta. http://plato.stanford.edu/archives/sum2012/entries/colonialism/.

Kramnick, Isaac. "The Left and Edmund Burke." *Political Theory* 11, no. 2 (1983): 189–214.

———, ed. *The Portable Edmund Burke*. New York: Penguin Books, 1999.

———. *The Rage of Edmund Burke: Portrait of an Ambivalent Conservative*. New York: Basic Books, 1977.

Lenman, Bruce P. "'From Savage to Scot' via the French and the Spaniards: Principal Robertson's Spanish Sources." In *William Robertson and the Expansion of Empire*, edited by Stewart J. Brown. Cambridge: Cambridge University Press, 1997.

Levy, Jacob T. Review of *Enlightenment against Empire*, by Sankar Muthu. *Perspectives on Politics* 2, no. 4 (2004): 829–830.

Lock, F. P. "Burke, Ireland and India: Reason, Rhetoric and Empire." In *Edmund Burke's Irish Identities*, edited by Seán Patrick Donlan. Portland, OR: Irish Academic Press, 2007.

———. *Edmund Burke*. 2 vols. Oxford: Oxford University Press, 1998, 2006.

Mahoney, Thomas H. D. *Edmund Burke and Ireland*. Cambridge, MA: Harvard University Press, 1960.

Mancke, Elizabeth. "The Languages of Liberty in British North America, 1607–1776." In *Exclusionary Empire: English Liberties Overseas, 1600–1900*, edited by Jack P. Greene. Cambridge: Cambridge University Press, 2010.

Mantena, Karuna. *Alibis of Empire: Henry Maine and the Ends of Liberal Imperialism*. Princeton, NJ: Princeton University Press, 2010.

Marshall, P. J. "Burke and Empire." In *Hanoverian Britain and Empire: Essays in Memory of Philip Lawson*, edited by Stephen Taylor, Richard Connors, and Clyve Jones. Rochester, NY: Boydell Press, 1998.

———. "Burke and India." In *The Enduring Edmund Burke*, edited by Ian Crowe. Wilmington, DE: Intercollegiate Studies Institute, 1997.

———. *"A Free Though Conquering People": Eighteenth-Century Britain and Its Empire*. Aldershot, U.K.: Ashgate, 2003.

———. *The Impeachment of Warren Hastings*. Oxford: Oxford University Press, 1965.

———. "Imperial Britain." *Journal of Imperial and Commonwealth History* 23, no. 3 (1995): 379–394.

———. *The Making and Unmaking of Empires: Britain, India, and America, c. 1750–1783*. Oxford: Oxford University Press, 2005.

———, ed. *The Oxford History of the British Empire: The Eighteenth Century*. Oxford: Oxford University Press, 2001.

———. Review of *Ornamentalism: How the British Saw Their Empire*, by David Cannadine. *History in Focus* (Institute of Historical Research), no. 6 (June 2001). www.history.ac.uk/ihr/Focus/Empire/reviews/marshall2.html.

Marshall, P. J., and Glyndwr Williams. *The Great Map of Mankind: Perceptions of New Worlds in the Age of Enlightenment*. Cambridge, MA: Harvard University Press, 1982.

Marshall, Peter. "British North America, 1760–1815." In *The Oxford History of the British Empire: The Eighteenth Century*, edited by P. J. Marshall. Oxford: Oxford University Press, 2001.

McBride, Ian. "Burke and Ireland." In *The Cambridge Companion to Edmund Burke*, edited by David Dwan and Christopher J. Insole. Cambridge: Cambridge University Press, 2012.

———. *Eighteenth-Century Ireland: The Isle of Slaves*. Dublin: Gill & Macmillan, 2009.

McCann, Andrew. *Cultural Politics in the 1790s: Literature, Radicalism and the Public Sphere*. New York: St. Martin's Press, 1999.

McCarthy, Thomas. *Race, Empire, and the Idea of Human Development*. Cambridge: Cambridge University Press, 2009.

McDowell, R. B. *Ireland in the Age of Imperialism and Revolution, 1760–1801*. Oxford: Oxford University Press, 1991.

McLoughlin, T. O. *Contesting Ireland: Irish Voices against England in the Eighteenth Century*. Dublin: Four Courts Press, 1999.

Mehta, Uday Singh. "Edmund Burke on Empire, Self-Understanding, and Sympathy." In *Empire and Modern Political Thought*, edited by Sankar Muthu. Cambridge: Cambridge University Press, 2012.

———. *Liberalism and Empire: A Study in Nineteenth-Century British Liberal Thought*. Chicago: University of Chicago Press, 1999.

Metcalf, Thomas R. *Ideologies of the Raj*. Cambridge: Cambridge University Press, 1995).

Morefield, Jeanne. *Covenants without Swords: Idealist Liberalism and the Spirit of Empire*. Princeton, NJ: Princeton University Press, 2005.

Morgan, Philip D. "The Black Experience in the British Empire, 1680–1810." In *The Oxford History of the British Empire: The Eighteenth Century*, edited by P. J. Marshall. Oxford: Oxford University Press, 2001.

Morris, Rosalind, ed. *Can the Subaltern Speak? Reflections on the History of an Idea*. New York: Columbia University Press, 2010.

Musselwhite, David. "The Trial of Warren Hastings." In *Literature, Politics, and Theory*, edited by Francis Barker, Peter Hulme, Margaret Iversen, and Diana Loxley. London: Methuen, 1986.

Muthu, Sankar, ed. *Empire and Modern Political Thought*. Cambridge: Cambridge University Press, 2012.

———. *Enlightenment against Empire*. Princeton, NJ: Princeton University Press, 2003.

Nechtman, Tillman W. *Nabobs: Empire and Identity in Eighteenth-Century Britain*. Cambridge: Cambridge University Press, 2010.

O'Brien, Conor Cruise. *The Great Melody: A Thematic Biography of Edmund Burke*. Chicago: University of Chicago Press, 1992.

O'Brien, Karen. "Robertson's Place in the Development of Eighteenth-Century Narrative History." In *William Robertson and the Expansion of Empire*, edited by Stewart J. Brown. Cambridge: Cambridge University Press, 1997.

O'Flaherty, Eamon. "Burke and the Irish Constitution." In *Edmund Burke's Irish Identities*, edited by Seán Patrick Donlan. Portland, OR: Irish Academic Press, 2007.

O'Gorman, Frank. *Edmund Burke: His Political Philosophy*. Bloomington: Indiana University Press, 1973.

Oldenfield, John. *Popular Politics and British Anti-Slavery: The Mobilisation of Public Opinion against the Slave Trade, 1787–1807*. Manchester, U.K.: Manchester University Press, 1995.

O'Neill, Daniel I. *The Burke-Wollstonecraft Debate: Savagery, Civilization, and Democracy*. University Park: Penn State University Press, 2007.

———. "Edmund Burke, the 'Science of Man,' and Statesmanship." In *Scientific Statesmanship, Governance and the History of Political Philosophy*. Edited by Kyriakos N. Demetriou and Antis P. Loizides, pp. 174–192. New York: Routledge, 2015.

———. "Empire." In *SAGE Encyclopedia of Political Theory*, edited by Mark Bevir. Thousand Oaks, CA: SAGE Publications, 2010.

———. "Rethinking Burke and India." *History of Political Thought* 30, no. 3 (2009): 492–523.

———. "Revisiting the Middle Way: The Logic of the History of Ideas after More Than a Decade." *Journal of the History of Ideas* 73, no. 4 (2012): 583–592.

———. "The Sublime, the Beautiful, and the Political in Burke's Work." In *The Science of Sensibility: Reading Burke's* Philosophical Enquiry, edited by Michael Funk Deckard and Koen Vermeir. New York: Springer, 2012.

O'Neill, Daniel I., and Margaret Kohn. "A Tale of Two Indias: Burke and Mill on Empire and Slavery in the West Indies and America." *Political Theory* 34, no. 2 (2006): 192–228.

Opal, J. M. "*Common Sense* and Imperial Atrocity: How Tom Paine Saw South Asia in North America," *Common-Place* 9, no. 4 (July 2009). www.common-place.org/vol-09/no-04/forum/opal.shtml.

———. "Thomas Paine and the Revolutionary Enlightenment, 1770s-1790s," in *Common Sense and Other Writings*, edited by J. M. Opal (W.W. Norton & Company, 2012), pp. vii-xxxv.

Pagden, Anthony. *Lords of All the World: Ideologies of Empire in Spain, Britain and France, c. 1500–c. 1800*. New Haven, CT: Yale University Press, 1995.

———. *Peoples and Empires: A Short History of European Migration, Exploration, and Conquest, from Greece to the Present*. New York: Modern Library, 2003.

Paine, Thomas. *The Complete Writings of Thomas Paine*. Edited by Philip S. Foner. 2 vols. New York: Citadel Press, 1945.

Pappin, Joseph L., III. *The Metaphysics of Edmund Burke.* New York: Fordham University Press, 1993.

Phillipson, N. T. "Providence and Progress: An Introduction to the Historical Thought of William Robertson." In *William Robertson and the Expansion of Empire,* edited by Stewart J. Brown. Cambridge: Cambridge University Press, 1997.

Pitts, Jennifer. "Burke and the Ends of Empire." In *The Cambridge Companion to Edmund Burke,* edited by David Dwan and Christopher J. Insole. Cambridge: Cambridge University Press, 2012.

———. "Political Theory of Empire and Imperialism." *Annual Review of Political Science* 13 (2010): 211–235.

———. *A Turn to Empire: The Rise of Imperial Liberalism in Britain and France.* Princeton, NJ: Princeton University Press, 2005.

Pocock, J. G. A. *The Ancient Constitution and the Feudal Law.* 2nd ed. Cambridge: Cambridge University Press, 1987.

———. *Barbarism and Religion,* vol. 4: *Barbarians, Savages, and Empires.* Cambridge: Cambridge University Press, 2005.

———. *The Discovery of Islands: Essays in British History.* Cambridge: Cambridge University Press, 2005.

———. "Edmund Burke and the Redefinition of Enthusiasm: The Context as Counter-Revolution." In *The French Revolution and the Creation of Modern Political Culture.* Vol. 3. Edited by François Furet and Mona Ozouf. Oxford: Oxford University Press, 1989.

———, ed. *The Varieties of British Political Thought, 1500–1800.* Cambridge: Cambridge University Press, 1993.

———. *Virtue, Commerce, and History: Essays on Political Thought and History, Chiefly in the Eighteenth Century.* Cambridge: Cambridge University Press, 1985.

Prior, James. *Memoir of the Life and Character of the Right Hon. Edmund Burke.* 2nd ed. London: n.p., 1826.

Rana, Aziz. *The Two Faces of American Freedom.* Cambridge, MA: Harvard University Press, 2010.

Rasmussen, Dennis. *The Problems and Promise of Commercial Society: Adam Smith's Response to Rousseau.* University Park: Penn State University Press, 2008.

Ray, Rajat Kanta. "Indian Society and the Establishment of British Supremacy, 1765–1818." In *The Oxford History of the British Empire: The Eighteenth Century,* edited by P. J. Marshall. Oxford: Oxford University Press, 2001.

Richardson, David. "The British Empire and the Atlantic Slave Trade, 1660–1807." In *The Oxford History of the British Empire: The Eighteenth Century,* edited by P. J. Marshall. Oxford: Oxford University Press, 2001.

Richter, Daniel K. "Native Peoples of North America and the Eighteenth-Century British Empire." In *The Oxford History of the British Empire: The Eighteenth Century,* edited by P. J. Marshall. Oxford: Oxford University Press, 2001.

Robertson, John, ed. *A Union for Empire: Political Thought and the British Union of 1707.* Cambridge: Cambridge University Press, 1995.

Robins, Nick. *The Corporation That Changed the World: How the East India Company Shaped the Modern Multinational.* London: Pluto Press, 2006.
Said, Edward. *Orientalism.* 1978. Reprint, New York: Vintage Books, 2003.
Schultz, Bart, and Georgios Varouxakis, eds. *Utilitarianism and Empire.* Lanham, MD: Lexington Books, 2005.
Sinha, Mrinalini. *Colonial Masculinity: The "Manly Englishman" and the "Effeminate Bengali" in the Late Nineteenth Century.* Manchester, U.K.: Manchester University Press, 1995.
Skinner, Quentin. "Meaning and Understanding in the History of Ideas." In *Meaning and Context: Quentin Skinner and His Critics,* edited by James Tully. Princeton, NJ: Princeton University Press, 1988.
Smyth, Jim. *The Men of No Property: Irish Radicals and Popular Politics in the Late Eighteenth Century.* Notre Dame, IN: University of Notre Dame Press, 1998.
Stanlis, Peter. *Edmund Burke and the Natural Law.* Ann Arbor: University of Michigan Press, 1958.
———. *Edmund Burke: The Enlightenment and Revolution* (New Brunswick, NJ: Transaction Publishers, 1991).
Strauss, Leo. *Natural Right and History.* Chicago: University of Chicago Press, 1953.
Suleri, Sara. *The Rhetoric of English India.* Chicago: University of Chicago Press, 1992.
Travers, Robert. "Contested Despotism: Problems of Liberty in British India." In *Exclusionary Empire: English Liberties Overseas, 1600–1900,* edited by Jack P. Greene. Cambridge: Cambridge University Press, 2010.
———. *Ideology and Empire in Eighteenth-Century India.* Cambridge: Cambridge University Press, 2007.
Tuck, Richard. *The Rights of War and Peace: Political Thought and the International Order from Grotius to Kant.* Oxford: Oxford University Press, 1999.
Tully, James. *An Approach to Political Philosophy: Locke in Contexts.* Cambridge: Cambridge University Press, 1993.
Vincent, R. J. "Edmund Burke and the Theory of International Relations." *Review of International Studies* 10 (1984): 205–218.
Wall, Maureen. *The Penal Laws, 1691–1760.* Dundalk, Ireland: Dun Dealgan Press, 1976.
Welsh, Jennifer M. *Edmund Burke and International Relations: The Commonwealth of Europe and the Crusade against the French Revolution.* New York: St. Martin's Press, 1995.
Whelan, Frederick G. "Burke on India." In *The Cambridge Companion to Edmund Burke,* edited by David Dwan and Christopher J. Insole. Cambridge: Cambridge University Press, 2012.
———. *Edmund Burke and India: Political Morality and Empire.* Pittsburgh, PA: University of Pittsburgh Press, 1996.
———. *Enlightenment Political Thought and Non-Western Societies: Sultans and Savages.* New York: Routledge, 2009.

Wilson, Kathleen. *The Island Race: Englishness, Empire and Gender in the Eighteenth Century*. London: Routledge, 2003.

———, ed. *A New Imperial History: Culture, Identity and Modernity in Britain and the Empire, 1660–1840*. Cambridge: Cambridge University Press, 2004.

———. *The Sense of the People: Politics, Culture and Imperialism in England, 1715–1785*. Cambridge: Cambridge University Press, 1995.

Winch, Donald. *Riches and Poverty: An Intellectual History of Political Economy in Britain, 1750–1834*. Cambridge: Cambridge University Press, 1996.

Zerilli, Linda M. G. *Signifying Woman: Culture and Chaos in Rousseau, Burke, and Mill*. Ithaca, NY: Cornell University Press, 1994.

INDEX

absentee taxation in Ireland, 16–17, 130–34, 137, 174, 216n26
absolutism, 23, 104–6, 146
Account of the European Settlements in America, An (Burke), 64–68, 75–76, 85, 96
Act of Union (Britain and Ireland), 128, 166–67, 226n128
Adams, John, 61
Address to the Colonists (Burke), 29
affinities in Ornamentalism, 2, 168, 180n5
Africa, 26, 172
African slaves/slavery: abolition of, 83–84, 85, 89; in American rebellion, 13; Burke defending, 146; civilizing of, 14, 77–78, 84–85, 146, 176; emancipation of, 14, 78–87; and liberty, 24, 84; and Orientalism, 63–64, 78–87, 172–73; reenslavement of, 87, 176; and religion, 14, 76–77; rights expanded for, 69–70; "savagery" of, 63, 175; sympathy for, 206n145; in the West Indies, 87–91
Agnani, Sunil, 205n144
Allahabad, Treaty of, 33
alterity: in American colonies, 63, 71, 81; justifying imperialism, 172; in Orientalism, 1, 14, 175. *See also* Orientalism
American colonies/colonists: alterity in, 63, 71, 81; in the British Empire, 19–20; character of, 51–52, 54–58, 59, 198n36; commerce in civilizing of, 21–22; conciliation and sympathy for, 13, 14–15, 51–52, 58–63; debate over, 47–49; and democracy, 13, 55–56, 58, 61; discipline in, 72; and English civilization, 52–54; features of, 55–58; and free trade, 59, 134–36; governance in, 55–56, 59; independence of, 25, 29, 49, 63; legitimacy of empire in, 28–29; leniency for, 49–52; liberty and subordination in, 50–51, 54–55, 57, 69; local autonomy for, 69; and Orientalism, 14–15, 172–73; and Ornamentalism, 13–14, 54–58; and Parliamentary representation, 60–61; religion in, 55, 56, 58; representative assemblies in, 42, 49; sovereignty of, 29, 49–52, 61; support for, 9; taxation in, 28–29, 55, 59–60, 61

American Crisis, The (Paine), 35
American Revolution, 62–63, 66, 71, 73–74, 134–36, 137–39
American South, 57–58, 78–79
American West, 69, 72–73
Amerindians: civilizing of, 77, 175, 176; compared to East Indians, 95–96; requirements to convert, 23; in the Royal Proclamation of 1763, 69; "savagery" of, 14, 65–68, 175. *See also* Native Americans
Ancien Régime: in defense of empire, 177; in India, 15–16, 94, 100–108, 110–23, 170–71; in Ireland, 18, 127–28, 144, 163–64; and liberty, 21
Anglo-Celtic frontier, 20, 40
Anglo-Dutch War of 1780-1784, 206n145
Anglo-Irish historical relations, 147

241

anti-colonialism and anti-imperialism: Burke described as defender of, 3–4, 12, 27, 140; in India, 115, 171; in Ireland, 127–28, 192–93n76; and Orientalism, 171, 173; and Providence, 41; in the West Indies, 205n144

Appeal from the New to the Old Whigs (Burke), 9–10, 155

Arcot, Nawab of, 114

aristocracy: of the American South, 57–58; Catholic, 17, 143, 149, 150–53, 163–64; in civilization, 5–6, 13, 52–53, 94, 95, 96; in civilizing, 169; in colonial America, 55, 58; in conservatism, 7; in the Hindu caste system, 99, 112; Indian, 15, 16, 107, 108, 110–16, 170–71, 210–11n50; Irish, 17, 148–49; lack of in savagery, 66–67; and Orientalism, 173; and the sublime, 53–54; West Indies, 89–90

Armitage, David, 11–12, 13, 20–21

Asaf-ud-Daula, nawab *wazir* of Oudh (Awadh), 117–18

Asia in ideology of empire, 25–26

atheism, 18, 144, 160, 161–62

Atlantic Archipelago, 20, 40, 48

Begams of Oudh (India), 116–21, 213n80

Bell, Duncan, 173

Bengal: destruction of nobles in, 111–12; famine in, 31–32, 34, 36, 92; infrastructure and institutions in, 102; looting of, 31, 36; revolution in, 30–31, 32, 92, 170, 187n37, 188–89n50, 189–90n56

"Black Codes," 87

Blaquiere, John, 131

Bolts, William, 31

Bourke, Richard: *Empire and Revolution*, 11, 37

bribery, 116, 120. *See also* corruption

Bristol, 81–83, 136–37, 145

British Empire, Burke's conception of, 42–46

Bromwich, David, 3

Burke, Edmund: biography of, 124–25; as MP for Bristol, 81–83, 136–37, 145; political career of, 42; and the United Irishmen, 153–58; as a Whig, 7–8, 9, 28, 182n22

Burke, Edmund, works of. *See under title of work*

Burke, Richard, 145

Burke, William, 64–65

Calcutta, capture of, 30

Calvin's Case (Coke), 22–23

Cambridge school historicism, 8–9

Canada, 25, 42, 70

Cannadine, David, 1, 2, 168, 169–70, 171, 172

Canny, Nicholas, 126

Caribbean colonies: in the British Empire, 20–21, 26, 42, 43; migration to, 48; Orientalism in, 172–73, 175–76; slave rebellions in, 15, 87–91; slavery in, 75, 77

Carnatic (India), 97, 98, 101, 114

Case of Ireland Stated, The (Molyneux), 138

Castle Party, 138

Catholic aristocracy, 17, 143, 149, 150–53, 163–64

Catholic Church, 42, 56, 149–50

Catholic Committee, 145, 156

Catholic lands, 126–30, 133–34, 144

Catholic rebellion of 1641, 129, 146–47

Catholic relief from penal laws: Burke's support for, 145–46, 154–55, 160–61; and free trade, 137; and Jacobinism, 160–61, 223n103; and Ornamentalism, 125; and the United Irishmen, 130, 143, 154, 221n91, 223n103; Wolf Tone in, 222n92

Catholics, Irish: Burke's support for, 141–42; defense of, 40; disenfranchisement of, 149; enfranchisement of, 125, 130, 143, 150–53, 160–61; and Jacobinism, 158, 223n103; and legislative independence, 218n60; penal laws imposed on, 17, 125, 130, 137, 142–53; and the Protestant Ascendancy, 150, 156–57, 161–62; and Protestant settlers, 147–48; sympathy for, 125

Catholic "Whiteboys," 145

Celtic Irish, 126–27

character: of American colonists, 51–52, 54–58, 59, 198n36; in Catholic enfranchisement, 151; in imperial sovereignty, 12–13, 44–45, 51–52; of Native Americans, 64–66

Christianity and Christian conversion: in civilizing African slaves, 77–78; in civilizing Ireland, 149–50; in civilizing Native Americans, 66; Hinduism compared to, 94; in ideology of empire, 22–23; and Jacobinism, 159; and the Protestant Ascendancy, 159–60; and the Royal Proclamation of 1763, 70
Church of Ireland, 153–54
citizenship, 24, 151–52
civilization: aristocracy in, 5–6, 13, 52–53, 94, 96; atheism threatening, 160; and conservatism, 5–7; degrees and levels of, 13, 46, 49; English, 52–54; in India, 94–98, 110–23; lack of for Others, 63–64; and Ornamentalism, 94–98, 107–10; religion in, 5, 95, 98, 114, 176; social hierarchy in, 114
civilizing: of African slaves, 14, 77–78, 84–85, 146, 176; of Amerindians, 77, 175, 176; commerce in, 21–22; economic development in, 65–66; enfranchisement in, 150–51, 153; history in, 13, 27, 45–46, 169; of India, 21–22; of Ireland, 125, 126, 142–53; liberty in, 219n69; of Native Americans, 14, 63, 66, 71–75, 146; organized religion in, 65–66, 149–50; and Orientalism, 72, 173, 175–76; and Ornamentalism, 72; religion and aristocracy in, 113. *See also* history as civilizing process
class, 2, 17–18, 114, 170. *See also* social hierarchies
Clive, Robert, 12, 29–37, 92–93, 177, 188–89n50, 189–90n56
coercion, 3, 87, 166
Coercive Acts, 59–60, 61
coherence. *See* consistency
Coke, Edward: *Calvin's Case*, 22–23
Colley, Linda, 23, 69
colonialism and colonization: and commerce, 20; defenses of, 28–29; etymology of, 19–20; in Ireland, 126, 128–29, 148, 165, 173; realities of, 24. *See also* American colonies/colonists
colonial legislatures, 13, 26, 49, 55–56, 59–60, 90
colonial trade, 51, 59, 136–37

commerce: in the defense of Clive, 32–33; in ideology of empire, 20–22; in India, 21–22, 92; in Ireland, 130; realities of, 24; regulation of, 26; slave trade as, 83
common law, 21, 42, 79, 105
Common Sense (Paine), 35
Company of Merchant Adventurers Trading to Africa (Africa Company), 81–83
conciliation policy and American colonists, 13, 14–15, 51–52, 58–63
Conciliation Speeches of 1775 (Burke), 43–44, 51–52, 54–58, 61, 71, 78–81, 83
confederate notion of empire, 60
conquest: and conservatism, 11; in expansion of empire, 176; in ideology of empire, 26; of India, 26, 29–32, 38–39, 191–92n70; of Ireland, 126, 128–29, 146–48; legitimized by time, 26; of Native Americans, 20; Providence in, 38–39
conservatism, 2–3, 5–7, 11, 73, 170, 184n35
consistency of Burke, 7–10, 155–58, 183n28, 183–84n30
corruption: in Burke's conception of empire, 43; by Hastings, 30, 39, 116, 189–90n56; in India, 30–31, 33–34, 39, 92, 115–16, 120–21, 122–23, 189n56; Indianism as, 123; national glory threatened by, 39; of the nawabs, 122–23; of voters, 60

Davies, John, 147
Davis, David Brion, 85
Declaration of the Rights of Man (French National Constituent Assembly), 88–89
Declaratory Act for Ireland (1720), 133, 138, 140
Declaratory Act for the American Colonies (1766), 28, 43, 49–50, 55, 140
democracy: and American colonists, 13, 55–56, 58, 61; churches in, 53–54; in civilization's break-down, 5–6; in Ireland, 17–18, 142–44, 147–49, 152–53, 154–55, 164–65, 166; rejected by Burke, 6, 169, 177–78; United Irishmen on, 17–18, 155
desirability of empire, 28–39, 47

INDEX · 243

despotism: Indianism as, 123; modern notions of, 2; national glory threatened by, 39; of the Nawabs in India, 123; Oriental, 104–6, 108, 172–73
diachronic explanations of belief, 183n29
Dirks, Nicholas, 37
discipline: in civilization, 5–6; in colonial America, 72; in emancipation of slaves, 85; in India, 100; against Jacobinism, 150; religion in, 56, 115; social, 5–6, 18, 53–54, 56, 58, 66–67, 150
Dissenters in Ireland, 18, 127, 129, 143–44, 158, 161–62
Diversity of empire, 42, 43–46, 69
diwani (grant of administrative and taxation rights), 30, 31–32, 33–34, 102, 103
Donlan, Seán Patrick, 146, 192–93n76
Drapier's Letters (Swift), 138
Dundas, Henry, 83

Eastern empire, 25–27, 90–91
East India Company: atrocities of the, 12, 34–35; compared to the French Revolution, 110–16; in conquest, 26, 191–92n70; corruption by, 92–93, 115–17, 120, 189–90n56; destruction of Indian nobility by, 110–16; in Indian imperialism, 30–32; in the Mughal Empire, 101–3; political power of, 38; regulation of, 32, 37, 39, 92–93, 95; sovereignty of Britain over, 106. *See also* India
economic development, 5, 65–66, 67
economics: in African slavery, 75–76, 78, 83; in Bengal, 102; in ideology of empire, 25
education: in civilizing African slaves, 85; in civilizing Native Americans, 66–67; of Irish Catholics, 152; of Munni Begum, 121
egalitarianism: and conservatism, 5–6; in the empire's end, 177; in Ireland, 143, 150, 162; in Jacobinism, 18; in the West Indies, 89–90
elected representatives, 53, 55
elites: in the American colonies, 57–58; in India, 107–8, 172; Indian, 26; Irish, 17, 18, 132–33, 138–39, 141–42, 150, 161

empire: conception of, defined, 42–46; new approach to, 50–52; and revolution, 10–11; second meaning of, 48
Empire and Revolution (Bourke), 11, 37
enfranchisement. *See* suffrage
Enlightened republicanism, 224–25n124
Enlightenment, The: in British Empire, 21; and equality, 201n73; and liberalism, 7; radicalized, 224–25n124; in settler colonialism, 174–75; and sympathy, 61
equality: in the American colonies, 56; in end of civilization, 5–6; and liberalism, 2–3, 4; and primitivism, 201n73; rejected by Burke, 169; of sameness, 109–10; and savagery, 67; in slave rebellions, 88–90
ethnicity, 66, 200–201n70
etymology of empire, 19–20
exemptions, local, 44, 50
expansion of empire, 2, 13, 71–72, 176
extractive imperialism, 21, 26, 101–2, 106, 170

Fitzwilliam, William, 162
"Flight of Earls," 126–27
Flood, Henry, 138–39
force. *See* conquest
Fox, Charles James, 9, 95, 98, 164
France, 25, 138–39
Francis, Philip, 103
Franklin, Benjamin, 60
freedom. *See* liberty
freedom of movement, 132
free seas in ideology of empire, 23–24
free trade: in the American colonies, 59; for Ireland, 16–17, 130, 134–37, 174; slave trade as, 82–83. *See also* trade
French civil law in Canada, 42
French Revolution: in Caribbean slave rebellions, 88–90; compared to East India Company, 110–16; in conservatism, 5–7; consistency on, 9–10; and imperial excess in India, 121–23; and Ireland, 130, 134, 143–44, 150, 153, 165; rights of man in, 14–15; savagery in, 74; secular atheism of, 160; and the United Irishmen, 153–58

Gaelic Irish, 126–27
"geographical morality" defense, 105
Gibbons, Luke, 202–3n96
global imperial vision, 27, 43, 130
"Glorious Revolution" (Ireland), 147
Gordon Riots, 145
governance: in the American colonies, 55–56, 59; aristocracy in, 52–53; in conception of empire, 42, 44–45; in India, 106–7; indigenous social hierarchies in, 170; as kindness, 40; local culture and elites in, 12–13, 172; in the New World, 50–51
Grattan, Henry, 138–39
Great Britain, defined, 20–21, 23
Grenada, 42

Haitian Revolution, 15
Hakluyts, Richard (elder and younger), 23
Hartley, David, 82
Hastings, Warren: as bad conscience, 209n41; and the Begams of Oudh, 116–21; corruption by, 39, 116, 120–21, 189–90n56; criticism of, 93; destruction of Indian nobility by, 110–16; in the famine, 35; impeachment of, 3, 15, 30, 39, 105, 107–9, 112–13, 116–21, 207n5; "Indianism" by, 170–71; and Muslim India, 101; on Oriental despotism, 104; religion in condemnation of, 176–77
heterogeneity in empire, 43–45
Hindu aristocracy, 99, 112
Hindu caste system, 15, 99–100, 171, 207–8n14
Hinduism, 15, 94, 98–100, 207n14
history as civilizing process: and American character, 58; in Burke's vision of empire, 45–46, 169; in Catholic relief and enfranchisement, 146; church and nobility in, 158–59; in global imperial vision, 27; Irish Catholics in, 142; levels of civilization in, 13; liberty and subordination in, 47; in Ornamentalism of India, 95
History of America, A (Robertson), 64, 67
Hoche, Lazare, 153
Holy Roman Empire, 96
Hume, David, 59

hybrid vision of empire, 69
Hyder Ali, Nawab of Mysore, 97

ideology of empire, 11–12, 13, 20–27, 42, 56, 168
idiosyncratic Ornamentalism, 54–58
immunities, local, 44, 50, 127
imperial unity, 43, 45, 133, 134–37
imperium, 19–20
Impey, Elijah, 119
independence: American, 25, 29, 49, 63; of Indian rulers and landowners, 106–7; Irish, 40–41, 143, 154–55, 156, 165, 192–93n76
India: administrative infrastructure in, 96, 98, 101–3; Ancien Régime in, 15–16, 94, 100–108, 110–23, 170–71; atrocities in, 12, 34–35; common people in, 113–14, 115–16; establishment of British rule in, 29–32; ideology of empire in, 13, 29–39; imperialism in, 19; infrastructure in, 96, 98, 101–2; military rule in, 26; Muslim, 15–16, 94, 100–107; and Orientalism, 15–16, 94–110; and Ornamentalism, 93, 94–110, 170–71, 172, 210–11n50; and Providence, 38–39, 92, 191–92n70; religion in, 15, 94, 98–100, 107; similarities of to France, 118–23; social hierarchies in, 15, 114, 115; and the "state of exception," 32–37; strangeness of, 206n1; sympathy for, 15–16, 94–95, 107–10, 210–11n50, 212n73, 212–13n74
Indian Affairs, Select Committees on, 31, 34, 37–38
Indian civilization: destruction of, 110–23; similarities of to Europe, 94–110, 210–11n50
Indianism and Jacobinism, 121–23
indirect rule, local hierarchies in, 172
inequality, 6, 54, 127, 148, 162
inheritance of Irish property, 133–34
injustice, 35–36, 165
internal empire, 44, 141–42
Ireland: and absentee taxation, 16–17, 130–34, 137, 174, 216n26; and the Act of Union, 128, 166–67, 226n128; Ancien Régime in, 18, 127–28, 144, 163–64; aristocracy of, 17, 148–49, 165–66;

Ireland *(continued)*
  Catholic emancipation and enfranchisement in, 17, 125, 130, 141–53, 150–55, 160–61, 164; Catholic/Protestant divide in, 125–26; civilizing of, 125, 126, 142–53; colonial status of, 157, 165; conquest of, 126, 128–29, 146–48; egalitarianism in, 143, 150, 162; free trade and commerce in, 134–37; French invasion of, 153–54; and the French Revolution, 130, 134, 143–44, 150, 153, 165; in the internal empire, 44, 141–42; Jacobinism in, 18, 150, 158–65, 221n91; as kingdom and colony, 19–20, 24, 47–48, 125–30, 192–93n76; legislative independence for, 17–18, 137–42, 165–66, 174, 218n60; in the logic of empire, 173–74; middle class in, 129, 143, 163; native lands appropriated in, 128–29; oppression in, 131–32, 145–47, 152–53, 156, 161, 192n76; and Ornamentalism, 17, 125, 142, 143–44, 153–67; Parliament of, 126, 129, 131, 134–35, 137–38, 142–43; penal laws in, 17, 125, 130, 137, 142–53; political exclusion and discontent in, 162–63; Protestantism in, 17–18, 24, 126–27, 129–30, 138–39, 142–44, 147–49, 162–63; and Providence, 40–41; rebellion in, 129, 146–47, 165–67; social inequality in, 127; status of, 16–17; suffrage in, 17, 125, 130, 141–43, 150–55, 160–61, 164. *See also* Catholics, Irish
Irish elites, 17, 18, 132–33, 138–39, 141–42, 150, 161
Irish nationalism, 40–41, 124, 130, 134, 155–58, 192–93n76
Irish patriot party, 130–31, 138–39
Irish uprising of 1641, 165–67
Irish Volunteers, 137–39
Islam in Ornamentalism, 94–95, 100, 104–5

Jacobinism, 18, 121–23, 150, 158–65, 221n91, 223n103
Janes, Regina, 109
justice, 45, 113–14, 195n101, 221n91

Keogh, John, 41, 141
King in Parliament, 43, 48, 61, 182n22

Knox, William, 60
Kramnick, Isaac, 172

landed nobility. *See* aristocracy
legal status of New World colonies, 48, 58–60
legislative authority, 28–29, 55–56
legitimacy of empire, 22, 27–39, 101–2, 189–90n56, 191n70
leniency for the American colonies, 49–52
Letters on a Regicide Peace (Burke), 89–90
Letter to Sir Hercules Langrishe (Burke), 147, 150–53
Letter to the Sheriffs of Bristol (Burke), 29, 50
liberal imperialism, 1–3, 169
liberalism, 2–3, 4, 7–8, 169, 170
Liberalism and Empire (Mehta), 4
liberty: and African slavery, 24, 84; for American colonists, 54–55, 57; in the Ancien Régime, 21; and authority, 45; in civilizing, 219n69; colonial definition of, 69–70; denied to Irish Catholics, 142–43; in ideology of empire, 12, 21, 23; modern notions of, 2; in the Mughal Empire, 103; and Protestant Ascendancy, 143–44; and religion, 56; in savagery, 67; in slave rebellions, 88–90; and subordination, 47, 50–51; and trade restrictions, 51; for upper-caste Indians, 146
local autonomy, 69, 106–7
local difference, 43–45
Locke, John: *Second Treatise*, 22–23
Louverture, Toussaint, 88, 89

Mahoney, Thomas, 192–93n76
manners, 55, 64, 72, 78
mare liberum (free seas), 23–24
Marie Antoinette, 54, 74, 110, 116–21, 213n80
maritime dominion, 12, 13, 20, 21, 23–27
Marshall, P. J., 26, 99, 106–7, 171, 172
McBride, Ian, 149
McCrea, Jane, 74, 202nn94,96
McDowell, R. B., 140, 166–67
McLoughlin, T. O., 192–93n76
Mehta, Uday, 94, 109; *Liberalism and Empire*, 4

Metcalf, Thomas, 171
metropole: and American colonial legislatures, 55–56; authority of over Ireland, 131–32; and Orientalism, 168, 180n5; and the periphery, 28, 38, 48; and provincial liberty, 45; social hierarchy in, 172
Middleton, Nathaniel, 119
military rule, 20, 24, 26
Miller, Michael, 82
Mir Jafar, Nawab of Bengal, 30, 31
Modest Proposal, A (Swift), 130–31
Molyneux, William, 147; *The Case of Ireland Stated*, 138
Montesquieu, Baron de La Brède, 22, 104, 108
morality, 5–6, 159
moral psychology of sympathy, 13–14, 15–16, 107–10, 114–15, 212n73
Mughal Empire, 100–107, 108
multiple monarchy, 138
Munni Begum, 120–21, 213–14n84, 214n87
Murray, John, Earl of Dunmore, 78–81
Muslim India, 15–16, 94, 100–107

national glory, 33, 39, 92, 193n77
Native Americans: civilizing of, 14, 66, 71–75, 146; common cause with, 70, 73; "ferocity" of, 65, 67–68, 73–74; in ideology of empire, 24; imperial conquest of, 20; and Orientalism, 63–64, 75, 172–73; rebellions by, 69; rights expanded for, 70; "savagery" of, 63, 64–68, 201n74, 202n94, 202–3n96; and *terra nullius*, 22; wars with, 24
natural law, 176–77
Navigation Acts, 26, 51, 59
nawabs, power of, 122–23
New English narrative of Irish history, 147
New World: civilizing in, 14, 65–66, 71–75, 77–78, 84–85, 146, 176; debate over American colonies in, 47–49; Ireland as, 128; and Orientalism, 14–15, 63–87; and Ornamentalism, 47–63; Protestantism in, 24; sovereignty and legitimacy in, 49–52; as territorial empire, 24; theoretical conundrums in, 13–14. *See also* American colonies/colonists

nobility. *See* aristocracy
nonintervention policy in India, 106–7
North, Frederick (Lord North), 37, 49
North America: in the British Empire, 19–22; and Orientalism, 47, 72, 75, 78–87, 91, 172–73. *See also* American colonies/colonists; New World

obedience, 54, 57–58, 77–78, 80, 149, 150
Observations on a Late State of the Nation (Burke), 28, 51, 198n36
Octennial Act of 1768, 139–40
O'Flaherty, Eamon, 140, 192–93n76
O'Hara, Charles, 52
"Old English" settlers, 125–26, 129
Opal, J. M., 34–35
opium production in India, 31
oppression: Burke's hatred of, 219n69; in India, 30–31, 212–13n74; in Ireland, 131–32, 145–47, 152–53, 156, 161, 192n76
Oriental despotism, 104–6, 108, 172–73
Orientalism: and African slaves, 63–64, 78–87, 90; and the American colonies, 14–15, 172–73; and civilizing mission, 72, 175–76; defined, 1–2; and empire, 25, 47, 169, 171–73; in imperial vision, 46; and India, 15–16, 94–110; in liberal imperialism, 1–3; metropole and periphery in, 168, 169, 180n5; and Native Americans, 75, 172–73; and the New World, 63–87; and North America, 47, 72, 75, 78–87, 91, 172–73; and religion, 66, 173; and universalism, 175
Ornamentalism: affinities in, 2, 168, 180n5; and American colonies/colonists, 13–14, 54–58; and civilizing, 72; in debates on empire, 47; and hierarchy, 2, 15, 168; in ideology of empire, 25, 168; in imperial vision, 46; and India, 93, 94–110, 170–71, 172, 210–11n50; and Ireland, 17, 125, 142, 143–44, 153–67; in liberal imperialism, 1–3; in logic of empire, 168–78; and Muslim India, 15–16, 94, 100–107; and the New World, 47–63; and religion, 98–100; sympathy in, 62, 107–10; and the West Indies, 89–90
Othering. *See* Orientalism
overseas expansion in ideology of empire, 25

Paine, Thomas, 34–35, 154, 165; *The American Crisis*, 35; *Common Sense*, 35; *Reflections on the Life and Death of Lord Clive*, 34; *Rights of Man*, 154
Parliament: colonial representation in, 60–61; and India, 92, 103, 106; of Ireland, 126, 131, 134–35, 137–38, 142–43; and King, 43, 48, 61, 182n22; virtual representation in, 60, 198n23
parliamentary career of Burke, 81–82
penal laws, Irish, 17, 125, 130, 137, 142–53
periphery: Ireland as, 131–33, 174; and metropole, 28, 38, 48; New World as, 52, 58–59, 63; and Orientalism, 168, 169, 180n5; and Ornamentalism, 168, 169, 170, 172; subordination of, 12, 28, 42, 45, 48
Philosophical Enquiry into the Origin of our Ideas of the Sublime and Beautiful, A (Burke), 107, 114–15
Pitts, Jennifer, 193n77
plantation society, 57–58
planting of Ulster, 126, 129
Plassey, battle of, 30, 31, 33
plebeian oligarchy in Ireland, 17, 148–50
Pocock, J. G. A., 128, 183n28
political power: of the East India Company, 38; in Ireland, 127, 148, 149, 150–53
poverty, 67, 162–63
Poynings' Law, 139–40
practices of empire, 24–25, 39, 41, 49
Presbyterians in Ireland, 129, 143, 162
prescription, doctrine of, 35–38, 85, 93, 146–48
privileges in the New World, 50, 69
"Proceedings against Clive" (Burke), 37
property, private: in conservatism, 6–7; in enfranchisement, 152; in India, 103, 108, 112; in Ireland, 126–30, 133–34, 144–45, 148, 162–63; Jacobinism threatening, 122; and liberty, 21, 22; in social order, 171. *See also* Catholic lands
Protestant Ascendancy: and absentee taxation, 133–34; and Catholic persecution, 150, 156–57; criticism of, 125; and Dissenters, 129, 161–62; in Irish legislative independence, 139, 142; Jacobinism encouraged by, 158–65; and liberty, 143–44; in the logic of empire, 174; and monarchical absolutism, 23, 146; and Ornamentalism, 161–62; as plebeian oligarchy, 148–49; policies of, 17–18; problems created by, 130, 219–20n73; and the United Irishmen, 153–58; war on fellow Christians by, 159–60
Protestant colonial narrative of Irish history, 146–47
Protestant patriots, 138, 139, 142–43
Protestants/Protestantism: of Burke, 16, 124; in colonial America, 13, 56; in ideology of empire, 22–23; in Ireland, 17–18, 24, 126–27, 129–30, 138–39, 142–44, 147–49, 162–63; and monarchical absolutism, 23, 146; in practices of empire, 24
Providence, 38–45, 71–73, 92, 191–92n70, 193n77
provincial liberty and metropolitan authority, 45
prudence, 36, 195n101

Quebec, 60, 61, 69, 88–89
Qur'an, 104

racial essentialism, 66
racial sensitivity, 113–14
Raleigh, Walter, 23
Rana, Aziz, 69
rebellion: in Ireland, 129, 146–47, 165–67; by Native Americans, 69; by slaves, 15, 87–91; and tyranny, 121–22. *See also* revolution
Rebellion of 1641 (Ireland), 129, 146–47
reenslavement for free blacks, 87, 176
Reflections on the Life and Death of Lord Clive (Paine), 34, 118
Reflections on the Revolution in France (Burke): as anticolonial masterwork, 4; aristocracy's role in, 52–53; consistency in, 9; and Irish nationalism, 155; Marie Antoinette in, 118; prescription in, 35; savagery in, 65; sublime in, 53–54; sympathy in, 114–15
Regulating Act of 1773, 37, 103
regulation: of commerce, 26; of the East India Company, 32, 37, 39, 92–93, 95;

of elites' movement, 132–33; of slavery, 83–85
religion: in civilization and civilizing, 5, 65–66, 77–78, 95, 98, 113–14, 149–50, 169, 176–77; in colonial America, 55, 56, 58; in conservatism, 7; in discipline, 56, 115; discrimination based on, 128; in English civilization, 53–54; in ethnicity, 66; in India, 15, 94, 98–100, 107; and Jacobinism, 159; lack of in Native American savagery, 65–66; and liberty, 56; in manumission of slaves, 85; and Orientalism, 66, 173; and Ornamentalism, 98–100; in the Quebec Act, 69; and slavery, 14, 76–77; and social order, 207n14; tolerance of, 42. *See also under religion name*
representative government, 21, 42, 49, 127, 138
resistance, 102, 127–28, 146–47
res nullius (empty things), 22
revolution: American, 62–63, 66, 71, 73–74, 134–36, 137–39; in Bengal, 30–31, 32, 92, 170, 187n37, 188–89n50, 189–90n56; and empire, 10–11; Haitian, 15; and imperial excess, 16; liberty and equality provoking, 88–90. *See also* French Revolution; rebellion
revolutionary secularism, 159–62
Revolution of 1782 (Ireland), 17, 139, 140
Reza Khan, Muhammad, 120
rights: in conservatism, 6; expanded for slaves, 69–70; in the French Revolution, 14–15; in Indian Ornamentalism, 210–11n50; as infectious disease, 89, 90; in Mughal India, 103; rejected by Burke, 169; universal, 143
Rights of Man (Paine), 154
Robertson, William: *A History of America*, 64, 67
Rohilkhand, 105
Rohilla War Charge, 105, 113
Royal Proclamation of 1763, 69
rule of law, 103–5, 107, 127

S
Said, Edward, 1–2, 169, 172–73, 175
Saint-Domingue, 88, 90

Saming. *See* Ornamentalism
savagery: of African slaves, 63, 175; of Amerindians, 14, 65–68, 175; and command, 67; and economic development, 67; in the French Revolution, 74; in imperial vision, 46; of the Irish, 126; of Native Americans, 63, 64–68, 74–75, 90, 175, 201n74, 202–3n96; in Orientalism, 14–15
Schoolbred, John, 81–82
Scotland, 44, 48
Scottish Enlightenment, 5, 21, 61, 64, 175, 201nn73,74
"Second Speech on Conciliation" (Burke), 83
Second Treatise (Locke), 22
secularism, 18, 159–62, 177
secular otherness, 66
self-governance in empire, 12
settler colonialism/colonies: authority and autonomy in, 26; and the Enlightenment, 174–75; in Ireland, 139, 142, 173–74; North America as, 20; Orientalism in, 173; place of in empire, 48; safety of and slavery, 76. *See also* American colonies/colonists
"settler nationalism" in Ireland, 129, 130, 138, 139, 142, 147
Seven Years' War, 25, 68
Shah Alam II, Mughal Emperor, 101
similarities: of American colonists, 13–14; in Ornamentalism, 2, 210–11n50; in sympathy, 62, 107–10
Singh, Chait, 117
Singh, Devi, 116, 212–13n74
Siraj-ud-Daula, Nawab of Bengal, 30
"Sketch of a Negro Code" (Burke), 83, 85–87
Skinner, Quentin, 183n28
slave rebellions, 15, 87–91
slave trade, 75–76, 78–81, 81–83, 176
Smith, Adam, 39, 59, 61; *The Theory of Moral Sentiments*, 107
social discipline: in civilization, 5–6, 53–54; in colonial America, 58; and Indianism, 122; of Irish Catholics, 18, 150; in Native American savagery, 66–67; religious dissenters in, 56

social hierarchies: aristocracy in, 152; in Bengal, 111; Christianity in, 159; in conservatism, 5, 6–7; democracy upending, 164; in India, 96, 99–100, 106, 114, 115, 122, 171; indigenous, 24, 170; in indirect rule, 172; in Ireland, 17–18; in Native American savagery, 66–67; in Ornamentalism, 2, 15, 168, 170; threatened by native rights, 70. *See also* Hindu caste system

social order/stability: in the American South, 57–58; Hinduism in, 207n14; in India, 207n9; in Ireland, 128; nobility in, 52–53; private property in, 171; and religion, 56, 207n14

South American Amerindians, 96

sovereignty: and the American colonies, 29, 49–52, 59, 61; in empire, 42, 43–44; *imperium* as, 20; in India, 93, 95, 106; of King in Parliament, 61, 106; and local character, 12–13, 44–45, 51–52; in a multiple monarchy, 138; over Ireland, 131–32; required for empire, 12; through war, 189–90n56

Speech at Bristol Previous to the Election (1780) (Burke), 82–83, 137

Speech at the Conclusion of the Poll (Burke), 43, 53

"Speech in Reply" (Burke), 104–5, 115, 118–19, 121–22

"Speech on Almas Ali Khan" (Burke), 118

Speech on American Taxation (Burke), 29, 59

Speech on Conciliation with America (Burke), 43–44, 51–52, 54–58, 71, 78–81

Speech on Fox's India Bill (Burke), 35, 39, 95–96, 100–101, 108–9, 111

Speech on the Nabob of Arcot's Debts (1785), 87

"Speech on the Opening of Impeachment" (Burke), 112

"Speech on the Use of Indians" (Burke), 73–74

Stamp Act, 50, 51, 59

Statues of Kilkenny, 147

sublime, 5, 53–54, 56

subordination: in Burke's vision of empire, 43; Christianity in, 159; in English civilization, 53–54; of imperial periphery, 12, 28, 42, 45, 48; and imperial taxation, 133; in India, 106; of Ireland, 139–41; and liberty, 47, 50–51; principle of, 29; in savagery, 67; of slaves, 88–89

suffrage: in American conciliation, 60–61; in English civilization, 53; in Ireland, 17, 125, 130, 141–43, 150–55, 160–61, 164

Swift, Jonathan: *Drapier's Letters*, 138; *A Modest Proposal*, 130–31

sympathy: for the Begams of Oudh, 119–20; for colonial America, 14–15, 61–63; for India, 15–16, 94–95, 107–10, 210–11n50, 212n73, 212–13n74; for Irish Catholics, 125; moral psychology of, 13–14, 15–16, 107–10, 114–15, 212n73; and social hierarchy, 114–15; in virtual representation, 198n23

synchronic explanation of beliefs, 183n29

taxation: absentee, in Ireland, 16–17, 130–34, 137, 174, 216n26; in the American colonies, 28–29, 55, 59–60, 61; granted, in India, 30; in India, 31–32, 34, 97; in the Mughal Empire, 102; right of, 50

terra nullius (empty lands), 22, 26, 70

Theory of Moral Sentiments, The (Smith), 107

Tone, Theobald Wolfe: and absentee taxation, 216n26; in Catholic relief, 222n92; death of, 166; and Enlightened republicanism, 224–25n124; and Irish nationalism, 40–41; in the United Irishmen, 17, 153–58, 162–63

Tracts Relating to Popery Laws (Burke), 145, 146–48

trade, 24, 51, 59, 134–37. *See also* free trade

tradition, 15–16, 38, 94, 104, 170–72

Travers, Robert, 103, 106

United Irishmen: and Catholic relief, 130, 143, 154, 221n91, 222n92; and the French Revolution, 153–58; in independence movement, 17–18; and Irish nationalism, 40–41; and Jacobinism, 162–63; rebellion by, 165–66

Vansittart, Henry, 30–31

Verelst, Harry, 30–31

Virginia Company, 23
Volunteers (Irish), 138–39, 218n60

warfare, mode of, 65–66, 73–74, 202n94
Wentworth, Thomas, 129
Western political thought on Oriental governments, 104
West Indies, 19, 42, 86, 87–91, 205n144
Whelan, Frederick, 109

Whigs: and the American colonies, 28, 50, 60–61; and Burke's liberalism, 8; conservatism of, 7, 182n22; and the Declaratory Acts, 61, 140; on the French Revolution, 9; and Ireland, 140; and the Mughal Empire, 103
Wollstonecraft, Mary, 115

zamindars, 107, 111

www.ingramcontent.com/pod-product-compliance
Lightning Source LLC
Chambersburg PA
CBHW030535230426
43665CB00010B/896